Lionel Kochan was born in London in 1922, and educated at Cambridge and London Universities. After serving in the Intelligence Corps during the war, he was Senior Research Fellow in International Relations at the London School of Economics, Lecturer in Modern European History at Edinburgh University, and Reader in Modern History at the University of East Anglia. Dr Kochan is presently Bearsted Reader in Jewish History at the University of Warwick. His previous publications include *Russia and the Weimar Republic*, *Acton on History*, *The Making of Modern Russia*, *Pogrom – November 10, 1938*, *The Struggle for Germany 1914–1945*, and *The Jews in Soviet Russia Since 1917* (ed.)

TO DÉGAGE

LIONEL KOCHAN

Russia in Revolution

1890–1918

PALADIN
GRAFTON BOOKS
A Division of the Collins Publishing Group

LONDON GLASGOW
TORONTO SYDNEY AUCKLAND

Paladin
Grafton Books
A Division of the Collins Publishing Group
8 Grafton Street, London W1X 3LA

Published in Paladin Books 1970
Reprinted 1971, 1974, 1978, 1981, 1983, 1986

First published in Great Britain by
Weidenfeld & Nicolson 1967

Copyright © Lionel Kochan 1966

ISBN 0-586-08011-2

Printed and bound in Great Britain by
Collins, Glasgow

Set in Monotype Bembo

To Nick, Anna and Benjy
and their Mother

Contents

Glossary   9
Preface   11
Introduction   15

Part 1
1. New Men in an Old Society   23
2. The Worker Abandoned   35
3. The Hungry Village Revives   51
4. The Ignorant Autocrat   60
5. Political Challenges   69

Part 2
6. On the Eve of 1905   79
7. Bloody Sunday   86
8. The Two Voices of St Petersburg   102
9. The Rise and Fall of the Duma, 1906–7   115
10. The Lessons of the Upheaval:
    1. The Wager on the Strong   133
    2. Theories of Revolution   140
    3. Permanent Revolution   146
11. The Mind Against Society   151
12. Before the Deluge   160
13. The Storm Breaks   176

Part 3
14. The Honeymoon of Revolution   199
15. Lenin Arrives   210
16. The First Crisis   216
17. The Government's Answer   225
18. The Revolution Gathers Strength   232
19. Unquiet on the Eastern Front   242
20. The Summer of Discontent   247

21. The Men on Horseback Fail 257
22. Mate in Two Moves 267

Maps 282
List of Abbreviations 284
Chapter References 285
Bibliography 315
Subject Index 327
Name Index 331

Glossary

Dessyatin – equal to 2·7 acres
Pood – equal to 3·1 pounds
Verst – equal to $\frac{2}{3}$ mile
Zemstvo – unit of local government at cantonal and provincial level, elected on restricted franchise

NB All dates are given according to the Julian Calendar, thirteen days behind the western Gregorian Calendar in the twentieth century. In cases of ambiguity both dates are given.

Preface

Why, to adapt a couplet from Auden, did 'old Russia suddenly mutate, into a proletarian state?' The present book attempts to answer this question. It is not, therefore, a history of Russia over a specific period. Rather, it is an attempt to identify, isolate and describe those factors that have promoted the mutation. This involves the presupposition that Russian society, however defined, found itself, at the turn of the nineteenth and twentieth centuries, in such a state of change as could not be contained within the limits of the existing order. The sheer ungovernability of the empire and the expectation of some cataclysm are commonplaces of political and literary comment from virtually all sections of opinion, both Russian and foreign. Were tsarism to be overthrown, Dmitry Tolstoy, the Russian minister of the interior, predicted to Prince Bülow in 1884, then its place would be taken by communism – 'communism pure and simple, the communism of Mr Karl Marx of London who has just died and whose theories I have studied with attention and interest.'[1]

Although the process of breakdown can, I hope, be identified, the final embodiment of this process is not presupposed. I do indeed take for granted what may be termed a state of latent revolution. But its issue in a Bolshevik victory remains merely one aspect of the process of change that must be shown in rivalry with other aspects. A balance has therefore had to be maintained between what was of contemporary importance and what was of importance as a contribution to the future. A batsman who scores a duck in one match may well learn how to score a century next time. It has been necessary not to anticipate the future but also not to neglect what was of relevance to the future. Without the *leitmotiv* of revolutionary change Russian history before 1917 would be unintelligible. But the sequel is also something that must be fought for.

I also presuppose the uniqueness of the Russian situation. Minimal use, I hope, has been made of general terms and terms of comparison. Where this is well-nigh unavoidable – as in the case of the term 'party', for example – I can only hope that the specific characteristics of a 'party' in Russian circumstances at a particular time will obviate confusion. Similarly with the term 'revolution': I have taken as my criterion of meaning the clearest and most specific of all descriptions – that moment when the new Bolshevik regime has created the two primary institutions of government, a police force and an army.[2] To be sure, the Cheka and the Bolshevik armed forces hardly enjoyed uncontested authority in 1917–18. But it is sufficient that they should have come into existence.

The assumption of Russian uniqueness does not preclude reference to points of contact with similar situations elsewhere, e.g. to industrialization in an under-developed country, or to those conditions in which systems of representative government may flourish. Such references illuminate differences and do not make untenable comparisons by postulating a common sequence of development.

Again, the same assumption also does not preclude some reflection on certain common causes or conditions of revolutionary change. These have recently been comprehensively and conveniently grouped, *inter alia*, into intellectual factors (the coexistence in a society of conflicting social myths); economic factors (growing poverty or unbalance between the production and distribution of goods), aspects of social structure (inadequate circulation of elites), political factors (estrangement of the rulers from the ruled), and such general characteristics of social process as rapid social change.[3]

All these factors were represented in Russia. That is why it is necessary to avoid treating the events of 1917 in isolation but to consider their origin at the end of the nineteenth century and to treat this whole period as a unit. The Russian revolution will never be understood outside a formula that fails to grasp the connexion between Tolstoy's anarchism and Lenin's Marxism, the character of the tsar and the disrespect for law and order, the alienation of the student and the influence of railway construction, the repression of the national claims of Poles and Finns and the character of revivalist sects, a demographic upsurge and great-power rivalry, bureaucratic corruption and western influences, etc., etc. No claim is made that any of these facets has been exhaustively dealt with. On the other hand, I do hope that I have been able to indicate their relative importance.

How may such a formula be found? How may a *point de départ* be selected from this host such as will at least serve to introduce the revolution? No doubt the Russian revolution was fed from multifarious and conflicting sources but I select that which seems to me to serve as the fountain-head of all the more significant future developments – and that is the disharmony between the resources of the state and its aspirations.

In Part 1 I try to give a dynamic analysis of the 'Vitte period', extending approximately over the last decade of the nineteenth century. I choose this as my starting point because it was then that the Russian situation became truly critical. The onset of a massive programme of government-inspired industrialization brought with it such tension as left no field of Russian society unaffected. Necessarily, the programme entailed, directly or indirectly, the rapid emergence of a restive proletariat, a sacrifice of agricultural (including peasant) interests, an intensified interest in Marxism and other revolutionary beliefs, and the emergence of a liberal movement hostile to the traditional ways of tsarism.

At some indeterminate point early in the new century, the further consequences of these factors made themselves felt in the form of a deepening revolutionary crisis, itself vastly intensified by Russian participation in the first world war. This brought about the collapse of tsarism and forms the second part of the book. Part 3 describes the collapse of the February regime and its replacement by a new, Bolshevik-dominated government. This merges into the beginnings of civil war between the new regime and the adherents of the old. A turning point has been reached.

Introduction

In August 1904, when the French ambassador, Bompard, had been in St Petersburg about a year, he sent to Paris a most alarming dispatch. 'All classes of Russian society are in a state of effervescence,' Bompard wrote. The peasants were 'a ready prey' for agitators. The proletariat, though of recent origin, had shown itself revolutionary from the outset; it expressed its claims 'in the most violent form'. Schools and universities were 'seed-beds of anarchists'. Students applauded terrorist attacks, if they did not participate in them. The merchant class, save for some honourable exceptions, was composed of 'rapacious and unscrupulous hawkers'. The nobility were *frondeurs*, blunderers and devoid of practical sense'. The bureaucracy was 'a scourge', the ministers progressively more mediocre, and the tsar clung to an authority 'that he was incapable of exercising'.[1]

Two years later, the British ambassador, Sir Arthur Nicolson, completed this sombre picture with a foreboding of 'some startling and terrible development. . . . Should the peasantry, excited by socialist and anarchist agitators, be led on whither the latter desire to draw them, and should the working classes simultaneously rise in the towns, there will be a catastrophe such as history has rarely witnessed.'[2]

How are these forebodings to be explained?'Why might the working classes rise?'Why might the peasants be so readily excited? Any answer must stress a flagrant contrast between the inherited forms of Russian social and political life and the emergence of new forces, vainly seeking a place in the existing order, and necessarily forced into opposition.

The undiminished prerogatives of tsarist autocracy; administrative centralization; a massive peasant population, imperfectly emancipated in 1861; a rapidly growing working class; a bare modicum of representative institutions; and a restless stratum of professional men and students – these salient features of Russian society were further aggravated at the end of the nineteenth century by a vast programme of industrialization. Industrial development, with all its implications – demographic, financial, sociological and psychological – undoubtedly introduced the most potent challenge to the *status quo*. 'The mighty inflow of the ideas of the west (in a union with the powers of capitalism) disintegrates patriarchal and communist conservatism . . .' Max Weber wrote of Russia early in 1906.[3] The late doyen of Soviet historians, Professor Pokrovsky, has outlined a Marxist model of this conflict in the form of the historical dialectic.

Landed property calls the railways into existence, in order to reach the wide and most profitable European market. The railway gives birth to metallurgy, metallurgy creates the most revolutionary section of the proletariat, which buries the ancestor of the whole system – landed property.[4]

Industrialization was no new phenomenon in Russia. It had been in progress since the Crimean war; the emancipation of 1861 gave some further impetus to the movement. But not until the 1890s did it enjoy the whole-hearted encouragement of the state in a compulsive effort to have done with Russian backwardness and overcome decades of weakness. The urge to industrialize expressed the deep need to unfold Russian greatness and power: '. . . Alexander III (1881–94) understood that . . . a country without a powerfully developed manufacturing industry could not be great,' wrote Vitte, the tsar's chief minister.[5] Vitte, the outstanding Russian statesman of this period, was the veritable embodiment of this urge, inspired by the vision of Russia as a great power, in fact as well as in name.

Much success was certainly achieved. In the heavy industries the rate of development was particularly rapid. The decade of the 1890s marked the point when Russian industry took off into maturity. By 1914 Russia was annually producing some five million tons of pig-iron, four million tons of iron and steel, forty million tons of coal, ten million tons of petroleum, and was exporting about twelve million tons of grain.

But the precipitate construction of a heavy industrial base unleashed enormous tensions throughout the whole of the Russian body politic. One of its concomitants, for example, was an unprecedented growth in population, far outstripping that of any other European country. Between 1867 and 1896 the average annual growth in population was 1·37 per cent. During this period the population increased (in round figures) from sixty-three million to ninety-two million. Between 1897 and 1913 the tempo of increase was even faster – at an average annual rate of 1·65 per cent, to produce a population of 122 million. The population almost doubled in less than fifty years. This phenomenon may be usefully compared with the demographic position elsewhere in Europe. If, between 1860 and 1910, the population of European Russia alone increased by 90·8 per cent, the comparable figure for

Germany was 72·2 per cent, for the United Kingdom 54·8 per cent, for Italy 40·6 per cent, and for France 10·6 per cent.[6]

The Russian demographic upsurge not only aggravated the endemic problem of agrarian over-population; it also promoted some degree of urbanization and the simultaneous growth of a discontented urban proletariat. In the upheaval of 1905, for example, the larger the town, the more important was the role of the proletariat. Between 1863 and 1897 the population of Riga and Kiev grew by more than three and a half times; that of Odessa only slightly less; in Baku, there was a more than eightfold increase; in Rostov-on-Don the increase was more than fourfold; in Ivanovo-Vosnesensk it was almost five-fold; in Ekaterinoslav and Tsaritsyn, later Stalingrad (now Volgograd) it was close on sevenfold.[7]

The magnitude of these figures made it impossible for industry, however fast it expanded, to absorb more than a small part of the population increase. As late as 1913, industry employed not much more than five per cent of the entire labour force and contributed only about one-fifth of the national income.[8]

Even this modest result was only achieved through the injection of massive foreign loans, investments and government subsidies, and with the aid of the high protectionist tariff of 1891 (though this had originally been introduced for budgetary reasons).

This fiscal and investment policy could not but arouse the hostility of the agricultural and the landed interest. The government's encouragement of heavy industry necessarily entailed the sacrifice of rural interests. The conflict of interest between industry and agriculture went yet deeper. In the last resort it was the peasantry who had to pay, far beyond their resources, for the development of industry. This was a sequel to the government's fiscal policy of indirect taxation and also to the high prices of imported goods following the imposition of the protectionist tariff. Industry, therefore, far from bringing benefit to the mass of Russians, actively contributed to their impoverishment. The famines of 1891 and 1898 gave tragic emphasis to this argument: had the peasantry not been too poor to lay aside a reserve of food, the ravages of hunger could hardly have been so extensive. Hostility to a rapid policy of industrialization had not only an economic but also a moral and emotional basis. Was it not putting Russia in pawn to foreign financiers and capitalists and introducing an alien way of life, rhetorically demanded the old-style Russian patriot? This contrast was early evident. Who is it whom Goncharov compares with the indolent, easy-going Oblomov but Stolz, the practical-minded German?

Vitte's attempt to convert Russia from its status as a colonial dependency of the western powers, importing manufactured goods and exporting raw materials, into a modern industrialized state bore with equal ruthlessness on the new urban proletariat. To the vast majority the transition from countryside to factory was precipitate and unwelcome. There was a great lack of tolerable hygienic and housing facilities, especially for married couples. The most that could be offered in many of the newly swollen towns was a corner in a factory barracks. Wages, let alone accommodation, would run to little else. This again conformed to Vitte's policy: he deprecated personal consumption and emphasized that saving and the accumulation of capital 'has a productive meaning only when it is applied to new productive processes. Saving merely for immediate use, for the increase of personal satisfaction, brings little to the country. . . .'[9]

The workers' position further suffered through the virtual prohibition of strikes and trade unions. In these circumstances, recurrent outbursts of disaffection could not but turn into open conflict with the government itself; and in these conflicts the use of troops and police was common. Until the end of the century the government even refused to acknowledge the existence of a Russian labour problem comparable to that of western Europe.

The inability of traditional Russian society to absorb, in all its ramifications, the impact of industrialization extended to the autocracy also. Tsarism, every whit as much as agriculture and the factory order, was involved in the all-enveloping crisis. A criterion of the tsar's reluctance to face the modern world can be found, for example, in his refusal to employ a private secretary, lest this limit his powers.[10] Nicholas II (1894-1917) found himself increasingly unable to dominate, let alone comprehend, the sources of unrest and upheaval. His isolation, alienation even, from his environment found its classic epitome in his words to Sir George Buchanan, the British ambassador. 'Do you mean,' the tsar asked, 'that *I* am to regain the confidence of my people or that they are to regain *my* confidence?'[11] These words were uttered on the very eve of the tsar's enforced abdication.

The inadequacy of a merely nominal autocracy was also inherent in the decay of the social system headed by the tsar. Social mobility and social differentiation were already characteristic of the years following 1861. They grew apace towards the end of the century. The old division of the population into the threefold estates of nobles, town-dwellers and peasantry disintegrated *pari passu* with the increasing diversification of society. A new outspoken stratum of *entrepreneurs*, professional men, technicians and merchants developed, defying classification within the old scheme. Such men were denied official participation in the government of the country. Societies of lawyers, professors, industrialists – all saw their activities crippled, if not positively suppressed. Only in the crisis year of 1905 did their calls for a constituent assembly based on equal, direct, universal and secret suffrage receive any heed.

The opposition of the intelligentsia and such national and religious minorities as Jews, Poles, Ukrainians, Finns and Georgians cut across the claims of class and caste. It was none the less effective. It will never be possible to estimate at its full extent the contribution made to the Russian crisis by the policy of Russification and the enforced conversion to Greek Orthodoxy of Catholics, Jews, Moslems, Lutherans and Uniates. But some indication may be found in the disproportionate membership of minority groups in the revolutionary parties.[12] To the members of the intelligentsia, whether organized in political groupings or not, there was little that the regime could do right. Hostility was their credo.

The contrast between the state of Russia and western progress, efficiency and orderliness, ultimately became so flagrant that it brought Russian institutions into discredit and disengaged large sections of the population from their traditional allegiances. It is in this sense that the European model has been identified as 'the primary agent of revolution in Russia'.[13] Inevitably, the greater the effort made to approximate to this model, through a planned policy of modernization, the more the original crisis was deepened. For all these reasons Russian society, at the end of the nineteenth and beginning of the twentieth century underwent not only a profound *crise de conscience* but also a structural crisis provoked by the modernizing urge. This convulsive change left no institution unscathed.

'Who can be happy in Russia?' the poet, Nekrasov, had asked in mid-century. Who, indeed? The question recurred with doubled force in later decades. A revolution in Russia was one of the most-heralded events of the decades before 1917. The upheaval of 1905 was significant in illuminating the future. It revealed an empire that was rapidly becoming, in the most literal sense of the word, ungovernable. It was collapsing into a state of internal war.[14] This awareness lay behind Vitte's remarks to a correspondent of the *Associated Press* shortly after the signature of the Russo-Japanese peace treaty in July 1905. 'The world should be surprised that we have any government in Russia, not that we have an imperfect government,' Vitte said.

With many nationalities, many languages and a nation largely illiterate, the marvel is that the country can be held together even by autocracy. Remember one thing: if the tsar's government falls, you will see absolute chaos in Russia, and it will be many a long year before you see another government able to control the mixture that makes up the Russian nation.[15]

In 1912 Vitte would argue that Russia enjoyed neither the advantages of 'absolute power' nor those of 'liberal government'.[16] What sort of government *could* it have, then, but the worst of both worlds?

Even in 'normal' times it seemed as though a state of lawlessness lay deeply embedded in Russian society. How else can be characterized such diverse phenomena as the violent dispersal of student meetings, punitive expeditions against the peasantry, mutinies in the armed forces, armed clashes between troops and strikers, the assassination of leading politicians and officials, and Bolshevik smash-and-grab raids on branches of the State Bank or state armouries?

The swan-song of the empire was compounded of the most heterogeneous and discordant strains – the crack of a Cossack's whip and the voice of Chaliapin, the roar of the most modern machinery and the poetry of Blok, the call for a constituent assembly and the agony of the famine-stricken, the assassin's high explosive and the music of Rachmaninov and Stravinsky, socialist agitation and the prayers of an effete autocrat, patriotic manifestoes and the tramp of a workers' demonstration. Disharmony was the *leitmotif* – and as the empire entered the twentieth century, disharmony turned more and more to open dissonance.

Part 1

1 New Men in an Old Society

Every step taken in the 1880s and 1890s towards a modern industrial Russia aroused the thrust and counter-thrust of controversy. Men as different as Tolstoy and Dostoyevsky gave voice to protests based on moral, ethical and religious criteria. Russian literature almost always made the merchant and businessman into figures of scorn. The *bourgeois* mind, with its calculation of profit and loss, its disregard of the human factor, its rationality, was inherently repugnant to wide circles of the Russian intelligentsia. The individual would be sacrificed to the factory order. The unnatural but inevitable division of labour would transform man into a diminished personality. A conservative thinker, Leontyev, for example, could see no way of reconciling the mores of the western industrialized order with the tsarist charisma, rooted as it was in an overwhelmingly agrarian, religious and quasi-patriarchal order. It was not yet understood – perhaps it could not be foreseen – that the media of mass-communication acted as a corrective instrument to the disenchantment brought about by industrialization.

Populist socio-economic thinkers such as Vorontsov and Danielson made the most cogent criticism of the industrial movement. It was argued that Russia suffered from manifold obstacles to a profitable capitalist development: transportation costs must necessarily be an onerous burden; the shortage of skilled labour would increase labour costs, whereas the abundance of cheap labour resulting from over-population would reduce the need to introduce modern machinery; an inclement climate would require additional expenditure on heating and lighting; and the conservative-minded Russian middle class would never provide a capable stratum of managers and *entrepreneurs*.[1]

All these inhibiting factors, however germane to the issue, were yet subordinate to the critics' basic contention that Russia could never succeed in developing capitalist industry to the point where its products would compete with the exports of the more economically advanced countries. Russia was also too weak to conquer markets abroad, in the normal imperialist fashion. The poverty of the domestic market completed the vicious circle. How could an impoverished peasantry ever provide a ready mass market for the products of Russian industry? A peasantry, moreover, whose position, as shown in the famine of 1891, was in fact growing ever worse through the very measures (high taxation, for example) taken in order to foster industry. The Populists concluded that Russian industry, lacking markets at home and abroad, was an essentially artificial creation, kept alive only by the massive injection of foreign loans and government subsidies.

Much of this analysis was true. Yet the battle had already been lost. In the 1870s it was already possible to talk of the initial phase of a Russian industrial revolution. The revolution proceeded at an accelerating rate. Between 1830 and 1860 the proportion of employed workers in the population never rose higher than one per cent. In the 1870s it began to grow and in 1887 the proportion was 1·4 million workers in a population of 110 million. The data of industrial production and mineral extraction showed a similar rise in tempo. In 1860 iron output amounted to 321,000 tons; in 1880 to 428,000 tons; in 1890 to 905,000 tons. In coal production the totals for 1880 and 1890 were respectively 3,290,000 tons and 6,027,000 tons. In addition, the beginnings of a banking and credit system and a capital market had come into existence.[2]

Yet by any standard of comparison, Russia remained a backward area. Home and foreign trade was at a low level; productivity in agriculture and factory compared most unfavourably with that of any other European great power; and the competition of large-scale grain exports from the Americas after 1870 not only reduced peasant earnings but made it more difficult than ever to earn the foreign currency required to service the loans contracted in the interests of railway building. Even that modest degree of industrialization achieved, say, between 1860 and 1890, had entailed unusual pressure on the population.

The unhappy career of each successive post-Crimean minister of finance clearly expressed the difficulties confronting Russia. Reutern, who did succeed in overcoming the recurrent budget deficit and an unfavourable balance of trade, eventually came to grief through the extraordinary expenditure incurred in the Russo-Turkish war of 1877–8. Bunge, his successor, was overwhelmed by the Bulgarian crisis of 1886. *His* successor, Vyshnegradsky, cut back the rate of railway construction and imposed a prohibitive tariff in 1891 in an endeavour to balance the budget. He in his turn came to grief through an intensified squeeze that he forced on the peasants, compelling them to export the very grain they needed for their own sustenance. That the peasants had no reserves with which to avert the inevitable crop failure followed ineluctably from Vyshnegradsky's policies.[3] The consequence was the famine of 1891. Given the burdens assumed by the Russian state – an active foreign policy, subsidies to industry, a balanced budget, and the need for a consistently favourable balance of trade, to say nothing of the normal expenditure of government – recurrent crises were inevitable. But could Russia not wait and, perhaps, not resort so easily to burdensome foreign loans? Time does not wait, came the answer; either we catch up or we fall further and further behind, and if we wish to catch up we cannot do without foreign help.

The awareness of the effort required was already a feature of the immediate post-Crimean decades. The first response to the challenge of defeat in the Crimea and later to the diplomatic defeat inflicted at the Congress of Berlin (1878) had been the recasting of such institutions as serfdom and the legal system. Some measure of local self-government in town and countryside through the municipal duma and the zemstvo had also been introduced. Economically, the response was most marked in a programme of railway construction that ranked as one of the first attempts to overcome Russian backwardness. This was in some instances undertaken with government financial participation, and sometimes with the aid of foreign loans. The new lines had four main purposes: there were strategic lines that facilitated the deployment of troops in the west (the lines St Petersburg-Warsaw, and Moscow–Brest Litovsk–Warsaw); lines that served the export trade, particularly grain (lines linking the Volga and the Ukraine with the Baltic, e.g. Riga–Tsaritsyn, and lines centring on Odessa); lines linking nascent industrial complexes in the Moscow, Ural and Ukraine industrial areas; and lines, such as the Trans-Siberian Railway, which were designed to serve both strategic and industrial purposes. The Trans-Siberian, for example, would link European and Asiatic Russia at a time of Japanese expansion in the Far East and the increasing disintegration of China, and also open up to intensified exploitation the mineral wealth of Siberia.[4]

At this juncture, in 1892, the arch-exponent of an industrialized Russia came to power – Sergei Yulievitch Vitte. Under his aegis and stimulus the empire entered on a period of unprecedented economic growth. Vitte, however mistaken his policies in social terms, must yet be considered one of the outstanding statesmen of the late-tsarist Russia. He was born in 1849 in Tiflis where his father directed the agricultural department in the office of the governor-general of the Caucasus. His mother was of noble birth. He studied mathematics at the Novorossisk University in Odessa. After graduation he entered the field of railway administration, on the advice of Count Bobrinsky, the then minister of communications. He began his career in the new railroads of the south; Vitte's first post was in the ticket office of the Odessa State Railway. From this unlikely rung he climbed ever higher in the hierarchy, mixing on all but equal terms with the railway tycoons of post-Crimean Russia – the Blochs, Poliakovs and Von Derviz'. Vitte's special achievement was the introduction of a vigorous tariff policy which put the South-Western Railway Company, covering the western Ukraine and Poland, on a profitable footing. After 1878, when the government began to take the railways into public ownership, Vitte was invited to form a railway department in the ministry of finance. This was in 1889. Three years later he was appointed, in rapid succession, minister of communications and minister of finance. The fall came in 1903. By then the cost of the policy of industrialization had become unmistakably evident. The economic crisis at the turn of the century was Vitte's *coup de grace* and a most powerful instrument in the hands of those who had opposed him throughout a whole decade. Renewed famine in the early years of the century and peasant unrest culminating in the upheaval of 1905 emphasized anew the hardships exacted by modernization. No less eloquent was recurrent unrest in the new industrial centres. Neither phenomenon can be divorced from Vitte's policies.

What motives justified Vitte in imposing a programme that knowingly entailed these consequences? A first approach to an answer may be found in the unease generated by the Crimean and later defeats and in the feeling that some sort of fundamental change was required if Russia were to retain its due place in the world. How could the empire continue to assert great power status, in actuality as well as in name, if its economy remained underdeveloped, its population illiterate, its agriculture unproductive, its way of life 'oriental' – all this, moreover, at a time when industrial development was constantly *widening* the gap that divided the great powers from the backward countries? If Russia were to continue to rank as a great power, then it would have to make a commensurate industrial and military effort.

This awareness was Vitte's *raison d'être*. He may be regarded as one of the first of the modern planners in his determination to effect from above a re-modelling of the Russian economy. It would cease to be dependent on an uncertain harvest and the export price of grain; rather, he would transform the empire into an efficient, industrialized and independent national unit of a type that alone could enable Russia to function as a world power.

Neither Vitte's aim, nor his policy, nor his *modus operandi* were altogether new. Yet in respect of each there was at work a consistent, clear-sighted and forceful vision that transformed his predecessors' haphazard efforts into a comprehensive plan for rapid industrialization. Vitte complained:

In spite of the vast successes achieved during the last twenty years (i.e. 1880–1900) in our metallurgical and manufacturing industry, the natural resources of the country are still underdeveloped and the masses of the people remain in enforced idleness. A considerable part of our peasant population does not know to what to put its hand in winter. In pre-reform Russia the huge natural wealth of the country was either not used at all or exploited only by extremely primitive means. To the present epoch has fallen the difficult task of making up for what has been neglected in an economic slumber lasting two centuries.[5]

Vitte's economic starting point was the consciousness of Russia's unrealized potential. His theoretical inspiration came from Friedrich List; and politically he equated economic and military power. It was characteristic also of the Russian tradition that although Vitte sought to create the conditions in which capitalists and *entrepreneurs* of any nationality might freely flourish, he never for one moment doubted that the initiative must come from the state.

Vitte gave the clearest *exposé* of his hopes and policies in a confidential memorandum to the tsar in 1899. Outstanding was his admission of the fact that 'years, even decades', would have to pass before the sacrifices imposed in the name of industrialization would bring their benefit. On the other hand, were Russia to remain a predominantly agricultural country, exporting raw materials and importing finished goods, then it could be nothing more than a colony of western Europe.

The economic relationship of Russia to western Europe is precisely similar to the relationship between the colonial countries and their metropolises: the latter look on their colonies as an advantageous market to which they can freely export products of their labour and their industry, and from which they can with a mighty arm draw the raw materials essential to them. . . . Russia was, and to a certain extent still is, a hospitable colony of this type for all the industrially developed states, generously supplying them with the cheap products of its soil and paying dearly for the products of their labour. But there is one radical difference between the position of Russia and that of a colony: Russia is a politically independent and mighty power; it has the right and the power not to want to pay tribute for ever to the economically more advanced states; it must know the value of its raw materials and natural richness . . . and it is conscious of the great labour power of its people, not yet fully displayed; it has the firm and proud power which jealously preserves not only the political but also the economic independence of its empire; Russia wishes to be a metropolis itself. . . .[6]

Vitte did not disguise – from the emperor at least – the fact that as a consequence of this programme 'the paying powers of the population are strained to the extreme, in many cases consumption is directly restricted'. He acknowledged that the tariff imposed 'heavy sacrifices which are borne by the whole people, not out of excess but out of current needs'. But he also argued that foreign loans could alleviate the burden by reducing the necessity to accumulate capital inside Russia. 'To wait,' he said,

for the natural accumulation of capital in a country where the majority of the population is living through a difficult economic period and hands to the Treasury a considerable part of its surplus in the form of taxes and to force it as before to pay dearly for what it buys – this is a too burdensome position for the population and its basic occupation – agriculture.

Vitte saw the solution to what he called this 'dilemma', typical of an undeveloped country, in the recourse to foreign loans and investments obtained from those states where capital existed in surplus.[7]

Vitte then went on to equate economic power with military power, and to argue that 'even the military preparedness of a country is determined not only by the level of its military organization but also by the degree of development of its industry. The Russian national political and cultural edifice lacks at its base an appropriate economic soil, so that the empire of Your Highness may become a great power not only politically and agriculturally but also industrially.' He contrasted, on the one hand, Britain, Germany and the United States with, on the other, India, China, Turkey and South America. The latter were 'politically impotent to the degree that they were economically dependent on foreign industry'.[8] Vitte was determined that Russia would go the path of Britain and not India, of Germany and not China, of the United States and not South America.

This policy brings Vitte close to Stalin. Both banged the drum of greatness and sang the same tune. 'To slacken the pace would be to lag behind,' cried Stalin at the height of the First Five Year Plan in 1931,

and those who lag behind are beaten. We do not want to be beaten. . . . [Russia] was ceaselessly beaten for her backwardness. She was beaten by the Mongol khans. She was beaten by the Turkish beys. She was beaten by the Swedish feudal lords. She was beaten by the Polish-Lithuanian *pans*. She was beaten by the Anglo-French capitalists. She was beaten by the Japanese barons. She was beaten by all – for her backwardness. We are fifty or a hundred years behind the advanced countries. We must make good this lag in ten years. Either we do or they crush us.

Vitte had, of course, to meet the same obstacles as had overcome his predecessors – unremitting opposition from the spokesmen of agricultural interests, ranging from populist economists to the members of the state council, peasant poverty, the lack of an educated managerial and technical elite (only in part overcome by the influx of foreign experts), the inadequacy of the Russian central and local bureaucracy, the absence of a skilled working class, and the sluggishness and deviousness of the Russian businessman. He was also aware of institutional barriers arising from the dispersal of authority amongst many different organs of the state.[9]

In the construction of a modern railway network Vitte enshrined his greatest hope of emerging victorious over these handicaps. In the earlier part of the century railways had been feared for their disintegrating effect on Russian life. In the 1840s Kankrin, Nicholas I's minister of finance, had called them 'the malady of the age' and accused them of fostering excessive mobility and increasing social equality. To Nicholas's contemporary, Francis I, emperor of Austria, railways were the harbinger of revolution. But to Vitte they were 'a mighty productive force'. They employed more than 400,000 workers – a larger number than any other branch of industry. The replacement and maintenance of Russia's 270,000 wagons and 11,500 locomotives was in itself an industrial undertaking. Lastly, railways had what Vitte terms 'a great cultural meaning'. The 95 million passengers carried annually on the Russian network represented so much cultural interchange. 'It is hardly possible to deny,' Vitte declared, 'that each journey from the depths of the countryside and villages to the powerful centres, and the reverse . . . facilitates the mutual intercourse of different social classes which is useful precisely in relation to culture.' Railways were from every point of view 'a ferment'.[10] He hoped that their beneficent influence, transmitted through the interchange of goods and persons, their stimulus to heavy industry and employment, their contribution to urban growth, would eventually raise the standard of living in the countryside.

Under Vitte's inspiration, the 1890s became *par excellence* the Russian railway age. The length of the major lines in 1885 was 23,500 versts; by 1895 it was 31,500 versts. Then the real upsurge began – by 1900 it was 47,800. It had doubled in less than fifteen years.[11] This effort was largely financed by the Russian Treasury. Out of a state debt totalling 6,000 million roubles in 1900 no less than 3,000 million roubles were invested in railways.[12] Furthermore, in order that the railways might play their part in the economic fertilization of the country, the Treasury systematically overpaid its suppliers. In 1897–8, for example, the price for rails was fixed at between 1 rouble 10 kopeks and 1 rouble 25 kopeks, although they could be produced at the best south Russian plants for 77–89 kopeks. English firms offered rails for the construction of the Trans-Siberian railway at a price of 75 kopeks, but the Treasury preferred to place its orders with Russian firms at a price of 2 roubles.[13] All in all, it has been calculated that between 1894 and 1902 more than two-thirds of the government's total expenditure was devoted to the economic development of the country. This represented the highest proportion of any period between 1861 and 1917.[14]

Railway construction, however important, was in itself only one aspect of the astonishing range of activity deployed by Vitte in his feverish pursuit of an industrialized Russia. He subsidized Russian steamship companies, sponsored industrial fairs and exhibitions, established nautical schools for the training of merchant navy personnel, manipulated freight rates, founded engineering schools and polytechnic institutes, pushed through the convertibility of the rouble, encouraged savings banks, remodelled the State Bank so that it might issue industrial loans, amended company law to facilitate the formation of private companies, subsidized journalists, both Russian and French, founded a bureau of weights and measures, and published a house organ of financial and industrial information. And all this is to say nothing of the ordinary fiscal activity of the ministry, and – even more important – the management of a vast but still growing foreign indebtedness. Finally, it was a most significant part of Vitte's function to maintain contact with the business lobbies, would-be concessionaires, company promoters, and the associations grouping oil-producers, private railway-owners, Polish mine-owners, and metallurgists – in short, all the multifarious media through which the ministry channelled its investments into the Russian economy.

Such was the range of Vitte's activity that contemporaries accused him of creating a state within a state.[15] A foreign observer found Vitte obliged to encroach on the work of all his colleagues. The ministries of war, the interior, agriculture, foreign affairs and education all suffered.[16] The exigencies of industrialization had the most far-reaching implications. Vitte, for example had at length to acknowledge the need to dissolve the peasant commune and to introduce into agrarian life the free play of market forces.

In foreign policy, he threw all his influence behind attitudes of passivity, not to say pacifism. Few things could more easily have upset his plans, as events would show, than unwonted military expenditure or a breakdown in international stability and confidence. The greatest praise that Vitte could lavish on Alexander III was inspired by the thirteen years of peace that Russia enjoyed during his reign (1881–94).[17] Not that Vitte did not energetically promote the imperialist penetration of China and Manchuria, but his chosen instruments were financial and economic – the Russo-Chinese Bank, for example, or the Russo-Korean Bank, or the Chinese Eastern Railroad. He strongly deprecated the Russian seizure of Port Arthur in 1898 and, in the words of a journalistic confidant, Dr Dillon (of the *Daily Telegraph*) 'grudged every rouble that he had to spend on armaments'.[18] Again, it was Vitte who swung the Russian government behind the policy which resulted in the first Disarmament Conference at The Hague in 1899. 'The ever-increasing financial charges strike and paralyse public prosperity at its source . . . ,' the Russian invitation argued.

> Economic crises, due in great part to the system of amassing armaments to the point of exhaustion and the continual danger which lies in this accumulation of war material, are transforming the armed peace of our days into a crushing burden, which the peoples have more and more difficulty in bearing.[19]

But the Russian effort to remain in the big league demanded not only a programme of modernization but also an ineluctable programme of rearmament, that all Vitte's 'grudging' could not gainsay. Russian naval expenditure rose from 55 million roubles in 1895 to 67 million roubles in 1898; military expenditure from 285 million roubles to 303 million roubles over the same period.[20]

What were the results of Vitte's policies? He had undoubtedly considerable success. Between 1892 and 1901 the index of industrial production rose from $31 \cdot 14$ ($1913 = 100$) to $61 \cdot 11$. The average annual percentage rate of industrial growth was $8 \cdot 03$. Between 1894 and 1899 it even came close to touching 9 per cent.[21] The percentage of the working class employed in 1890 in heavy industry grew from 43 per cent of all industrial workers to close on 50 per cent by 1900, with particular growth in mining and metal-working.[22] Oil production grew between 1892 and 1901 from 286 to $706 \cdot 3$ million poods; the production of cast-iron from $65 \cdot 4$ to 175 million poods; of coal from $424 \cdot 1$ to 1,009 million poods.[23] In certain respects Russian production far outstripped that of its competitors. The number of spindles in Russia between 1890 and 1900 increased by 76 per cent – the comparable figure for Britain and the United States was respectively $3 \cdot 8$ per cent and $25 \cdot 6$ per cent.[24] Over the whole period from 1870 to 1900 manufacturing production increased in Russia $4 \cdot 5$ times; the equivalent figure for the United States was $4 \cdot 1$, Germany $3 \cdot 7$, Britain $1 \cdot 7$, France 2 and Italy $3 \cdot 3$.[25]

Was all this enough? Alas no! It had always been Vitte's hope that the programme of industrialization, to which everything else was sacrificed, would in time communicate its benefits to the peasantry and the rapidly growing working class and raise the standard of living all round. But during this transition period, he had to acknowledge that taxes and import duties reduced a standard of living that was already at a bare subsistence level, that taxes were paid 'not out of surplus but out of current needs'. Furthermore, the burden of taxation, because it was mainly indirect, and because the government depended so largely on the export of grain to service its foreign loans, was distributed most unequally.[26] The Vitte system was tantamount to squeezing the peasantry tighter and tighter for the sake of a problematic future benefit. Rarely has national greatness, the *raison d'être* of the system, ever been so dearly purchased. In essence, the Vitte system was a gamble on the ability of industry to produce some show of improved living conditions before the peasantry and proletariat found the burden of greatness intolerable.

This gamble did not come off. In 1898–9 famine once again struck at the peasantry, this time in the central Volga area; and in 1901 and 1902 the sky in the Poltava and Kharkov areas turned red with the burning of manor houses. Simultaneously, the international crises of the end of the nineteenth century – Fashoda, Spanish-American War, Boer War, Boxer Rebellion – combined to reduce the supply of foreign capital to Russia. This severely curtailed the state's orders to industry – and there was no domestic market to take up the slack. Expansion came to a sudden stop. In 1900, 1901 and 1902 there was virtually no change in the volume of industrial output; over the period 1900–1906 the average annual rate of growth declined to 1·43 per cent.[27] This of course meant unemployment, strikes and wage reductions for the urban proletariat.[28]

In 1902 the mounting criticism of Vitte's programme found expression in the annual report to the emperor of General Lobko, the state comptroller:

At present there is no more doubt that the crisis is caused by the artificial and excessive growth of industry in recent years. Industry, based on the protective tariff, extensive government orders, and the speculative increase of cheap foreign capital, grew out of proportion to the development of the consumer's market, which consists chiefly of the mass of the agricultural population, to which eighty per cent of our population belongs. An entirely sound existence for industry is guaranteed only by a corresponding development of the domestic market representing a sufficiently broad and constant demand for manufactured goods. That condition is particularly important for a young industry developing under the influence of protective tariffs, as it is in no position to count on the international market. Furthermore, the economic condition of our agriculture cannot be called satisfactory. The strenuous efforts of the government to plant industries has not been accompanied by equally intensive measures for the support and raising of the agricultural base of the welfare of the Russian people. In view of the inadequacy of the government measures the negative sides of the protective system show up all the more strongly in the agricultural population. The chief burden of that system lies undoubtedly upon the agricultural mass, seriously impairing its purchasing power. It has to bear almost the entire burden of direct and indirect taxes. As a result the demand of our domestic market cannot keep up with excessive growth of our industry. The equilibrium between industry and the domestic market has been destroyed and with it the basis of successful economic development. This, according to my deepest conviction, constitutes the chief cause of the present difficulties.[29]

At this time Vitte had himself to admit the incompatibility of his policy with the needs of the peasantry. The military and naval budgets could not be reduced; and customs duties could not be lowered without detriment to industry. All he could suggest to relieve the agricultural crisis was greater freedom for the peasantry but this could only be a long-term solution. At the end of the year, Vitte, like Vyshnegradsky before him, had to admit that 'the paying power of the population are exhausted'.[30]

From one point of view the overall crisis may be seen, in Lenin's words of 1908, as the result of the contradiction between 'the most retarded agriculture' and 'the most advanced industrial and financial capitalism'.[31] From another, it confirms the populist analysis of the flaw at the heart of any Russian capitalist development. In any event, the crisis that befell the Vitte system at the turn of the century revealed not only a poverty-stricken peasantry, whose full despair would not emerge until 1905, but also a disaffected working class. This was the new dimension added to the perennial crisis of the Russian economy.

Over and above this, the economic development of the latter half of the century, in particular its last decade, had changed the very framework within which the crisis unfolded. Rapid economic growth brought with it a considerable degree of social and political instability. Those ninety-five million railway journeys every year were bringing the countryside closer to the town, displaying and creating new ways of life, disrupting social groups, but as yet providing no cohesive force to replace them. The railways were truly serving as a 'ferment'. One society with its inherited norms and values was in decline; it was assailed by a new society struggling to come to birth.

Vitte gave unstinted support to these new forces. 'On the new paths opened up by the general improvement in economic conditions,' he wrote, 'there always enter first only the most enterprising economic units, only people of bold beginnings, only men of success – *udachniki* – not until later . . . do the weak, inert masses begin to stir themselves.'[32] The new men who came to the fore in the Russian industrial revolution were not only businessmen but also the multifarious groups of men with technical and professional qualifications – managers, teachers, lawyers, scientists, journalists, economists, engineers. All this entailed some re-distribution of economic power and also the emergence of political aspirations, for which the existing order made no provision.

Discontent over the lack of political opportunities was perhaps confined solely to the new men. But there was certainly no predisposition for revolutionary change amongst those who suffered by such change – the peasantry and industrial workers, the 'weak inert masses'. Only the whip of poverty drove the peasant from the countryside into the factory; and once there he rarely lost all contact with his native village. Those who gained by modernization and those who lost by it brought further instability to an already unstable society.[33]

2 The Worker Abandoned

Where and how did the proletariat live and work? In the first half of the nineteenth century two main industrial areas were in existence – the Urals, producing iron and copper, and the central industrial area, producing mainly textiles. By the end of the century this pattern had become much diversified. In 1896 a survey based on total economic plant showed eight main industrial areas – the Moscow region (textiles, metal-processing, chemicals); St Petersburg region (machine-building, metallurgy, textiles); Poland (textiles, coal, iron, chemicals); south Russian Ukraine (coal, iron ore, basic chemicals); the Urals (mining and metallurgy); the Baku petroleum region; the south-western sugar beet industry; and the Trans-Caucasian manganese and coal region. These eight areas alone accounted for fifty-eight per cent of the total factory labour force of European Russia, such was the degree of Russian industry's geographical concentration.[1] This feature later became even more pronounced: by 1912 the central industrial area, the north-western (St Petersburg) area and the Ukraine, which occupied thirty per cent of the area of European Russia, produced sixty-two per cent of all industrial output and employed sixty-three per cent of all workers.[2]

Factory employment was by no means synonymous with urbanization. Between 1860 and 1914 the urban population approximately trebled; but the *proportion* of the total population living in cities grew only from 11·6 per cent to 14·6 per cent.[3] This was not only due to the continuing importance of agrarian activities but also to the establishment of enterprises in rural areas outside towns, where industry developed faster than in urban centres. Some seventy per cent of all workers were employed in such locations. It was most marked of course in the extractive industries but applied also in high degree to metal-working and textiles.[4] The *entrepreneur* had to build roads, houses, hospitals, schools, churches, and establish such services as water-supply and postal communications – yet the availability of cheap labour made the additional expense worth while. It was more profitable to bring the factory to the worker than vice versa. Only in the St Petersburg province was there a high proportion of urbanized workers. Elsewhere, the norm was the company 'town' in a rural area. Occupational mobility, however stimulated by Vitte's policy of cheap passenger fares, had still to make its full presence felt. Many factory workers did not have to venture far beyond their native commune to find industrial employment.

The concentration of industry had not only a geographical but also a functional aspect. A most striking feature of the Russian economy and further testimony to its advanced technical nature was its concentration in large enterprises. This derived from its adoption, almost without preliminary, of the latest European models. In the coalmines of the Donetz Basin in 1890, for example, the thirty-seven largest mines (those with over a hundred workers) employed nearly three-fifths of the total number of workers and produced seventy per cent of the total coal output. The remaining output and employment was accounted for by 223 mines.[5] Furthermore, an increasing number of workers was being employed in factories employing more than a thousand workers. In 1866, factories with a thousand workers and over employed twenty-seven per cent of the total number of workers in factories with a hundred or more workers; in 1879, forty per cent; and in 1890, forty-six per cent. Similarly, the larger the factory the greater the increase in the volume of output.[6]

A contrary trend was also at work – the growth of small enterprises. It is surprising to note, for example, that by 1913 there were almost as many workers in small enterprises, employed in the employer's home perhaps, as in factories and mines. The respective percentages were 16·8 per cent and 18·8 per cent – in round figures, three million as against 3,350,000.[7] There was a dual trend operative – towards the foundation both of mammoth factories and of small producing units.

Who were the workers and where did they come from? Quite a high proportion were women – in 1904 no less than 27·5 per cent of those engaged in manufacturing industry.[8] The remainder was formed of peasants suffering from lack of land, shortage of land, the effects of bad harvest, those burdened with arrears and debts or those peasants who were 'superfluous'.[9] It was only the whip of the extremest poverty or the heaviest financial stress that could force the peasant to leave his village. It is also clear that most of the workers were amazingly young – according to one source about fifty per cent in 1905 were between twenty and twenty-nine.[10] Perhaps, by the end of the 1890s, only one-half formed a hereditary proletariat in the western sense, i.e. were the offspring of fathers who had themselves been factory workers.[11] The working class, if in such circumstances it can be said actually to exist, grew to a large extent by a constant process of accretion from the countryside and not by natural increase.

Ties of the most varied type continued to exist between the factory employees and the villages they came from. It is no matter for surprise that for the best part of two decades Populists could seriously challenge the Marxist contention that a working class was in fact coming into existence in Russia. Was not the new factory population composed merely of peasants in disguise, displaced peasants, as it were? For the same reason the government could repeatedly deny the existence of a labour problem in Russia. In the first place, the worker still remained legally classified as a peasant. Similarly, he also remained a member of his village commune, entitled to share in the periodical redistribution of land and also obliged to contribute his share towards the taxes levied by the commune. It was also of course the commune which issued the passport entitling the peasant to seek work beyond its confines.

Even though the peasant's decision to seek factory work broke his physical bond with the village, the 'worker's' attachment to his allotment of land frequently remained unbroken. Relatives might till it during his absence and he himself would very likely make periodic returns to the village to help at harvest-time or in the fields. In the intervals he would remit to his family such savings as could be spared from his scanty wages. In other cases the absentee allotment-holder could lease his land to other peasants; or he might hire hands to raise his crops for him. The connexion between factory and village may have been tenuous, but to many a factory worker it was an unforgotten reality. To the worker who lost his job, fell ill, or was disabled, the village offered the only sanctuary available, however poverty-stricken it might be. He could go nowhere else in adversity.

Perhaps the most notable evidence of the factory–village attachment was the continuing proportion of workers to whom the factory was only a part-time occupation. The rest of the year, particularly at harvest-time, they worked on the land. In this respect there was tremendous variety as between one industry and another, one region and another. Over the whole country perhaps one-quarter of the workers might be affected. The proportion was greatest in the food processing and textile industries and lowest in the metal trades. The highest proportion of permanent workers – almost nine-tenths – was in the St Petersburg factory region.[12]

The factory–village link slowed down the process of industrialization and the formation of a permanent working class. A further obstacle, in the worker's viewpoint, was the low level of wages. He could barely support himself on his average wage of some two hundred roubles a year. How then could he support a wife, let alone a family? The unskilled worker, typically, lived a single life in a factory barracks or, if he was married, lived apart from the family he had left behind in his native commune. The number of married workers living a normal conjugal life in their own accommodation was extremely limited. This separation was at its worst in the congested cities; it was less evident in the factories located near villages.

Living conditions were amongst the worst in the new extracting industries. At Baku, at the end of the century, almost all the workers lived in barracks built by the oil firms, according to a report issued by the department of mines in 1893. Mud huts had been prohibited following an outbreak of cholera the previous year but the buildings that replaced them lacked light, had no ventilation, and were crammed full with plank beds. Heating came from oil stoves which produced smoke, dirt and soot and easily caused fires. Some firms, in the interests of economy, built barracks for only half their workers; they were occupied in shifts. There were also barracks in which married and unmarried workers lived side by side; barracks in which food was cooked and bread baked; and in every barrack hut the overcrowding was intense. Benckendorff, head of one of the oil-producing firms, told the eleventh congress of oil producers in Baku in 1903 that it was impossible to pass 'without horror and trembling' in the vicinity of a workers' barracks. 'The workers, all in greasy, soot-covered rags, covered with a thick layer of grime and dust, swarm like bees in the extremely dirty and congested quarters. A repulsive smell hits you as soon as you try to approach the window.'[13]

In Moscow and St Petersburg the characteristic working class dwelling was a hideously overcrowded tenement on the outskirts of the city. Here land was cheap. A report of 1902 in the journal of the Moscow municipal corporation described rooms where 'the atmosphere was intolerably stuffy because of the density of the inhabitants. The apartment is damp and unbelievably dirty. In two rooms there is complete darkness. The ceiling is so low that a tall man cannot stand upright. A specific smell.' Another report: 'The apartment has a terrible appearance, the plaster is crumbling, there are holes in the walls, stopped up with rags. It is dirty. The stove has collapsed. Legions of cockroaches and bugs. No double window frames and so it is piercingly cold. The lavatory is so dilapidated that it is dangerous to enter and children are not allowed in. All the apartments in the house are similar.' Yet another: 'An impossible atmosphere – exhalation of people, wet clothing and dirty linen; everywhere dampness and dirt. Draughts in every corner; in rainy weather water on the floor two inches deep.' There was no separation of the sexes in the apartments surveyed. In one and the same room the inspectors found old women, young girls, twins, juveniles and old men. All these people lived, settled their accounts, changed their underclothing, slept side by side, half an inch apart, only rarely screening their bed with a curtain. And in these surroundings 38,000 children were growing up, the inspectors reported.[14] In the new mining and manufacturing centres of the south, zemstvo investigators in the middle 1880s found workers and their families accommodated in bare, exposed huts, overcrowded and un-hygienic to the last degree. 'We often met in the wooden huts poor women somehow covered with dirty rags, sitting on the bare earthen floor with darning in their hands, nursing a child, rolling around on a pile of dirty, stinking rags, and surrounded by other children. . . . In one hut of this type a sick boy was lying in a corner, barely recovered from smallpox, but fallen ill again with a fever. All around cocks were walking and clucking and young pigs were grunting.'[15]

There were indeed examples of model factory housing built by paternalistic employers, but here peasant habits had to be eradicated by strict discipline and such establishments had the worst strike record.[16] They also had the social disadvantage of alienating the worker physically from the rest of the population. Let us visit, with a contemporary German observer, a model textile factory in the Moscow region employing many thousands of people:

Contact between the workers and the outside world was almost entirely limited to the relationship of the people to their native village where they would go on leave from time to time. This isolated life of whole bodies of workers was the more pronounced the more remote the factory from the town centre, the more the factory administration had considered all the needs of the worker's life and the more certain the children were to find work in the same factory. The short summer season, poor communications and the infrequent and expensive means of transport prevented any active contact with the town and there was also no need for this. The expenses of the people were limited to food and clothing which they could obtain in the factory shop at cost price; all other arrangements were completely or almost cost-free. I saw factories which contained heated and illuminated dwellings for the married and unmarried, communal kitchens, eating rooms, washrooms, baths, hospitals, confinement apartments, children's nursery, school, shops, bakery, fire-station and even its own police force.[17]

Conditions of labour were on a par with those of living. Wages, as already mentioned, were insufficient to support a wife. Accidents were another hazard. In mining, in 1904, they amounted to 11·1, and in manufacturing industry to 4, per 100 workers.[18] The actual conditions of labour were not only hazardous but also insanitary; the working day was heavy – perhaps eleven or twelve hours; corporal punish-ment might be inflicted even, and fines were imposed for a multitude of offences. The sole mitigating feature was the large number of public holidays – almost a quarter of the year, from the Feast of the Circumcision of Christ to Christmas.

Were the mills of St Petersburg and Moscow perhaps not even darker and more satanic than those of Lancashire? Russian industry, after all, was a late-comer to the European scene, and had to fight against entrenched rivals for its place in the sun. It also suffered under geographical handicaps – the lengthy distances and poor communications which inflated transport costs, and the climate which necessitated additional expenditure on heating. There were institutional difficulties – the need, for example, to establish schools and hospitals, the expenses of which, in the western countries, were borne by the state. Again, interest rates in Russia were high owing to the poverty of the country. Lastly, it would of course have utterly contradicted Vitte's policy of capital accumulation should the Russian employer have dissipated his profits in paying higher wages to his men rather than in extending his business. Not for nothing did Vitte write with gratification of the 'modest habits' engendered by rural life. 'The Russian peasant is much less demanding that the western European or particularly the North American worker,' he claimed, 'and a low wage is for Russian enterprise a fortunate boon, which complements the riches of Russian natural resources.'[19]

All these factors – to say nothing of the constant influx of peasants seeking work – pressed down on the wage fund of Russian industry. The striking contradiction between Russian industrialization and the preservation of the standard of living, let alone its improvement, could not be more clearly demonstrated. 'There is no doubt . . . ,' writes one distinguished analyst of the Russian economy, 'that in no western country did the periods of "industrial revolutions" exact sacrifices from the populations comparable to those made in Russia in the closing years of the last century.'[20] Vitte's policy of robbing the present for the sake of the future, of guns before butter, of establishing Russian greatness by impoverishing the peasantry and exploiting the proletariat was most intimately linked to the progress of the Russian revolution.

All in all, therefore, because seasonal work was so much a part of the industrial picture, because the physical distance between factory and commune was in many cases not so great, because manifold legal and family links still tied the peasant to his commune, because factory life offered to the vast majority no possibility of a stable existence with wife and family, because it was only under the stimulus of poverty that he had entered the factory at all – for all these reasons the factory worker still looked on himself as a peasant; and this was no less characteristic of the full-time worker.

The dichotomy in the consciousness of a worker, half-peasant and half-proletarian, cannot but have been sharpened by his experiences in the factory and town. There was a massive and self-evident contrast between the easy-going, time-consuming, time-hallowed ways of the village and the regularity and discipline required by factory life. In this new world such skills as the peasant did possess were of no value. His illiteracy left him unfitted for any but the most mechanical tasks and, psychologically, made it difficult to encompass the adjustment to factory life. No doubt the sense of cohesion and solidarity engendered by life in a large factory mitigated to some extent the sense of alienation; but it could never replace the closeness of traditional life in the commune. Moreover, the peasant's acute resentment at having to undertake factory work in the first place was intensified by the unavoidable comparison between his own lowly status and that of his employer. Industrialization necessarily involved social mobility. Though there were no doubt significant differences in the village amongst the village shop-keeper, the peasant with two horses and the peasant with no horse, the contrast in any large town or factory encampment between employer and worker was a thousand times more flagrant. These circumstances made it easy for the radical and revolutionary intelligentsia to open the eyes of the factory masses to the relative opulence of their exploiters. There was all the less disposition to accept the factory and urban world as unalterable.

By any standards a social problem of some magnitude had emerged in Russia in the 1890s. The government did its best to avert its gaze. 'In our industry,' ran a secret circular issued by the ministry of finance in 1895,

there prevail patriarchal relations between the employer and the worker. This patriarchy in many cases is expressed in the concern of the factory owner for the needs of the workers and employees in his factory, in his anxiety for the maintenance of harmony and agreement . . .
    'In Russia, fortunately, there does not exist a working class in the same sense and significance as in the west, and therefore there does not exist a labour question . . .[21]

This view could undoubtedly draw substance from the very small proportion of workers in the population; from the fact that most of them were peasants, legally registered as such, and owners of allotment land; even if they worked in a factory or mine, they were often not so far removed from their native village. But to deny the existence of a labour problem *per se* was pure self-deception. A decade earlier, the men on the spot in certain areas already saw through the official denial. In 1885, a police report from Moscow, summarizing the labour situation for the previous year, pointed out that

the former family and patriarchal relationship, so to speak, between employers and workmen has vanished to be replaced by regulations based on formal agreements and conditions, determining the number of working hours in the week, the size of wages, fines for loafing and spoiling goods, the right of the employer to dismiss the worker from the establishment and the right of the worker to withdraw from work. However, the position of the worker has not improved through this.[22]

Had such a relationship ever really existed? The government's own actions suggested the contrary. In 1882 the first important factory legislation was passed during Bunge's tenure of the finance ministry. It prohibited the employment of children under twelve and restricted the working hours of those aged between twelve and fifteen. Night work was banned entirely. In order to give effect to these decrees, a factory inspectorate was created under the aegis of the ministry of finance. Its personnel, drawn from the academic and the medical profession, operated under a chief inspector in St Petersburg. The inspectorate's first reports on labour conditions played the same role in Marxist agitation in Russia as had British Blue Books in the composition of Marx's *Capital*. The reports created such a furore that they had to be banned. In 1896 Lenin justifiably commented:

The government fears more than the plague publicity for factory practices and incidents. It banned the publication of strike news in the press, it forbade factory inspectors to publish their reports, and it even put a stop to the hearing of strike cases in the ordinary courts open to the public.[23]

From this point on the government wavered between a policy of repression and a policy of legislation, designed to display its role as the protector of the worker against exploitation by the employer. In either case, however, any attempt by the workers to better their position at their own initiative contravened the law. It was illegal to strike; it was illegal to form a trade union or any collective organization and in those few instances where mutual aid societies did exist, they were removed from the workers' control. The young Lenin did not exaggerate when he wrote in one of his earliest works:

The conditions of the Russian workers are such that they are deprived of the most elementary civil rights. They must not dare to gather together, to discuss their affairs together, to organize unions, to publish statements . . . (there is) such scandalous abuse of power by officials and such a violation of the rights of the common people as are hardly possible in any European country.[24]

The weight of government repression was all the more effective in that the peasant-workers in factory and mine brought with them from their native village a certain tradition of social passivity. Moreover, the worker was under the strongest possible pressure not to jeopardize his wages; he also had no strike fund or friendly society to fall back on. Even so, strikes did rapidly become a feature of Russian industrial life. But because of the inhibiting circumstances, political and traditional, they tended to be of short duration and by no means fully supported. Strike statistics for the years from 1895 to 1904 show, for example, that only about half of the labour force in any one factory took part in any particular strike, and the strikes themselves rarely exceeded an average duration of ten days. Also noteworthy was the close relationship between the size of a factory and the number of strikes. The larger the factory, the greater the number of strikes.[25]

Large scale incidents forced the government to mitigate repression with some show of concession. In 1885 a particularly ferocious strike involving some four thousand workers broke out at one of the textile mills in Vladimir province owned by the Morosov family. The fight rapidly took an ugly turn when the governor called in police and troops. Subsequent investigation revealed such abuses on the part of the management that, in order to avert further unrest, the minister of the interior was forced to recommend to the tsar new measures to determine relations between employer and workman. Alexander III concurred in this and a commission under von Plehve, the deputy minister of the interior, drafted a law, published in 1886, which remained a basic factor in the tsarist labour code. This law incidentally illuminates much of Russian management practice.

Its *rationale* was the principle that 'the hiring of factory labour is not merely a civil contract but a matter of public interest irretrievably connected with public order and peace'. The law then defined in meticulous detail the essentials of the contract binding employer and worker; wages must be paid at fixed times and only in cash; they must not be reduced once the initial contract has been made; no payment might be expected for the use of tools, medical aid or lighting; fines might only be inflicted in accordance with a fixed schedule and the funds thus accumulated could only be expended, with the government's permission, on behalf of the workers. The need to give black and white definition to the contract came from the need to facilitate the task of the factory inspectors who now received extended powers of inquiry and added responsibilities. The inspector was also appointed to a newly created factory council in each locality, consisting of the governor, vice-governor, chief of police and representatives of the zemstvo or municipal duma. This body, under the terms of the act of 1886, was empowered to take all the necessary steps for the maintenance of peaceful industrial relations in the localities.

The law was not applied at once throughout the empire. In some respects it can be seen to have had a beneficial effect – for instance, in reducing the price of foodstuffs in factory shops and in curtailing fines.

Also, no doubt, it did something to remove the grosser forms of exploitation. It went no further; this is abundantly evident from the strikes of the later 1880s and 1890s. As it was, the scales, given the employer-oriented government, remained weighted on the side of capital. Thus, in return for state intervention on their behalf, the workers had to abandon all claim to form trade unions. They also might not form assemblies to discuss their common interests – the police practice was to regard all such assemblies as illegal unless they had been authorized in advance. It was, moreover, typical of the government's approach that employer and worker should not be equal before the law: in the case of non-payment of wages it was necessary for the aggrieved worker to initiate a civil suit – a virtual impossibility. But it was a criminal offence should a worker, for example, quit his employment before the expiry of his contract.

For all these reasons, then, the law of 1886 failed to fulfil its purpose. It failed completely to remove the fundamental grievances of the workers in respect of pay and conditions. The strike movement gathered irresistible pace and weight, especially and most ominously in the large-scale textile mills and metallurgical plants. More ominous still, the strikes of the 1890s had political overtones and were organized. This latter was a feature of some sixty per cent of all the strikes that took place between 1895 and 1904.

The new phase in the Russian labour movement originated in the early 1890s in the west of the empire – in Poland and among the Jewish proletariat of Vilna and the Jewish Pale of Settlement.[26] It reached St Petersburg a few years later and soon manifested itself in the first mass strikes ever to take place in Russia – the textile strikes of 1896 and 1897.

The occasion was the coronation of the new tsar, Nicholas II. The governor of St Petersburg decreed the closure of all factories – those privately owned for one day and the state-owned for three days. These holidays were to be paid. Workers privately employed might also have the two extra days but without pay. This limitation produced a serious misunderstanding when some of the latter returned to work after taking three days off: they found that they had forfeited two days' pay.

The immediate response was a strike by the workers affected. Messengers quickly took the news from factory to factory. Within two days almost all the city's mammouth textile plants lay idle. The whole labour force of 30,000 was on strike. Russia had seen nothing like this before. Also new was the absence of the customary violence and drunkenness on the part of the strikers. This self-discipline was partly a consequence of the workers' formation of primitive strike committees and the election of representatives to maintain liaison between one factory and another. In these may be seen the germ of the future soviets (workers' councils) and trade unions.

Colleagues in other trades gave the textile workers financial support. A small body of Social-Democrats, including Lenin, grouped together in the Union of Struggle for the Emancipation of the Working Class, published leaflets and appeals in support of the strikers.

But within a week it was all over. Lack of financial resources forced the strikers to return to work. Their main demand – a reduction in the working day from thirteen hours to ten-and-a-half – remained unfulfilled. This defeat was temporary. A second great strike broke out in January 1897. Three months later the government was forced to concede the eleven-and-a-half hour working day.[27]

The government's policy of alternating repression with enforced conciliation was unsuccessful. It could not be otherwise, for the object of most strikes was to secure increased wages, and in this matter the government never intervened, having regard to the low wage policy of the ministry of finance.

The workers suffered not only from inadequate wages but also from humiliation and a sense of resentment. Deprived of any official form of organization or representation, uprooted from the countryside, at the constant mercy of employers and police, they existed only as an amorphous mass. They were no longer men and women but the outcasts of society. Listen, for example, to a leaflet put out in 1898 by the Ekaterinoslav Union of Struggle for the Emancipation of the Working Class. It is a protest against accidents at the Bryansk factory. Literate radicals may well have composed the leaflet; but were such people not in the best position to know how the workers felt?

Every day we must hear, now here, now there, that a man has died and our blood-suckers continue to stuff their pockets, giving *no* consideration to the men who have died, whose families have lost their bread-winner and are perhaps *dying of starvation*. The whole day we work, pouring out our blood and sweat. Every minute we expose our life to danger, we have no chance to use an essential break, and when there are accidents they accuse us of carelessness! *The greed of the capitalists, the long working day, the meagre wage – there is the cause of all accidents.* Even the holidays which we have had until now, have seemed too much to these beasts of prey and they have persuaded the government, *which is always on the side of the capitalists*, to reduce the number of holidays in the year. . . . Comrades, they have fooled us, they have fed long enough on our blood and sweat. Our only salvation can be *Friendly Workers' Unions*, against which nothing can stand. *Let us join together, comrades, in one general union and demand from the office new changes in the regulations.*[28]

Listen also to a leaflet put out by a Riga Workers' Committee of the Djutova factory in 1899:

On the evening of 5 May at the Alexandrovsky gate an utterly violent killing took place, whose victims were people of the working class – even our children were not spared. The terrible murderer is the government itself. Who will avenge our killed and wounded fathers, mothers and brothers? Who will judge the guilty? Will the government do so? But who will judge the government? The government pronounces judgement on itself and declares itself innocent! This has already happened. This is confirmed by the declaration of the governor who is not afraid even to lie to make us appear the greatest criminals in the eyes of the public. The governor lies when he says that the strike at the Djutova factory was begun by the male workers only, who are fewer here than the female workers; he does not say a word of the daily wage of these women workers – they receive thirty-five kopeks which even the director of a Riga factory called a dog's wage. The governor lies when he denies what is most important – that there were about fifteen killed and sixty wounded, the governor also lies when he says that the disorders took place following a previously planned criminal conspiracy . . .

Taking into consideration the present favourable circumstances, i.e. (1) strikes are taking place in almost all south Russia and Poland and also in Libau, where all the workers and even the policemen have demanded higher wages; (2) in almost all factories here wages have been reduced; (3) as a result of the latest crime of the government we feel ourselves more united – *we therefore summon the factory workers of Riga to begin a general strike*, demanding a rise in wages and a reduction of the working day . . .

Our enemy, as you see, has finally thrown off his sheep's skin and now flaunts his wolfish nature, and let hot hatred for him, for our common enemy, be our bond of unity! And while this hatred burns in our wounded hearts like a violent flame, while the whistle of the bullets and the boom of the drums still sounds in our ears, while the warm blood is wafted to the clouds – let us take each other's hands, brothers, in a new serious struggle![29]

It was rare at this time to find a strike call couched in terms other than those of protest at administrative abuse, low wages, repression and intolerable working conditions. But since the government repressed virtually any step taken collectively by the workers at their own initiative to improve their position, political aims must soon become dominant. In 1900 an organization known as *Socialist* brought this theme to the fore:

Noting that in every strike, every disorder, the police, gendarmes, soldiers, factory inspectors are the obedient servants of the employers, the workers have come to realize that it is necessary to wage a struggle not with the capitalists alone and not for economic interests alone. They have begun to realize that without political freedom, i.e. without the right of participation in the government through elected representation, without the right to form unions, to hold meetings, and the freedom of speech, press, conscience, person and movement, the worker cannot develop as he should.[30]

This initiative was isolated and strikes continued to have a mainly economic motivation. There is no doubt that the whole movement was on the increase at the turn of the century. Measures of repression grew *pari passu* with labour's restiveness. This affected the work of the factory inspectors – in 1897 they were instructed more forcefully than ever to inform strikers of the punishment to which they had made themselves liable. The inspectors must also make it possible for those workers who did not participate in a strike to enter the place of work.[31]

As part of this policy the authorities increased the police forces in the industrial districts. In certain factory areas the employers had themselves employed police at their own expense. The government now followed suit and established a new ratio of one policeman per 250 workers and one police inspector per 3,000 workers. These forces, according to the ministers of the interior and of finance, were 'designated exclusively for service in the areas of industrial establishments. Moreover, these police forces must have a mobile character, being grouped and directed to those localities where at any given moment there is felt the greatest need for an organization of correct and adequately powerful police supervision.'[32]

If police were insufficient, there was always the army. No symptom speaks with greater eloquence of the increasingly disturbed state of Russian industrial relations than the use of troops to quell strikes and demonstrations. The army was called in more and more frequently – 19 times in 1893, 50 times in 1899, 33 times in 1900, 271 times in 1901 and 522 times in 1902.[33] One particularly bloody encounter took place at the Obukhovo steel foundry in St Petersburg in May 1901. In order to crush a strike, troops and police had to institute a regular siege of the plant.[34]

When Svyatopolk-Mirsky, deputy minister of the interior, investigated the situation here and at other Petersburg plants, he found much to excuse the workers' mood of rebellion. Their conditions of housing and work were equally deplorable; they could make no provision for old age or illness; they were bullied by management; most of all, they had no legal means of making their grievances manifest.[35]

This sympathetic attitude clearly suggested that repression was not enough. As early as 1884 an alert police captain was already thinking in a somewhat similar strain. He suggested that the workers be supplied with books and reading matter 'which would explain in a concise and popular form a basic understanding of political economy'. He also recommended the employment of the church to teach 'Christian morality'.[36] This was an early and embryonic anticipation of what became the tsarist regime's sole constructive policy in dealing with the tense labour problem, based on the view that repression was not enough. General Trepov, head of the police department, elaborated the rationale of the new departure in 1898.

If the minor needs and demands of the workers are exploited by the revolutionaries for such profound anti-governmental aims, then is it not up to the government as soon as possible to seize this weapon, that is so rewarding for the revolutionaries, from their hands and itself to assure the fulfilment of the task . . . the police are obliged to be interested in the same thing as the revolutionary.[37]

The first step in this direction was taken in 1901 under the auspices of Colonel Zubatov, head of the Moscow security police. This figure from the political *demi-monde* of tsarist Russia had behind him a sordid past, first as revolutionary and then as *agent provocateur* in the students' revolutionary movement. He would win the confidence of those whom he intended to betray.

Zubatov's socialism represented a serious attempt to satisfy the workers whilst at the same time preserving the framework of the autocracy. What Zubatov would do was create the regime's own labour movement, separating the workers' economic action from the revolutionary political struggle. If the regime were to satisfy certain justified demands of the workers, then it might hope to withdraw them from the influence of revolutionaries. By satisfying the workers, Zubatov would emasculate the revolution.

The affinities of this view with the ideology of the Nazi Labour Front are manifest. Hence the *Zubatovshchina* is not to be regarded as an aberration on the part of the tsarist government but as a development that lies in the mainstream of the labour movement, and, more particularly the trade union movement, of the twentieth century. It is also related to Bismarck's labour policy. 'Give the workman the right to work as long as he is healthy,' said Bismarck, 'assure him care when he is sick, assure him maintenance when he is old. . . . If you do that . . . then I believe the gentlemen of the Social-Democratic programme will sound their bird-calls in vain.'

Zubatov's *point de départ* was the fear that he detected amongst the revolutionaries at the prospect of government activity on behalf of the workers. '*Such a policy leaves the revolutionary staff without an army* and the struggle with the government becomes physically impossible.' He therefore proposed the organization, with government encouragement, of cultural societies for the workers and the dissemination of suitable literature. On more orthodox lines, Zubatov also recommended the extension of mobile police detachments and the decentralization of the secret agent organization. Were this programme to be adopted, he concluded, 'then a vast benefit would be achieved (without any political concession of principle) and the revolution would be dealt a blow such as the most violent repression could never bring about.'[38]

The movement began in the western provinces of the empire. A police drive against the Social-Democratic General Jewish Workers' Union (the Bund) resulted in the arrest and subsequent conversion of a number of party members into police spies. They returned to the workers and now agitated for the abandonment of political aims and concentration on a purely economic struggle. The establishment of evening classes satisfied the workers' urge for education.

In 1901 Zubatov transferred his activities to Moscow where he organized a remarkably successful Mutual Assistance League of Workers in the Mechanical Industry. This was accompanied by the provision of lecture courses and workers' discussion groups, all demonstrating the benefits of a non-revolutionary approach to social problems. A lecturer at these gatherings compared the workers there to 'a parched soil, thirstily drinking in the first drops of moisture and this thirst for knowledge seized us; I felt that we were bringing a light, but this light did not penetrate a glass wall – yet it remained a light and those sitting in the darkness were stirred and dragged themselves to the light at its first gleams . . .'[39] This is testimony to the workers' yearning for some recognition of their problems.

Similar unions sprang up in Odessa, Kharkov, Kiev, Minsk, and elsewhere, in such disparate industries as weaving, baking, perfumery and tobacco. There is no doubt that the Zubatov movement successfully met a demand amongst the workers for a broad and open organization. In 1902 Zubatov organized a demonstration of 50,000 workers to Alexander II's memorial in the Kremlin.

Zubatov's success was also his undoing. It created great alarm amongst the industrialists. These fears were not unfounded. In 1903 Zubatov unions broke loose from their government-imposed framework and took a leading part in that year's general strike in south Russia.[40] Employers brought correspondingly great pressure to bear on Vitte, who in any case advocated a free contract between capital and labour. It also had an unfavourable effect on the attitude of foreign investors. In June 1903 the *Zubatovshchina* came to an abrupt end with the dismissal of its organizer. All that remained of this phase of tsarist labour legislation was one act providing for industrial accident insurance and a second act that established the workers' right to elect representatives to put their problems to management. But the first was far too narrowly conceived to calm disquiet, and the second the workers largely ignored.

The limited nature of these measures, in conjunction with the failure of the Zubatov experiment, had momentous consequences. As ever, the workers remained outside society, deprived of any stake in the existing order.

3 The Hungry Village Revives

Those revolutionaries who went to the villages in the 1870s in order to rouse the peasantry to an awareness of their plight met with little response. The nihilists and anarchists could establish no contact with the villagers. 'Blind faith in the nearness of the Russian revolution prevented us from acknowledging that our people were far from being as revolutionary-minded as we wished' – thus the sober reminiscence of a survivor of those days, Debagory-Mokrievitch. True, the peasants had an unappeased yearning for more land; but they also had un-diminished confidence in the generosity of the tsar. Only landlords and officials, they said, prevented the tsar from carrying out a further redistribution of land to complete the emancipation of the previous decade. For the moment the peasant was content to wait: 'In general, the picture was extremely passive in character.'[1] Turgenev's novel, *Virgin Soil*, which chronicles the beginnings of this movement, depicts a hero unable to engage in any meaningful dialogue with the peasan-try. When he tries to talk to the men of one village, they make him drunk on vodka. Zhelyabov, one of the revolutionaries who helped to organize the assassination of Alexander II in 1881 had an equally discouraging experience: he once asked a peasant, supposedly con-verted to socialism, what the man would do if he had 500 roubles: the answer came pat, 'Well, I will open a saloon.'[2] That is not the stuff of which peasant revolts are made. Faith in the tsar took long to fade. 'The expectations of a new division of the land have, with rare excep-tion, become everywhere stronger in the province,' reported the Voronezh correspondent of the underground journal *Narodnaya Volya* in September 1881. 'The redivision must, in the general conviction, take place on the basis of a decree of the tsar.'[3]

At the end of the nineteenth and beginning of the twentieth century the mood of the villages was very different. There would be no more waiting for the tsar. The peasants were taking matters into their own hands. Consider, for example, report No. 4894 issued on 17 July 1898:

From reports reaching the ministry of the interior it is seen that in certain provinces, predominantly southern and south-eastern, there has recently emerged a series of peasant disorders in the form of systematic damage to the landowners' fields and meadows, together with the driving away of cattle under the protection of men armed with sticks, staves and pitchforks, and attacks on the landowners' watchmen and guards or considerable illegal timer-cutting in the landowners' woods, and brawls with the foresters. When the guards seize the peasants' cattle, the peasants, hoping to free it, *often moving by whole villages*, carry out armed attacks on the buildings and farmhouses of the landowners and divide up the working and even the living quarters, attacking and wounding servants and guards.[4]

By 1905, peasant rioting in certain of these areas, in Poltava for example, was reminding a certain Khrulov, a government legel official in Kharkov, of a new Time of Troubles. There was 'a ferment' amongst all classes. People were rethinking the foundations of the whole existing order. No need existed for any further 'going to the people' in the manner of the 1870s. The villages had their own local intelligentsia to spread socialist and anti-governmental views.[5]

This 'ferment', this end of rural isolation can only be appreciated by reference to the salient conditions of serf emancipation in 1861, as modified by subsequent developments in rural life and industry. Far from breaking *in toto* with the past, the emancipation perpetuated many of the undesirable features of landlord Russia. The peasant remained a member of what has been called 'a caste confined in peculiar legal limits'.[6] He undoubtedly gained a great deal in the way of personal freedom, but much of this was nullified by the coercive role of the village commune. This institution isolated the peasantry from the remainder of the population, subjected them to special laws and made of them second-class citizens.

The commune existed before the emancipation. But because the government wished to avert the emergence of a class of landless labourers; because, too, it was easier for the landlord to deal with the peasants as a whole rather than individually, the commune's powers were in certain respects reinforced and even extended.

To the commune, for example, was assigned the land granted to the peasants as a result of emancipation. The peasant himself only 'owned' that portion of the commune's allotment land to which his family responsibilities, as head of a household, entitled him. In many areas it was also the commune that periodically redistributed the land in accordance with changing family obligations. Furthermore, the authority of the commune controlled the individual peasant's freedom of movement. A peasant wishing to relinquish his holding had first of all to pay certain redemption fees. He then had to obtain permission from the village assembly and the head of the household to which he belonged. This latter was in many cases not lightly given; the loss of a household member would automatically, *ceteris paribus*, reduce the amount of land available at the next partition. Should the peasant's departure from the commune be short-term – in order to work in a factory, for example – then he still remained attached to the commune as a taxpayer and the head of the household to which he belonged had the right to a share in the earnings of the absent peasant. The commune had it within its power to control the peasant's entry into such institutions as a monastery, for example, or a university or a government office.

The powers of the commune over peasant mobility far transcended matters of administrative convenience; they may also be seen as a function of the commune's fiscal purpose. Its members were collectively responsible for the payment of taxes and also of redemption dues. This circumstance shows how essential it was not to lose control of the individual member. In short, the commune was 'first and foremost a weapon in the hands of the government for assessing and levying taxes. . . .'[7] For this reason, when a trend towards individual holdings did set in, involving, despite every obstacle, the division of family plots, a law of 1886 erected any number of further legal obstacles to this process. In 1893 further legislation made it even more difficult for a peasant to relinquish his claim to a holding or to leave the commune altogether.

The quasi-emancipated peasant was not only economically weak and tied closely to the commune; he also remained under the unremitting scrutiny of the government. The new administrative unit created in 1861 – the *volost*, or canton, grouping one or more villages – functioned as a state institution. In 1889 the newly established office of land captain – *zemski nachalnik* – increased the degree of state supervision. The new official was almost invariably appointed from within the ranks of the local landowning nobility. Through the peasant courts and elected peasant officials, he enjoyed quasi-omnipotence *vis-à-vis* the individual peasant. And what were these peasant courts and peasant law? They were founded on custom, maintained a system of corporal punishment and were so arbitrary that they 'very often proved to be no law at all'.[8]

Increased efficiency in no way compensated for the commune's powers over the individual. On the contrary, the commune perpetuated the old three-field system, whereby one field lay fallow every third year. Each field was divided into a number of strips so that a single household would have a holding dispersed over any number of fields. This had many disadvantages: it increased the physical effort of farming and wasted much time; it took up much space with boundary marks; it forced all the peasants to move in step, for if the commune wished to leave a field fallow then it was all but impossible to sow one isolated strip by reason of the fact that mutual rights-of-way existed over all the strips. The odd-man-out would be unable to prevent his neighbour's cattle from grazing on the strip that he hoped to sow. By the same token, the system also made it impossible to use artificial fertilizers, to develop rotating or diversified crops or introduce deep-ploughing techniques. It is also to be remembered that the peasants' allotments were often unbalanced by reason of the proportion of meadow and pasture-land as against arable. This was particularly true of the northern part of the country where arable land tended on the whole to be of lesser value than pasture-land.[9] Again, in those communes in which the land was periodically redistributed, the fear that any benefit might be garnered by someone else at the subsequent redistribution engendered a natural reluctance to improve the holding overmuch.

According to a survey made at the beginning of the 1890's, thirty-two per cent of the peasantry were well provided with land, forty per cent adequately endowed and twenty-eight per cent insufficiently so.[10] It was some decades therefore before economic problems began seriously to affect the majority of peasant households and radically to undermine their position. A cluster of factors interacted to produce this result. Amongst the most important must be accounted intensified financial pressure on the peasantry. This was inaugurated by the redemption dues, those annual payments to the state which ostensibly covered the cost of emancipation. In the early years after 1861 their burden actually outweighed the income derived from the land. In 1881 the mounting total of arrears was so great that a start had to be made with the phased reduction of the dues. In 1905 they were cancelled altogether. By now the poll tax had also been remitted. In the meantime however, what the one hand of the state had relinquished, the other had seized. Most prominent amongst the new burdens was indirect taxation. In 1890 more than one-third of the ordinary and extraordinary revenue of the state came from the excise tax on spirits – the notorious vodka monopoly – and indirect taxes on tobacco, sugar and kerosene. Indirect taxes produced 16·5 million roubles in 1881 and 109·5 million roubles in 1895.[11] In the last decade of the century the tax on sugar and matches rose by one hundred per cent, and on kerosene by fifty per cent. In all, it is estimated that the average annual per capita contribution to tax revenue was something over one-fifth of the annual per capita income.[12] Even this understates the element of discriminatory taxation: an acre of peasant land bore almost seven times as much tax as an acre of land in the hands of a private owner.[13]

The peasantry not only suffered financially, through their tax-enforced contribution to the imperial revenue, i.e. to the policy of industrialization; the government's fiscal policy also forced the peasantry to export grain and other agricultural produce in order to provide the state with foreign currency, essential if Russia were to continue to be able to raise loans abroad and service a foreign debt. The country did enjoy a favourable balance of trade for every year between 1882 and 1913 (except for 1899). But this was at the expense of home consumption. The per capita share of the harvest, after deducting exports, was about eighteen poods in 1883; by 1897 it had dwindled to fourteen.[14]

This was the situation that validated the contemptuous reference of the anarchist, Kropotkin, to 'order' in Russia:

... It is misery and famine become the normal state of society ... it is the peasant of one-third of Russia dying of diphtheria, typhus, of hunger from hardship, amidst piles of grain making their way abroad.... It is land taken from the peasant in order to raise cattle to feed the wealthy; it is land left fallow rather than restored to him who asks for nothing more than land for cultivation.[15]

Further pressure on the peasant standard of living came from the increase in population, unaccompanied by any increase in agricultural productivity or proportionate increase in peasant-controlled land. It has been tentatively estimated that whereas the number of peasants in the village grew by some 27·8 per cent between 1877 and 1905 (from sixty-one millions to seventy-eight millions) the land area at their disposal grew only by 24·2 per cent, from 118,181,000 dessyatins to 146,825,000 dessyatins. The average size of allotments per family, over the same period, shrank from 12·9 dessyatins to 10·37 dessyatins.[16] Population pressure was at its most intense in certain of the central agricultural provinces south of Moscow and the middle Volga provinces. Here, between 1861–5 and 1911–13, population increases took place of the order of 51·7 per cent (Penza), 31·7 per cent (Tambov), 34 per cent (Voronezh), 21 per cent (Orel), 59·4 per cent (Nizhni-Novgorod), 51·3 per cent (Simbirsk), 23·8 per cent (Saratov), 18·3 per cent (Kazan). These compare with the average population growth of 18·3 per cent in the fifty provinces of European Russia.[17]

It is not fortuitous that peasant rioting was so frequently associated with areas suffering from a shortage of land, either for purchase or for leasing. The disturbances of 1902 in Kharkov, Poltava and Kherson, for example, were found to be due to a shortage of grazing and pasture land and fodder. Here the supply of land for leasing was also diminishing because estate-owners were more and more frequently turning their land over to sugar-beet cultivation.[18] Similarly, the perennial restiveness of the Volga provinces is attributable to the fact that here the peasants had lost more land than elsewhere at the emancipation. Two-thirds of *all* the peasantry received slightly less land after 1861 than they had hitherto farmed. But in Saratov, for example, two-fifths of the peasants received less than one-half of the land they had previously held.[19]

There were of course certain economic advantages to the possession of a large family in that its 'surplus' members could earn cash in a factory wherewith to purchase agricultural tools and horses. More-over, in the repartitional communes such as prevailed in the Volga and central provinces, the commune was bound to extend the farm-holding in accordance with the number of 'eaters'. This, it has been asserted, accounts for the extreme population growth in these areas.[20] Be that as it may, these were certainly the areas of maximum over-population and land shortage. But the inability of the peasantry, through a low technical level, to create a viable economy, was general. At the end of the nineteenth century the peasants' income from allotment land fell short by one-half or three-quarters of the amount necessary for bare subsistence.[21]

This situation could be alleviated in a number of ways. A man could work in a factory, for example, during the idle winter season or become a seasonal worker on the land. He might also purchase land, either collectively or individually; and the foundation of the Peasant Bank in 1883 helped this movement forward. Between the emancipa-tion and 1905 nearly twenty-four million dessyatins came into peasant ownership in this way. But the competition for land brought about a steady rise in its price. Again, a peasant might lease land from a neighbouring landowner; but this had overtones of serfdom about it. Renting might not be only in the form of cash; it might also involve working on one part of a landowner's estate in return for permission to cultivate another part; or the landowner might allow a peasant to work a part of his land in return for part of the crop. Whatever the method of payment, the very practice of leasing could be nothing more than a palliative. The same lowly level of technique prevailed and therefore the return to the peasant was less than the cash value of his labour or the cost of the rent expressed in money terms. What made the operation alone worth while from the standpoint of the peasant was the additional sustenance it produced. On the other hand, since the majority of leases were short-term, perhaps for one year only, the peasant lessee's natural desire to maximize his production led to wasteful and ruinous methods of cultivation. The large amount of land held on lease was no criterion of peasant wealth – rather, of peasant poverty. From the landowner's point of view, it was a system whereby he exploited the land hunger of the peasantry. But although he secured more dependable labour than might otherwise have been possible, he did so at the price of impoverishing the land and of contributing to the gradual decay of large-scale landownership – the most productive type present in contemporary Russia.[22]

More indirectly, the landlord in this position also contributed to his own downfall; for the practice of leasing land, actually paying for its use, ran clean counter to the peasant notion that the land belonged to those who worked it and lived by it. The fundamental commune principle of periodically dividing the land in proportion to need was in itself a denial of the right to private property in land. This sentiment could not but be offended and inflamed by the economic compulsion to pay heavily, in cash or labour, for what belonged to the peasant as a matter of justice. The notion of private property did not prevail in the commune. Why, then, should it prevail outside?

All this adds up to a picture of many millions of people, the bulk of the population of the empire, caught up in a situation of irredeemable poverty. True, a small stratum of wealthy peasants did crystallize out of the mass, but the overwhelming majority led a life poised precariously between poverty and actual destitution. Wherever the peasant turned for relief he found a cul-de-sac. If he bought or leased land, he fell into debt; if he entered a factory he was exploited; if he became a seasonal summer worker elsewhere he barely earned enough to see him through the winter.

Any number of indices and criteria illuminate peasant poverty. His consumption of common foodstuffs was inferior to that of any other European country. The annual consumption in kilogrammes of wheat, rye, barley, yeast and maize was 235·2 per head of population in pre-war Russia. For Germany, France, Austria-Hungary and Italy the totals were respectively 443·8, 420·4, 404·6 and 274·3.[23] The peasant's living conditions produced sickness, ill-health and overcrowding.[24] In 1903, Kuropatkin, the Russian commander-in-chief, not only feared peasant poverty because of its effect on morale but also because 'impoverishment is at the same time reflected in the low physical standards of the new recruits'.[25] The growing number of emigrants and settlers in Siberia was closely related to hunger and hardship at home (though towards the end of the century more positive motives came into play).[26]

The increase in the number of peasants without horses served perhaps as the most telling criterion of peasant poverty – and this in a rural economy where the horse provided almost the sole source of power. Between 1888 and 1905 in the provinces of Ryazan, Tula, Tambov, Orel and Voronezh the number of horseless peasants increased from 24 per cent to 28·8 per cent of the whole; the number with only one horse grew from 25·8 per cent to 28·5 per cent; the number with two horses remained virtually static; but there was a decline from 21·1 per cent to 16·6 per cent and from 7·9 per cent to 4·8 per cent in the numbers of those owning respectively three to four and five or more horses. The other troubled provinces of Saratov, Penza, Simbirsk, Kazan and Nizhegorod displayed similar features.[27]

'Your Majesty has 130 million subjects,' Vitte wrote to the tsar in 1898. 'Of them barely more than half live, the rest vegetate.' How long could this situation last? And why did it become increasingly intolerable towards the turn of the century? A large part of the answer is without doubt the sheer economic plight of the peasantry. A police report of 1905 summed this up in lapidary style:

Very often the peasants do not have enough allotment land, and cannot during the year feed themselves, clothe themselves, heat their homes, keep their tools and livestock, secure seed for sowing and, lastly, discharge all their taxes and obligations: to the state, the zemstvo and the commune.[28]

As for the rest, cause and effect are indistinguishably intertwined. The harnessing of the village to the town by way of the grain trade, railway construction and migrant labour brought to the village radical ideas. Those ninety-five million railway journeys every year, of which Vitte wrote with such pride, were indeed serving as a 'ferment', though not in the sense that he intended. They exposed the young men of the village to urban agitation and when this flowed back to the countryside it helped to undermine the authority of the village elders.[29] To this must be added a growth in literacy: in 1868 only eight out of every one hundred peasant recruits to the army could read and write; by 1882 the figure was twenty. The census of 1897 disclosed that the proportion of peasants able to read had doubled, from about one-quarter for men over sixty to one-half for those under twenty. Over the span of one generation the peasantry had more than tripled their share of individuals having secondary training.[30] No doubt also, the discredit suffered by the Orthodox church and the growth of movements of religious dissent, frequently of a utopian character, both expressed and deepened the prevailing ferment and denial of the state. The favoured themes of sectarian poems all concerned, in the Russian tradition indeed, a flight from the world, the wilderness, a wandering life, the monastery, the subjugation of the flesh, celibacy, chastity, a holy life, the boon of learning.[31]

Over and beyond all this, there was perhaps the psychological after-effect of the emancipation. Despite all its manifest defects, the emancipation did at least give the peasant a new consciousness of his status. 'A new generation, which has not known slavery, has had time to grow up,' wrote one observer in the late 1880s.[32] And this new generation, finding itself in a rapidly changing Russia, was, by every external symptom, no longer content to bend the knee in the manner of its forebears. Peasant acquiescence in serfdom had never of course been universal or even prolonged. But at the end of the nineteenth and beginning of the twentieth century the first taste of a new life brought with it the conviction that intolerable conditions could no longer be tolerated.

4 The Ignorant Autocrat

'The emperor of all the Russias is an autocratic and unlimited monarch. God himself commands that his supreme power be obeyed, out of conscience as well as fear.' Thus ran Article I of the Fundamental Laws of the empire (published in 1892). Nicholas II, who ascended the throne in 1894, was determined that this should remain so. The tsar alone nominated the members of the ministerial council, amounting to some ten in all. The absence of any doctrine or practice of collective ministerial responsibility further enhanced the tsar's power. Each minister was independently and individually responsible to the tsar personally; although, then, an informal chief minister might emerge to act as the tsar's closest adviser – or a small group of particularly influential ministers might work in this capacity – the council *per se* never confronted the tsar as a united body. On the contrary, the chief minister might not even be present when 'his' ministers reported to the tsar. The latter could also appoint or dismiss ministers *à son gré* and take the chair at the meetings of ministers.

Further power devolved on the autocrat through his control of nominations to the council of state. This was composed of some sixty members drawn from ministers (past and present), members of the imperial family and prominent state servants. It had consultative function in relation to legislative matters. This loose system made it possible for the autocrat to call for advice on personalities who lacked any other qualification than loyalty; it also opened the way to backstairs influence. Such was the tsar's relationship to the tsarina and to Rasputin (who made his first appearance at court at the end of 1905).[1]

How well did this system work? And what sort of man was its mainspring? Polovtzov, a member of the council of state, confided to his diary in 1901 an alarming picture of disarray at the very centre of government:

There is nothing consistent, considered or firmly directed. Everything is done spasmodically, haphazardly, under the influence of the moment, in accordance with the intrigues of this or that person, or the lobbying of those crawling out from their different corners in quest of fortune.

The young tsar is filled more and more with contempt for the organs of his power and begins to believe in the beneficient force of his absolute power, asserting it sporadically, without preparatory debate, without connexion with the general movement of affairs.

He was even reminded of the mad tsar Paul, the diarist confessed.[2] As for the ministerial council, the system of individual responsibility to the tsar evoked in one close observer, Izvolsky (foreign minister, 1906–10), the 'wonder that such a system did not bring about, long before, a complete disorganization of the vastest empire known to modern times'. To a maliciously acute British diplomatist, Russia had 'no real government'. Each minister acted on his own, 'doing as much damage as possible to the other ministers'. The emperor himself was surrounded by a legion of thirty-five grand dukes, 'with a few priests and priestly women behind them'.[3]

Foreign affairs suffered as much as any other department of state, if not more so. In 1902, for example, two governmental bodies were in diplomatic contact with Japan – a committee for the Far East as well as the usual ministry of foreign affairs. The command of the military and naval forces was divided three ways – between the ministries of war, of marine and Admiral Alexeyev (viceroy of the Russian possessions on the Pacific coast). 'Hopeless controversy was the result,' commented the British ambassador.[4]

Weaknesses of character compounded the tsar's failure to exert the power at his disposal – an inability, for example, to say or do anything disagreeable to a person in his presence. When he decided to dismiss a minister he would never tell him so to his face; he would treat the man with double courtesy – and then write a letter.[5]

Furthermore, the tsar held himself aloof from the main currents of contemporary Russian life. He withdrew more and more from St Petersburg, and, in the words of one observer, 'shrank back into the seclusion of Tsarskoe Selo and Peterhof'.[6] No student of the tsar's immediate *milieu* and daily round can but be impressed by his incomprehension, if not ignorance, of the changes undermining the old traditional ways. Did Nicholas II ever visit a factory? A declining village? Did he ever tour a strike area? The St Petersburg bourse? The industrial exhibitions organized by Vitte? Yet it was all these that determined the Russian fate. The tsar's sole knowledge of such phenomena was mediated through the reports of officials; and these were no doubt frequently distorted through the fear of giving offence or conveying unpalatable truths. In this respect of course, the revolutionaries of whatever stamp, although they too had their illusions, enjoyed at least the great boon of immediate contact with the most urgent needs of Russian society, in factory and village.

The tsar's forte was not political and public life but the private, domestic and family side of things. Not for nothing did he and his consort, Alexandra Feodorovna, make their home in one wing of the Alexander Palace in Tsarskoe Selo. They had it fitted out in the style of a fashionable-minded wealthy bourgeois of the day, of no great taste. An extraordinary cult of the photograph further emphasized the family aspect. No article of furniture in the imperial wing but was decked out with a photograph of one or the other member of the imperial family. The lavatory, even, was not exempt. Each member of the imperial family had his, or her, own photograph album, and an expert photographer was employed solely to develop and print the imperial snapshots. The cult of the family image, on a par with the empress's partiality for icons, denoted a withdrawal from the political to the private.[7]

The tsar's inclination in this respect was confirmed by the wishes of Alexandra Feodorovna. 'Any talks with people unconnected with "the Services", any receptions not absolutely necessary for reasons of state, were, in her eyes, simply and purely a waste of time,' wrote one intimate of the court. 'She did all she could to reduce to a minimum the occasions when the tsar undertook such "duties". . . . Then the sacrosanct hours of reading aloud in the evening. I find it difficult to imagine any affair of state of sufficient importance to induce the empress to forego a single one of these fireside evenings tête-à-tête.'[8]

This was the character, and this the entourage, of the man who sat at the centre of the imperial government, at a time of unprecedented change. Each problem that came his way he met with the reassertion of his autocratic prerogatives – and a call to arms. No trait perhaps was more characteristic of the tsar than his taste for violence. This was early revealed. In 1895, the year following his accession, the tsar telegraphed to a grenadier regiment that had distinguished itself in suppressing workers' disorders: 'Highly satisfied with the calm and bold conduct of the troops during the factory riots.'[9] He sounded the same note in 1905: 'Terror must be met with terror,' he wrote to his mother in December 1905, in commending the repression of the rebellious Baltic peasants. 'Orloff, Richter and the others are doing very good work. Many seditious bands have been dispersed, their homes and property burnt.'[10] A little while later, on hearing that Riga had been captured, and that 'Captain Richter had not only shot but also hanged the chief agitators,' the tsar commented: 'Fine fellow!'[11] Whether it was strikers, tribal rebels, demonstrators anarchists, revolutionaries, the tsar's unvarying answer was a call for violence.[12]

He had a particular animus for the Jews. When Stolypin, the chairman of the council of ministers 1906–11, proposed to relax certain restrictions imposed on the Jews in the Pale of Settlement, the tsar replied: 'In spite of the most convincing arguments in favour of an affirmative decision in this matter, an inner voice ever more insistently confirms that I should not take this decision upon myself. So far my conscience has *never* deceived me. Therefore in this case also, I intend to follow its dictates.'[13] Not for nothing did the tsar become a member of the anti-semitic Union of the Russian People, subscribe to the Union's funds and receive its president, Dr Dubrovin, on friendly terms. He had no sympathy for the victims of the pogroms that followed the publication of the manifesto of October 1905.[14] On the contrary, he saw in them a revolt against 'the impertinence' of the socialists and revolutionaries,

and because nine-tenths of the trouble-makers are Jews, the people's whole anger turned against them. That's how the pogroms happened. . . . In England, of course, the press says that these disorders were organized by the police. They still go on repeating this worn-out fable. But not only Jews suffered; some of the Russian agitators, engineers, lawyers and such-like bad people suffered as well. Cases as far apart as in Tomsk, Simferopol, Tver and Odessa show clearly what an infuriated crowd can do; they surrounded the houses where revolutionaries had taken refuge, set fire to them and killed everybody trying to escape.[15]

The identification of the mob as loyalists and the 'bad people' as consisting of Jews, engineers and lawyers showed a strong capacity for evasion and self-deception. This blindness to reality persisted until the very end of the dynasty. As late as February 1917, a bare week or two before the revolution, the tsar remonstrated with the head of the court chancellery who had suggested that the position of the dynasty needed to be 'assured'. 'People are continually harping on this supposed peril,' Nicholas replied. 'Why, you have been with me and have seen how I was received by the troops and the people. . . . Let us go into dinner. The empress will be waiting for us already.'[16]

How could this institution, and this man, be fitted into the new Russia? Plainly, it was impossible – all the more so as the tsar would surrender none of his prerogatives or in any way consent to any remodelling of his autocratic power, except under the severest constraint (and then merely await the opportunity to seize back what he had lost).

Even so, even in the face of this inflexibility, the argument whereby an intellectual defence of the system might be devised merits appraisal. What was the protean character of the autocracy that it could appeal to such diverse men as Pobedonostzev and Vitte? To an archreactionary and to the boldest of bold innovators?

To the former it was precisely the inflexibility of tsardom that confirmed its merit. Pobedonostzev saw 'the works of the devil every-where, in telegraphs, telephones and railways . . . ,' wrote the German ambassador.[17] In this new world of flux, when all manner of alien institutions and alien political and philosophic doctrines threatened Russia's precarious stability the autocracy was more necessary than ever as an agent of the status quo. This was the message that Pobedonostzev, as Procurator of the Holy Synod, gave to both Alexander III and Nicholas II. In a manner that later fascist doctrine has made more familiar, autocracy denoted a practice and a theory that initiated and justified the enforcement of uniformity of belief and conduct in every sphere of life. The church and the schools must inculcate the virtues of conformity to the whole prevailing order, through the media of panoply and a circumscribed education. On this basis, Pobedonostzev defended the censor and denounced freedom of the press as an avenue to the dissemination of falsehood; parlia-mentarianism as a façade for intrigue; Jews, Poles and Catholics as enemy aliens within the Russian body politic; and an indepen-dent and irremovable judiciary as a shackle on the freedom of the state.[18]

By contrast, almost by way of antithesis, Vitte saw in the autocracy an instrument of change. This was quite natural. Without the tsar's support, more forthcoming in the case of Alexander III than Nicholas II, the policy of forced modernization would hardly have been poss-ible, so much hostility did it arouse. The convertibility of the rouble, for example, was introduced by administrative measures alone, by way of imperial decrees that circumvented the normal process of legislation. It also did not accord with Vitte's imperious nature that he should have to manoeuvre and lobby his policy through, let us say, a hostile assembly. It was bad enough to have to deal with the tsar and the council of state! The depth of Vitte's commitment to the auto-cracy may be gauged from his youthful participation in a secret plot to avenge the assassination of Alexander II. Not for nothing did Vitte contemptuously spit on the ground when asked for his views on the October manifesto of 1905, which brought the Duma into existence.[19] But these were personal matters. Of far greater moment was the socio-political role of the autocracy. In his memorandum *Samoder-zhavie i Zemstvo* (Autocracy and the Zemstvo, 1899), Vitte established a well-merited antithesis between the principle animating the auto-cracy and the principle of independent elective authority embodied in the zemstvo. For Vitte this was a concept alien to Russia, something imported from Britain and the west with their tradition of opposition between the government and society. By way of contrast, with due regard to Russian circumstances, he looked forward to the harmonious interaction of government and society.

The development of social forces, abundant and many-sided, does not only not contradict the principles of absolute monarchy, but, on the contrary, gives it vitality and firmness.

Fostering the development of public activity, listening, so to speak, to the beating of the public pulse, the government does not however, enter into the disposition of society, remains a force of reason and of consistent authority, always clear as to its own aims, constantly aware of the means to their accomplishment and knows where it is going and leading.

Such a government does not run the risk of its measures being divorced from the past, from the national soil, or that they will show themselves inappropriate to the social level, or that society will develop outside and beyond the government, or that the state will cease to be the guide of the whole sum of public activity.[20]

But could 'the development of the social forces, abundant and many-sided', be fitted into an autocracy, however streamlined? All Russian experience denied this possibility. It is certainly true, of course, that no antithesis exists between industrialization and an authoritarian political system. On the contrary, industrialization supplies its own, improved methods of social control. Yet to suppose that a nascent capitalism, beset with social problems of great magnitude, could somehow be integrated into a fundamentally unchanged socio-political pattern, geared to an agrarian order, especially if its *fons et origo*, the tsar, saw no need for change, was surely utopian on Vitte's part.

In Russian conditions one of the few thinkers to see the connexion between political pattern and social change was Konstantin Leontyev. His intelligence forced him to contemplate this problem full face – and to advocate, not a mere streamlined autocracy but a reinforcement of the agrarian order. Leontyev wrote:

A democratic constitution (the highest stage of capitalism and of some limp and impotent mobility), surely means a weakening of the *central power*; a democratic constitution is bound up most intimately with equalitarian *individualism*, taken to its ultimate point. It will creep up on us imperceptibly. Give us a constitution – and the capitalists will at once destroy the land commune; destroy the commune – the hasty destruction will lead us to the final liberal stupidity – to a house of representatives, i.e. to the rule of bankers, lawyers and landowners, not as *gentry* (that is still nothing) but again as representatives of such *landed property* as is very easily transformed into movable property when it is convenient, without asking anybody and nowhere encountering any obstacles.

Salvation does not lie in *strengthening the movement*, but in *arresting* it somehow or other; if it were possible to find a law or a means *to strengthen landed property*, then this would be well.[21]

This was not of course possible, although in the 1880s a number of governmental measures had attempted to inject financial aid into the declining gentry. The gentry continued to decline *pari passu* with the rise of industry. Leontyev sighed to no avail. Yet precisely because of this and for all the unrealism of his advice he saw the problem of the autocracy in a more uncompromising light than either Pobedonostzev or Vitte.

In the event, it was not until after the turn of the century that the autocracy revealed its inability to master the problems it confronted. It continued to enjoy the allegiance of the overwhelming majority of its subjects. It held the undisputed support of the police, the armed forces and the machinery of government. The bureaucracy contained liberal sympathizers, but as a body, its loyalty was unquestionable. No less was that of the Orthodox church. The autocracy served also as apex to the declining yet still influential class of large and middle-sized landowners. To the workers and peasants the autocracy had a special importance for it was precisely from the tsar that alleviation might be expected. However, what it could not do was embrace the growth of all manner of independent bodies – an independent bar, for example, or the zemstvos, or students' corporations, to say nothing of the striving of the workers for some form of representative organization. When, as in the Zubatov episode, the autocracy did endeavour to take the workers under its wing, the attempt was so half-hearted that it collapsed at the first sign of opposition. The autocracy could neither make its peace with such bodies nor repress them entirely. It wavered between conciliation and forthright opposition.

This was the situation when an unexpected ally came to the aid of Nicholas II – the nascent industrial *bourgeoisie*. The latter, to be sure, was a weak social force. Russia had happily not known 'three scourges' which had retarded the west, Herzen told a London audience in 1855 – these were Catholicism, Roman Law and the rule of the *bourgeoisie*.[22] The Russian *bourgeoisie*, a modern French historian has said, 'never conquered the town. . . . The Russian towns have no belfry testifying to the power of an urban *bourgeoisie*. . . .'[23] From at least the seventeenth century onward the number of town-dwellers had remained only a small proportion of the total population: in 1630, 2·5 per cent, in 1724, 3 per cent, in 1796, 4·1 per cent.[24] By 1897 it was 12·4 per cent. Over the whole period from 1861 to 1914, although the urban population showed a three-fold increase from seven to some twenty million, the proportion of town-dwellers to the total population increased only from 11·6 per cent to 14·6 per cent. Apart from Moscow (one million) and St Petersburg (1¼ million) only eighteen other towns had a population exceeding 100,000 – and this out of a total population of more than 130 millions.[25]

The emergence of a moneyed class did indeed produce friction, but only at a social level. Alexander III was unsympathetic, for example, to what Vitte called the 'private tsardoms' that grew up in his reign, ruled over by 'little railway kings' such as Polyakov, Bloch, Kronenberg, Gubonin. And these men were not always models of tact vis-à-vis the monarchy. In 1883, after a party given by the tsar at Gatchina, the numerous guests went to the railway station where they were to await a special train. 'Suddenly, instead of this train,' Vitte relates, 'another train pulled in, a very light train, in which sat State-Secretary Polovtzov with his wife and when he had invited a few acquaintances he moved away in front of everybody and thus held up the train prepared for the people invited by the tsar, he delayed the tsar's guests.' Polovtzov of course was the chief shareholder in the company running the line. Similarly, when the Grand-Duke Sergei Alexandrovitch came to inspect the palatial Moscow villa of Savva Morozov, the textile tycoon, he was received by Morozov's major-domo. The owner himself stayed away.[26]

Such incidents were however no symptomatic pointer to the socio-political role of the bourgeoisie. 'The political impotence of the Russian bourgeoisie corresponded to its inner weakness.'[27] This had its reason not only in the social history of the bourgeoisie but also in the whole policy of planning from the top. If governmental orders were the chief nourishment of Russian heavy industry, if control over such matters as freight rates and fiscal policy gave the government power to determine the price of mass consumption goods, if industry could only flourish behind a government-imposed tariff, if governmental credit institutions controlled the flow of capital into industry, if the operation of the vodka monopoly determined the receipts of distilleries and sugar refineries, if the government supplied police and troops for service in factory districts – then, in the face of all this, not only could no independent capitalism develop but there was also no need for such development to take place. There was, inevitably, occasional friction between industry and the government – in respect of factory legislation, for example, or the Zubatov movement. But this remained insignificant. As a result the bourgeoisie may fairly be described in the word of a recent Soviet historian as 'a satrap' of the regime.[28] There existed what Pokrovsky called 'a firm alliance between the autocracy and capitalism'.[29]

The state, by virtue of its economic policy, was the senior ally. Nothing showed this to greater advantage than the state's domina-tion of the congresses which grouped together the largest *entrepreneurs* in every important branch of Russian industry – oil extraction, mining and metallurgy, iron-foundries, sugar-refining, flour-milling, etc. The industrialists were, to be sure, privileged in enjoying permission to form an association of a representative type not allowed to other citizens. But they had to pay for the privilege by submitting to the close tutelage of the state at their assemblies. It was the minister of finance who nominated the chairman of the annual meetings of each congress, who approved the agenda and whose representatives were in attendance. The agendas alone show the narrow scope within which the congresses operated. They only covered a wide range of economic matters – railroad tariff policy, improved postal and telegraph services, port and canal facilities, factory legislation, the adoption of the metric system, insurance cover for accidents to workers, etc.[30]

Conversely, the role of the members of the congress in the implementation of governmental policy gave them a strong lobbying position. 'Almost all the more substantial interventions of preceding sessions have been satisfied either wholly or to a considerable extent,' declared the chairman of the fourth session of the Polish congress of mines and metallurgy. 'Many of the interventions furthered the conduct of affairs in a sense desirable to the congress. Literally not one of them was a voice sounding in the wilderness.'[31]

Nowhere, however, is there any mention of political intervention. Industry did not find it necessary to enter into the politcal struggle against tsarism or in any way to oppose the regime on any minor issue, at least, not until 1905–6, and then only fleetingly. This political passivity and close association with tsarism served to impress a characteristic stamp on the Russian revolution. Herzen had already pointed in 1855 to the non-existence of the Russian *bourgeoisie* as a distinctive feature of the Russian social structure. Marx took up this insight towards the end of his life and again predicted, albeit with many reservations, an evolution for Russia so unique that the country might by-pass the capitalist stage of development altogether. In his turn, Trotsky, in 1905, made of this same distinctive feature the sociological presupposition of the theory of permanent revolution – the most satisfying anticipation of the actual events of 1917.[32]

5 Political Challenges

In a state where the autocracy sought to monopolize all forms of political life no political parties could legally exist. Yet within a bare two years three parties, all necessarily illegal, took the field against tsarism: the Socialist-Revolutionaries (1901), a liberal party (1903), and the Social-Democrats (1903). The quickening of political life epitomized, as could nothing else, the increasingly fluid internal state of Russia at the turn of the century.

The Socialist-Revolutionaries inherited from the populists of the 1870s the pro-peasant orientation and a belief in the use of terror in the early stages of the struggle. Twentieth-century populism, in its Socialist-Revolutionary reincarnation, was formed of two main populist groupings, the one centred on Kharkov (the party of the south) and the other on the turbulent province of Saratov (union of the north).

The Socialist-Revolutionaries did not possess a coherent organization or ideology. What they did have, in respect of either, they largely owed to Victor Chernov, who had learnt his populism in Samara, Saratov and Tambov. Chernov bent his mind to arguing that a great peasant upheaval must come, such as would enable the peasantry to confiscate all land not already held by the communes. The land would be socialized and made available to the peasant toiler in accordance with his needs. The peasants might either become members of a co-operative or till the soil as small 'proprietors'. But this was the final outcome. As a minimum first stage the Socialist-Revolutionaries demanded limited measures of reform – political liberty, the eight-hour day in factory and village and a constituent assembly. Simultaneously, they would gradually develop 'collective forms of control over the economy at the expense of purely individual forms'; i.e. the liquidation of private land-holding based on Roman law, and 'factory constitutionalism'. The land would become a 'possession of the whole nation'. This was not yet socialism, but it would clear the way for socialism.[1]

Agitation amongst the peasantry, especially in the central agricultural and Volga provinces, formed the main activity of the Socialist-Revolutionaries. Of fifty-seven publications issued in 1902 only one was devoted to the labour question; in 1903 it was one out of thirty-four.[2] More spectacular was their programme of assassination, a task assigned to a special combatant group that enjoyed complete independence within the party. It was staffed solely by volunteers whose identity was not known even to the central committee of the party. The latter designated the targets but only the combat organization determined and put into practice the mode of execution.[3]

What did the combat organization hope to achieve? First, it sought to disorganize the enemy; second, terrorism would serve 'as a means of propaganda and agitation, a form of open struggle taking place before the eyes of the whole people, undermining the prestige of government authority'. Lastly, it was a means of self-defence and of 'protecting the organization against the injurious elements of spies and treachery'.[4]

Given the conspiratorial *demi-monde* in which terrorism operated, the combat organization inevitably attracted its due share of the corrupt – a man such as Azev, for example. He combined leadership of the organization with activity as a trusted agent of the police. Azev's sole redeeming feature was his share in the assassination of von Plehve in 1904.[5] Terrorism charmed also the idealist, Maria Spiridonova. She shot and killed General Luzhenovsky in 1906 for his part in burning down the villages of rebellious peasants. In Spiridonova's eyes to be a Socialist-Revolutionary meant to dedicate 'one's life, one's thoughts, one's feelings to the realization of the party's ideas; it means owning nothing but the interests and ideals of the party; utilizing every moment of one's life in such a way that the cause may be the richer for it.'[6]

The most lucid guide to the outlook of the Socialist-Revolutionary was perhaps the speech made by Kalayev to his judges. This young man hurled the bomb that killed Grand Duke Serge in Moscow on 4 February 1905. He gave himself up after the coup. He told the court:

I am not a defendant here, I am your prisoner. We are two warring camps. You – the representatives of the imperial government, the hired servants of capital and oppression. I – one of the avengers of the people, a socialist and revolutionist. Mountains of corpses divide us, hundreds of thousands of broken human lives and a whole sea of blood and tears covering the country in torrents of horror and resentment. You have declared war upon the people. We have accepted your challenge. Having taken me prisoner, it is now within your power to subject me to the torture of slow extinction or to kill me outright, but you cannot hold trial over me. No matter how much you may seek to exercise your sway, there can be no justification for you as there can be no condemnation of me. Between you and me there can be no reconciliation, as it cannot be between absolutism and the people. We are still the same enemies, and if, having deprived me of liberty and the opportunity to speak directly to the people, you have seen fit to institute this solemn judgement upon me, I am in no way obliged to recognize you as my judges. ... Let us be tried by this great martyr of history – the Russia of the people.[7]

Russian liberalism was 'not *bourgeois* but intellectual,' declared Paul Milyukov, one of its most prominent adherents and exponents.[8] Max Weber saw in it 'the bearer of a political and socio-political idealism', isolated from the forces of industry and finance.[9] This movement, despite the absence of an economic leverage, none the less constituted, by virtue of its numbers, resources and articulateness, the most serious opposition that tsarism had to contend with – at the beginning of the century, that is.

It consisted of three groups: the gentry represented in the zemstvos; the technical experts they employed – teachers, doctors, statisticians, veterinary experts; and members of the free professional classes – academics, lawyers, engineers. The unyielding policy of the government in regard to any united public initiative on the part of these people veritably forced them into opposition. The government's frequent refusal to confirm elected zemstvo officials in office, its rejection of zemstvo petitions, its prohibition of joint zemstvo activity, its close supervision or even outright suspension of professional societies and associations – all this forced the zemstvos leftwards, forced the most literate and cultured sections of Russian society into an attitude of quasi-permanent opposition and led necessarily to the moral isolation of the autocracy.

This division went a stage further in 1902 when the journal *Osvobozhdenie* (Liberation) began publication in Stuttgart. It was financed in large part by the landowner Zhukovsky. Peter Struve, a former Marxist and associate of the young Lenin, edited the journal. His initial programme called for a broad united front (later somewhat modified in a leftward sense) of oppositionist groups ranging from revolutionaries to gentry liberals. Struve demanded the proclamation of personal and civil liberties, and the summoning of an assembly to draft an electoral law that would culminate in the election of a national parliament.

The founding of *Osvobozhdenie* was very soon followed by the establishment of the underground Union of Liberation which grouped the journal's sympathizers throughout Russia. 'This was not a party,' Rodichev, one of its supporters has written, 'it was a union of people of different tendencies who were drawn together by one object, the achievement of emancipation.'[10] This came clearly to the fore in the Union's first programme, adopted at a clandestine congress in St Petersburg in January 1904. It called for 'the political liberation of Russia'; it sought to abolish the autocracy and to inaugurate a constitutional regime on a democratic basis. 'Above all, it recognizes as fundamentally essential that the principle of universal, equal, secret and direct elections be made the basis of the political reform.' As to social policy, the programme gave priority to 'the defence of the interests of the labouring masses'. In the national question it acknowledged the right of self-determination on the part of the different nationalities constituting the empire.

To the Socialist-Revolutionary view that the peasants would lead the revolution, to the liberal demand for a constitution, the Social-Democrats opposed the priority of the proletariat. 'The Russian revolution will triumph as a proletarian revolution or it will not triumph at all,' proclaimed Plekhanov, the father of Russian Marxism, to the foundation congress of the Second International in 1889 in Paris. This was the *leitmotif* of the second (foundation) congress of the Russian Social-Democratic party in 1903 – that the development of Russian capitalism and the concomitant formation of a Russian proletariat constituted the first step towards the eventual achievement of socialism. Thus the newly refounded party gave its principal attention (until 1905) to agitation in the factories, mines and workshops of Russia.

It was not a united party. From the outset it suffered from a division between Bolsheviks and Mensheviks. The issue involved in this division had been foreshadowed in a pamphlet – *What is to be Done?* – written in 1901–2 by Lenin, the future Bolshevik leader. Here was Bolshevism *avant la lettre*.

In this pamphlet Lenin enunciated three basic principles that must govern social-democratic political activity. First, 'The history of all countries shows that the working class, solely by its own forces, is able to work out merely trade-union consciousness, i.e. the conviction of the need for combining in unions, for fighting against the employers, and for trying to prevail upon the government to pass laws necessary for the workers, etc.'; second, 'The spontaneous struggle of the proletariat will not become its "class struggle" until it is led by a strong organization of revolutionaries'; third, 'He who wants a *broad* organization of workers, with elections, reports, universal voting, etc., in conditions of absolutism is simply an incorrigible utopian . . . attempts to apply the "broad democratic principle" in fact only facilitate widespread arrests by the police and . . . divert the thoughts of the practical party workers from the serious and urgent task of training themselves as professional revolutionaries to the compilation of detailed "paper" statutes on election systems.'[11]

At the congress in 1903, Lenin's Menshevik opponents, such as Axelrod and Martov, accused him of aspiring to turn the party into a collection of generals without an army, of 'throwing people overboard who, although they cannot be directly taken into the organization, are nevertheless party members'. 'A man can be . . . sincerely devoted to the cause but quite unsuited for a strongly centralized militant organization consisting of professional revolutionaries. For this reason the party of the proletariat must not limit itself to the narrow framework of a conspiratorial organization because then hundreds, and even thousands of proletarians would be left outside the party.' 'We can only be glad if every striker, every demonstrator . . . can describe himself as a party member. The conspirators' organization makes sense to me (Martov) only in so far as it is surrounded by a broad social-democratic workers' party.'[12] In short, the future Mensheviks placed greater trust in the spontaneity of mass action, and therefore thought and worked in terms of a broad party organization embracing all forms of proletarian mass action, even though this might entail the sacrifice of some degree of party control. Lenin and the future Bolsheviks, on the other hand, whilst enthusiastically participating in agitation amongst labour organizations (such as trade unions) remained distrustful of untrained spontaneous mass action, fearing constantly that it might degenerate into contentment with the struggle for immediate economic aims. Hence the strictest party control would always remain essential.

The full implications of this division did not reveal themselves at the time. Plekhanov, for example, supported Lenin at the congress, but later denounced his views as 'unmarxist'. Rosa Luxemburg opposed Lenin from the start. Yet Lenin's conception of a small dedicated body of professional revolutionaries, identifying itself with the leadership of what it took to be the most advanced historical force, formed the mainstream of the Russian revolutionary tradition, both theoretical and practical. The polarity of individual and general, of elite and mass, of personality and society, lay deeply embedded in Russian political thought.

The sociological basis for this division between leaders and led was undoubtedly the autocracy as an institution and this was compounded by the isolation of the intelligentsia amongst the mass of the 'dark people'. In the 1840s a population of some forty million included only 3,000 university students in any one year; in the 1860s, 4,500; in the 1870s a little over 5,000, out of a population that had grown to some seventy-five million. In these circumstances, given the example of the omnicompetent autocracy it might well seem that initiative and enlightenment could only come to the masses from outside.

It is in this light and in this respect that Lenin is to be seen as the successor to a long line of Russian political thinkers. Tchaadayev, for example, in the 1820s, wrote that 'the masses are subject to certain forces located at the summit of society. They do not think themselves, there is among them a certain number of thinkers who think for them, who give impetus to the collective intelligence of the nation and make it go forward. Just as this small number thinks, the rest feel, and the general movement takes place.' Herzen, writing in 1871, likewise found the masses passive, requiring '. . . apostles, men whose faith, will, convictions and force coincide perfectly with their own. . . . The masses want a social government that will govern *for them*, and not against them, as at present. To govern themselves – this idea never occurs to them.' Tchernyshevsky and Lavrov were other thinkers given to similar opinions.[13] To the same socio-political context belongs the call of the anarchist, Bakunin, for 'a revolutionary general staff'. These must be men 'without either ambition or vanity (who) are able to build a bridge between the revolutionary idea and the instinctive longings of the people. There is no need for any very large number of such men. For an international organization covering the whole of Europe one hundred revolutionaries bound in one fixed and earnest common aim would suffice. Two to three hundred revolutionaries are enough to organize even the largest country.'

The roots of Bolshevism in the Russian milieu can also be seen in the absolute congruence between Lenin's view of the workers' mentality and that taken by the Trepovs and Zubatovs. They too identified the urge to a 'trade-union consciousness' and thought in terms of an elite that would give direction to the unthinking mass. The difference was this: whereas the police-socialists feared the revolutionary mentality and hoped to foster trade union conscious- ness, Lenin feared trade union consciousness and hoped to foster the revolutionary mentality. Trepov's remark was very true – what concerned the policeman, concerned also the revolutionary.

As it happened, both the policeman and the revolutionary took full account of a sociological insight formulated by Max Weber as 'the "principle of the small number", i.e. the superior manoeuvrability of *small* leading groups (which) always dominates political activity. This caesarian stamp is ineradicable (in mass states).'[14] This was the insight denied to Lenin's critics – to the Mensheviks, to Plekhanov and to Luxemburg with their old-style idealization of the mass.

The affiliation between Bolshevism and certain aspects of the Russian political tradition, together with the western orientation of Menshevism, is illuminated by their respective geographical sources of strength. In 1907, for example, a line drawn from Astrakhan to St Petersburg separated the Menshevik areas to the west from the Bolshevik areas to the east. This separation was not absolute. In each area there were men of the other faction. Yet Bolshevik committees and links lay mainly in the Moscow area, Ivanovo-Vosnesensk and the Urals; Menshevik committees in the Caucasus, the Ukraine and the western provinces. This geographical division further corresponded to and overlapped with national groupings. Thus, again for the congress of 1907, the Bolsheviks comprised eighty-two Russians (78·3 per cent), with twelve Jews (11·4 per cent), three Georgians (2·7 per cent) and two Armenians (1·9 per cent). The Mensheviks, on the other hand, consisted of only thirty-three Russians (34 per cent); border nationalities were correspondingly more densely represented, e.g. Jews twenty-two (22·7 per cent), Georgians twenty-eight (28·9 per cent) and Ukrainians six (6·3 per cent). An analysis of the age-structure in 1907 shows that nine Bolshevik leaders had an average age of thirty-four; the corresponding Menshevik figure was forty-four. There existed no significant differences between the two groups in respect of education or social status.[15]

All three political groupings – Socialist-Revolutionaries, Liberals and Social-Democrats – remained marginal phenomena until the eve of the Russo-Japanese war. The war brought into prominence every source of disaffection within the empire. It subjected tsarism to the sternest ordeal it had yet had to face.

Part 2

6 On the Eve of 1905

Few sides of Russian life escaped the threat of reality of violence in the early years of the new century. Student revolutionaries claimed two notable victims in 1901 and 1902 respectively – Bogolepov, minister of education, and Sipyagin, minister of the interior. This betokened a revival of political interest amongst the student body, after the student strikes and demonstrations of 1899. Kiev University, the largest after Moscow and St Petersburg, seems to have taken particular prominence. The national question helped to account for this. The strongest organizations at Kiev belonged to the Polish, Ukrainian and Caucasian students.[1] In these years also, government-inspired anti-semitism took on new life. In 1903, the government instigated ruthless attacks on the Jewish communities in Kishinyov (Bessarabia) and Gomel (White Russia). At least one minister, von Plehve (interior) saw in these attacks 'an anti-revolutionary counter-action'.[2] He hoped they might serve to divert the unpopularity of the regime on to the Jewish scapegoat.

The time was long past, if, indeed, it had ever existed, when such measures might suffice. In 1902 peasant disorders once again broke out, mainly in the troubled provinces of Poltava and Saratov. In Poltava, to the perennial burdens of the peasant, was added a bad harvest. In the absence of government relief the peasants took the law into their own hands; they ransacked the landowner's stocks of grain and foodstuffs, even seizing stretches of land. All sorts of utopian rumours flew amongst the crowds – 'it was allowed', 'new laws had come out', 'the tsar has ordered no shooting' (by the troops), 'each man is to have six dessyatins of land'. In Saratov the situation was more tense and complex. Here, too, rumours of land redistribution were rife. There was arson, open seizure of land, boycott and strikes. The aim was to limit the extent of the landowner's exploitation or, more frequently, to destroy his property.[3] Similar restiveness gripped other provinces – Tambov, Voronezh, Kherson and Ekaterinoslav, for example.

In 1902 and 1903, the workers' movement paralleled that of the peasants. At Zlatoust, a Ural mining centre, troops killed sixty-nine striking workers before order was restored. Bogdanovitch, the governor who summoned the troops, was later assassinated. In the south of Russia and Transcaucasia the most significant movement took place. It began in the early summer of 1903 in Baku. Oil-plants, engineering workshops and railway depots went on strike for the eight-hour day, sick-pay, increased wages, improved conditions of work, and the construction of schools and hospitals at the employers' expense. The strike quickly spread to other towns in Transcaucasia: Tiflis, Batum and Poti. Zubatov unions were prominent. Now the other end of the Black Sea coast flared up. By the middle of July the strike had paralysed the great port of Odessa. The spark next flew to Kiev ... Ekaterinoslav ... Nikolayev ... Elizavetgrad ... Kerch ... It was on an unprecedented scale. In 1903 governors called in more troops than ever before – 160,385 – but on fewer occasions than in 1902 (427 as against 522). This testified to the relatively concentrated nature of the movement.[4] The strikes, demonstrations and mass meetings took on such dimensions that police and army prohibitions could be braved with impunity.[5] It seems that the strikers' main object was economic but the local Social-Democratic committees were very active in putting forward political demands. Most frequently, perhaps, the two were blended. The Don committee cried: 'Stop work and demand the eight-hour day, the abolition of fines, a rise in wages, an end to searches when leaving the workshop, decent treatment by foremen, free medical aid, free factory schools, and end to work at two o'clock before holidays. Up with the strike! Down with autocracy!'[6]

A symptom of the disarray in town and country may be seen in the ever-widening imposition of a type of emergency regime which gave governor-generals the right to extend summary administrative punishment. By 1904–5, 'the larger half of the country (lay) outside the law,' declared a leading St Petersburg advocate, Vladimir Nabokov. 'There is no citizen,' commented Durnovo, head of posts and telegraphs in the ministry of the interior in 1904, 'who can be assured that his home will not be subject to administrative search and he himself be arrested.'[7] A secret review of public opinion for 1903 (compiled on the basis of censored correspondence) concluded that 'universal attention ... was utterly transfixed by the unusual growth of the anti-governmental, oppositionist and social-revolutionary movement, and equally by the measures taken by the Russian government in the struggle against this movement.'[8]

In January 1904, in this context – a strike-prone working class, an impoverished peasantry, widespread contempt for the law, unremitting political hostility, an alienated intelligentsia of students, liberals and professional men – war broke out between Russia and Japan.

'Alexey Nikolayevitch, you do not know the internal condition of Russia,' Plehve had once protested to Kuropatkin, minister of war. 'In order to hold back the revolution, we need a small victorious war.'[9] But when war in the Far East actually became imminent, Plehve lost his enthusiasm and urged a compromise. This brought him closer to Kuropatkin himself, and also to Muravyev, minister of justice. Both opposed a forward Far Eastern policy lest internal security be unfavourably influenced.[10]

Events of course thoroughly justified this apprehension. The years 1904–6 brought into the open political arena a four-fold force of vast hostility that left incurable scars on the body of the autocracy. Workers, peasants, liberals and national minorities (especially Poles, Finns and the Baltic peoples) moved *en masse*, though without co-ordination. None of these forces was new, but never had they over-lapped so closely. They put tsarism to an unprecedented ordeal. It withstood the attack and fought back. Yet the truth of Trotsky's dictum could not be gainsaid: 'La révolution est morte, vive la révolution!'

The war met a mixed reception. But it did at least, if only pro-visionally, do something to still the voice of opposition. Government-organized demonstrations in its favour helped to encourage the waverers. By directing the call-up away from the more revolutionary-minded larger towns and industrial centres, the government hoped to prolong the relatively favourable atmosphere.[11] Only in the border-lands – Finland, Poland and the Caucasus – were there major symp-toms of disaffection and hostility to the war. But continuous military failure – all the more unwelcome in that it was so unexpected – quickly shook the government. The war became a catalyst that brought about an ever-deeper internal crisis. Each major Russian defeat in the Far East unleashed tremors thousands of miles to the west.

The government's continued defiance of moderate opinion magni-fied the effect of defeat. On the eve of war Plehve suspended from office the whole of the zemstvo board of the province of Tver. After the war had broken out he not only obstructed *à outrance* a joint zemstvo organization to care for the sick and wounded in the Far East; he also refused to confirm in office Shipov, the grand old man of the zemstvo movement, as chairman of the zemstvo board of Moscow province.

The Union of Liberation now began to divide into 'defeatists', i.e. those who welcomed military defeat in the hope that it would accelerate internal reform; and into 'defencists', i.e. those who gave greater stress to a Russian victory.

A first token of the inter-relationship between defeat and revolution followed the Russian defeat on the Yalu river in April 1904. Not only did it stimulate the Polish public and left-wing parties to a renewed wave of anti-Russian demonstrations; in Russia proper it produced an outburst of left-wing hostility that led directly to the assassination of Bobrikov, the governor of Finland, and to the assassination of the execrated von Plehve. The latter's death, on 15 July 1904, really broke the government's front.

Sazonov, of the Socialist-Revolutionary combat organization, threw the crucial bomb. It was no mean achievement to frustrate the extraordinary security precautions surrounding the minister. His office could only be reached by way of circuitous corridors. He dared not travel without an escort of police-cyclists and police droshkys, in a carriage protected by closed blinds of nickel-plated steel, proof against revolver bullets and shrapnel. To no avail. The two terrorists, Sazonov and Sikorsky, made use of a vehicle disguised to simulate the type of van used to collect letters from the pillar-boxes of the capital. With this they intercepted Plehve's entourage as it passed by the Warsaw railway station in St Petersburg. The momentary halt gave Sazonov and Sikorsky their chance.

What happened next? The invaluable Dr Dillon, *Daily Telegraph* correspondent in Russia, was the very exemplar of the ubiquitous journalist, always on the spot when big news breaks. On that historic 15 July he was driving in a cab to the landing-place for steamers to meet a friend who was coming from Ireland. His droshky was in the street leading to the Warsaw railway station 'when two men on bicycles glided past, followed by a closed carriage, which I recognized as that of the all-powerful minister. Suddenly the ground before me quivered, a tremendous sound as of thunder deafened me, the windows of the houses on both sides of the broad streets rattled, and the glass of the panes was hurled on to the stone pavements. A dead horse, a pool of blood, fragments of a carriage, and a hole in the ground were parts of my rapid impressions. My driver was on his knees devoutly praying and saying that the end of the world had come. . . . Plehve's end was received with semi-public rejoicings. I met nobody who regretted his assassination or condemned the authors.'[12]

Why should Plehve's assassination be so much more significant than that of other ministers, governor-generals or police-chiefs? Because Plehve was the very embodiment of the government's policy of repression, contempt for public opinion, anti-semitism and bureaucratic tyranny. Furthermore – his successor was the relatively moderate Svyatopolk-Mirsky, governor-general of Vilna. This change precisely marked the transition to new danger for the autocracy; it was the moment when repression gave way to some measure of accommodation to the demands of society. But reform can never proceed fast enough to satisfy rising expectations . . .

Mirsky began his ministerial career to general acclaim from the press and amidst his own repeated declarations that 'the government should base its efforts upon an attitude of sincere trust in public and class institutions and in the people. . . . Without confidence no desirable results can be attained.' He spoke to members of his ministry in the same terms.[13] Mirsky's deeds matched his words. He reinstated certain exiled zemstvo leaders in office, allowed others to participate again in public life and gave permission for a zemstvo congress to be held on 6 November 1904. He won great popularity thereby – 'almost universal rejoicing throughout the country'.[14]

When Mirsky proposed, however, to introduce into the state council representatives elected by public institutions he aroused the hostility of influential ministers, particularly Vitte and Pobedonostzev. Mirsky left his meeting with them in despair. 'Everything has failed,' he told his sympathizers. 'Let us build jails.'[15] Mirsky tendered his resignation – which the tsar refused to accept.

In the meantime the liberal and zemstvo campaign continued apace. The defeat of the Russian fleet at Vladivostok in August 1904 gave it fresh impetus. Further disorders followed in Warsaw, Baku and Riga. For the moment, however, the tsar could only bring himself to make a number of minor non-political concessions: a partial amnesty, the abolition of corporal punishment and the cancellation of certain peasant dues.

The programme of the 'Paris bloc' of oppositionist groupings showed the inadequacy of such measures. The bloc came into existence following a conference in September in Paris of eight of the major opposition groupings. Milyukov, of the Union of Liberation, sat side by side with Chernov and Azev, the Socialist-Revolutionaries. The conference also included four peasant socialist parties from Latvia, Georgia, Armenia and Poland and two non-socialist parties – the Finnish Party of Active Resistance and the Polish National League. A final joint declaration urged the abolition of the autocracy, its replacement by a democratic regime based on universal suffrage, and the right of national self-determination. On the basis of these 'fundamental principles' the eight groupings undertook to 'unite their efforts in order to hasten the inevitable fall of absolutism which is equally incompatible with the realization of all the ulterior purposes pursued by each of the parties'.[16]

The Union of Liberation also pressed ahead with a banquet-campaign, inspired by the French example of 1848. Ostensibly, the members of the Union foregathered in November and December in order to celebrate the fortieth anniversary of the legal reforms of 1864. In actual fact the banquets were designed as a demonstration against the regime. Appropriate resolutions were formulated as, for example, at a banquet attended by 676 members of the intellectual professions in a St Petersburg hotel. The legal reforms had proved a failure, they declared – 'under the autocratic-bureaucratic regime which rules the country the most elementary conditions for a proper civil community cannot be realized'; they demanded a re-organization of 'the whole state structure of Russia along constitutional principles', to be achieved by a freely elected constituent assembly, and they proclaimed the inalienable rights of the citizen – freedom of conscience, speech, assembly, equality before the law, and no taxation without representation.[17] Professional men acclaimed similar resolutions in such major urban centres as Moscow, Kiev, Odessa and Saratov.

In November a conference in St Petersburg brought together zemstvo and gentry liberals in greater numbers than ever before. Present were more than a hundred delegates from thirty-three of the thirty-four provinces in which zemstvo institutions operated. Four days of discussion culminated in an eleven-point resolution which denounced the alienation of the government from the public and the abuses of the bureaucracy; it demanded freedom of conscience, religion, the press, speech and assembly; it claimed equality of rights for the peasantry and an extension and democratization of the zemstvo. The constitutional question aroused dissension. Here the zemstvo men showed themselves markedly less exigent than the Union of Liberation. Should the powers of the proposed national assembly include legislation or be limited to 'regular participation in legislation'? The former had seventy-one votes to the latter's twenty-seven. Both versions were incorporated in the final draft. With but two dissentients the conference, in its final resolution, voiced the hope that 'the supreme authority will summon freely elected representatives of the people in order with their cooperation to lead our fatherland on a new path of state development in the spirit of the establishment of the bases of justice and the mutual action of state power and the people.'[18] There was no support for the idea of a constituent assembly. This presupposed a state of anarchy, it was claimed.

At the end of November a conference delegation presented the resolutions to Mirsky, for transmission to the tsar. Prince Serge Trubetskoy, a leader of the zemstvo-men, submitted a covering memorandum, stressing the urgency of the reforms. He also exhorted the tsar to take the initiative: 'As at the time of the emancipation of the peasants, the government must stand *in the forefront* of society *and not in its rear* if it wishes to lead and retain its supreme directing position.' Trubetskoy called on the government 'actively *to organize* the political freedom of Russia, to organize society on the basis of popular representation and in this way to strengthen society'.[19]

The tsar's response was an undertaking to accord a degree of religious toleration and non-discrimination, to relax the laws governing press censorship and to enlarge the powers of the zemstvos. Whatever mollifying effect these undertakings might have had was more than nullified by an intransigent communique of 14 December. This heartily condemned all violations of public order and illegal gatherings. It warned zemstvos and all other organizations, societies and institutions 'not to go outside their proper sphere and not to examine questions for the study of which they have been given no legal rights'.[20]

This was a slap in the face of the Union and the zemstvos. It brought the deadlock between the public movement and the tsar to a new pitch of intensity. The loss of Port Arthur in December, and the massacre of Bloody Sunday on 9 January 1905, broke the deadlock. These twin catastrophes took the anti-governmental movement to a new height of exultation. Workers and peasants moved into action as never before.

7 Bloody Sunday

Lenin spent the end of 1904 and the beginning of 1905 in Geneva. Remoteness from the scene of action did not blind him to the significance of Russian events. In an article published at the end of December he expressed wonder at the unprecedented 'political ferment'. Never before, Lenin wrote, had the average Russian heard on every hand such bold and passionate appeals for liberty. Liberal gatherings turned into open public meetings and street demonstrations. As for the workers: 'Although the proletariat . . . seems to be standing somewhat aloof from the polite conferences of the solid citizens . . . everything points to the fact that the workers are eager for big public meetings and open street demonstrations.'[1] A recent British diplomatic visitor to St Petersburg also anticipated an increase in the activity of extremists; their ranks would be swollen by moderates who had lost all hope of peaceful reform.[2]

Events very soon confirmed the prognoses of both observers to the full. Less than a fortnight later St Petersburg witnessed the mightiest demonstration in its history hitherto: some 200,000 workers, their wives and families, crossed the boulevards and bridges leading to the Winter Palace. At the head of the main procession marched Father Georgei Gapon.

Who was this turbulent priest? Surely one of the most mysterious persons in the whole Russian revolution: a man in whom are centred the most disparate hopes and policies, a man who is *persona grata* with the most highly placed members of the government, marches side by side with Pinchas Rutenberg, a Socialist-Revolutionary, narrowly escapes death at the hands of the tsar's troops, is sheltered by Maxim Gorki, becomes a companion of Lenin in Geneva, takes part in a conference of left-wing parties, gambles at Monte Carlo with money earned by cheque-book journalism, returns to Russia and then, to cap it all, sends a letter to Durnovo, minister of the interior, in which he attempts to rehabilitate himself and once again apparently offers his services to the government.[3] He is finally killed in Finland in March 1906 by order of the very Socialist-Revolutionary he had earlier marched alongside.[4]

Gapon was born in 1870, of a peasant family from the troubled province of Poltava. He was touched by revolutionary influences in his youth and this debarred him from entering a university. In its place he entered the Theological Academy of St Petersburg. Gapon combined his studies with missionary work amongst the poor and chaplaincy duties at a St Petersburg deportation centre for convicts.

Gapon, a handsome, bearded man, with a rich baritone voice, had oratorical gifts to a spell-binding degree. Himself the son of a peasant, he stood close to the peasant-workers of St Petersburg and could give voice to their moods as none other. In the tense days of early January 1905 he had the aura of a leader and prophet: '. . . for each of his words men were ready to give their lives; his priest's cassock and crucifix were the magnet that drew these hundreds of thousands of tormented people,' wrote one observer.[5] To a man of Lenin's views, such symbols were of course anathema. Yet Lenin appreciated in Gapon a man who stood close to an could influence the masses.[6]

It was precisely this feature of Gapon's personality that also drew him to the attention of the police authorities. He was invited to continue his missionary work amongst the masses in the spirit of Zubatov, i.e. to direct their grievances into the path of economic reform and away from political discontent. Thus, with the encouragement of the ministry of the interior, Gapon was authorized in February 1904 to form 'the Assembly of Russian Factory Workers of St Petersburg'. Its aims, *inter alia*, were to affirm 'national consciousness' amongst the workers, develop 'sensible views' regarding their rights and foster amongst the members of the Assembly 'activity facilitating the legal improvements of the workers' conditions of work and living'. The Assembly officially opened its doors on 11 April 1904.[7]

What ultimately developed was a cross between a trade union, a mutual aid society and even an underground revolutionary organization; for Gapon, if he is to be believed, sought to form inside the Assembly a nucleus of assistants who would be 'ready to lead the people when the critical moment came'.[8]

By the end of 1904 the Assembly had a membership divided into eleven sections with cells in most of the larger factories, including a particularly strong contingent at the Putilov works. The overall total has been variously estimated at more than two thousand, or between six thousand and eight thousand.[9] Whatever the true figure, and whatever Gapon's true intentions may have been, the strength of the Assembly and of its sympathizers exceeded by far that of the political parties. In St Petersburg at this time, for example, the local Menshevik and Bolshevik committees could muster no more than three hundred members each.[10] This disparity accounts no doubt for the interest that Liberals, Social-Democrats and Socialist-Revolutionaries all took in Gapon's Assembly.

The 'critical point' foreseen by Gapon came at the turn of the year. At last the agitation amongst the professional men was beginning to communicate itself to the masses. The initial spark was the dismissal of four Putilov workmen at the end of December. They were all members of the Assembly with many years of employment behind them. Gapon assumed, justifiably enough perhaps, that their membership was the reason for their dismissal. He resolved to take up their cause lest the Assembly lose all credit.[11] Gapon now tried to intercede for the dismissed men with the Putilov management, the local factory inspector and the governor-general of St Petersburg. To no great avail. As a mode of additional pressure, Gapon also organized a strike movement at the Putilov works. This enjoyed instant success. By 3 January all the thirteen thousand workers were on strike, the department of police reported to the ministry of the interior.[12] Soon the only occupants of the factory were two agents of the secret police.[13]

The strikers demanded the eight-hour day, a ban on overtime, improved working conditions, free medical aid, higher wages for women workers, permission to organize a representative committee and payment for the period of the strike. Bolshevik attempts to gain influence were rejected. Their speakers were beaten up, their leaflets destroyed, and only 'unwillingly' was a donation of 500 roubles accepted.[14] A mass meeting of strikers on 5 January 1905 also acclaimed petitions that called for the immediate convocation of a constituent assembly, the establishment of personal liberties, an end to the war with Japan and an amnesty for political exiles.

Within a few days the strike spread at a fantastic rate throughout St Petersburg. It was virtually a general strike in the Russian capital. By 5 January, 26,000 men had ceased work; by 7 January, 105,000; by 8 January, more than 111,000.[15] During these last days, 'St Petersburg seethed with excitement,' writes Gapon. 'All the factories, mills and workshops gradually stopped working, till at last not one chimney remained smoking in that great industrial district. . . . Thousands of men and women gathered incessantly before the premises of the branches of the Workmen's Association.'[16]

The authorities were also not idle. By 7 and 8 January they had assembled troops, including many picked guards regiments, at electrical stations, gas works, telephone exchanges, railway stations, water supply installations, the larger factories and the Treasury and the State Bank. Special concentrations guarded the environs of the Winter Palace and the junctions joining the centre of the city to the industrial districts on the periphery. The troops set up braziers in the streets to warm themselves.[17] It needs little imagination to see in St

Petersburg in those January days a city on the verge of open conflict.

Amidst this mounting tension Gapon conceived the idea of a direct approach to the tsar. Let the workers, with their wives and children, march to the Winter Palace! There let them plead their case for redress of their grievances before the All-Highest! Let them at least make contact – over the heads of policemen, officials, foremen, factory inspectors, governors and factory-owners – with the one man who could right the wrongs of the insulted and injured!

Gapon, aided by some sympathizers, drew up a petition for presentation to the tsar. It was redolent of unappeasable longing and utopian hopes, incongruously juxtaposed with soberly factual political and social claims. Few other documents can convey so truthfully the Russian workers' sense of exclusion from society, the *état d'âme* of the rejected. 'O Sire!' they called on the tsar,

we working men of St Petersburg, our wives and children, and our parents, helpless and aged men and women, have come to you, our ruler, in quest of justice and protection. We are beggars, we are oppressed and overburdened with work; we are insulted, we are not regarded as human beings but are treated as slaves who must suffer their bitter lot in silence. We have suffered but are driven further and further into the abyss of poverty, injustice and ignorance; we are strangled by despotism and tyranny, so that we can breathe no longer. We have no strength at all, O Sovereign. Our patience is at an end. We are approaching that terrible moment when death is better than the continuance of intolerable sufferings . . .

Our first wish was to discuss our needs with our employers, but this was refused to us: we were told that we have no legal right to discuss our conditions. We were told also that it is illegal to insist on the eight-hour working day and on the fixing of wage-rates in consultation with us. We were not allowed to discuss our complaints over the behaviour of the lower administrative staff. We asked that wages of casual labourers and women should be raised to one rouble a day, that overtime should be abolished and that more adequate medical attention should be provided for us with care and without humiliation. We asked that the factories should be rebuilt so that we could work in them without suffering from draughts, rain and snow . . .

Your Majesty! We are here, many thousands of us; we have the appearance of human beings, but in fact we have no human rights at all, not even the right to speak, to think, or to meet for discussion of our requirements or the steps to be taken for the improvement of our conditions. We are turned into slaves by your officials. Any one of us who dares to raise his voice in defence of the working class is thrown into prison, sent into exile. The mere fact of having a kind heart or a sensitive soul is regarded as a crime; to show sympathy with the lowly, the oppressed, the tortured is to commit a heavy crime. Every worker and peasant is at the mercy of your officials, who accept bribes, rob the Treasury and do not care at all for the people's interests. The bureaucracy of the government has ruined the country, involved it in a shameful war and is leading Russia nearer and nearer to utter ruin. We, the Russian workers and people, have no voice at all in the expenditure of the huge sums collected in taxes from the impoverished population. We do not even know how our money is spent. The people are deprived of any right to discuss taxes and their expenditure. The workers have no right to organize their own labour unions for the defence of their own interests.

Is this, O Sovereign, in accordance with the laws of God, by whose grace you reign? And how can we live under such laws? Break down the wall between yourself and your people. . . . The people must be represented in the control of the country's affairs. Only the people themselves know their own needs. Do not reject their help, accept it, command forthwith that representatives of all classes, groups, professions and trades shall come together. Let capitalists and workers, bureaucrats and priests, doctors and teachers meet together and choose their representatives. Let all be equal and free. And to this end let the election of members to the Constituent Assembly take place in conditions of universal, secret and equal suffrage.

This is our chief request; upon it all else depends; this is the only balm for our sore wounds; without it our wounds will never heal, and we shall be borne swiftly on to our death.

But this measure alone cannot remedy all our ills. Many others are needed besides; and these we shall put before you directly and openly, O Sovereign, as to our father . . .

The petition now enumerated certain political and economic demands 'to overcome the ignorance and legal oppression of the Russian people'. These resembled those earlier put forward by the Putilov workers. But they also included demands for universal and compulsory education, freedom of the press, association and conscience, the liberation of political prisoners, separation of church and state, replacement of indirect taxation by a progressive income tax, equality before the law, the abolition of redemption payments, cheap credit, transfer of the land to the people, the execution of Admiralty orders inside Russia and not abroad, and an end to the war against Japan.

Lastly, in order to prevent the oppression of labour by capital, the petition demanded the abolition of factory inspectors, a permanent commission of workers to represent them in each factory, freedom of cooperatives and trade unions, freedom of struggle between labour and capital and the state insurance of workmen.

'There are only two paths for us; either freedom and happiness, or the grave,' the petition ended. 'Let our life be a sacrifice to agonizing Russia. We will not grudge this sacrifice, we gladly give it.'

Gapon spent the days immediately preceding the projected march in haranguing meetings of the strikers. 'His passionate, burning speeches electrified the crowds and in reverential ecstasy they repeated after him: "To the tsar!"' But what if the tsar should refuse to receive them? Then, said Gapon, 'for us there is no tsar.' And this the crowds also repeated after him. 'Many people wept, stamped their feet, banged their chairs, beat their fists on the walls, and raising their hands high, swore to stand firm to the end.'[18]

Gapon, meanwhile, gave notice of the impending demonstration to the minister of the interior, Svyatopolk-Mirsky, and to the tsar. He emphasized its peaceful nature and implored the tsar to receive the petition.[19] No response came. On the contrary, Mirsky's deputy ordered Gapon's arrest.[20]

In this threatening situation – with labour *élan* about to face troops in battle order – a group of liberal and radical spokesmen sought to avert the imminent clash. They included, amongst others, Maxim Gorki, A. A. Shakhmatov, linguistic scholar and member of the Academy of Sciences, V. M. Hessen, Professor of Law at St Petersburg and editor of the liberal journal *Pravo*, E. I. Kedrin, liberal lawyer, well known for his role as defence counsel in political trials, N. F. Annensky, zemstvo statistician and publicist, A. K. Arsenev, zemstvo leader, and A. V. Peshekhonov, left-wing radical. The deputation hoped to secure an interview with Mirsky through whom they would persuade the tsar to withdraw the troops to barracks and receive a delegation from the workers. In the night of 8–9 January Gorki and his party called first at Mirsky's residence, then at his deputy's and then at Vitte's house. Everywhere they met with answers that ranged from a shrug of the shoulders to outright hostility.[21]

Calmness prevailed in court circles. 'A clear, frosty day,' the tsar noted in his diary entry for 8 January.

There was much activity and many reports. Fredericks came to lunch. Went for a long walk. Since yesterday all the factories and workshops in St Petersburg have been on strike. Troops have been brought in from surroundings to strengthen the garrison. The workers have conducted themselves calmly hitherto. Their number is estimated at 120,000. At the head of the workers' union some priest-socialist Gapon. Mirsky came in the evening with a report of the measures taken.[22]

Sunday, 9 January, was fine and cold, the Neva covered with a thin layer of ice.[23] From mid-morning onwards the workers assembled at four or five points on the outskirts of the city and thence marched to the centre in a converging movement. They wore their Sunday best, sang hymns, carried portraits of the tsar and religious banners. There were perhaps some 200,000 demonstrators in all. 'I shall never forget that Sunday in January 1905,' wrote an English eye-witness, when, from the outskirts of the city, from the factory regions beyond the Moscow Gate, from the Narva side, from up the river, the workmen came in thousands crowding into the centre to seek from the tsar redress for obscurely felt grievances; how they surged over the snow, a black thronging mass . . .[24]

Gapon himself marched at the head of one throng. He was flanked by a priest to one side and Rutenberg to the other. When the procession approached the Narva Gate it found infantrymen barring the road; in front a company of cavalry was drawn up, its swords glinting in the sun. Without warning the Cossacks bore down on the crowds. Cries of alarm and fear rang out. The front ranks broke before the attack, opening to right and left, and down this lane Gapon saw the soldiers drive their horses, striking to both sides. 'I saw the swords lifted and falling, the men, women and children dropping to the earth like logs of wood, while moans, curses and shouts filled the air.'[25] Infantrymen took a hand and poured volley after volley into the crowd. Massacres took place all over St Petersburg that Sunday morning. Prince Vassilchikov, commander of the Guards division, gave the order to fire. From the windows of his embassy by the Troitzka Bridge, the British ambassador saw soldiers shooting at men, women and children, too tightly packed to disperse.[26] No figures give the precise numbers of killed and wounded. There may well have been more than a thousand.[27]

For the most part the crowds offered no resistance. But here and there revolutionaries amongst them set up barricades, flourished a red flag or two, broke into the occasional arms store, and set telegraph poles on fire.[28]

In the immediate sense Gapon's demonstration failed. Yet after Bloody Sunday Russia was never the same again. The massacre of an unarmed, hymn-singing crowd undermined the standing of the autocracy to an incalculable degree, not only in Russia but also abroad. 'All classes condemn the authorities and more particularly the emperor,' reported the United States consul in Odessa. 'The present ruler has lost absolutely the affection of the Russian people, and whatever the future may have in store for the dynasty, the present tsar will never again be safe in the midst of his people.'[29]

This was clearly an exaggeration, attributable to the heat of the moment. Yet for most of the next two years the tsar was *not* safe amongst his people. At Peterhof in September 1906, nearly two years later, he still dared not venture beyond the grounds of the Villa Alexandria, the imperial residence. The tsar, his consort, and the children had eventually to take refuge in the imperial yacht and cruise round aimlessly off the coast. At night a squadron of the fleet illuminated the yacht's surroundings with searchlights. The tsar found it 'a most beautiful sight on the whole'. In October his ministers still advised the tsar not to attend ceremonies whose date had been announced beforehand.[30]

This was a passing phase; but this can by no means be said of the other major sequel to Bloody Sunday – the political activization of the masses. The massacre, super-imposed on the ferment already provoked by the war, made political concern a mass phenomenon in Russian society. Lenin did not exaggerate in his appreciation of a thoroughly new situation in Russian political life: 'The revolutionary education of the proletariat made more progress in one day than it could have made in months and years of drab, humdrum, wretched existence.'[31] Old patriarchal, humble Russia had turned into the Russia 'of the revolutionary proletariat and the revolutionary people'. The events of January 1905 'furthered the extension and intensification of Social-Democratic ideas amongst the population,' a member of the Bund remarked. 'New members came in, the demand for literature grew – social-democracy sent down deep roots, the movement gripped wider circles.'[32] Bloody Sunday completed what the Japanese war had begun. 'Even in the very recent past, of several thousands of proclamations distributed by the socialist parties, it might be expected that a hundred-odd, not more, would reach the people and be read by them,' a Social-Democrat noted.

Now tens of thousands of revolutionary pamphlets were swallowed up without remainder; nine-tenths were not only read but read until they fell apart. The newspaper which was recently considered by the broad popular masses, and particularly by the peasantry, as a landlord's affair, and when it came accidentally into their hands was used in the best of cases to roll cigarettes in, was now carefully, even lovingly, straightened and smoothed out, given to the literate, and the crowd, holding its breath, eagerly listened to 'what they are writing about the war'. . . . Not only did the soldiers moving along all the lines of the railway network almost fight for a newspaper or other printed sheet thrown from the windows of a passing train, but the peasants of the villages near the railways from then on, and also for some years after the war, continued to ask travellers for 'a little newspaper'.[33]

In the border areas – Poland, the Baltic, Finland, the Caucasus – Bloody Sunday gave a fresh goad to nationalist violence and resentment. The armed forces were necessarily affected; here and there soldiers and sailors attacked their officers, ran up the red flag, disobeyed orders. For the rest of 1905 and well into 1906 the Russian empire became a panorama of strikes, demonstrations, petitions, banquets, peasant unprisings, student riots, assassinations – all ultimately quelled by repression and anti-Jewish pogroms. The movement died down in one area – but flared up elsewhere, in a variegated criss-cross of violence.

On the morrow of Bloody Sunday there were 125,000 men and women on strike in St Petersburg. From then on there was a slow drift back to work. By 18 January the immediate mass movement was over, at least in Russia proper.[34]

This was only a lull. The events of the next few months abundantly justified Rosa Luxemburg's identification of the Russian mass strike with the very history of the Russian revolution – 'the unconscious precedes the conscious, the logic of the historical process the subjective logic of its bearers.'[35] Not only were there individual strikes in all the principal industrial and mining areas; repeated strikes paralysed these areas to an unprecedented degree. Amongst the worst affected areas were St Petersburg, Petrokov (Poland), Livonia, Baku and Warsaw. In Livonia each worker struck nearly five times; in Baku only slightly less. The reason for this higher rate as compared with Russia proper was the conjunction of the national with the class struggle.[36]

A special feature was participation by workers who had not previously engaged in strike activity – bakers, and transport and harbour workers, for example. This in itself epitomized the growing radicalization of the masses. Of special importance were the railway workers. They brought traffic to a standstill in many areas of South Russia. The needs of war forced the regime to negotiate with the railwaymen and eventually to mobilize them. But this did not prevent the formation of an important railway union which later joined the Union of Unions.[37]

The student body of St Petersburg (and later of the whole empire) was another fiery element – all the more so through its articulation of explicit political demands. The students' immediate reaction was to assemble at the Technological Institute in the capital, express their solidarity with the workers and declare a strike. We cannot study when the ground beneath our feet is soaked with blood, they said; we cannot accept education from the hands of a government of murderers.[38] On 7 February, by a majority of 2,378 to 66, the students demanded the summoning of a constituent assembly on the basis of universal, equal, direct and secret suffrage, and the freedom of press, assembly, strike, trade unions and political parties. The students' prime duty was to participate in the struggle of the people against the autocracy, declared a Vyborg congress later in 1905 of representatives from higher educational institutions all over the empire.

They must mobilize their forces in the powerful towns and create the possibility of using higher educational institutions for revolutionary agitation and propaganda in the broad masses of the people and undertake measures to organize student fighting squads so that the students, when necessary, can join the general political strike and armed uprising.

Only by way of revolution could a constituent assembly be attained.

Where the students led, their professors, lecturers, the members of the Academy of Sciences, and professional men were not far behind, if, indeed, they were not in the vanguard. In innumerable manifestoes they condemned the autocratic regime as a bar to the free functioning of intellectual life. No understanding was possible with 'the hangman of the people', declared Struve in *Osvobozhdenie*. All opposition forces must unite to annihilate tsarism.[39]

The strikes were relatively non-political in character apart from those in the border regions. 'To present the Russian working class,' Pokrovsky comments, 'as being all the time during the whole period of the first revolution on the same topmost level of revolutionary consciousness would mean, in the first place, rejecting Marxist dialectic; and secondly it would make it impossible to understand why it took twelve years to overthrow Nicholas II and not twelve weeks.' Pokrovsky cites in substantiation the reaction of the workers at the textile centre of Ivanovo-Vosnesensk to the slogan 'Down with the autocracy!' They backed away in horror, loudly protesting.[40] Economic and social demands, at least in the early part of the year, corresponded far more closely to the workers' feelings. In Kharkov, a typical example, the workers demanded the eight-hour day, medical aid, improved sanitary conditions, a workers' elected council, decent treatment, etc.[41] The Social-Democrats did indeed try to give the strike movement a political direction – but to no avail. Given the nature of the workers' interests it may well seem that the Bolshevik slogans, conceived in terms of a revolution for socialism, democratic republic, or a constituent assembly found little resonance. Demands for the eight-hour day and wage increases came very low on the Bolshevik list of priorities.[42] The Marxist Bund, on the other hand, a party closer to the workers than were the Bolsheviks, devoted itself, at least in the provinces of Minsk and Mogilev, to pointing out 'the difficult economic position' of the workers and called sympathy strikes.[43] But when the members of the Bund tried to agitate against the autocracy, they found no echo. This was the case during a performance of Gorki's play *Dachniki* at the Pushkin Theatre in Kishinyov. Several people cried out in uncertain tones 'Down with the autocracy!' and bundles of hectographed leaflets were thrown into the stalls. Five Jews were arrested. 'The incident did not meet with sympathy from the public,' the local police department reported.[44]

The failure of the Social-Democrats to bring political influence to bear was attributable, first, to their disunity and, second, in the words of a Menshevik analyst, to the fact that 'the connexion between the intelligentsia of the party and the workers was purely external, affixed by the pressure of circumstances but having extremely weak roots in the past of the whole movement and its organizational work.'[45] Perhaps also, the admixture of semi-proletarian elements new to the struggle diluted the influence of more seasoned groups such as the metal and textile workers.

In the face of this unremitting hostility the tsar had no choice but to give ground. As early as 17 January he had confessed to Yermolov, minister of agriculture, that 'the position of the government was impossible if it relied only on troops'.[46] Yet the tsar's initial measures were weak in the extreme. The government took but the feeblest of feeble actions to restore its moral authority. On 19 January a special train brought a random selection of thirty-four workers from St Petersburg to Tsarskoe Selo. The tsar delivered a little homily. He regretted the deaths of the innocent victims led astray by thieves and rogues. 'I believe,' he continued, 'that apart from a handful of worthless and abandoned people the overwhelming majority of the workers were, and will be truly Russian, orthodox people, loving God, the tsar and their country, true sons of Russia and I forgive them their guilt. The life of a working man is hard,' Nicholas added, but he, the tsar, would ensure that the workers' just demands were satisfied, whilst observing similar justice to the employers.[47]

In addition, Kokovtsov, minister of finance, undertook a hasty inquiry into labour legislation outside Russia. He recommended, *inter alia*, that Russia follow the western European model, no longer consider strikes a breach of public order (hence a punishable offence) and only interfere in case of violence.[48] Far stronger advice came from Yermolov. In two verbal reports to the tsar he did not hesitate to assert that there was 'in reality no government; only separate ministries'; and that the tsar must grant a constitution, when the time was ripe, and summon an all-Russian duma of freely-elected representatives of the people.[49]

The government's actual programme remained much more modest. It amounted to nothing more than the establishment of a commission under Senator Shidlovsky. Its object was 'to ascertain the causes of the dissatisfaction of the St Petersburg factory workers and to elaborate proposals for its elimination.'

The commission was to work with and through workers' delegates from the factories, elected at two levels; 150,000 workers voted: twenty per cent for the Social-Democrats, forty per cent for 'leftish inclined' workers and thirty-five per cent for the workers with economic demands.[50] Mensheviks and Bolsheviks differed in their approach to the commission. Whereas the latter were hostile, the former hoped to expand the body of delegates into a representative tribune of the workers of Russia. In the event, under Bolshevik influence, the workers' electoral delegates, already disaffected by the arrest of certain of their colleagues, demanded freedom of speech and assembly, full freedom of discussion with their electors and the release of their arrested colleagues. The government rejected these demands; the delegates thereupon resolved to boycott the commission and called on the workers to carry on the fight for the eight-hour day, state insurance, popular participation in government and an end to the war. The next day the commission was dissolved. Its failure marked the bankruptcy of the regime's only attempt to establish contact with the workers. But it also helped to inaugurate the idea of an elected organization that would represent the workers of a given factory – in other words, a soviet.[51] Later in 1905 and, still more prominently in 1917, this institution became the characteristic feature of the Russian revolution.

In the meantime however, the growing turmoil, pinpointed in the assassination of the Grand Duke Sergei, uncle of the tsar and military commander of Moscow, at length forced the tsar to yield further ground. On 18 February he issued a rescript to Bulygin, newly-appointed minister of the interior, undertaking to call in representatives of the people in preparing new laws. The tsar also issued a manifesto and an ukaze. The first denounced all those who sought 'to disrupt the existing state structure'; the second ordered the council of ministers to examine all the proposals submitted to the tsar 'concerning improvements in the state organization and the betterment of the people's existence'. These actions took the tsar's ministers by surprise – the public also. Well they might – 'in the morning (the public) read the tsar's appeal to support the autocracy, and in the evening it read his decision to attract the people's elected representatives to the work of legislation.'[52] These were not, strictly speaking, contradictory, but they relied on a distinction which could not be apparent in the turmoil of the time.

In any case, the repercussions of the Russian defeat at Mukden a week later and the even greater catastrophe of Tsushima in May when the Baltic and Black Sea fleets were destroyed, entirely nullified the government's hopes. On 24 May 1905 a council of war decided that 'internal order (was) more important than victory'.[53]

This change of emphasis clearly took time to put into practice. Failing its immediate realization Tsushima gave the national upheaval renewed strength – not only in Russia proper but also in Poland, the Baltic provinces and the Caucasus. In these areas the movement had a political content hitherto lacking in the Russian movement. This was due of course to the presence of the national question. In Poland, for example, although bourgeois groups such as textile manufacturers saw their future linked to a continuance of the Russian empire with its markets in the Far East, and although the left wing was divided between the nationalist socialists of Pilsudski, the Marxist Social-Democratic Party of Rosa Luxemburg, and the Jewish Bund, there was a strong national and political content in the recurrent waves of unrest that swept across Poland in 1905. During the whole of that year there were never less than 250,000 Russian troops quartered in the country. The Polish movement embraced strikes, demonstrations – those on 1 May had to be suppressed by force – and armed uprisings led by Pilsudski. He hoped to secure the financial support of the Japanese General Staff in Tokio; but the attempt was negated by the intervention of Dmowski, leader of the bourgeois National League (later, National Democratic Party). None the less, in the second half of 1905, Poland was never far from a nation-wide outbreak of violence. At the end of June workers' barricades in Lodz defied the Russian army for three days.[54] In the Baltic the movement took the primary form of attacks by the native peasantry on the German landowners.

In their different way the middle-class intelligentsia and zemstvo-men matched the radicalism of the workers. The first pressed on with their banquet campaign and formed the nucleus of a movement that aimed to group together the scattered professional societies. In May this endeavour culminated in the foundation of the Union of Unions. It embraced fourteen constituent groups: academics, lawyers, pharmacists, agriculturalists, teachers, accountants, engineers, writers, railway workers, doctors, veterinary specialists, zemstvo constitutionalists and unions for the emancipation of women and the emancipation of the Jews. The Union of Unions was by far the most radical of all the bourgeois groupings. It sanctioned terrorism and it passed a resolution in the most violent terms:

All means are admissible in the face of the terrible menace contained in the very fact of the continued existence of the present government: and every means must be tried. We appeal to all groups, to all parties, all organized unions, all private groups . . . and we say: with all our strength, with all the means at our disposal, you must hasten the removal of the gang of robbers that is now in power, and put in its place a constituent assembly.[55]

The zemstvo-men remained relatively moderate – but at successive congresses in February, April and May the tone became ever more radical. They finally came out in favour of what was virtually a constituent assembly to be elected by equal, direct, universal and secret suffrage which would cooperate with the tsar in remodelling the state.[56] On 6 June, in the name of the Zemstvo Congress, one of its members, Prince Trubetskoy, professor of philosophy at the University of Moscow, led a small delegation to the tsar and delivered an oral memorandum. Trubetskoy veritably implored the tsar to meet the liberals half-way. He stressed their loyalty, their sentiment of duty; he pointed out that in the confusions of the time, the most dangerous factor was the general disorganization. In order that this might be overcome the tsar must follow the path he had himself laid down, i.e. summon representatives of the people. The delegation could not determine the precise form of such a national assembly, continued Trubetskoy, but it must not be elected on a class basis. Lastly, he warned lest the bureaucracy usurp the prerogatives of the tsar, and he stressed the need for freedom of assembly and of the press to discuss these problems.[57]

The tsar gave a friendly but non-committal reply. But the next conference of the zemstvo-men, scheduled to be held in July at the residence of Prince Dolgoruki in Moscow, was banned. The resulting disillusion marked a notable step in the radicalization of the left wing of the zemstvo movement. At the conference – held in defiance of the police – Petrunkevitch advocated a 'going to the people'.

Till now, he said, they had hoped for reform from above, but henceforth their only hope was in the people [*loud applause*]. . . . We cannot keep the storm in check, but we must at least try to avert too much turmoil. We must tell the people that it is useless to destroy factories and estates. We cannot regard such destruction as mere vandalism: it is the peasants' blind and ignorant way of remedying an evil which they instinctively feel but are unable to understand. The authorities may reply with the knout. It is nevertheless out duty to go to the people. . . . We must tell the peasant that we stand with him.[58]

What did this mean? How were the Russian peasantry reacting to the turmoil that had first seized the liberal elements, and then the workers and national groupings?

The reaction of the countryside to the events of Bloody Sunday was not immediate. Not until 21 March 1905 did the ministry of the interior circularize provincial governors with a request for information on the state of public opinion. Furthermore, several governors (e.g. those of Kursk, Voronezh, Tambov, Nizhni-Novgorod, Kazan and Penza did not make their first reports until April or May.[59] Was this purely gubernatorial inertia? Is it not perhaps permissible to conjecture that in these provinces few untoward signs had thus far revealed themselves? Be that as it may, the early calm was thoroughly deceptive; by the middle of the year the peasant movement touched its first peak with close on five hundred disturbances. Rural rebellion took the primary form of rent and labour strikes, illegal timber-cutting and the illegal pasturing of horses and cattle. There was as yet relatively little pillaging of estates or their forcible seizure. This corresponded to the peasants' main grievances – the shortage of pasture-land, high rents and low wages. There were also cases of arson.[60]

In May, some attempt was made to coordinate the agrarian struggle through the organization of a Peasant Union. The initiative came from certain peasants of Moscow province, it seems. The governor was trying to persuade them to pass patriotic resolutions in support of the war. In reply, the peasants decided to form a Union with five members to represent each province.[61] By the end of July the Union was ready to hold its first conference. More than a hundred peasants from twenty-two provinces attended, as well as Social-Democrats and Socialist-Revolutionaries. The party-political members were kept in a distinctly subordinate position. 'Private property in land should be abolished . . . ,' the conference resolved after almost two days of discussion. 'The land should be considered the common property of the whole people.' Politically, the conference called for an elective constituent assembly that would include a duma with extensive legislative and financial prerogatives.[62]

Eventually, at the beginning of August, the government made a further political concession and issued a decree that called into existence a consultative assembly 'for the preparatory elaboration and discussion of draft laws and for the supervision of the budget'. The tsar would summon this body and could dissolve it at any time. The state council continued to exist. Delegates were to be elected for five years by a complex process of indirect election for which purpose a number of electoral curiae divided along class and property lines was instituted. The government allotted forty-three per cent of all seats to the peasants, thirty-four per cent to private land-owners and twenty-three per cent to town-dwellers with house and property. The proletariat in town and country and large sections of the intelligentsia and professional men would not, on this basis, be entitled to vote. Nor would most of non-European Russia. This was a world away from universal, equal, direct and secret suffrage, and merely followed the tenor of the February undertakings.

However inadequate this scheme, it had at least the merit, in the government's view, of blunting the opposition. This may have been fortuitous; it was none the less effective. Ever since the February decrees the industrial bourgeoisie had urged the government to go further in conciliating the workers lest a real popular uprising took place. The government could no longer rule by repression alone, industrialists argued. It would therefore have to make concessions – lest worse befall. The Duma proclaimed in August, therefore, with all its limitations, went some way to meeting this argument. Moreover, it also created some disarray in the ranks of other middle-class and intellectual opponents of the aurocracy. Should they cooperate with the government in the hope of extracting further concessions? Or should they reject the Duma as contemptibly inadequate?

Dissensions such as these were not the only factor to strengthen the government. Of equal importance was a palpable decline in the strike movement – from 150,000 in July to 78,000 in August and 36,000 in September. Lastly, peace with Japan was concluded on 23 August. The significance of this may be gauged from the earlier reaction of the St Petersburg Stock Exchange to the defeat of Tsushima – Russian Consols at once rose half a point. In other words, the more closely peace approached, even at the cost of military defeat, the stronger the position of the government. But peace alone was not enough.

8 The Two Voices of St Petersburg

The printers of Moscow renewed the strike movement. They downed tools on 19 September:

We must have the right to meet freely, to discuss our affairs freely and to use for this any time and place. . . . They will probably interfere but this cannot hold us back; our vital interests are at stake, and we must defend them. . . . The strike must continue until all our demands are satisfied or our strength has given out.[1]

Strikers soon clashed with police and Cossacks; this brought in all the workers of Moscow. Close links bound the workers of the two capitals.[2] This led to a printers' sympathy strike in St Petersburg and then, on 6 October, to a strike by the workshop men of the Moscow–Kazan railway. Earlier discussions of a railwaymen's general strike formed the background to this move. In a flash this turned to reality when a rumour spread that delegates to a railwaymen's conference in St Petersburg to discuss pension rights had been arrested. The rumour was untrue. But the correction came too late to prevent a crescendo strike movement. By 16 October virtually all the Russian and Finnish railway tracks were paralysed. The line Moscow–Yaroslav–Archangel; Moscow–Brest; Moscow–Kiev–Voronezh; Warsaw–Vienna; St Petersburg–Warsaw; the Trans-Siberian; Riga–Orel – the railwaymen brought them all to a standstill or cut services to the odd passenger or goods train.[3] Factory workers and professional men joined in. In the van were Moscow and St Petersburg, setting the pace for the smaller urban centres.

This vast movement raised once again the economic and social demands of the earlier months of 1905. But political demands in the autumn began to take more prominence. A multitude of pamphlets, fly-sheets and manifestoes, published in such numbers that the police could not interfere, demanded powers threatening the very foundations of tsarism. In a resolution sent to Vitte the first All-Russian conference of railwaymen's delegates demanded, in addition to every type of economic concession, an end to capital punishment, freedom of conscience and the press, the inviolability of the person, freedom to form trade unions, to declare a strike, the immediate convocation of a constituent assembly, freely and secretly elected, 'for the erection of a basic law of a new state order in Russia'. Workers in Moscow put this in the forefront of their demands; students at Kharkov University and Technological and Veterinary Institutes did not lag behind. In Perm leaflets proclaimed 'the electoral rights of women', 'the rights of man and the citizen', 'how the people's money must be spent', 'the palace of representatives'; in Zhitomir crowds thronged the streets, crying 'Down with the autocracy,' 'Down with the tsar, greetings to revolution and the democratic republic.'[4]

For the first time in 1905 tsarism confronted a united force of all opposition groups. The Kadet party, meeting in St Petersburg for its foundation congress precisely at this time declared its 'full solidarity' with the strikers.[5] The Union of Unions helped to organize the participation of professional men. Factory owners allowed their workers to meet on their premises, paid wages as usual and made no dismissals for participating in the strike.[6] 'Complete chaos' – this was Vitte's impression of Russia when he returned to St Petersburg from Portsmouth, New Hampshire (where the peace negotiations with Japan had taken place).

The press came out without any supervision or respect for the law. The municipal railways were on strike, almost all traffic on the streets had ceased, street lighting was no more, the inhabitants of the capital feared to go out on the streets at night, water supplies were cut off, the telephone network was out of action, all railways to St Petersburg were on strike. The ruler with his most exalted family was in Peterhof and communication with him was only possible by means of crown steamers.[7]

In December 1905 the movements of the imperial family could still not be guaranteed. The tsar warned his mother against returning from Amalienborg (Denmark) to St Petersburg – the railways were unsafe, and he cited the case of a train carrying two squadrons of cuirrassiers to Livonia to which explosives had been attached.[8]

Provincial capitals followed the example of St Petersburg. Rabut, the French consul at Kharkov, wrote to Paris in mid-October:

Work stopped everywhere: on the railways, in all factories, workshops, in shops of all types, in the University, in all schools, in all administrative offices, even the telegraph offices . . . the whole population was on the streets, either as sightseers or as demonstrators. From the evening, people began to ransack arms stores and to smash the windows of the large stores and conservative journals. On the 24th, students directed by lawyers, doctors and teachers and helped by workmen and Jews, seized the district neighbouring the University and set up ten barricades made of heavy oak planks, telegraph and telephone poles, electric light standards and large paving stones. The rioters seized the law courts where the archives were and threw them into the streets.

All the police could do was organize a poor demonstration at one rouble a head, with a portrait of the emperor and the national flag. This demonstration failed pitifully before the student's revolvers – they tore the tsar's portrait and the flags to shreds.

Officially, more than a thousand people were killed and wounded before Cossacks mastered the crowds.[9]

Events had paralysed the government, reduced it to complete disarray. Vitte found Trepov (minister of the interior)

utterly at his wits' end, he moved now to the right, now to the left . . . and dreamed of how he might retire from the chaos he did not understand. . . . The wise old man, the sceptical K. P. Pobedonostzev, had completely retired from clear influence on events. . . . The remaining ministers, colourless bureaucrats . . . sat quietly by and said nothing. By the way, Schwanebach (agriculture) submitted to the committee of ministers a project for the distribution to the Manchurian army of lands in Siberia. This idea originated in the fear that when the army returned home after all its failures it would join the revolution and then everything would really collapse. . . . The government had lost its power to act, everybody was either doing nothing or moving in different directions, and the authority of the regime and of its supreme bearer was completely trampled down.[10]

In the face of this mighty wave of opposition, Vitte, now restored to favour following the Japanese negotiations, saw only two choices open to the tsar; either he must put himself at the head of the popular movement for freedom by making concessions to it, or he must institute a military dictatorship and suppress by naked force the whole of the opposition, 'even at the price of mass bloodshed'.[11] But there were no applicants for the post of dictator. The tsar, willy-nilly, had to take what he called 'this terrible decision' to grant a constitution.[12] October 17 saw the publication of what came to be known as the October Manifesto.

This had three main provisions. It granted the fundamental civil liberties of the subject – freedom of the press, of opinion, assembly and association; it undertook to extend the electoral law of 6 August so as to enfranchise those groups which had been excluded; and it undertook to enlarge the Duma's prerogatives so as to give it a legislative instead of merely a consultative competence.

The policy embodied in the Manifesto went far to allay public unrest. Vitte sold the new policy with all the forcefulness at his command. Tsarist ministers were no strangers to the manipulation of the press but Vitte took what was probably the unprecedented step of summoning a press conference in St Petersburg for the morning of 19 October. Present were representatives from thirty-three newspapers and periodicals – French, German and Yiddish, as well as Russian. Vitte appealed for cooperation – 'help me to calm opinions . . .', he urged the assembled journalists.

I need support. I turn to you. Help me. If you calm public opinion, if a genuinely popular representation emerges, everything will be easier. The heavy burden will fall. Then the government will play the part that it does in civilized countries. If you wish, gentlemen, you can bring great benefit to all. Not to me, not to the government but to all Russia. It is impossible to live any longer with such scattered and diffused feelings and thoughts.

There was too much distrust of the government for this appeal to meet with success. The journalists demanded an immediate amnesty. Vitte pleaded for time; whereupon Professor Khodsky of St Petersburg University, editor of *Nasha Zhizn* (Left-Kadet) exclaimed, 'Count, you are under a delusion. We do not demand, and we do not ask. We are saying what is essential. An amnesty before anything else. Also, General Trepov must be removed from his post as governor-general of St Petersburg.' Vitte protested again when the journalists demanded that the troops be withdrawn and a popular militia formed. 'Withdraw the troops?' exclaimed Vitte in horror. 'No, better stay without newspapers and electricity. . . . If I withdraw the troops, then hundreds of thousands of people, women and children will say "Vitte is mad."'[13]

This was clearly not a satisfactory encounter. None the less, the government *did* declare an amnesty only three days later, and there soon followed the remission of the peasants' redemption dues and a liberalized press law.

Taken all in all, these measures had a favourable effect. The strike movement diminished in volume, the railway began to function once more and in a general way the united front of the anti-government forces was broken. This came most noticeably to the fore in the attitude of right-wing zemstvo and commercial and industrial circles. The latters' hostility to the government rapidly declined. From the second half of October, writes one Menshevik analyst, 'the temperature of their oppositionist fever falls, at first slowly, and then more and more precipitately.'[14] In this reaction to the October Manifesto, the Octobrist party came into existence in November 1905. It took its stand on the commitments contained in the Manifesto, and had no desire to go further.[15] The Kadets, on the other hand, continued to press for a constituent assembly though they hoped to realize this through the projected Duma and not through any revolutionary upheaval; and by December even certain members of the Kadet Central Committee were forswearing any sympathy with the strikers. Some, such as Petrunkevitch, looked on the later armed uprising in Moscow and the formation of the St Petersburg Soviet as proof of the 'stupid and harmful actions of the revolutionaries . . .'[16]

On the morrow of the Manifesto Vitte hoped to profit from this more accommodating attitude shown by his erstwhile opponents and bring Octobrists and even Kadets into his government. But the latter refused because Vitte found their demands for a constituent assembly and full political amnesty unacceptable; and the former could not stomach P. N. Durnovo, an old-style repressive bureaucrat of questionable moral standards, as minister of the interior. But this was an appointment that Vitte would not relinquish. He had to keep the police apparatus in safe hands. But this meant that the rest of the government would be reduced to the role of passive participants in a policy directed by the police, Shipov, one of Vitte's opponents, complained.[17] However, whilst refusing to join the government, the right wing, both Octobrists and Kadets, though to very varying degrees, had at least relaxed their hostility to the tsar. The later events of 1905 – intensified agrarian disturbances and a week-long outbreak of street fighting in Moscow – probably helped to reinforce the change in outlook.

Had the tsarist leopard lost its pre-October fangs? Trotsky, in a striking image, denounced 'a cossack's whip wrapped in the parchment of a constitution'. Within a day the literal truth of these words was manifest in the hundreds of pogroms that swept over the villages and townships of the Jewish Pale of Settlement in the west and southwest of the empire and in such cities as Kiev. The mob perpetrated its worst atrocities in Odessa, where with the assistance of the police, troops and the local governor, more than three hundred Jews were killed and several thousand wounded. Prince Urussov (deputy minister of the interior in 1905–6) later revealed to the Duma the complicity of the police department in these massacres.[18]

The capacity to organize these attacks over areas that were hundreds, if not thousands of miles apart, with the coordinated action of civil and military authorities testified to the unbroken, if shaken, machinery of tsarism.[19] This was part of the resurgence of the Russian right. Such a reaction had been in train since the tsar's rescript to Bulygin in February. Not until then, writes a right-wing bureaucrat, 'did the conservative elements of the Russian public realize that in order to apply their ideas and to preserve Russia . . . from a precipitous change in its entire organization . . . they would have to unite into political organizations.'[20] First fruit of this awareness was a number of ephemeral right-wing groupings – 'The White Flag', 'People's Union', 'League of Struggle Against Sedition', 'Autocracy and Church', 'For Tsar and Order'. They propagated dynastic and clerical loyalty and opposed all such alleged sources of disaffection as Jews, liberals, students and socialists.[21] Their support came chiefly from impoverished gentry, artisans, and the petty bourgeoisie of town and countryside – all those whose livelihood the strike movement had jeopardized. Towards the autumn some of these scattered right-wing groupings came together in the Union of the Russian People. This body enjoyed a degree of official patronage when the tsar, for example, welcomed a deputation of the Union and accepted its badge.[22]

For the moment, however, neither the Union nor the government felt strong enough to indulge in any greater degree of counter-revolutionary activity than was connoted by the pogroms of 18 October. A certain balance had been established between reaction and revolution. 'The autocracy is *no longer* strong enough to come out against the revolution openly,' was Lenin's assessment of the situation. 'The revolution is *not yet* strong enough to deal the enemy a decisive blow. This fluctuation of almost evenly balanced forces unavoidably engenders confusion among the authorities, makes for transitions from repressions to concessions. . . .'[23] This was as true of countryside as of town. The police-chief of Smolensk province reported (on 14 November) that after the publication of the October Manifesto 'all the means of legal struggle (i.e. against the peasant outbreaks) are paralysed, and the authorities, knowing their complete impotence, have given up'. A land captain of the same province was forced to witness increased activity by urban agitators whom he was powerless to repress.[24]

This rough equilibrium of forces gave birth to the 'days of freedom' – the period between the issue of the October Manifesto and the suppression of the Moscow uprising in December. This was the halcyon autumn of 1905. 'How can those days be described?' asked the Socialist-Revolutionary Vladimir Zenzinov who returned at this time to St Petersburg from his exile in Geneva.

How can you express the feeling when all the best and hallowed dreams are realized? The heavy nightmare of despotism had moved into the past: *Russia was free*! . . . Free papers, free public meetings, free political activity. And all this for people who were used to the underground, used to persecution . . . used to being ready to sacrifice their freedom and their life. . . . The soul lay open to all that was fine and radiant, all men seemed brothers, it was as though evil had disappeared from the earth.[25]

The St Petersburg Soviet, meaning 'Council', was the characteristic manifestation of these days and weeks and also one of the most significant and prophetic episodes of the whole of 1905. It was an unlooked-for phenomenon. It fitted into no known categories and was unique to Russia – so much so that the word 'soviet' has given its name to the very revolution itself. It may be seen as yet another embodiment of the hitherto thwarted Russian workers' urge to collective organization and action. Did not the Soviet also perpetuate the rural-communal tradition of the deliberations of the village elders? Very few of the workers, after all, were more than one generation away from the village. The unusually high concentration of workers in large factories in a few urban areas may also help to explain the soviet movement.

Be that as it may, the first soviet ever to come into existence was apparently at Ivanovo-Vosnesensk in the Moscow textile country in the middle of May 1905. The soviet began as a strike committee but developed into an elected representative body of all the town's workers, acknowledged as such by the authorities and police. It confined itself to making economic demands, though a political undertone was not absent. During the spring and summer therefore, the idea that elected representative bodies in the factories should defend the workers' interests, help to organize strikes, act as spokesmen of the workers – all this was no longer new. Moreover, the idea that such bodies should extend beyond the confines of a single factory and embrace the factories of a whole town had become familiar through the operation, however short-lived, of the Shidlovsky commission.[26]

In some such similar spontaneous way, at the height of the October strike movement, the St Petersburg Soviet originated. Here, where Menshevik influence was relatively strong, the idea of a representative council of the workers fitted in well with Menshevik advocacy of workers' self-government and a workers' congress. The spontaneous movement of the workers in this sense had been encouraged throughout the year. Clearly, a widely representative working-class body, such as the soviets were, offered the Mensheviks the opportunity of creating the broadly based party to which they aspired. Here lay the possibility of turning a small illegal grouping into a mass party, or at least of giving it more of a representative character. Certain Mensheviks had already anticipated a 'council-style' development. Martynov and Martov, for example, had submitted to the third Menshevik Congress in Geneva in April 1905 a resolution proposing the establishment of revolutionary communes in one or the other city or district. They would serve to spread the insurrection and further disrupt the government.[27] In August 1905, Martov devised a plan whereby those workers excluded from the franchise by the terms of the 'Bulygin Duma' would participate in elections by universal suffrage to 'peoples' agitation committees'. These would encourage genuine popular representation and establish their own representative body, 'able at the right moment to come forward as the country's provisional organ of the people's will . . . a constituent assembly'. Whether this could be achieved in full Martov left open to doubt; but it would be furthered 'by the increasing disorganization of the government apparatus and the growth of an effective power among the people'. In any case, he argued, 'a movement along these lines will serve to organize revolutionary self-government, which will smash the shackles of tsarist legality, and lay the foundation for the future triumph of the revolution.'[28] Later in the year, therefore, when the soviet movement unfolded its full scope, it seemed to many Mensheviks that this was 'the battleground on which alone the cadres of a broad mass party could be developed'.[29]

Lenin first took stock of the soviet movement early in November 1905, shortly before his return to Russia. He rejected the antithesis of certain Bolsheviks who argued in terms of soviet *or* party. On the contrary, the soviet workers' deputies should strive to include representatives of all occupations, no matter what their political allegiance, so long as it was hostile to tsarism. What is more, Lenin wanted the soviet of workers' deputies to be regarded as 'the embryo of a *provisional revolutionary government*'. This would constitute an all-Russian political centre whence it should summon new deputies 'not only from the workers, but, first of all, from the sailors and soldiers, who are everywhere seeking freedom; secondly, from the revolutionary peasantry, and thirdly, from the revolutionary bourgeois intelligentsia'. Such a government would proclaim the full freedom of press, speech, association, assembly, convoke a constituent assembly, proclaim the eight-hour day and the transfer of all the land to the peasants. The party, Lenin insisted, must retain its independence; yet it might conclude a temporary alliance with a reorganized soviet, whilst upholding 'the more important interests of the socialist proletariat. . . .'[30] In general, however, the party played very little part in this analysis.

Lenin later became much more cautious and fought shy of non-party organizations. He rejected their boycott since this would in certain circumstances 'amount to a refusal to participate in the democratic revolution'. But such participation must be by way of exception, to preach socialism to 'vaguely democratic audiences', or to form 'a fighting agreement for the achievement of definite revolutionary aims'. In either case, the Bolsheviks' independence must be safeguarded and the party must 'control and guide its members and groups "delegated" to non-party unions or councils'.[31]

In St Petersburg therefore, with a view to extending the strike movement, both the local Menshevik group and the strike committees of individual factories, each from its own point of view, promoted the idea of an organization grouping *all* the workers of the city. Trotsky, who returned from Finland to St Petersburg at precisely this time, had with him a plan for 'an elected non-party organization', in which each delegate would represent a thousand workers. He therefore welcomed the Menshevik appeal for a revolutionary organization to be elected on the basis of one delegate per five hundred men: 'This was the right thing to do.'[32] This proportion was taken from that proposed by the Shidlovsky Commission.

The Soviet, in the event, began with only forty members; of these a bare fifteen had been specifically elected for the purpose. It held its first meeting on the evening of 13 October in the hall of the great Technological Institute in St Petersburg. 'The general strike has begun,' declared the Soviet's first news-sheet. 'We deputies from the different factories and workshops of St Petersburg, having weighed the position, call on all workers to support the great cause of the fight for freedom, for the happiness of the people and to join the general strike . . . the working class must close its ranks, must step forward as one organized force.'[33]

The Soviet grew rapidly – the next day its numbers had almost doubled, representing some 40,000 workers from about forty giant factories. On the third day it had 226 members from ninety-six factories and also representatives of five trade unions. It was decided at this meeting to admit three representatives from each of the three left-wing parties – Mensheviks, Bolsheviks and Socialist-Revolutionaries. But they had only a consultative voice and, in general, the Soviet was hostile to identification with any one political party or, indeed, to the political influence of intellectuals. Voting both in and for the Soviet was on a somewhat rough and ready basis – by a show of hands in open assembly, but deputies were freely chosen and subject to repeated re-election so that the Soviet reflected with great fidelity the changing opinion of its electors. Inside the Soviet, an elected executive committee dealt with current business.[34]

By now the Soviet held its meetings in the premises of the Free Economic Society, founded by Catherine the Great. Henry Nevinson, the English journalist, found the big chamber and ante-room crowded with workers.

Some of the men wore the ordinary dingy clothes of English or European factory-hands, making all as like as earwigs. Some had come dressed in the national pink shirt with embroidered flowers or patterns down the front and round the collar. But most wore the common Russian blouse of dark brown canvas, buttoned up close to the neck, and gathered round the waist by a leather belt.

The executive committee sat at a long green table in the middle of the hall. Khrustalev-Nosar, the chairman, was 'pale, grey-eyed, with long fair hair, not a strong-looking man, but worn with excitement and sleeplessness. For there was no time now for human needs, and his edge of collar was crumpled and twisted like an old rag.' The committee sat in almost continuous session.[35]

The St Petersburg Soviet formed the model for perhaps forty to fifty soviets in the lesser urban centres, as well as soviets of peasants and soldiers. Here again the origin was often a strike committee, fanned into organizational flame by a political party. Of these lesser soviets, the most important was that at Moscow. But this was not formed until the 21–22 November with about 180 deputies representing some 80,000 workers. The lag came from local Bolshevik opposition; it was feared that the party would be swamped in a non-party organization.[36] But by the beginning of December the Moscow Soviet was strong enough to form the centre of an armed uprising against the autocracy.

The St Petersburg Soviet maintained liaison with these lesser soviets and, with its own militia, conducted itself as though it were an alternative government.[37] Even if only for a matter of weeks, this ill-kempt, ill-organized body could yet defy the government, in the imperial capital itself. Starting out with the limited aim of furthering the general strike, the sheer force of working-class pressure held the government at bay. Here lay in embryonic form one side of the dual power that emerged fully fledged in 1917.

Even in 1905 the Soviet juxtaposed its own policy to that of the government. Two contending voices came from St Petersburg: one, the October Manifesto of Vitte and the tsar; then came the Soviet's reply – withdraw police and troops from the city, grant a political amnesty, lift martial law from the country, summon a constituent assembly, introduce the eight-hour day.

Here lay the Soviet's Achilles heel. The workers tried to enforce the eight-hour day on their own. They met with lock-outs and strict employer opposition.[38] Many thousands became unemployed. This weakened the unity of the Soviet. It suffered a further blow when a general strike to protest at the extension of martial law to Poland proved a failure. The government, for its part, succeeded in suppressing a sailor's mutiny in Kronstadt and in breaking a strike of postal and telegraph employees. The equilibrium of forces was slowly changing in favour of Durnovo, now minister of the interior.

Durnovo exploited to the full his strengthening position. On 27

November he arrested Khrustalev-Nosar (whose position as chairman of the Soviet was taken by Trotsky). The Soviet's counter-manifesto, calling on the public to start a run on the banks, had no great influence. Durnovo, growing bolder, attacked the Soviet itself. His troops surrounded the building on 3 December and imprisoned all the members.

Vitte's face turned chalk-white when he heard this news. His voice broke. 'All is lost,' he told his assembled ministerial colleagues in tones of great agitation. Some sprang from their seats, others trembled like aspen leaves. All debate came to a rapid stop.[39]

But all was not lost. The Moscow Soviet, hoping to take up the fight where St Petersburg had capitulated, issued a call for a general strike. The declared intention was to make the strike into an armed uprising. But by now the government had so far recovered its nerve that it allowed these preparations to go ahead, confident of its ability to deal the uprising a crushing blow.[40] In the event, there resulted a number of ill-prepared, scattered actions marked by great brutality on the part of the troops, commanded by Colonel (later General) Min (later to be assassinated). Artillery shelling of the working-class district of Presnya marked the climax of Min's ruthlessness. Then came the cold-blooded shooting of prisoners, driven out of their shattered tenements . . .[41]

The arrest of the St Petersburg Soviet and the government's victory in Moscow by no means brought the upheaval to an end. On the contrary, 'it was precisely at the end of the year that railwaymen and reservists in such Far Eastern centres as Chita, Krasnoyarsk and Harbin made common cause against the government.[42] At this time also agrarian riots in the Baltic provinces reached their peak, measured by the number of killings, destruction of estates and the looting and sacking of government-owned spirit stores and public buildings. 'In the localities of Livonia and Courland adjacent to Vitebsk there is complete anarchy . . .' the governor of Vitebsk reported to the ministry of the interior on 6 December. 'The police are powerless to restrain many bands of insurgents excellently armed with long-range weapons, before which regular troops are in retreat.'[43] Similar upheavals also characterized Transcaucasia and the south. The French ambassador compared the situation here to civil war.[44]

To all these the answer of Vitte and Durnovo was a punitive expedition. The former, according to the tsar, was a changed man after the Moscow uprising: 'Now he wants to hang and shoot everybody.'[45] The government dealt with the Trans-Siberian situation by ordering one punitive expedition under General Meller-Zakomelsky to move eastwards from Moscow; another, under General Rennenkampf, moved westwards from Harbin. With flogging parties and firing squads as their chief instruments of pacification, the two generals eventually cleaned up the line, making it possible to bring back the Manchrian and Far Eastern armies for duties in the interior. By the same methods Prince Orlov and General Sollogub were able to pacify the Baltic provinces.

Transcaucasia and the south presented special problems, in so far as troops do not seem to have been available for service in these regions. This lack was a perennial complaint of Vitte – no less than the fact that the strategic dispositions of the military did not accord with the requirements of internal policy.[46] Here therefore, Vitte had to rely, *faute de mieux*, on the local authorities. All he could do was issue orders. Thus he ordered the authorites in Novocherkassk 'to stop at nothing' in putting down the revolt at Rostov. He had no contact with the authorities in Novorossiisk – the governor was held by the revolutionaries and his deputy was not available – so he turned for help to the Kuban *araman*; and he strongly advised the governor-general of Turkestan to introduce martial law 'and decisively put an end to strikes and revolutionaries . . .'[47]

'I fear the 8th of January,' i.e. the eve of the first anniversary of Bloody Sunday, Vitte told the tsar.[48] He was determined that the dreaded date should find the government with its power restored. It seems, so far as the outlying areas were concerned, that this hope was on the way to achievement. But it leaves out of account certainly the momentous problem of the *Russian* peasant.

The October Manifesto had all but a negligible influence on the mood of the peasantry. In the Ukraine at least it may even have had an inflammatory effect, for here it was interpreted as a victory over the government and as token of its weakness.[49] Moreover, the Manifesto concerned itself with political and social demands whereas, to the peasants, land was the all-important criterion of sympathy.

But land, though primordial, was by no means the only peasant demand. The whole spectrum of peasant claims would include, for example, all the items mentioned at the village assembly of Makarevka in Smolensk province on 7 December 1905: adequately equipped village schools; provision for free secondary and university education; confiscation of church land, and payment of clergy by the state; equality of taxes and status; removal of the police; release of political criminals; reduction of taxes on liquor, tobacco, matches and other goods; increase in the number of hospitals; and the condemnation to death of all those guilty of the war with Japan.[50]

Thus the second conference of the Peasant Union, held at the beginning of November, was no less radical on the land question, and considerably more representative, than the first. It rejected the Manifesto, denounced participation in the elections to the proposed

Duma and added to its previous resolution the condition that the use of the land should only be permitted to those who tilled it themselves. A few days later the police arrested several of the leading members of the Union. At the last moment it joined hands with the St Petersburg Soviet in signing the December appeal urging the populace to refuse to pay taxes or redemption dues.[51]

It was at this time that the June peak of disorders was surpassed; there were 796 and 576 outbreaks in November and December respectively.[52] The autumn movement affected the provinces of Saratov and Tchernigov. Then Tambov, Voronezh and Kursk succumbed. In December the movement engulfed Samara and Simbirsk, Tula, Orel and Penza. The black-earth zone was at the centre of the unrest. Somewhat inadequate statistics show that three-quarters of all revolutionary incidents occurred in this zone, and one-quarter in all other areas of the empire. 'At night ominous pillars of flame could be seen in all directions,' wrote the Socialist-Revolutionary Breshko-Breshkovskaya ('the little grandmother of the Russian revolution'). 'It was easy to agitate in the period from 1903 to 1906.'[53] Arson, the destruction of estates and the fight for woodland were the most common forms of peasant violence.[54] In October and November the peasant movement took on such dimensions that it became 'factually impossible' to impose on offenders the punishment decreed earlier in the year, i.e. deprive them of their land. 'It would have led to the formation of vagabond gangs and, of course, would only have strengthened the peasant movement,' reported Durnovo, on 28 February 1906.[55]

The government fought on the landlord's behalf. Events in the Far East and the Baltic were now paralleled in the Russian interior. Admiral Dubasov led a punitive expedition to the provinces of Kursk and Tchernigov; General Strukov to Tambov and Voronezh; and General Sakharov to Saratov and Penza. The latter, on his assassination, had to be replaced by General Maximovitch. Assuredly, there was much truth in the argument of the opposition that tsardom was at war with its own people.

9 The Rise and Fall of the Duma 1906–7

A number of 'important but tiring conferences' took up the tsar's time during the first week of December 1905. They dealt with the electoral law for the promised Duma. 'The whole future' of the institution hung on the right solution to this problem, Nicholas wrote to his mother.[1] Eventually, on 11 December, amidst the first flare-up of the Moscow uprising, Vitte issued the new law. This broadened considerably the narrow franchise of August and brought it into accord with the promises of the October manifesto. It enfranchised a large section of the industrial workers, the urban intelligentsia and the lower middle class. The arrangements for worker representation in the Duma were informed by precisely the same principle as representation in the St Petersburg Soviet. *Both* the Soviet *and* the Duma elected their worker-members on the basis of factory representation. The Soviet had elected one delegate for every five hundred workers; in the Duma the proportion was one electoral representative per factory employing fifty to a thousand male workers, and one such representative for each one thousand workers in the case of a factory that employed several thousand workers. This disproportionate representation was intended to outweigh the influence of the larger establishments, where the workers' mood was more militant. These arrangements are of great sociological import: they show vividly how the worker existed solely in relation to his place of work. He lived outside society proper and was a pure proletarian. It also helps to explain why trade unions played so small a part in Russian labour history (although the influence of government repression must of course also be borne in mind). The factory was the trade union.

Even with this extension of the franchise, ninety thousand workers and two thousand landowners still enjoyed the same representation – one deputy in each case. Those 'tiring conferences' had not been a waste of time. Furthermore, through the exclusion from the franchise of factories employing less than fifty, of building labourers, casual labourers and artisans, it is calculated that sixty-three per cent of the urban male working population had no vote.[2]

Limited as it was, the franchise law of December 1905 marked a significant governmental retreat. It was also the last such retreat. The government now moved over to the offensive, eager to exploit the prestige culled from the defeat of the Moscow uprising. This new policy took form in a less cooperative, not to say hostile, policy *vis-à-vis* the Duma and in a planned campaign of repression against the peasantry and the political opposition. The balance of power in the strange and sporadic civil war between the government and the opposition began to readjust itself in favour of the former.

The tsar never reconciled himself to the Duma. He had even ordered that publication of the manifesto of 6 August be postponed, lest it accidentally coincide with the first anniversary of the birth of his heir, Alexey.[3] In other words, no shadow must fall across the future autocratic rights of the heir. When, despite everything, the tsar had to yield, he was resolved that the Duma should be as unrepresentative as possible. He firmly declined to agree, for example, to a system of universal suffrage. 'God alone knows how far people will go with their fantastic ideas!' Nicholas commented.[4]

Government policy in this respect first manifested itself in legislative decrees of February and April 1906. The fledgling Duma must have its wings clipped, even before it left the nest. It was clear to Vitte, who attached great importance to the timely issue of these decrees, that the Duma would otherwise 'turn itself into a constituent assembly, that this would arouse the necessity of intervening with armed force and that in the upshot the new structure would collapse'.[5] The Duma, in other words, must work within a framework determined from above. The pattern came from the Prussian, Austrian and Japanese systems of government, i.e. there might be a constitution but certainly no parliamentary rule.[6]

Thus it was that the decrees of February and April included the conventional autocratic formula: 'By the grace of God, We, Nicholas the Second, emperor and autocrat of all the Russias, tsar of Poland, grand duke of Finland . . .'; and one principle of the decree not only emphasized the emperor's 'supreme autocratic power' but went on to claim that 'submission to His power, not only from fear but as a matter of conscience is enjoined by God Himself.' The decrees did, none the less, unquestionably curb the absolute power of the tsar, but there still remained highly powerful prerogatives at his disposal. The tsar enjoyed the right of legislative initiative and was required to give his sanction to all legislation. He enjoyed executive power, in his own right, or through his ministers or other subordinates. He exercised complete control over foreign affairs including the right to declare war, conclude peace and enter into treaties with other powers. He also directed naval and military affairs and appointed and dismissed governmental ministers. The laws functioned in the name of the autocrat and he alone was empowered to intervene in the course of justice through exercising his power of clemency, commutation of sentence or the staying of proceedings.

Side by side with the elective Duma the fundamental laws also created a counterbalancing upper house, the Imperial Council. In part this consisted of members appointed by the tsar, and in part of members elected by the church, the universities, zemstvos, assemblies of the nobility, chambers of commerce and the Academy of Sciences. The Duma and the Imperial Council enjoyed co-equal power. They could amend or repeal existing legislation (except the fundamental laws) and could enact new legislation. Both houses had to be in agreement in any such action; and the tsar had to approve the resulting legislation before it could enter into force.

The exclusion of many budgetary items from its surveillance deprived the Duma of further power. It could not, for example, examine sums set aside by the government to repay loans or other state obligations. It had no control over emergency credits or loans contracted in time of war, all of which remained subject to the tsar and *his* ministers.

Both the Duma and the Imperial Council had a life-span of five years. Imperial decree called them into being and determined the length of the annual session. Both could be dissolved by imperial decree which must also, however, determine the date of the next session. It was characteristic of the new system that in the periods of recess and in 'exceptional circumstances' the emperor could legislate on his own initiative by virtue of Article 87 – always providing that within two months of the resumption of the Duma's session such legislation was submitted to the Duma. Since 'exceptional circumstances' were broadly interpreted and since it was always difficult to annul or amend measures which had passed into law, Article 87 offered an opportunity for autocratic legislation that bypassed the Duma entirely.

This constitution placed the tsar and the government in an extremely strong, if not impregnable, position. The Duma was not, remotely even, a constituent assembly. It did not enjoy legislative parity with the monarch but only in conjunction with the Imperial Council; and large and significant areas of the government's activities were excluded from its purview. All that remained of the Duma was a body of limited legislative power under the supreme authority of the tsar.

In the early months of 1906 the successful return of the troops from the Far East further strengthened the government's position. Both workers and peasants, though by no means quiescent, were growing less active. The struggle of the liberals was diverted into parliamentary channels. Conversely, the forces of the right were strengthening. The most notable feature in the government's revival was the conclusion with a French-dominated banking syndicate of what Vitte proudly claimed to be the largest foreign loan ever made – two and a quarter million francs.

The Russian financial position had been steadily weakening from the summer of 1904 onwards. But the first mention of a loan on this scale seems to go back to the time of Vitte's peace negotiations with Japan in the summer of 1905. Hardly had he set foot in America than Kokovstsov informed him that on his return by way of Paris, he must insist on 'the vital necessity of a loan as the only means of not driving us (i.e. Russia) into financial recklessness'. Negotiations between Vitte and J. P. Morgan followed in August, as a result of which Morgan offered to participate in an international loan for Russia jointly with Britain, Germany and France.[7] In October, a group of French bankers arrived in St Petersburg for further negotiations. The circumstances were most distressing for the bankers – those representatives of the Crédit Lyonnais, Le Comptoir National d'Escompte de Paris, La Banque de Paris et des Pays-Bas. This was strike-bound Russia, and their train stopped now at stations and now in the open country. They arrived, no in the morning as scheduled, but in the late afternoon. Hardly had they had time to make themselves comfortable in the Hotel d'Europe in St Petersburg than the electric lights failed and they were obliged to spend the first night in darkness. They even considered returning to France the next morning.[8] The milieu of the actual negotiations was equally depressing – darkness, and a reinforced police patrol. In a day or so the bankers returned to Paris on board a specially chartered *Finnish* steamer.

But the task of rescuing Russia from bankruptcy could not wait on the susceptibilities of French bankers. The empire was in a desperate position. To the cost of war was added the cost of internal upheaval. Revenue came in very slowly; depositors were making heavy withdrawals from savings banks and overwhelming the commercial banks with demands for payments in gold. A panic flight of capital abroad was in progress. At the end of November and beginning of December no less than two hundred million roubles in gold was withdrawn from the vaults of the State Bank. As if this were not enough, Russian funds had to be made available for the redemption of certain short-term loans, issued by the German banking house of Mendelssohn, and falling due in January–March 1906. Very soon the limit for the note issue was reached, if not exceeded. Would the crisis push the country off the gold standard? Would troops have to be sent to guard the banks, if payment in gold were stopped? This frightening vision faced the finance committee of the council of ministers.[9]

In these unpromising but exigent circumstances Vitte sent Kokovtsov to Paris to solicit French financial aid and avert the collapse of Russian finances. Kokovtsov took with him promises of Russian support for France at the imminent conference at Algeciras.[10]

The fate of the Romanovs lay in the hands of *haute finance* and the French government. Here no autocratic pretensions could carry weight. The Romanovs, and their advisers, need not have worried. The French bankers had doubts concerning the financial stability of Russia, but the French government saw the advantage to be gained by exploiting Russian embarrassment in the interests of the Franco-Russian alliance. They could thus dispel the nightmare of a Russo-German *rapprochement* and create the possibility of British alignment with the Franco-Russian front.

With all this at stake the French government prevailed on the bankers to make a first loan of one hundred million roubles. This enabled Russia to avert an immediate financial collapse. In April 1906 the final loan followed, effected through a consortium of French, British, Dutch, Austrian and Russian banks. German banks were forbidden to participate – 'vengeance for Algeciras and for *rapprochement* with Britain,' said Vitte.[11]

The loan was of course at least as important to Russian internal as to external developments. In Vitte's summary, it enabled the government 'to survive all the ups and downs of the period 1906–10, gave the government a supply of money, which, together with the troops brought back from Transbaikalia, restored order and confidence in the actions of the authorities.'[12]

Less than two weeks later, on 27 April 1906, the first Duma convened. The government faced it in a far more commanding posture than would have seemed possible a bare few months earlier. This was just as well. When the first election returns showed peasant victories, there was great rejoicing in the council of ministers. 'Thank heaven!' exclaimed Vitte, 'the Duma will be predominantly peasant.' 'And a clerical one, too,' added Obolensky, ober-procurator of the Holy Synod.[13] Alas for these confident expectations! The full returns showed a striking anti-governmental majority. Of the 497 members only forty-five belonged to the right. The dominant party was the Kadets (184 seats). The opposition also included left-wing parties (124), and certain national and religious groupings, e.g. Poles, Moslems, Kazaks (32). It is true that there was also a large number of peasants amongst the left-wing parties and an additional 112 non-party deputies: but many of these, whilst looking to the tsar for the securing of their rights, still laid claim to large-scale land transfers. Assuredly, there was little comfort anywhere for the government. By religious affiliation, more than three-quarters were Greek Orthodox, 14·1 per cent Roman Catholic, Protestant and Muslim 3·3 per cent each and Jews 2·7 per cent.[14] The average age of the deputies was thirty-nine – clear evidence of the Russian demographic upsurge. It compared with fifty in the contemporary French Chamber of Deputies and fifty-one in the German Reichstag. Other characteristics of the Russian social structure showed themselves in the presence, despite the limited franchise, of a thirty per cent Duma membership of workers and peasants – more than in any other European parliament.

The results of the election were so unwelcome that pleas were made for the dissolution of the Duma even before it had convened. Either complete parliamentarization must be permitted or the Duma dissolved and a new electoral law introduced, it was argued. Supporters of the autocracy, such as Kokovtsov, continued to maintain that Russia was 'not yet mature enough to have a one-chamber constitutional monarchy of a purely parliamentary type'. The tsar fully agreed. He disclaimed any intention 'to renounce that which was bequeathed to me by my forefathers and which I must hand down unimpaired to my own son'.[15] Not until the middle of May was the actual decision taken to dissolve – thenceforward it was merely necessary to await a favourable opportunity.[16]

Unaware of its impending sentence of death, the Duma was solemnly opened by the tsar in the throne room of the Winter Palace. Had its walls ever enclosed such a strange scene, one ministerial onlooker wondered to himself. To one side stood the uniformed members of the Imperial Council and the tsar's retinue, the ladies of the court liberally bedecked with pearls and diamonds. To the other stood the members of the Duma, dressed overwhelmingly in the garb of workers and peasants. Prominent amongst the latter stood a tall workman named Onipko; he surveyed the throne and those about it 'with a derisive and insolent air'. In less than three months Onipko would be a leader of the Kronstadt insurrection. So threatening was his mien already that one minister turned to his neighbour, whispering: 'I even have the feeling that this man might throw a bomb.'[17] The dowager empress also felt herself surrounded by enemies – she could not stop herself looking at certain faces, 'so much did they seem to reflect an incomprehensible hatred for all of us,' she confessed.[18] This atmosphere could hardly have been improved by the tsar's speech of welcome. 'For the spiritual greatness and welfare of the state, freedom is not the only essential but also order based on justice,' he pointedly emphasized.[19]

The Duma met in the eighteenth-century Tauride Palace, once presented by Catherine the Great to viceroy Potemkin. The lobby resembled a gigantic white ballroom built in the late Louis Seize style. Here, and in the chamber itself, the whole spectrum of the population of the empire stood revealed in all its clash and diversity. An English observer saw

peasants in their long black coats, some of them wearing military medals and crosses; popes (i.e. priests), Tartars, Poles, men in every kind of dress except uniform. . . . You see dignified old men in frock coats, aggressively democratic-looking '*intelligents*', with long hair and pince-nez; a Polish bishop dressed in purple, who looks like the Pope; men without collars; members of the proletariat, men in loose Russian shirts with belts; men dressed by Davies or Poole, and men dressed in the costume of two centuries ago. . . . There is a Polish member who is dressed in light-blue tights, a short Eton jacket and Hessian boots. He has curly hair, and looks exactly like the hero of the *Cavalleria Rusticana*. There is another Polish member who is dressed in a long white flannel coat reaching to his knees. . . . There are some socialists who wear no collars and there is, of course, every kind of headdress you can conceive.[20]

On the eve of the Duma's first session Milyukov took the chair at an assembly of deputies summoned in the hope of forming a united opposition. This did not formally come about, except in so far as the Trudovik-Labour group of unattached peasants was occasionally concerned. But in many respects almost all the deputies found themselves opposing the government. Very soon the French ambassador could see no prospect of any collaboration between the Duma and the government.[21] Opposition took many forms but deadlock was soon evident in the dispute over the political powers of the Duma. The Duma, inspired by the Kadet vision of a Parliament *à l'anglaise*, demanded a cabinet responsible to the legislature, a political amnesty, universal, equal, direct and secret elections to the Duma, abolition of the Imperial Council, equality before the law and a number of personal freedoms – the right to strike, and the freedom of press, assembly and thought.

To the cabinet such ideas were inadmissible – every whit as much as the projects for land reform put forward by the various party groupings. The Duma then passed a vote of censure on the council of ministers. But it did of course remain without response. It merely demonstrated the absence of any common ground between the regime and most of the Duma members.[22]

In these unpromising conditions the government initiated in June 1906 certain discussions with a view to forming a Duma ministry. General Trepov, palace commandant, and Stolypin, minister of the interior, were the government's intermediaries. Their principal objective was Milyukov and some degree of Kadet support for and/or participation in a coalition government. Governmental responsibility would tame the extremists, it was hoped, induce a sense of responsibility for the policies followed by the government and thus inhibit destructive criticism. These attempts failed. Milyukov refused to countenance any abrogation or sacrifice of Kadet policy. 'He wished to exploit the revolutionary situation in order to create a Kadet parliamentary ministry with a *Kadet* programme. This would be a *complete* victory of the Duma over the historical power,' wrote a right-wing Kadet, critical of Milyukov.[23] But this was to overestimate the power of a mere Duma majority.

The dissolution of the Duma came perceptibly closer. The tsar had always looked askance at the proceedings in the Tauride Palace; his ministers likewise. The land question brought the final conflict. The Duma talked of the forced alienation of private lands; the government, on the other hand, was concerned with nothing more than improving conditions on those lands already owned by the peasantry and with extending their area by normal means, i.e. by means other than alienation. It is possible to argue, as does a repentant Kadet, that these two programmes were not irreconcilable.[24] They differed sufficiently however – and especially so because of the delicacy of the topic – for this question to provoke the final breach between the government and the Duma.

The Duma then appealed to the country to be patient and await the results of its deliberations. But this appeal was by no means unanimous – too bold for some, too timorous for others. The government seized the opportunity to proceed with the long-prepared dissolution.

This decision brought to the fore P. A. Stolypin, one of the last 'strong men' of the empire. The tsar appointed him chairman of the council of ministers very shortly before the dissolution. Stoypin at first wished to refuse the position. But the tsar remonstrated with him. 'No, Petr Arkadievitch, here is the icon before which I often pray. Let us make the sign of the Cross over ourselves and let us ask the Lord to help us both in this difficult, perhaps historic moment.' After this little ceremony the tsar then asked Stolypin 'on what day it would be best to dissolve the Duma and what instructions he proposed to give to ensure order chiefly in St Petersburg and Moscow. . . .'[25] With the aid of divine guidance, the dissolution was fixed for the following Sunday, 9 July 1906. The city and province of St Petersburg were simultaneously subjected to special security measures. Some two hundred deputies of the Kadet and labour groupings travelled to Vyborg in nearby Finland where the writ of the Russian police did not run. There they issued the famous Vyborg manifesto: the populace must pay no taxes and furnish no recruits. But there existed no organization to implement the appeal and it fell flat, to say nothing of the fact that the bulk of taxes were levied indirectly. The signatories were debarred from the second Duma and deprived of their electoral rights.

The first Duma died not with a bang, but with a whimper. Would there not at least be a general strike, a railway strike, barricades, demonstrations? No – 'everything was calm; not the slightest excitement on the streets.'[26]

Stolypin's background was landed provincial gentry. He owned 2,850 acres in Penza, 2,500 acres in Kovno. His wife, daughter of a high official of the imperial household, owned 14,500 acres in Kazan province in her own right. After his graduation from St Petersburg University, Stolypin worked in various ministries before he was appointed marshal of the nobility in Kovno district and then Kovno province. In 1902 he became governor of Grodno and the following year governor of Saratov. His draconian measures in suppressing one of the most turbulent of the Volga provinces in 1905–6 made him notorious. His own words are suggestive: of one action against the peasants he reported to the ministry of the interior, 'the whole village, almost, went to prison on my instructions. . . . I billeted Cossacks in the houses of the worst offenders, left there a squadron of Orenburgers and imposed a special regime on the village.'[27]

This conduct brought Stolypin to the attention of the tsar. In his new ministerial capacity Stolypin opposed any transition from constitutionalism to parliamentarianism. An assembly representing the majority of the population would never work. 'It is no use trying to transform the whole world all at once,' he explained to an English visitor. 'We want not professors but men with roots in the country . . .'[28]

Stolypin came into office with a threefold programme: to secure the support of some at least of the Duma for a coalition ministry; to introduce a far-reaching land reform; and to repress disorder and terrorism.[29] In the first he failed. His attempts to persuade Shipov and Prince Lvov, moderate conservatives, to join his cabinet met with a dusty answer. They insisted that public men be included in Stolypin's cabinet explicitly in order to establish contact between the government and the public; that government bills be introduced to make the liberties proclaimed in the October manifesto operative; and that capital punishment be suspended until the legislative bodies had approved its employment in principle. Lvov and Shipov would not settle for less than seven portfolios out of thirteen – internal affairs, justice, education, agriculture, commerce, high procuracy of the holy synod and comptroller.[30] However, the absence of response to the dissolution of the first Duma and to the Vyborg Manifesto made it less and less necessary for the government to seek to conciliate its opponents.[31]

In respect of public order Stolypin faced not upheaval *en masse* so much as a multitude of attacks on governmental personnel. Between November 1905 and June 1906, from the ministry of the interior alone, 288 persons were killed and 383 wounded. Altogether, up to the end of October 1906, 3,611 government officials of all ranks, from governor-generals to village gendarmes, had been killed or wounded.[32] 'In no country,' Stolypin justifiably told Bernard Pares in 1906, 'is the public more anti-governmental than in Russia.'[33]

The atmosphere generated by this hostility on all sides converged on the premier first and foremost. 'Soon after the dissolution,' wrote a journalistic acquaintance of Stolypin, 'one morning about ten o'clock, I found the premier in his study, in his dressing gown. "Are you unwell?" I asked. "No, but they wired me after midnight from Kronstadt that a cruiser had mutinied, and was coming to bombard St Petersburg. I had to telephone all night before I could find a field battery and post it at the entrance of the canal to sink her. By great good fortune the cruiser went out to sea. But I could not sleep the whole night."'[34]

The first attempt on Stolypin's life was a failure. In August 1906 two unidentified terrorists hurled a bomb into the minister's summer villa on an island in the Neva delta. It killed twenty-seven persons and injured thirty-two, including Stolypin's daughter, who had both legs broken, and his son. Stolypin later moved into the Winter Palace for greater security. He was not assassinated until September 1911. It happened during a gala performance at the Kiev theatre of Rimsky-Korsakov's opera *The Tale of Tsar Saltan*. The assassin was Dmitry Bogrov, the Kiev-born son of a wealthy family of converted Jews. He began life as a police spy and informer. He repented of these activities and, though he was intimidated by the anarchist groups amongst which he worked, his assassination of Stolypin was apparently an attempt to atone for his past.[35]

The tsar, with Olga and Tatyana, his two elder daughters, had just left their box during the second interval. Then they heard two sounds, 'as if something had been dropped'. Perhaps an opera-glass had fallen on somebody's head, thought the tsar. He ran back into the box to look.

To the right I saw a group of officers and other people. They seemed to be dragging someone along: women were shrieking, and directly in front of me in the stalls, Stolypin was standing. He slowly turned his face towards us and, with his left hand, made the sign of the cross in the air.

Only then did I notice that he was very pale and that his right hand

and uniform were blood-stained. He slowly sank into his chair and
began to unbutton his tunic . . .[36]

Five days later Stolypin was dead.

The right was no less active than the left. The Union of the Russian
People, organized in Black Hundreds, was active in inciting race-riots
and carrying out assassinations. A most notorious case was the murder
in July 1906 of the Kadet deputy and journalist, Professor Herzenstein.

Stolypin faced his first test in uprisings at the naval bases of
Kronstadt, Sveaborg and Reval, and in an attempted strike in St
Petersburg. All were easily dealt with. This cleared the way for a
thoroughgoing policy of repression. Field courts-martial virtually
annulled all civil liberties in the areas where they operated. They were
introduced by virtue of Article 87 of the Fundamental Laws, which, it
will be remembered, authorized the government to introduce
legislation in the interval between sessions of the Duma, provided
that such legislation be submitted to the subsequent Duma for
approval. But Stolypin's legislation never was submitted to the
second Duma, where it would certainly have been rejected.

These regulations were enforced between August 1906 and April
1907. They gave to governor-generals of any region declared to be
under martial law the right to hand over an accused person to a court
composed of a chairman and four military or naval officers; the case
must be investigated in secret, within twenty-four hours, and concluded within forty-eight hours. Sentence must be executed at once,
and on no account more than twenty-four hours after it had been
pronounced. The tsar gave warm approval to the field courts-martial.
Through the minister of war he explicitly informed the chief of the
St Petersburg military district that he required 'the unconditional
application' of the new laws. Commanding officers were ordered to
'take care that no telegrams with pleas for clemency be sent to his
majesty the emperor in these cases.'[37] Field courts-martial ordered the
execution of more than one thousand persons between August 1906
and April 1907. Ordinary courts-martial were also not inactive:
between 1905 and 1908 they were responsible for the execution of
2,239 people.[38] The areas to suffer most were those where social,
religious and national disaffection coincided – the Baltic provinces
(324 executions), Poland (212), the Caucasus (195) and the province
of Ekaterinoslav.[39]

This policy gradually brought disorder under control. But it was at
the cost of further alienating much of the public from the nominal
custodians of public security. Not for nothing did Samuel Harper, the
American Russian expert, note that exceptional measures had so
demoralized both officials and population that lack of respect for law

and order was 'unquestionably characteristic of present-day Russia'.[40] One of the prime institutions of government had forfeited much public sympathy.

Stolypin's success in mastering the revolutionary trend gave impetus to, and also benefited from, a revival of pro-monarchist and pro-governmental activity. In the winter of 1906–7 spokesmen for the church and for nobles' associations were loud in their denunciation of the Duma, the revolution, the infringement of the rights of property, etc. Kryzhanovsky, assistant minister of the interior, was in the meantime preparing a revision of the electoral law of 1905, in the 'strictest secrecy'. This necessity seems to have first made itself evident when the composition of the first Duma became known.[41]

The convocation of the second Duma was finally scheduled for 20 February 1907. During the election campaign in the winter of 1906 and the early part of 1907 a certain amount of governmental intervention was evident in the suppression of the press, in the exclusion of the signatories of the Vyborg Manifesto from eligibility as candidates and in discrimination against opposition parties. A law of 1 March 1906 removed the requirement of prior permission for the formation of unions and societies. But in a secret circular of 15 September, Stolypin informed governors that they could ban a political party 'if its aim, while being legal in form, was insufficiently clear'. This referred to parties which, 'although they are not counted amongst the revolutionary parties, by their programme and even by the declarations of their leaders (e.g. the Vyborg appeal) reveal none the less a tendency to struggle with the government.'[42] Right-wing leaders such as Dubrovin (of the Union of Russian People) and Purishkevitch were also receiving subsidies from the ministry of the interior.[43]

In the event, the government's attempt to influence the elections can only be considered a tremendous failure. The second Duma had an even more radical membership than the first. Most evident was the result of the decision taken by the left-wing parties to drop their boycott of the elections. Thus there were now sixty-five or sixty-six Social-Democrats (eighteen Bolsheviks, thirty-six Mensheviks and eleven Menshevik sympathizers). Once again, the tendency of the Marxists to serve in some measure as one of the reflectors of national discontent was manifest in the fraction's ethnic composition. Only thirty were great-Russians; there were eight Ukrainians, seven Georgians, six Lithuanians, two Esthonians, one Lett, one Armenian and one Jew.[44] The Poles, on the other hand, expressed their national feeling through the National-Democratic party which ranged all the way from millionaire estate-holders to landless labourers. The left also included thirty-seven Socialist-Revolutionaries. Together with the Labour group (Trudoviki) of ninety-eight unattached radical peasants and intellectuals the left wing formed the largest bloc. The right wing, both moderate and extreme, also emerged stronger with fifty-two seats. National and religious groups increased their mandates from thirty-two to ninety-four. The great sufferers in the elections were of course the Kadets: they shrank by almost a half – from 184 to 99.

What was the social composition of the Duma? Overall, it corresponded to the party's political outlook. The parties on the right, the extreme wing of which was explicitly anti-Duma and closely linked to the Black Hundreds and the secret police, included thirty-seven landlords, the remaining fifteen being farmers and professional men. The Kadets had twenty-four landlords, twenty-three farmers, with the remainder from middle-class occupations. The Labour group consisted predominantly of small farmers (seventy-one out of ninety-eight); of the socialist-revolutionaries more than half were professional men or holders of some official position; workers comprised thirty-nine per cent of the Social-Democrats but there were also four middling landlords and eighteen professional men. There was a conspicuous absence of businessmen or industrialists. Only fifty-one per cent of the members of the second Duma were property-owners.[45] From the demographic view-point, the Duma had a quite remarkable youthfulness, corresponding to the growth in the Russian population. No less than 56·6 per cent of the members were below forty, only nine per cent were over fifty years of age. Youthfulness was a particular feature of the Social-Democrats – thirty-five were aged between twenty-five and thirty; twenty between thirty-one and forty; only eight were over forty. Their chief spokesmen, Tseretelli (Menshevik) and Alexinsky (Bolshevik) were aged twenty-five and twenty-seven respectively.[46] Every member of the Social-Democratic Duma fraction had served his term of arrest, imprisonment or exile.

The strengthening of the extremes and decline of the centre gave satisfaction to those, such as Lenin, who looked forward to new upheavals and a new sharpening of the class struggle. 'The most reactionary election law in all Europe. The most revolutionary popular representative body in Europe in the most backward country!' Lenin exclaimed. 'The days of the Russian constitution are numbered. A new clash is inexorably approaching: either the revolutionary people will be victorious or the second Duma will disappear as ingloriously as the first, followed by the repeal of the election law and a return to Black Hundred absolutism *sans phrases*.'[47]

The second of Lenin's prognoses came closest to fulfilment. From the outset the Duma clearly expressed all the forces disrupting Russian life. In his opening speech, Stolypin, it is true, did indeed assert the government's readiness to work with the Duma on a whole range of proposals – famine relief, police reforms, legal reforms, taxation reforms, the legalization of economic strikes, workers' insurance, agrarian reform, etc. To the first Duma the government offered too little; to the second it offered too much.[48] But Stolypin gave no hint of any concession to the demand for a Duma ministry – and, in any case, a mere speech against the background of the field courts-martial, the terror in the countryside and governmental interference in the elections, could make no impression on opposition deputies. Tseretelli, the young Georgian Menshevik, followed Stolypin to the tribune. His fighting demagogic speech, much interrupted by the right, condemned the government for throwing the country into the chains of martial law, dissolving the first Duma, wasting the people's money, executing the best of its sons, letting Herzenstein's murderers go untouched – 'Your hands are stained with blood,' Tseretelli shouted to the right wing of the Duma. Where were the promises of the October manifesto? he demanded. The freedom of association, assembly, the press, of speech? 'They had turned into a hollow sound.' The Social-Democrats, he concluded,

base their hopes on the movement of the whole people who can put an end to the rule of arbitrariness and violence and give the people's representatives the power to open the prisons, establish freedom, solve the land question, open the way to the struggle of the proletariat and transfer the burden of taxes from the poor to the wealthy.[49]

This presupposed a union between the defence of the Duma and the defence of the interests of the masses. The Bolshevik fraction, on the other hand, was more radical in abjuring any semblance of cooperation with the moderate parties that might make the Duma a workable instrument of government.[50] The Kadets, severely reduced in number, played a far less active role than previously, lest the dissolution of the Duma be prematurely provoked. 'In order not to . . . give reason to think that the second Duma was more peace-loving than the first but also not to destroy it at once, the Kadet leader (i.e. Milyukov) recommended a harmless way out: silence.' Kizevetter, a Kadet deputy, saw the essence of his party's policy in working in that sphere where it could attain 'definite, practical results'.[51]

Right-wing members were openly provocative. They told an English liberal, Bernard Pares, that

they aimed at dissolution and a curtailment of the franchise, which they described in detail, very much as it was to be fixed later. . . . Purishkevitch at the outset got up and shouted the national anthem, and a Kadet member who failed to join in was shortly afterwards officially excluded from court rank. Shulgin (another right winger) introduced a cleverly worded mock bill for the socialization of all brains and once began a speech by asking the Socialist-Revolutionaries if any of them happened to have a bomb in his pocket. . . . On the other hand, ministers speaking in the Duma were interrupted by the lefts; sometimes at unsatisfactory answers as to abuses of official and police authority, the lefts would confine themselves to a deep-voiced and very effective 'Oh'. A genuine thrill ran through the house when an old Socialist-Revolutionary peasant, Kirnosov (from Saratov), with flaming eyes and shaggy hair and beard, intervened in a debate which touched the rights of property. 'We know all about your property,' he said, 'we *were* your property. My uncle was exchanged for a greyhound.'[52]

The land question remained of primordial importance, inside no less than outside the Duma. Listen, for example, to a speech by Sakhno, a non-party peasant from Kiev province. He speaks for the unknown millions who make history. 'Gentlemen, people's representatives,' said Sakhno, 'it is difficult for peasants' deputies to get up on this rostrum and reply to the rich landed gentry. At the present time the peasants are living very poorly because they have no land . . .' If they sent their children to work for a landowner, then they might, through inexperience, be injured by agricultural machinery; if they sent them to a town to earn wages, then the children might be lost altogether. Who would wish to return to a village 'where life is bitter'? If the peasants on a landlord's estate asked for higher wages, Sakhno continued, then they were called 'rioters'. Police and guards at once appeared and flogged and imprisoned them. 'We are told when the priests in church speak to the poor peasants: "Do not chase after riches, do not ask for land for yourself, remember what is written in scripture – true Christians, seek ye first the kingdom of heaven, the rest will be added."' But why, asked Sakhno,

why can a landlord own a lot of land, while all that remains to the peasant is the kingdom of heaven? And so, people's representatives, when the peasants sent me here they instructed me to stand up for their needs, to demand land and freedom for them, to demand that all state, crown, private and monastery lands be compulsorily alienated without compensation [applause from the left] – because even in scripture it is written: 'The land shall not be sold for ever: for the land is mine. For ye are strangers and sojourners with me.' This is written in the book of Leviticus, chapter 25, verse 23. I have read it myself [applause from the left]. And so, people's representatives, there cannot be any peace with us, because the people are suffering from hunger, the people are poor, they have no land, nothing to work at. They go to the landlords and there they give him a tiny wage. If he receives thirty kopeks, and he has a family of six or seven, then how can he feed his family on this money . . . ? I want you to know, people's representatives, that a hungry man cannot sit quietly when he sees that in spite of his suffering, the powers are on the side of the landlords. He cannot help demanding land, even if it is against the law; his needs force him to demand it. A hungry man is capable of anything, because his hardship makes him take account of nothing, because he is hungry and poor [*applause from the left*].[53]

Views such as these not only illustrate peasant outlook – they also illuminated the tension at the heart of the Duma. On what common ground could its members meet? What conceivable common ground could there be between a Bolshevik, say, and a member of the Black Hundreds? Between a liberal lawyer and a reactionary cleric? Between a Baltic peasant and his Russian overlord? Between a hungry peasant and a millionaire estate-owner? Walk-outs, cries of 'Order', challenges to duels, incidents galore – these were the visible and audible signs of that absence of agreement necessary to the working of a representative system. This was the type of situation that validated Vitte's outburst to an American journalist. It was as true in 1907 as it had been at its original utterance in 1905:

The world should be surprised that we have any government in Russia, not that we have an imperfect government. With many nationalities, many languages and a nation largely illiterate, the marvel is that the country can be held together, even by autocracy. Remember one thing: if the tsar's government falls, you will see absolute chaos in Russia; and it will be many a long year before you see another government able to control the mixture that makes up the Russian nation.[54]

The Imperial Council was very different from the Duma. There, far below, the spectator in the visitor's gallery would see 'long rows of bald heads reposing in capacious armchairs. . . .' All was dignified deportment, grave authority, formality, for those bald heads belonged to elderly councillors burdened with years of experience in chancellery, bureaucracy, the church, commerce, the groves of academe and the seats of provincial government. This had left them sensitive to 'the gradations of rank and authority', and to the unwisdom of holding views unacceptable to one's superior. Yet for all the 'exceptional cogency, subtlety of argument and wealth of illustration' with which original views were presented, the net result was to leave reforms 'decorously buried'.[55]

The tsar himself was no less hostile to the second than to the first Duma. Not much more than a month after its convocation he wrote to his mother: 'One must let them do something manifestly stupid or mean, and then – slap! And they are gone!'[56] Ten days later, complaining that the chairman did not restrain left-wing speakers from introducing serious threats to calm in the countryside, the tsar and Stolypin were corresponding in terms that suggested an imminent dissolution. Stolypin, for example, objected to accusations of 'governmental roguery' made in the Duma by Rodichev, a prominent Kadet from Tver. He also reported to the tsar that Kirnosov, that shaggy, bearded peasant from Saratov, had told the Duma that he had been sent 'to seize the land, and not to buy it'. 'I am convinced,' Stolypin continued, 'that a firm word from your highness to Golovin will be a first serious precaution against the revolutionization of the people from the Duma tribune.'[57] Wider court circles shared this hostility.

What had now to be awaited was the opportunity. This came at the beginning of June. Using 'evidence', originating with a police spy, of Social-Democratic membership in an illegal revolutionary society, Stolypin charged the Social-Democratic fraction with preparing plans for the convocation of a constituent assembly and the violent over-throw of the monarchy. He thereupon demanded the raising of parliamentary immunity and the surrender of the offending deputies. The majority of the Duma, apart from the right, fearful of this threat to its existence, established a committee to examine the government's accusations. The committee was by no means satisfied with the government's case. It therefore refused to deliver up the Social-Democrats. Stolypin proceeded with the prearranged dissolution of the Duma. Once again there was no repercussion in the country.

The supreme imperial Decree called for new elections to be held on 1 September 1907, and for a new Duma to be convoked on 1 November. It also announced the introduction of a new electoral law pre-pared earlier in the year. This was of such a radically revised nature as to amount to a veritable *coup d'état* by the government against its own creation. The new law had a threefold aim: to reduce the representa-tion of the non-Russian and non-Orthodox sections of the population; to raise the representation of the large landowners and wealthy urban bourgeoisie; and to reduce that of the peasantry and industrial workers.[58] Thus Polish representation was pushed down from thirty-seven to fourteen and that of the Caucasus from twenty-nine to ten. As for the rest, the highly complex electoral rules provided for the direct election of eight Duma members by the wealthy voters of five large cities (St Petersburg, Moscow, Riga, Kiev, Odessa); eight other members were similarly elected by the poorer voters of the same cities. The remaining 387 members of the Duma were elected by fifty-three separate electoral colleges with a franchise so weighted in favour of high property qualifications that a large part of the urban population, including nearly all wage-earners, was disenfranchised. In rural areas the franchise was enjoyed by large numbers but the system of three-or-four-stage indirect voting ensured the practical nullification of the voice of the peasants and the smaller landowners. The effect of this may be gauged from the fact that one elector represented 230 large landowners – and 125,000 workers.

The government followed up its restriction on the franchise by other measures to preserve public order. It placed student gatherings under police supervision and student organizations under the control of the authorities. Let there be a single lecture criticizing the government, warned the city prefect of Moscow, and the University would be at once closed down. A renewed token of the old days was the insistence of the authorities on limiting the number of Jewish students matriculating in centres of higher learning.[59] Stolypin also effected a policy of selective repression by the systematic arrest of oppositionists and the prohibition and censorship of meetings. 'Have you personally seen and experienced revolution amongst us?' he proudly demanded of a correspondent of *Le Matin* in August 1907. 'In Russia there is no revolution whatever.'[60] True enough. But repression was by no means synonymous with the solution of the empire's problems, as Stolypin's own land policy recognized. Moreover, some of the keenest minds in Russian history were already debating how best to give the lie to Stolypin's boast.

10 The Lessons of the Upheaval

1. *The Wager on the Strong*

The relief of the peasant problem – amongst a host of others this stood out most prominently in the government's assessment of 1905-6. The fear of a renewal of peasant violence in the summer of 1906 reinforced the lesson. This accounts for a number of concessions made to the peasants at the end of 1905.[1] In November 1905, a law cancelled outstanding redemption payments as from 1 January 1907. This made each peasant the legal owner of his plot, within the framework of the commune. Early in 1906 it had further to be acknowledged that it would be impossible to enforce a decree making the peasants responsible for the destruction they had wrought in 1905 and punish them accordingly.[2] But the element of coercion through violence, as a factor in agrarian policy, must also be juxtaposed to developments in the land question itself.

At the turn of the century, following intensive study of the peasant economy, the view gained wider and wider ground that the authority of the commune must be limited.[3] It had been the original intention of the emancipation of 1861 gradually to eliminate communal tenure, when redemption payments had been completed. But in the 1880s, following the assassination of Alexander II, legal obstacles had arrested this trend, and even reversed it. The commune must at all costs be preserved as a means to prevent the peasantry from leaving the soil and swelling the ranks of the restive urban proletariat.[4]

Over a period legal restrictions were unable to contend with the economic decay of the commune. A number of measures expressed and furthered this reality. Of these the most important was the abolition in March 1903 of the joint liability of the commune for redemption payments and taxes. This measure, when added to the cancellation of redemption payments altogether, largely eliminated the fiscal necessity of the commune. This accelerated a process that was already in train, as a result of the growing inclusion of the peasant world in a market economy. Increasing contact with urban life, increasing internal movement of men and goods, were slowly dis-integrating the legal viability of the commune. Not only had it lost its *raison d'être* as a tax-collecting agency functioning on behalf of the government; it was also losing its socio-legal function. All this prepared the way for the commune's eventual abolition.

Over and above all this a very strong political motive was at work: how might the turbulent peasantry, once regarded as the apotheosis of a tsar-centred allegiance, be re-converted into a pillar of society? Stolypin, on the basis of his experience as governor of Saratov in 1904 and 1905, came early to the conclusion that 'individual ownership (is) the pledge of order because the small proprietor is in himself that nucleus on which is based a stable order in the state'. At the moment the more enterprising peasant throve only by exploiting his fellow members of the commune, Stolypin continued. Here lay his sole escape from 'poverty and darkness'. As an alternative, let him be given a separate portion of land: 'Then an independent, wealthy settler would arise, a firm representative of the land. Such a type has already grown up in the western provinces and he is particularly desirable now . . .'[5]

The implementation of such a policy involved a complete re-casting of the peasant's role in Russian society. He must receive the same treatment as other classes 'in relation to civil law and order, administration and justice'; the limitations on his rights of ownership in communal land 'must disappear'; he must, where necessary, be enabled to acquire more land and improve his low level of producti-vity – these were amongst the points made to the Duma on 13 May 1906 by Goremykin, Stolypin's immediate predecessor as chairman of the council of ministers.[6]

In December 1908, Stolypin gave a full *exposé* to the Duma of his aspirations. Politically, he envisaged 'a strong individual landowner' who would reorganize Russia 'on solid monarchical foundations' and serve as 'a barrier' to revolution. Economically, 'through the use of individual labour in individual ownership . . . it is necessary to raise the productivity of our poverty-stricken, our weak, our exhaus-ted land. . . .' These new men, in Stolypin's oft-quoted words, were 'the solid and the strong' as opposed to 'the weak and the drunk'.[7]

The task which the tsarist government had set itself was one of the most momentous and costly in its long career. It would ultimately embrace between sixty and seventy million peasants, more than three hundred million acres of land, and employ more than six thousand surveyors, land registrars, etc. The government's ideas, necessarily vague and tentative in the initial stages, did of course conform to the economic reality of the declining commune. Even so, nothing less than an agrarian revolution was to be undertaken. The enclosure movement in England provided the closest comparison. But in Russia an attempt would be made to compress into decades what had elsewhere taken centuries.

The policy first began to take shape in a number of measures that further reduced the powers of the commune. In November 1905, a decree permitted peasant families to sell their share of communal land and leave the village. Less than a year later the communal assembly was deprived of its right to impose forced labour on any member who had defaulted on his public obligations. No longer, also, could the heads of households or elective peasant officials deny a passport to a would-be seceding peasant. This materially reduced the hold of the commune both over those peasants who remained within its aegis and those who had left or wished to leave. On both counts, therefore, although the peasantry remained subject to a differential legal position, some *rapprochement* took place between them and the remainder of the population.

All this was but an *avant-goût* of the main corpus of Stolypin's legislation. Its purpose was defined as 'the formation of independent farms through the concentration in one place of all the lands of different types of various tenures which pertain to a given holder'.

The legislation finally took shape in three separate enactments in 1906, 1910 and 1911 which collectively affected every rural household in Russia. Clause I of Section I of the decree of November 1906 inaugurated the revolution. 'Every head of a peasant family holding allotment land by right of communal tenure is entitled at any time to claim the appropriation to him as private property of his due share of the said land.' In those communes where no general redistribution of land had taken place within the last twenty-four years, the withdrawing peasant had the right to claim as his personal property, apart from his homestead, all the land in his actual possession as a member of the commune at the time the request was made. Where redistribution had taken place within the previous twenty-four years Clause 3 of the decree allowed the seceding peasant to claim his due share of communal land. If, at the time the claim was made, the peasant's actual holding was greater than his share, then he could purchase the excess from the community at the average price determined for land redemption at the Emancipation of 1861. Such a peasant however, still retained his right to use those parts of the village land – e.g. pasture-land and woods – which were exploited jointly by the villagers and therefore remained undivided.

A peasant who seceded in this way from the commune had the right to claim his share of land in a single plot, i.e. to consolidate all his scattered strips into one enclosure. The whole weight of the state's influence was directed to securing this specific aim. A further section of this decree marked a sharp break with existing peasant custom whereby the holding was regarded as the joint possession of the household. This section enacted that 'individual peasant holdings . . . are the private property of the heads of the households in whose possession they are.' Lastly, 'whole village communities, whether holding land in common or in perpetuity, can effect the enclosure of the holdings of their members by a majority of two-thirds of all the peasants enjoying the right to vote in the village assembly'.

The Act of 1910 made a distinction between those communes with communal tenure which had redistributed their land since 1 January 1887 and those which had not. The first category was now legally deemed to have assimilated itself to a commune in which land was held by right of heredity. This at one stroke enormously simplified the process of enclosure since the preliminary phase of securing appropriation of the title was thereby rendered unnecessary. In 1910, also, where communes held land in perpetuity, a simple majority of votes in the village assembly was declared sufficient to proceed to a general system of enclosed holdings. A two-thirds majority still remained operative where a commune held its land subject to periodical re-allotment.

The intent of the Act of 1911 was to codify and accelerate the process of enclosure by introducing an element of compulsion and by lessening the voting requirements. Thenceforth, any number of individuals could insist on enclosure at a general repartition of the land provided the application had preceded the village assembly's decision to proceed to a repartition. On other occasions enclosures might be enforced if the request was made by a group amounting to not less than one-fifth of the total (or to at least fifty in communes with a membership of more than 250 families). Even one member of the commune might ask for enclosure provided no harm to the village was likely to result.

In 1911 also the work of the land settlement commissions came into greater prominence. These had been originally established in 1906 with instruction to cooperate at the peasants' request in the re-allotment of land; they were, in 1911, given a more forceful part in supervising the actual work of enclosing and exchanging land. By 1913 there were 463 district land settlement commissions at work in the 468 districts affected.[8] Both at district and government level the commissions were controlled by the bureaucracy and non-peasant landowners (although there were of course peasant representatives on the commissions). Given this disproportion the commissions almost invariably acted as agents of the government's policy of enclosures.

What subsequently happened? What contribution did the land reform make to the solution of the agrarian problem? Its limitations must first be considered. First, its aim was not *re-distribution* of the land but purely its *consolidation* in separate holdings. A secret instruction issued in November 1906 specifically warned officials that 'because of the limited amount of land available even the most extensive acquisition of land can accomplish only a very small part of what is required.'[9] Second, the reform was conceived in isolation, i.e. it took no account of a tremendous variety of climatic and geographic conditions, or, for example, of the way in which the railway network served strategic rather than economic purposes; or of the high tariffs which increased the price to the peasant of artificial fertilizers or manufactured implements.[10] Lastly, the peasants themselves opposed the reforms, though there were indeed highly significant exceptions.[11] For this reason the full persuasive power of the state, whether exercised by land captains or land settlement commissions, had to be brought to bear on the recalcitrant.[12]

In the upshot, about 10·5 per cent of all peasant households in the decade between 1906 and 1 January 1917 moved over to enclosed landholdings.[13] The peasants thus affected lived either on an *otrub* – that type of holding where the land was consolidated but where the family homestead remained in the village, possibly at some distance from the land; or they lived on a *khutor*, where the farmhouse was actually sited on the landholding.

The latter, the *khutor*, must serve as the criterion for assessing the success of Stolypin's reform. The *khutor* was its supreme object and the *khutoryanin* the model farmer to whose realization the regime devoted a titanic effort.

The *khutor* depended for its successful establishment on a combination of factors – adequate and sufficiently varied land, a water supply, either natural or by irrigation, proximity to the railway network, and sufficient free capital or access to credit to cover the expense of moving from the old establishment, constructing the new homestead and perhaps preparing the ground for cultivation.[14]

To what extent, and where, did these conditions obtain? These were the determining factors. The south and south-east were areas of poor irrigation systems and deep underground deposits of water. Cultivation was extensive and had not yet made the transition to fertilization by manure; building materials were costly; and homesteads included fruit orchards. All these factors severely militated against any successful introduction of the *khutor* economy. In the central area a shortage of land, combined with non-agricultural pursuits in industry, also hampered independent farming. In the north absence of communications and the need for great expenditure of labour in clearing wooded areas again had the same effect.

This only left the western and north-western provinces, and here, in such provinces as Volhynia, Minsk, Pskov and Smolensk, natural and historico-institutional factors combined to favour the *khutor*. In Pskov, for example, hilly contours, hollows and gullies that divided the soil into small areas, varying soils, and accessibility to sub-soil water all encouraged the emergence of a *khutor* economy. As a result, the percentage of peasant homesteads on allotment land to become *khutory*, as compared with the total number of private holdings, ranged from fifty-seven per cent to seventy-five per cent. This is to be compared with a range of 11·4 per cent to eighteen per cent in the north and a range of a half to ten per cent in the centre and south.[15]

The operations of the Peasant Bank did something to redress this balance in so far as it significantly increased the percentage of *khutory* in the centre and south-east. But here the *otrub* continued to remain the favoured form. This was particularly the case in those areas where peasant farming was already largely commercialized. Thus the percentage of enclosed peasant allotment land in the Petrograd region was 15·6, in the western region 17·6, in the Ukraine 11·1. Similarly, in the southern and eastern parts of the black-earth belt, where cereals were extensively produced for the home and foreign market, the proportion of enclosed plots reached as high as 28·1 per cent in the province of Samara and 22·1 per cent in Saratov.[16] However, in such key provinces as Voronezh, Nizhny, Kazan, Penza, Ryazan, Simbirsk and Tambov the proportionate total of enclosed holdings, *including* both *otruby* and *khutory*, ranged only between four per cent and 8·9 per cent.[17]

The enclosed and consolidated homesteads, whether in the form of *otruby* or *khutory*, had significantly different destinies. Whereas the former did not reveal any improvement in technique, at least in the first years of their existence, the latter developed an improved system of crop-rotation, fodder grass and took to more advanced implements. This was natural; only the more progressive-minded peasant would in any case venture to establish himself on a *khutor*.[18] However, it remained very rare for even the most prosperous *khutoryanin* to employ hired labour outside the family. Furthermore, the expense involved in running a separate farm exceeded that of the old allotment and was beyond the capacity of the poorer peasant. If, on the other hand, the *khutoryanin* or even the *otrubnik* purchased further land from noble or state sources through the instrumentality of the Peasant Bank, then he was liable to find himself heavily indebted. At the end of 1914 about three-sevenths of the non-allotment land in forty-seven provinces was mortgaged to the Bank for a total sum amounting to more than three-quarters of its official valuation.[19]

It does not seem that there was any significant decline in the number of peasant households consolidating their share of the communal land between 1909 and 1915.[20] On the other hand, the fact that *khutory* were confined, as any significant component of the new agricultural order to the western provinces, must cast an unfavourable light on the prospects of the reform, even had the war not intervened. It is not even clear that there existed the amount of land necessary, pasture-land in particular, to provide *khutory* of sufficient dimensions in sufficient quantities. The reform made only a minimal contribution to the heart of the agrarian problem in the central agricultural and Middle Volga provinces. In one important respect, furthermore, it aggravated it, for it worsened the position of the poorer peasantry who could not afford the more expensive maintenance of an *otrub*, were progressively denied the opportunity of renting estate land (since this was being disposed of at an accelerating rate) and were less able to borrow from the Peasant Bank.[21]

The consequences of Stolypin's failure did not fully reveal themselves until 1917. In the meantime, however, the whole corpus of the land reform – the division of the commune, resettlement in Siberia, technical aid to agriculture, the cooperative movement, the finance pumped in via the Peasant Bank – did improve agricultural standards of living. The average death rate per 1,000, for example, declined from 31·0 in 1901–5 to 27·2 in the period 1911–13. (The comparable figures for France and England and Wales were respectively 19·4 and 15·4.) It is notable also that the area sown with grain increased from 88·8 to 93·8 million dessyatins between 1908 and 1912. Over the same period the grain yield rose from 4,056 to 5,072 million poods and the potato crop from 1,817 to 2,319 million poods.[22] Matters were further improved by a number of above-average harvests (in 1909, for example). A rise in prices abroad for agricultural produce and a growth in their consumption inside the country brought further benefit. Rye (per pood) at Libau, for example, fetched an average price from 1906–10 of 98·8 kopeks; in 1901–5 the comparable price had been 78·9 kopeks. The average price per pood of wheat and barley at Odessa over the same period rose respectively from 91·9 to 113·8 kopeks and from 63·3 to 77·7 kopeks; Siberian butter at Moscow rose from 12·1 to 15·4 roubles per pood. For the most part these increases were maintained in 1911 and 1912.[23] The overall result was a relatively contented countryside. The number of recorded peasant outbreaks dwindled from 1,337 in 1907 to 96 in 1915.[24]

Gone are the days when migrant workers besieged the estates for work. Now the landowner of his bailiff must meet the migrants at the railway station – they have travelled third-class perhaps, no longer on foot. What is more, higher wages have to be paid.[25] The level of Russian agricultural productivity still remained very low relative to that of the western European countries; likewise the standard of living in the countryside. Even so, the improvement in agricultural incomes in the period after 1906 produced an increased demand for agricultural machinery and implements, ironware and lead roofing. The peasant was no longer a purchaser of consumption articles alone; he was in the market for capital goods also.[26]

This contentment was not well-founded. The agrarian problem had by no means been overcome. Nor did it even give the appearance of forthcoming success. Hardly a dent had been made in the critical areas of the middle Volga and the central agricultural region. Adventitious circumstances masked this failure – but only for a time.[27]

2. *Theories of Revolution*

'La révolution est morte! Vive la révolution!' Such was Trotsky's response to the upheaval of 1905-6. It was echoed by Lenin's cry: '1905 will come again.' But *when*? How could its return be best accelerated? The years after 1905 provoked much rethinking whose revolutionary relevance would not become fully apparent until 1917. However minor the role of the left-wing parties in 1905, as distinct of course from that of the workers and peasants, the activity of the latter forces did open up the prospect of greater scope for conscious party-political direction. Relations with the Duma, say, or the liberals or the soviets, or the peasantry, would have to be examined and elucidated afresh.

Policy *vis-à-vis* the Duma was first considered by the fourth Social-Democratic congress at Stockholm in 1906. Mensheviks predominated and the decision was taken to participate in the elections to the Duma, to use the Duma fraction as a nucleus for all revolutionary elements, and by the introduction of political questions to sharpen the conflict between the Duma and the government. The Bolsheviks, led by Lenin, dissented from this decision in the mistaken expectation that the revolutionary wave would rise again and that premature participation in a Duma could only blunt the party's cutting edge. By reason of this division, and the short interval before the electoral campaign, Social-Democracy played no role in the first Duma.

To the second Duma sixty-five (or sixty-six) Social Democratic delegates were elected, most of them Mensheviks or Menshevik-sympathizers. This impressive result did not still Bolshevik misgivings and Menshevik tactics in the Duma fraction met severe criticism at the, subsequent party conference in 1907 in London. Had they not been over-prone to stress the legislative as opposed to the agitational and revolutionary significance of the Duma? Had they not forfeited con-tact with the working class beyond its walls? Had they not made too many concessions to tsarist 'legality'? But intransigence in the Duma, the Mensheviks replied, would only hinder its transition from a weak body into a strong body capable of rallying wide sections of the population in the struggle against tsardom and its transformation into a genuine constituent assembly.

At the heart of this dispute lay the issue of relations with the liberals in the Duma. Were they an ally or not? In Bolshevik eyes there could be no question of cooperation with the middle class. Time and again Lenin argued that the Kadets were fearful of the revolution and would have no hesitation in coming to terms with the autocracy. They were part and parcel of the autocracy and unable to divorce themselves from its fate. Bolshevism made little distinction between the liberal critics of the autocracy and the autocracy itself, and in the Menshevik aspiration for a ministry responsible to the Duma saw only an opportunity for such a ministry to come to terms with the autocracy at the expense of the workers and peasants. Moreover, the Kadets strengthened the illusion, particularly amongst the peasantry, of reformist amelioration and thus confused them as to the necessity of socialism. In the light of this criticism the Bolsheviks attacked the participation of the Social-Democratic fraction in the Kadet-convened conference of oppositionist groups.

To the Mensheviks the problem of the liberals presented itself in an altogether different light. As early as 1898, Axelrod, a Menshevik *avant la lettre*, had made a distinction between those capitalist members of the bourgeoisie whose interests were indeed identical with the survival of the autocracy and those other bourgeois elements – the professional men, the intelligentsia, the 'third element' in the zemstvos, and even part of the bureaucracy – who suffered under the autocracy and represented a quasi-revolutionary force. Western influences, as mediated through these strata of society, were permeating tsarism and thus creating the presuppositions for the development of the proletariat. Thus it became a principle of Menshevik policy to support liberalism, in the hope of pushing it further along the revolutionary path. In the Duma the Mensheviks looked on tsarism as the main enemy, whose destruction would enforce the cooperation of all opposition groups. Why split the opposition, it was argued, by turning against the liberals? It was true, of course, that no identity of ultimate aim existed between Social-Democrats and liberals. But this belonged to the future, not to the present. In the meantime the two parties might well cooperate.[1]

The counterpart to the relationship with the liberals was that with the peasantry. Here was another contentious topic to arise in the wake of 1905. In a way the respective roles of Menshevik and Bolshevik were reversed: whereas the former looked somewhat askance at peasant support, the latter enthusiastically took up the peasant cause. The matter was first considered at the Fouth Congress in 1906 when both factions, as a result of the rural upheaval, were compelled to define their attitude to this new force in the revolutionary situation. The Mensheviks presented a policy of 'municipalization' whereby peasants would retain their allotments and be released from all semi-feudal burdens and personal restrictions. Local re-formed communes would take over large private holdings for leasing out to the peasants in return for a tax in lieu of rent, based on the productivity of the land. Other forms of land tenure – the lands held by the church, state and imperial family – were scheduled for nationalization.

Lenin countered 'municipalization' with 'nationalization'. This followed from his earlier studies of the peasant question which had persuaded him that the peasant struggle must in the first instance be bourgeois in nature, i.e. directed against feudalism and large landed estates. His interpretation of 1905 reinforced this view. By reason of this analysis Lenin later looked forward at least to a working arrangement with the Socialist-Revolutionaries and the Trudoviks in the Duma. The latter represented the 'incredibly downtrodden' peasants who dreamt of the equal division of the land, and who were 'capable of waging a resolute and self-sacrificing struggle into which they are being driven by the whole course of events and by the whole conduct of the government'.[2] In particular, the peasant parties must be prevented from succumbing to the influence of the Kadets.

How did 'nationalization' fit into Lenin's anticipated schema of revolutionary development? The policy was first devised in 1906; only later, in the context of the Stolypin land measures, did it acquire its full significance. Lenin, somewhat unnecessarily, was alarmed lest Stolypin succeed. This represented one way of carrying through a bourgeois revolution, Lenin thought. 'Stolypin tried,' Lenin wrote, 'to pour new wine into old bottles, to turn the old autocracy into a bourgeois monarchy. . . .' Such a policy had succeeded elsewhere; it might also succeed in Russia. In this case the whole future of the Russian revolution would stand in jeopardy.

If the land were cleared of such feudal-medieval survivals as the commune, Lenin argued, then the unhindered development of farming and the creation of a rural bourgeoisie would become inevitable. But under whose aegis, in whose interests, would this process take place? Stolypin was attempting 'a bourgeois evolution of the landlord type'. The Social-Democrats, on the other hand, would propound 'a bourgeois evolution of the peasant type'. Both were progressive but only the second offered the more rapid development of productive forces and, in the circumstances of commodity production, a more tolerable mode of existence for the mass of the peasantry. Whereas Stolypin's scheme only amounted to giving the kulaks *carte blanche* to rob the peasant masses and ruin thousands of peasant farms, really free farming would follow from nationalization of *all* the land. If *all* private ownership in land were abolished, if all land were transferred to the state, then feudalism in the countryside would disappear finally and for ever.[3]

With a programme such as this in hand Lenin looked forward to united action by workers and peasants in opposition to the *ancien régime*. In fact – and this marks the great advance in Bolshevik thought as a result of 1905 – only on condition of such united action could any attack on tsarism be successful. Lenin concluded from the experience of 1905 that the Russian revolution could be victorious 'only as a peasant agrarian revolution', and this could not completely fulfil its mission unless the land were 'nationalized'.[4] This prognosis of 1907 had much in common with the actual course of events a decade later.

No less far-sighted was Lenin's assessment of the soviets. Despite his cautious attitude *vis-à-vis* a non-party body, despite the fear that the soviets might open the way to 'non-party political' influences in the proletariat.[5] Lenin saw in them potential nuclei of revolution. For all their 'rudimentary, spontaneous, amorphous and diffuse character', they were yet 'organs of *revolutionary authority*'. The St Petersburg Soviet in 1905 'acted as a government' when it seized printing plants, when it arrested police officials, when it appealed to the whole people to withhold money from the old government. 'Yes,' said Lenin,

these were undoubtedly the embryos of a new, people's, or, if you will, revolutionary government. In their social and political character, they were the rudiments of the dictatorship of the revolutionary elements of the people. . . . This new authority said, in effect: are you a working man? Do you want to fight to rid Russia of the gang of police bullies? You are our comrade. Elect your deputy. . . . We will willingly and gladly accept him as a full member of our soviet of workers' deputies, peasant committee, soviet of soldiers' deputies and so forth.[6]

There is here a remarkable contrast between Lenin's dynamic view of the soviets as the embryo of a revolutionary government, under the independent control of the party, and the somewhat passive role of a workers' congress ascribed to them by the Mensheviks. In 1905 this difference was theoretical only. Its practical bearing did not become apparent until 1917 when Lenin's readiness to exploit the power inherent in the soviet movement – far more widespread than it had been in 1905, of course – gave him a vast tactical advantage over the Mensheviks. This was not the least of the tactical lessons that Lenin gleaned from the 'dress-rehearsal' of 1905–6.

The differing views of Bolsheviks and Mensheviks in relation to the socio-political role of the peasantry and the bourgeoisie, the importance of the soviets, policy towards the Duma – all these matters in dispute found their focal point in the two factions' respective doctrines of revolution. How could Russia become a socialist state?

Following Plekhanov, it was accepted by both Bolsheviks and Mensheviks that the next stage in Russian development must be a bourgeois revolution, i.e. a revolution that would give power to the bourgeoisie and allow full play to the development of capitalism and the proletariat. Given the semi-feudal and retarded nature of Russian society there could be no thought of an immediate transition to socialism. The next stage could only be the erection of a bourgeois and democratic republic. At this point the difference began.

To the Mensheviks it appeared self-evident that in a bourgeois revolution the bourgeoisie must take the lead. This had as consequence that the proletariat and the Social-Democrats, the party of the proletariat, must play a subordinate role. 'The proletariat cannot win political power in the state, either wholly or in part, until it has made the socialist revolution,' wrote Martynov, the Menshevik theoretician, in his pamphlet, *Two Dictatorships*.[7] At this stage, it must therefore limit itself to exerting pressure lest the bourgeoisie fail to fulfil its allotted historical role. 'There must be compulsion on the part of the more democratic "lower strata" of society to bring the "upper strata" into agreement to carry through the bourgeois revolution to its logical conclusion.'[8] The Mensheviks hoped in this way to further the establishment of a bourgeois government, that would in no circumstances include the representatives of the proletariat. Any such participation could only lead to mass proletarian disillusion. 'The Social-Democrats, despite the seizure of power, would not be able to satisfy the pressing needs of the working class, including the establishment of socialism . . . and, on the other hand, *would cause the bourgeois classes to recoil from the revolution and thus diminish its sweep*.'[9]

The proletariat could, however, in this interim period, in the Menshevik view, develop a mass party by associating the present small illegal faction with the mass organizations emerging in 1905, develop trade union activity and in the elections to the Duma organize a network of 'people's agitation committees' throughout the country, disorganize the tsarist administration, and establish a sort of workers' congress. This might develop into a constituent assembly but it would at least bring pressure to bear on the government to make concessions to the workers.[10] On one condition only did the Mensheviks envisage directing their efforts at seizing power: should the revolution spread to the west where conditions for the advancement of socialism were more mature than in Russia, then the limited historical scope of the

Russian revolution could be 'considerably widened and the possibility will arise of entering on the path of socialist reforms'.[11]

Menshevik policy derived from the example of western Europe, and Germany in particular. The Mensheviks were prepared to place greater reliance on the deterministic aspect of the Marxist schema, waiting until conditions were ripe for revolution in Russia and more closely resembled those in the west, i.e. until a further development of capitalism and the proletariat had taken place. How could there be talk, in Russian conditions, of socialist participation in a bourgeois government, when the proletariat and its party constituted such a small minority of the population? All that could be hoped for in such conditions was a bourgeois revolution with the proletariat functioning as a ginger-group. Yet this view, for all its apparent acknowledgement of the Russian situation, did in fact fail to take account of two counter-vailing factors, Russian *par excellence*, that vitiated the Menshevik analysis: first, the weakness of the Russian bourgeoisie, which, apart from its liberal elements, was far too closely dependent on the government to constitute a centre of resistance to the government, and second, the contribution that the peasantry might make to a revolution. Only in recent years have former Mensheviks come to realize the nature of their primary error.[12]

Bolshevism as formulated by Lenin spoke a very different language on all these counts. Lenin had nothing but scorn for 'the faint hearts who have lost faith in the revolutionary energy of the working class'; or for those who adhered to the theory of 'uprising as process'.[13] He took full advantage of the voluntaristic side of Marxism to evolve, in 1905–6, a specific theory of revolution which had a certain similarity to the actual circumstances of 1917. Lenin accepted the prognosis that it was impossible to go beyond the limits of a bourgeois-democratic revolution. But – 'there is bourgeois democracy and bourgeois democracy.' It was not the same in America as in Switzerland, in Britain as in Germany. One must discriminate, become aware of these differences, and in Russia the boundaries of a bourgeois-democratic revolution could be 'vastly extended'.[14] At the same time, it was 'absurd' and 'semi-anarchist' to talk in terms of a socialist revolution.[15]

These were the two extremes. Where did the middle lie? The revolution would be bourgeois in so far as it remained limited to a social order based on the institution of private property. But it would be proletarian in so far as the proletariat, owing to the weakness of the Russian bourgeoisie, took the leading part in the revolution. Moreover, the peasantry, although by no means socialist or ceasing to be petty-bourgeois, was 'interested not so much in the absolute preservation of private property as in the confiscation of the landed estates'. This made it an ally of the proletariat, 'a whole-hearted and most radical adherent of the democratic revolution'.[16]

Lenin envisaged a sequence of events whereby the proletariat seizes power in the democratic revolution; the liberals passively wait on developments; the peasants actively assist, as well as the radical, republican intelligentsia and the corresponding urban strata of the petty-bourgeoisie. 'The rising of the peasants is victorious. The power of the landlords is broken.' There then follows the revolutionary-democratic dictatorship of the proletariat and the peasantry.[17] This is exercised by way of a provisional revolutionary government, in which of course the proletariat participates. The last battle is now engaged – between the proletariat, anxious to preserve its gains, and the bourgeoisie which has moved over to counter-revolution. This stage is intimately linked to the struggle in Europe as a whole. 'The Russian proletariat *plus* the European proletariat organize revolution. In such conditions the Russian proletariat can win a second victory. The cause is no longer hopeless. The second victory will be *the socialist revolution in Europe*. The European workers will show us "how to do it", and then, together with them, we shall bring about the socialist revolution.'[18]

This schema brought Lenin very close to the analysis that he followed in April 1917. It also borders on the Parvus-Trotsky theory or permanent revolution, another insight of 1905 which did in fact, in Trotsky's words, give 'the prognosis of the October revolution'.[19]

3. Permanent Revolution

The relative absence of a bourgeoisie made more complex the meaningful introduction of Marxism to Russia. The respective theories of Mensheviks and Bolsheviks, each in their different ways, had taken hold of this problem. But it was also envisaged that this very absence might, as it were, enable Russia to outpace the more advanced western world. Herzen, in 1855, had already associated Russia's ignorance of a threefold 'scourge' – the bourgeoisie, Roman Law and Catholicism – with the capacity to achieve some form of historical leap. 'We will meet you half-way in the coming upheaval,' he told his London audience.

For this we do not have to pass through those swamps through which you have passed; we do not have to exhaust our strength in the semi-darkness of those social forms which may be called between *the wolf and the dog* and which have nowhere produced anything great and powerful except where they were born.

It is not at all necessary for us to perform your long, great epic of emancipation. . . . Your efforts, your sufferings are for us a lesson.

History is very unfair, to the *late-comers* if does not give gnawed bones but the first place in experience.[20]

In a different perspective Marx himself had been sufficiently unortho-dox – '*Moi, je ne suis pas marxiste,*' he once said – to suggest on several occasions towards the end of his life that on the basis of the peasant commune and in conditions of successful western socialist revolution Russia might avoid the full capitalist stage of development and pass directly to socialism. It was precisely this lacuna in Russia's internal structure that conditioned a successful endeavour to predict the course of the Russian revolution – the theory of permanent (better, 'uninterrupted') revolution, as worked out by Trotsky and Parvus. Lenin had seen what force the peasantry could wield and built them into his revolutionary schema. Trotsky and Parvus now performed the same function for the proletariat – drawing in particular on the phenomenon of the mass-strike as operative in 1905.

Parvus, a Russian-born member of the German Social-Democratic party, was respected by Trotsky as 'unquestionably one of the most important of the Marxists at the turn of the century'.[21] Parvus won this tribute through his trenchant attacks on Bernstein's revisionism in the later 1890s. Parvus's experiences in Russia in 1901, and still more the outbreak of the Russo-Japanese war, well accorded with the pre-supposition of his earlier polemics against Bernstein – that revolution must not be considered a far-off event but an imminent possibility. By a dialectic act of truly unimaginable proportions it was in the fortress-prison of SS Peter and Paul that Trotsky made of Parvus's insights the *point de départ* of the theory of permanent revolution. 'Perfect for intellectual work,' was Trotsky's appreciative description of his cell.[22]

The outbreak of the Russo-Japanese war was 'the bloody dawn of coming great events', Parvus argued.[23] It denoted a new cycle of imperialist wars that would shatter the bases of existing world order.

The war began because of Manchuria and Korea, it has already become a battle for hegemony in Eastern Asia, it will extend into the question of the world position of autocratic Russia and will conclude with a transformation of the political balance of the whole world. Its first consequence will be the fall of the Russian autocracy.[24]

Parvus argued in terms identical to those of Vitte – either Russia must modernize its institutions or it must cease to remain a great power. Vitte had thought it possible to combine modernization with the retention of the autocracy and the existing social order; Parvus denied this and argued that only revolution could accomplish the task. Other-wise there was no difference between right and left. In this light

Parvus became persuaded of the interdependence of war and social revolution.

Moreover, he envisaged the world capitalist system as a whole in which account must be taken not of the socio-economic development of each country as a national unit but of the inter-relationship of the system. It could thus be anticipated that the collapse of Russia would communicate itself to the remainder of the capitalist world.

Shortly afterwards, the mass-strikes that followed Bloody Sunday were confirmation to Parvus and Trotsky, as also to Rosa Luxemburg, of 'the exceptional role' which the proletariat of backward Russia was called upon to play.[25] Parvus supported his high estimate of the proletariat by an historical analysis of the Russian social structure. Owing to the highly centralized autocratic system, no bourgeoisie, outside St Petersburg and Moscow, had been able to develop. The provincial towns had only been able to produce a small class of officials, too closely tied to the autocracy to make common cause with the liberal professions. As for the peasantry, whilst forming the overwhelming majority of the population, they were politically unawakened, lacked a class organization and could only contribute to the extension of anarchy. The proletariat, on the other hand, was concentrated in factories from the outset. But if, in the absence of other forces, the proletariat was to take the leading role in the overthrow of tsarism, then it could only function effectively so long as it maintained its tactical and strategic independence. In November 1904 Parvus had already written in an open letter to Lenin that 'in the interests of the class struggle of the proletariat, Social-Democracy must pursue an independent policy.... Whether it is a matter of overthrowing the autocracy or saving the republic, Social-Democracy goes its own way.'[26] To be sure, even a Social-Democratic provisional government could not bring about a socialist insurrection but it would at least create 'fertile ground' for political activity.[27]

Parvus's experience of the following year with its clear demonstration of the power of the proletariat and the mass strike must have confirmed him in his earlier analysis of the independent role of the proletariat. Yet even this prominent component of the theory did not, as a whole, denote any break in the continuity of the orthodox revolutionary process.

There was much here that coincided with Lenin's own anticipations and desires – particularly the emphasis on the leading role of the proletariat. Lenin, however, doubted the capacity of the proletariat, unaided, to erect an enduring revolutionary dictatorship.[28] The Mensheviks had other reasons for rejecting Parvus; only too clearly did he reject their theory of a bourgeois revolution in which the proletariat must play second fiddle, refrain from the assertion of independent political and social demands and confine its activity to supporting the liberal-democratic movement.

It was left to Trotsky, writing in 1906 in the calm of his prison cell, to extend to its fullest Parvus's insight into Russia's ripeness for revolution and to embed the 'quite peculiar character' of the Russian revolution in the actual conditions of Russian society and thus open up 'quite new historical perspectives'.[28]

What was this character and what these perspectives? Like Parvus, Trotsky began by pointing to the uniquely strong position of the autocratic state which had stultified the development of the bourgeoisie and urban craftsmen.[30] Then, following the onset of rapid industrialization in the last decade of the century Trotsky saw 'the proletariat . . . concentrated in tremendous masses, while between these masses and the autocracy there stood a capitalist bourgeoisie, very small in numbers, isolated from the "people", half foreign, without historical traditions and inspired only by the greed for gain.' Trotsky then went on to envisage the coming revolution in Kautskyan terminology, as '*a single combat between absolutism and the industrial proletariat*, a single combat in which the peasants may render considerable support but cannot play a leading role.'[31]

Trotsky further revised Marx. His error in thinking in terms of national revolution arose, according to Trotsky, from his position relative to a period when capitalism had not yet attained world-wide dominance. Trotsky, on the other hand, saw in the global nature of capitalism at the turn of the century a confirmation that what determined revolutionary ripeness was not the internal development of this or that country but the development of the system as a whole.

If these two aspects – the Russian and the *global* – are correlated, Trotsky's theory of permanent revolution emerges in all its clarity. 'For backward countries,' he writes, 'the road to democracy passed through the dictatorship of the proletariat. Thus democracy is not a regime that remains self-sufficient for decades, but is only a direct prelude to the socialist revolution.'[32] In other words, 'the Russian revolution will create conditions in which power can pass into the hands of the workers . . . *before* the politicians of bourgeois liberalism get the chance to display to the full their talent for governing.' However, given the backwardness of Russian social development, Trotsky had also to affirm that although the Russian proletariat in power could win the support of the peasantry by appropriate measures, it would be unable to maintain itself in power or pass over to a socialist regime in Russia '*without the direct state support of the European proletariat*'. Only in this way could 'temporary domination' be converted into 'a lasting socialistic dictatorship'.[33]

This encapsulation of the bourgeois into the socialist revolution is what distinguishes Trotsky's contribution from that of Parvus. It is this also that gives the theory its validity as a guide to the events of 1917 in Russia (within Trotsky's terms of reference, of course). It anticipated with great accuracy the tactics Lenin would follow when he returned to Russia in April of that year (although Lenin himself may not have been fully aware of all the details of the theory). Where the theory fell down of course was in its optimistically erroneous assessment of the prospects of revolution in the western world. Yet if it was no guide to what happened *after* 1917, it retains its undiminished importance as a dynamic diagnosis of the weakness of tsardom and of the force required to overthrow it.

11 The Mind Against Society

'The nightingale of poetry . . . is heard only after the sun is set . . . all through history, the mind limps after reality.' Thus wrote Trotsky in his *Literature and Revolution*. But may the mind not anticipate reality? Can the nightingale of poetry not make itself heard *before* the sun descends, although its song may well be informed by the imminence of the sunset? This is the truth contained in poetry. The nightingale is a herald. What song did it sing in Russia in the 1900s?

It has often been pointed out – by Theodor Adorno, for example – that a period of dissolution releases forces which become, through their opposition to contemporary life, 'the haven of the better'.[1] In Russia these forces drew their sustenance both from the disturbed present and from the future which the present was becoming. In Europe generally, the sentiment of collapse, of unreason and destruction waiting to be unleashed – as embodied in the increase of military expenditure, in the rapidity of international crises, in the growing acuteness of social and national conflict – found expression in the works of such thinkers as Freud, Sorel and Nietzsche. There was a change of atmosphere at the turn of the century. Since the Paris commune in 1871, the Russian upheaval of 1905 first demonstrated to all Europe a major threat to the existing social order. It was accompanied of course by the war in the Far East and by the first Moroccan crisis. Thenceforward crisis followed crisis, continually extending the area of uncertainty. Not fortuitously had Parvus seen in the Russo-Japanese War 'the bloody dawn of coming great events'.[2]

This foreboding and anticipation, this awareness of dangers yet unknown, was common to all Europe. In Russia it was perhaps sensed more acutely than elsewhere. There was the original unease generated by the problematic nature of the relationship to the west. To this must be added the yet more specific disabilities endured by the Russian intelligentsia. Did not the articulate forces of society live under a far more repressive regime than elsewhere? Was not assassination an accepted method of dealing with political opponents? Arbitrary violence, whether exercised by peasants against landlords, by police against revolutionaries, by troops against the public, by the Black

Hundreds against Jews, was of such dimensions as infallibly to arouse the liveliest fears concerning the survival of such a society. 'The bloody struggle that flared up anew in 1902 between state and society – the murder of Sipyagin in 1902, the murder of Plehve in 1904, the murder of the Grand Duke Sergey Alexandrovitch in 1905, in the same year the shooting before the Winter Palace – robbed life of every feeling of stability, of all confidence in the possibility of any lasting calculations and plans,' writes Feodor Stepun, a survivor of those years.[3] 'How beautiful the world will be in three hundred years!' Chekhov was wont to exclaim. But what was it like in 1900, say? Listen to the prophetic words of Baron Tuzenbach in *Three Sisters* (1901):

The time has come, an avalanche is moving down on us, a mighty wholesome storm is brewing, which is approaching, is already near and soon will sweep away from our society its idleness, indifference, prejudice against work, and foul ennui. I shall work, and in some twenty-five or thirty years everyone will work too.

In the same apocalyptic spirit a student in Bely's novel *St Petersburg* (1910), returning home late at night, apostrophized the Bronze Horseman, Falconet's statue of Peter the Great: 'You, Russia, are like that horse. Your front hooves stretch out into darkness and emptiness; but the rear hooves are firmly fixed in granite soil.' The Bronze Horseman will overcome this division by a leap over history;

There will be a great turmoil; the earth will split; the hills themselves will burst from the great fear. . . . Petersburg itself will vanish.

In these days all the peoples of the earth will hurl themselves apart; there will be a great cursing – a cursing that was never heard before: yellow hordes of Asiatics, stirring from their age-long homes, will turn the fields of Europe red with oceans of blood . . .

On that day the last sun will shine over my native country.

Again in that same spirit Bryusov asked: Where are 'the Huns' who are hanging like a cloud over the world? 'I hear your leaden tramp on Pamirs yet hidden from our eyes. Fall upon us from your dark camp, a drunken horde, and quicken our decrepit body with a wave of flaming blood.' Is there not also rejoicing at the defeat of the world of bourgeois science in Blok's laconic diary entry for 5 April 1912: 'The sinking of the Titanic made me unutterably happy yesterday (there is still an ocean).'

Chekhov's distinctive contribution to the revolt against society was couched primarily in peronal terms. To politics *tel quel* he was more or less indifferent. He was explicitly apolitical and liked to think of himself as a free artist. 'Great artists and writers,' he wrote, defending Zola's intervention in the Dreyfus case, 'must take part in politics only in so far as it is necessary to put up a defence against politics. There are enough prosecutors and gendarmes already, without adding to the number.'

Yet Chekhov, in his own way, and despite himself, was also a prosecutor; and the indictment that he drew up against Russian society is redolent in Gogol's *Dead Souls*. But it is expressed with a mitigating touch of sympathetic humour where Gogol had been satiric. Chekhov saw in Russia a country where men, kindly men and men of goodwill, were isolated both from each other and from society. It was a chaotic, frustrating world of alienated individuals, victims of their own sentiment of inferiority *vis-à-vis* an impossibly imposing environment. It was a world where the individual was powerless and reduced to finding his *raison d'être* in the expression of his own feelings. It was a world where nobody was happy.

Chekhov did indeed have faith in a better future. His vision was not irretrievably and inconsolably bleak. But the situation was so desperate that half-measures were a mere palliative; and he could not conceive of revolution. In the end all that was left to comfort him was the belief, as he himself put it, 'in individual personalities, scattered here and there throughout Russia, whether they be intellectuals or peasants'. How substantial could this hope be, in the face of the overwhelming preponderance of the oppressive, the trivial, the humdrum, the shoddy and the pretentious?

The 1900s manifestly witnessed a great revolt by youth against the values of its forebears. The younger generation was alienated. This was no new thing in Russian socio-intellectual life. It had formed the mainspring of Turgenev's *Fathers and Sons*. But it must be doubted whether such a wide gap between the generations had ever existed as in the new century. The large numbers of radicals, terrorists, populists and *révoltés* of all types who came from families where the father was perhaps a governor-general, merchant, estate-owner, senior bureaucrat, respected member of the professions, was surprisingly large, irrefutably testifying to the inability of the fathers to transmit their values to the sons. Between 1905 and 1908, for example, it seems that as much as 22·9 per cent of those tried for political crimes were by occupation members of the liberal professions or students; as much as 9·1 per cent were by social origin members of the gentry class. At the same time the number of workers and peasants had of course increased enormously.[4] At the end of the nineteenth century a French observer noted this high proportion of scions of the nobility amongst the revolutionaries and shrewdly compared the receptivity of Russian society to radical ideas with that of French society before 1789.[5]

Inquiries conducted amongst the students of Moscow University in the period between 1906 and 1909 clearly established, however fragmentary the data, the existence of a crisis of confidence and continuity in the social order. Two thousand one hundred and fifty students were asked what influence their families had had on the formation of their ethical ideals, aesthetic tastes, friendships, etc.; of the 1,706 students who answered, fifty-six per cent denied family influence, forty-four per cent acknowledged it. As regards family influence in the choice of faculty, eighty-four per cent of the 2,061 answers denied such influence, and only sixteen per cent gave affirmative answers. In reponse to a further question eighty-six per cent of the students asserted that they had had no 'spiritual intimacy' with any of their teachers in secondary schools. Had their family influenced their elaboration of a definite outlook on the world? Fifty-eight per cent of the 1,794 responses denied such influence; only forty-two per cent gave an admission. 'The Russian intelligentsia has no family,' the old-style Kadet, Izgoyev, inferred from these data.[6]

Student alienation from the government matched that from family and school. A survey of a representative selection of students made in 1910 disclosed that twenty-five per cent were affiliated to the Social-Democrats; twenty-one per cent to the Kadets; twenty-one per cent non-party; twelve per cent to the Socialist-Revolutionaries; ten per cent left wing; three per cent to the anarchists; and two per cent each to the Octobrists and moderate right. Students of minority peoples were particularly radicalized; thus eighty per cent of Jewish and Caucasian students belonged to left-wing parties. Also noteworthy was the trend towards greater radicalism – i.e. Social-Democratic affiliation – amongst the older students.[7]

'I knew students,' Prince Eugene Trubetskoy, professor at the University of Kiev, wrote in 1904, 'who only read banned writings and formed their outlook in accordance with these because everything that could be openly published in Russia aroused from the start their distrust . . . revolutionary proclamations . . . replace the daily press.' Trubetskoy characterized the student by his passionate readiness to put himself at the service of the social ideal. 'Marxism itself was taken up by our students as a sort of religious faith.' They had 'a need for self-sacrifice, a yearning for martyrdom'. To these radical political views corresponded a radicalism of character that recalled the French revolutionaries of the eighteenth century. Russian students had the same incapacity 'to comprehend historical formation, the same incli-nation to think *moro geometrico*, the same dogmatism and faith in the possibility of being able to remodel reality in a moment, in accordance with the dictates of reason'. Their standpoint was 'the ideal of absolute perfection'. There were no transitions between absolute darkness and the fullness of light. They saw mankind divided into heroes and scoundrels. They lacked critical judgement and the faculty of cool analysis. Yet they could be forgiven a great deal because they loved greatly, they were unreservedly devoted to the people and in the cause of freedom they were ready to sacrifice their all, Trubetskoy concluded.[8]

The Russian *fin de siècle* did not begin in earnest until after the failure of the 1905 revolution. A schoolboy of the time remembers: 'Now it was no longer Marx and Engels, but Nietzsche and Baudelaire and Wagner and Leonardo da Vinci whom we passionately discussed; we did not sing revolutionary songs but recited to one another poems of contemporary symbolist poets and our own imitations of them. A new period had begun.'[9] The specifically Russian form of the decadent movement emphasized the impossibility of communication between one human being and another – this is the *leitmotiv* of Andreyev's work, for example. There was also the turning away from public themes to private pursuits – the glorification of sex, the resurrection of myth and legend, the invocation of death, the exploration of the emotions. These last were the favoured matter of the symbolist poets, the closest Russian equivalent to the western European exponents of art for art's sake. The social counterpart of this was a certain reluctant acquiescence in the existing order of reality. 'The radical sons of petty merchants submitted to their fate and took up positions behind the counters of their fathers' businesses. One or other of the socialist students buried himself in knowledge as in a monastery.'[10]

The justification of this quietism was provided in the symposium, *Vekhi (Landmarks,* 1909). This was not only the socio-political equivalent to the artistic, non-civic, private concerns of a Chekhov, say, or a symbolist poet, or a religious mystic; it was also an explicit attack on the whole gamut of ideas cherished by the students and their mentors.

Vekhi, therefore, created a furore, a *succès de scandale* in the words of one of its contributors, Frank, the religious philosopher. Four impressions were exhausted in the year of publication alone; the symposium provoked no less than 156 articles, brochures, open letters *pro et contra*. Milyukov even undertook a sgecial lecture tour in order to denounce the slim subversive volume.

The message of *Vekhi* was simple. It has significance less for its intrinsic philosophical interest – which is small enough – than for the advocacy of what Gerschenson, its editor, called 'the theoretical and practical priority of spiritual life over the external forms of society, in the sense that the inner life of the personality is the only creative force in human existence and is . . . the only firm basis for any social reconstruction.' From this viewpoint the contributors made a threefold attack on the contemporary Russian intelligentsia. First, it had sacrificed its intellect in that it judged philosophical systems by reference to their social utility and purpose, rather than by reference to their truth-value; second, the intelligentsia's belief in progress, science, socialism and atheism had led to the development of a nihilistic morality in which all absolute moral claims had gone by the board – Frank, indeed, defined nihilism as the denial of objective, absolute values; third, the intelligentsia had no consciousness of law or a legal order of society.

This indictment had no lasting significance. By virtue of its emphasis on the primacy of the spiritual, *Vekhi* could not but lead to some form of reconciliation with the *status quo*. It did not release men from the allegiance to the official values of official society – it simply left the task in abeyance. The message of *Vekhi* was tantamount to a withdrawal from politics into political passivity. It revealed the same uncritical onesidedness as the students and intellectuals it excoriated.

The Russian *fin de siècle* was, in this way, marked by a retreat from public into private concerns on the one hand or by a total rejection of the official values of society, or by some combination of the two. It is the voice of Feodor Sollogub: 'I am the god of a mysterious world, all the world is in my dreams alone.' It is the voice of Rozanov: 'All religions will pass but this will remain, simply sitting in a chair and looking in the distance.'

But this was far from being the last word. That the mind could attack society, non-politically, was shown by the philosopher Shestov. Wisdom and society had been 'artificially joined', he maintained in his *Apotheosis of Groundlessness* –

by orators who have taught the public and philosophers to think that only those tasks merit attention which have absolutely everything on their side: social utility and morality and even metaphysical wisdom. . . . Why so much? It would be enough if some new project proved itself useful! Why invoke in addition the sanctions oᶠ morality and metaphysics? On the other hand, given that the laws of morality must be autonomous and ideas prevail over the empirical needs of mankind means that it is impossible to oppose to them social considerations, even the possible collapse of the country. *Pereat mundus, fiat philosophia: if Athens died because of the very wisdom of Socrates – this is no argument against his wisdom.* That is how an autonomous thinker must argue. But a *de facto* thinker does not like overmuch to quarrel with his native country.

What was necessary, however, was to bring the values of the mind into the closest possible proximity to the ways of society. This was the task of the later Tolstoy. In works such as *What Then Must We Do?*, *The Kingdom of God is Within You* and *The Restoration of Hell* he assailed the more dangerous institutions and views of the contemporary world in such terms as to prefigure the circumstances of the First World War and the revolution. Here was no general impersonal vision of collapse but a precise identification of the forces of decay.

Tolstoy, no doubt, showed little, if any, awareness of the deep-rooted complexity of the evils he stigmatized; no doubt, also, his positive doctrine was thin enough – the gospel of universal love, undogmatic Christianity, sexual abstinence, non-resistance to evil, the renunciation of tobacco and alcohol – for all that, his later work constitutes an anarchist programme of profound strength. His un-bridled criticism of society and its values, his corrosive and derisive scepticism, made him an anarchist more anarchic, a nihilist more nihilistic and a revolutionary more destructive than any whom Russia had yet brought forth – far more consistent and humanistic than Bakunin, far more hard-headed than Kropotkin.

What is science? he asked. Had it done anything of value to human life in determining the weight of Saturn's satellites? What was universal suffrage? A means whereby the prisoners elected their own gaolers. Had industrialism raised the standard of living? Then look at the slums and doss-houses of Moscow. Tolstoy derided division of labour as a device for turning men into machines, book-printing as a medium for communicating 'all the nasty and stupid things that are done and written in the world', and reform for teaching people 'that though themselves bad they can reform bad people'. What did the church do but maintain idolatry 'in the most literal sense of the word – worshipping holy relics and icons, offering sacrifices to them and expecting from them the fulfilment of the worshippers' wishes'? What did compulsory education do but 'teach the savage superstition of patriotism and the same pseudo-obligation to obey the state'? What was the press but a means for 'exciting feelings of mutual hostility between the nations'? What were the governments of the time, despotic and liberal alike, but – and here Tolstoy quotes Herzen's phrase – 'Genghis Khans with telegraphs'? The modern state was a mechanism so interlocked and interdependent that it became impossible to discriminate between the guilty and the inno-cent: 'Some people demand the perpetration of a crime, others decide that it shall be done, a third set confirm that decision, a fourth propose its execution, a fifth report on it, a sixth finally decree it, and a seventh carry out the decree.' Tolstoy's apocalyptic vision of a state given over to destruction culminates in an anticipation of the imminent First World War:

The bells will peal and long-haired men will dress themselves in gold-embroidered socks and begin to pray on behalf of murder. . . . The editors of newspapers will set to work to arouse hatred and murder under the guise of patriotism and will be delighted to double their sales. Manufacturers, merchants, and contractors for army stores will hurry about joyfully in expectation of doubled profits. . . . Army commanders will bustle here and there, drawing double pay and rations and hoping to receive tinkets and crosses, stripes and stars, for murdering people. Idle ladies and gentlemen will fuss about, entering their names in advance for the Red Cross and getting ready to bandage those whom their husbands and brothers are setting out to kill – imagining that they will be doing a most Christian work thereby.

Only when Tolstoy came to describe the attitude of the common soldier did his unsentimentality desert him and disguise from him the initial enthusiasm of the masses. In 1914 a life for the tsar was no empty phrase. But of the later stages of the war he has a vision of the men who

will trudge wherever they may be driven, stifling the despair in their souls by songs, debauchery and vodka. They will march, freeze, suffer from hunger, and fall ill. Some will die of disease, and some will at last come to the place where men will kill them by the thousand. And they too, without themselves knowing why, will murder thousands of others whom they had never before seen, and who had neither done nor could do them any wrong.

By virtue of this prognosis of a war 'which will devour in a year more victims than all the revolutions of a century', Tolstoy made a complete and utter *tabula rasa* of the Russia of his time and, indeed, of the world also.

Tolstoy's apocalypse was pessimistic. There were others in an optimistic strain – that, for example, of the 'Scythian' movement of Ivanov-Razumnik and the peasant-poet Essenin. The 'Scythians' saw the revolution as the outburst of a new-born, unlimited, maximalist spirit that would sweep away the corrupt old world, as Christianity had once burst asunder the decadent Roman Empire. In the *International* Ivanov-Razumnik could hear the words, 'Peace on earth, goodwill to men.' This cast of thought reached its climax in Blok's poem, *The Twelve*, of 1918. Blok, probably the greatest of the symbolist poets and a sympathizer with the left socialist-revolutionaries, who were themselves allied for a time to the Bolsheviks, depicts twelve riotous, rowdy Red Guards marching through the snowy streets of St Petersburg, shouting, shooting, cursing, blaspheming. A man bearing the red flag leads them – Jesus Christ.

In his essay of 1918, *The Intelligentsia and Revolution*, Blok compared the revolution to a mighty phenomenon of nature. 'We Russians,' he proclaimed, 'are living through an epoch which has had few things equal to it in grandeur.' The aim is –

to remake everything. To build everything anew, so that our lying, dirty, boring, monstrous life becomes a just and clean, a joyous and beautiful life. . . . The range of the Russian revolution aimed at embracing the world. A true revolution cannot wish for less. . . . 'The peace and the brotherhood of the people' – that is the symbol under which the Russian revolution is taking place. It is of this that its torrent is roaring. This is the music which those with ears must hear.

This outburst was by no means typical of all the intelligentsia. Blok himself died disillusioned in 1921. But his dithyramb gives effective voice to the intelligentsia's alienation from the *ancien régime*.

12   Before the Deluge

An industrial upsurge followed the suppression of the revolt of 1905–6. In the immediate pre-war years this movement swelled remarkably the size of the proletariat – from some 1·8 million in 1910 to two and a half million in the summer of 1914. This rise in numbers made no notable difference to the position of the workers. Stolypin's reforms combined with a rise in the price of agricultural produce to improve peasant welfare. No such benefit came the way of the urban masses. On the contrary, the failure of the revolution may have led, in certain important respects, to a veritable weakening of the proletarian position. The revolutionary parties, after their brief emergence into the light of day, were forced back into the underground, decimated and reduced to impotence. The workers' militancy rapidly declined, and the number of strikers, in round figures, sank precipitously from 740,000 in 1907 to a mere 46,000 in 1910.[1] As before, we hear of workers unable to lead a normal family life. A survey of workers' budgets in 1908–10 showed that only the skilled or semi-skilled, earning a minimum of four hundred roubles a year, could afford to maintain a family. The majority, with an average wage of less than three hundred roubles a year, could not usually support a wife. The number of children stood in a direct relationship to the worker's wage.[2] The unremitting fiscal policies of the government continued to exert their pressure on living standards. Tax receipts grew from 996·3 million roubles in 1900 to 1,746·2 million in 1910 and to 2,111·1 million in 1913; of these totals, direct taxes accounted respectively for 131·9, 216·1 and 272·5 million roubles; indirect taxes (including receipts from the spirits monopoly) accounted for 775·7, 1,359·7 and 1,607·4 million roubles.[3] The latter of course were levied on articles of mass consumption and thus became an immediate charge on the mass standard of living. It was characteristic of the Russian fiscal system that direct taxation, as opposed to indirect, should yield such a low proportion of state revenue. It was also characteristic that so little attempt should have been made by Russian industry to develop an internal market for its products. This would have entailed a complete *volte-face* in the policy of guns before butter – a reversal all the less likely, the more the frequency of international crises accelerated the arms race. Moreover, considerable institutional and social obstacles held back any attempt at raising the low urban living standards – the serf tradition, international competition, and the orientation of Russian industry towards capital goods.[4]

In sum, therefore, very little remained to the worker for his militancy of 1905–6 – some representation in the Duma, perhaps, and a law of March 1906 legalizing the formation of trade unions. But in 1907 Stolypin, by a veritable *coup d'état*, had cut the workers' franchise; and from the outset the trade union law had serious limitations. Each union's charter had to be approved by the bureaucracy, and a specific prohibition prevented the combination of individual unions into larger units. The movement as a whole also suffered from sporadic police repression.

Trade unionism, therefore, remained extremely weak. In 1907 its membership is estimated to have amounted approximately to 245,555 workers – about one-seventh of industrial labour – divided amongst 652 unions. Only six unions had more than five thousand members; 108 unions had between one hundred and two hundred members. Three hundred and forty-nine unions had less than one hundred members.[5] After 1907 the number of unions and their membership actually declined. In 1907 Moscow had forty-six unions with 48,000 members; in 1909 there were twenty-one unions with 7,000 members. In 1907 St Petersburg had forty-four unions with 51,782 members; in 1908 the figures were respectively twenty-eight and 29,300.[6] In sum, the small number of unionized workers, the unions' lack of funds, their fluctuating membership and the disabilities imposed by the government, combined to nullify any benefits that might otherwise have accrued to the workers. In the best of circumstances perhaps, it is also debatable whether the geographical dispersion of the proletariat in large clusters may not inherently have lent itself to the soviet form of representative organization rather than to unionization.

It is not surprising therefore, that the first signs of a fresh upsurge swiftly followed the nadir of strike action in 1910. All the causes, apart of course, from the war, that had produced working-class militancy in 1905–6, were still operative. But the place of the war was taken by the heightened political awareness of the masses in the period before 1914. In 1910 there had been a mere 222 strikes, affecting 46,000 workers. In 1911 these figures more than doubled, to 466 and 105,110 respectively. What is equally striking is the rise in the number of strikes for political, rather than economic motives – from eight (1910) to twenty-four (1911).[7]

Then, in 1912, came the massacre of the miners in the Lena goldfields in Siberia. In February 1912, five thousand of the miners went on strike, in protest against low wages, the truck system of payment, degrading working conditions and a working day that effectively extended from 5 a.m. to 7 p.m. The strikers demanded a rise in wages, the eight-hour day, the abolition of fines and of the truck system. They held out for a month; then the authorities called in troops. In a clash between troops and strikers 170 workers were killed and 372 wounded. Nothing like this had happened since Bloody Sunday in 1905; and the response was the same. 'From a peaceful economic strike on the Lena river to political strikes in Russia,' wrote the young Stalin at this time, 'from political strikes in Russia to innumerable demonstrations of students and workers in the very centre of Russia – that is what the representatives of the government have achieved in their struggle with the workers.'[8]

This was the precise truth. The massacre of the Lena goldfields served the same purpose in precipitating a widespread strike movement as Bloody Sunday had done five years earlier. In April 1912 alone, 500,000 men struck in sympathy with the Lena workers – more than in the whole of the previous four years. This was no passing phase. It was but part of a rolling movement that engulfed larger and larger numbers of men. In 1912 the total number of strikes, 2,032, was almost fivefold that of the previous years; the number of strikers rose almost sevenfold – 105,110 (1911) as compared with 725,491 (1912). Similarly, the number of politically motivated strikes soared from twenty-four (1911) to 1,300 (1912).[9]

In this context, it was natural that Beletsky, vice-president of the Department of Police, should echo his former colleague, Zubatov: 'The better the workers are safeguarded financially, the less will the mass of the working population be influenced by revolutionary propaganda.'[10] True enough, and the government, under the pressure of the strikes, did take some steps in the direction of social welfare. It authorized the establishment of sick benefit funds, financed jointly by workers and employers and managed in part by labour. A scheme of accident insurance was also introduced, the total cost of which was covered by the employer. This provided medical aid in case of an industrial accident, as well as disability pensions and family pensions in the case of the breadwinner's death. But accident insurance did not operate at once and excluded large numbers of workers – agricultural labourers, for example, those employed in undertakings with fewer than twenty employees and workers in the building industry. Such a measure at a time such as this could scarcely be effective. The figures for the first eight months of 1913 bore this out. Over this period the number of strikes totalled 1,671 of which 761 were political in nature.[11]

A number of ministerial conferences examined the situation in the summer and early autumn of 1913. A diagnosis of remarkable gravity, made in October 1913, referred to sudden strikes flaring up

> sometimes for the most trivial causes and embracing with extraordinary rapidity wide areas with tens of thousands of workers. . . . But apart from that, the strike movement we are now experiencing has a yet more threatening social significance in that it arouses hostility and bitterness between employer and worker, unites the workers on the basis of an irreconcilable relationship to the existing state and social structure and in this way creates amongst the workers ready cadres to reinforce the revolutionary parties. Under the influence of agitators and the printed organs of the Social-Democratic press, with the moral and material support of different workers' circles, there has recently developed amongst the workers a harmony of action such as indicates their close solidarity and organized nature. The places where strikes take place are put under a boycott, those workers who approach are exposed to bitter persecution and are excluded from work. Orders at strike-bound factories and plants are also placed under a boycott and any factory that might accept them risks a strike amongst its own workers.[12]

The provinces of St Petersburg and Moscow stood out, both in respect of the number of strikes and of their political content. The situation here convinced the council of ministers that 'the strike movement is definitely growing to threatening dimensions, more and more taking on a political colouring. It is also apparent that in respect of the number of lost working days political strikes are less prolonged than economic but are more intensive by reference to the number of workers who participate.' The ministers saw it as their 'most imperative task' to prevent a further intensification of the strike movement. This was so, not only in order to maintain production but also 'to preserve order and the security of the state'.[13]

What would the ministers actually do? They were well alive to the need to avoid administrative repression and thereby 'disarm the revolutionary parties'. But all they could propose was some system of 'arbitration chambers' to adjudicate disputes between workers and employers, press the latter to be more 'responsive' to the workers' claims and institute more police supervision.[14]

This could hardly suffice, than which there is no greater proof than the ascendancy of Bolshevik leadership amongst the proletariat. In the autumn of 1912 in the elections to the fourth Duma Bolsheviks were victorious in six of the nine labour curiae, including all six curiae in the major industrial areas. They ousted their Menshevik opponents from control of the Union of Metalworkers, the strongest union in St Petersburg in August 1913; in January 1914 they were voted into a dominant position in the workers' section of the administration of the state insurance boards established in 1912; and on the eve of the First World War Bolsheviks were dominant in most of the trade unions in St Petersburg and Moscow.[15]

What did all this mean? In October 1913, Colonel von Koten, of the St Petersburg division of the secret police and an expert on the labour movement, foresaw the probability of a general strike in the capital. He noted growing discontent amongst the workers, such that '. . . the slightest cause (was) sufficient to make them strike. . . . As in 1905 the idea has been circulating of organizing combinations of workers in the most diverse categories – postal and telegraph employees, railwaymen, tramway workers, water-supply employees, gas workers, etc.' So inflamed was the atmosphere that it might be harmful to liquidate the unions, von Koten continued. This might 'only accelerate the explosion of the strike movement'.[16] The first seven months of 1914 fully justified this alarm. The number of strikes increased by some fifty per cent to 3,466 as compared with 1913. Of this total some 2,500 were politically motivated, embracing more than a million workers.[17]

All this culminated in the great St Petersburg general strike of July 1914. The immediate cause was a general strike in Baku, itself provoked by an outbreak of plague in the neighbourhood of the oilfields. This at once made the housing conditions of the oil-workers a crucial issue. Bolsheviks had long been influential in the oilfields and used the opportunity to raise a broad programme of economic demands. A month-long struggle between the Baku strikers and police and Cossacks began.

Liaison between Bolsheviks in Baku and St Petersburg brought the strike to the capital, where little excuse was in any case needed. On 1 July the St Petersburg branch of the party called for a one-hour strike in solidarity with the Baku workers, adding the slogans: 'For the eight-hour day! For a democratic republic and the confiscation of private land! For socialism!'[18]

On 3 July, in the agitated atmosphere generated by the workers' meetings, demonstrations and collections, two Putilov workers were killed by police, about fifty wounded and more than a hundred arrested. This ugly incident inflamed the atmosphere yet further. It marked a turning point. That same evening the Petersburg Bolsheviks called for a three-day strike – 'Let a shout of protest and indignation spread throughout all St Petersburg, all Russia . . . only through our own strength will we throw off the autocrat and his gangs of brigands.'[19] Within a few days a crescendo strike wave brought virtually all the capital's workers on to the streets. In the working-class districts such scenes now took place as had no parallel in the city's history. Amidst the unfurling of red flags and the chanting of the *Marseillaise* and other revolutionary songs, workers engaged in running fights and street battles with police, troops and Cossacks. The two sides exchanged shots, workers hurled stones at their enemies, and set up barricades made of overturned tramcars and telegraph poles. It needed all the forces of the government to prevent the riots spreading to the central districts of the city.

On 9 July, foreseeing eventual defeat in the absence of sufficient weapons, the local Bolshevik committee called off the strike.[20] But it had lost effective control. The influence of what the police called 'green young men', i.e. fresh worker-peasants from the countryside, had always been militantly to the fore.[21] A group of these party-members defied their leaders and tried to convert the street fighting into an armed uprising. Not until the eve of Russia's entry into the war on 16 July were the workers finally subdued. They had once again demonstrated their 'irreconcilable relationship to the existing state and social structure . . .'[22]

The Economy, Society and Politics

When agriculture transmitted its post-1906 prosperity to industry, a certain impetus naturally resulted. The years of crisis, 1900–1903, and of depression, 1903–1906, were followed (apart from a slight set-back in 1908–1909) by a period in which each year set a new production record. Between 1903 and 1907 there was an average annual growth of six per cent in the value of production. In 1913 the value of production was 54·2 per cent higher than it had been in 1909. Over the same period the number of workers rose from 1,805,000 to 2,357,000. This denotes an increase of 30·6 per cent which, when juxtaposed to the growth in the value of production, shows a clear growth in productivity. The increasing modernization of Russian industry was also evident in the growing concentration of industry. In 1901 46·7 per cent of the workers had been employed in factories employing five hundred or more workers; in 1910 the comparable figure was fifty-four per cent.[23] Railway construction was less important than in the past. Not until 1912 did a strong pick-up in this sector become evident (owing to strategic considerations, i.e. ease of mobilization). This continued until 1916.

As an immediate political corollary to this industrial and agricultural upsurge, radicalism declined, both in town and village. This was of course much more protracted in the latter than in the former. Spokesmen of both the major parties lamented their fragmentation and organizational disarray.[24]

For this reason perhaps, and also because of the initial smoothness of the renewed economic upsurge, the years after 1906 brought no immediate change to the political aspirations of the industrialist flank of the bourgeoisie. Though it certainly had affiliations with the Octobrist party, no specifically 'industrial' party emerged. The decision to support the government, taken in the second half of October 1905, precisely after the publication of the October Manifesto, was not rescinded until a year or two before the war.

Industrialists more and more put themselves at the service of the government in the economic development of the empire. An Association of Industry and Commerce, founded in 1906, and its journal *Industry and Commerce*, devoted themselves specifically to this purpose. The association was a federation of industrial organizations formed along geographic and functional principles, e.g. the mine owners of south Russia or the Baku oil producers. By the beginning of 1914 it embraced thirty-four banks and insurance companies, 251 industrial undertakings, eleven transport companies and nineteen trading concerns.[25]

The association consistently advocated the further economic development of the empire through a policy of high entrepreneurial profits combined with austerity in consumption. It argued against free competition – 'the anarchy of the market and a chaotic fluctuation of prices' – and in favour of a five-, a ten- or even a fifteen-year plan, that would overcome Russian backwardness and free it from dependence on agriculture. It proposed cooperation between industry and the government in, for example, the irrigation of Turkestan for the cultivation of cotton, the construction of the Volga–Don canal, and the intensive exploitation of the Magnitogorsk iron deposits in conjunction with Siberian coal. 'The constant fear of atmospheric caprice, in order that our economic calculations may finally become less dependent on the barometer and on the problematical aspects of the harvest' – this was the motivation of industry. Planning from above, with the sympathetic stabilizing and regulatory intervention of the vast resources at the disposal of the Treasury would enable trade and industry to take their full share in industrial development, it was hoped. In the last resort, the association envisaged a type of corporate state in which industrial and commercial interests would play a co-determining role *vis-à-vis* the government in relation to economic policy.[26]

For this reason the association scheduled its own congresses to take place during the Duma sessions – the membership overlapped in many cases – and 'sometimes its debates were the more interesting and important of the two,' noted one observer.[27] The association functioned as a vast pressure-group: '. . . Russian industry and commerce must, in the interests of self-preservation,' declared an early initiator of the association, 'express not only its broadly based views but also know how to present these views to those institutions and groups on whom will depend the putting into practice of this or that law or policy. . . . Here lies the whole root and the whole meaning of the All-Empire congresses of the representatives of industry and commerce.'[28]

The association spoke with all the louder voice because its constituent bodies came more and more to enjoy positions of monopoly in their respective pursuits. The connexion between protectionism and the formation of cartels and trusts has often been pointed out.[29] The economic crisis of the turn of the century which bankrupted many of the weaker concerns fostered this inherent predisposition in Russia. No less than 150 monopolistic associations are estimated to have come into existence.[30] They began on a large scale in railway construction in 1901; in 1904 they spread into the field of locomotive construction; and then embraced carriage manufacture, the mining industry (*Produgol*), metallurgy (*Prodamet*) and oil extraction (*Nobmazout*). A monopoly with a territorial basis was *Krovlya*; this grouped a number of Ural sheet metal manufacturers into a sales syndicate so that they might more effectively compete with the technically advanced plants of south Russia. *Prodamet* was one of the most powerful of these syndicates in that it controlled the output, prices and distribution of its constituent firms; furthermore, these firms were themselves amongst the largest in the metallurgical sector of the economy. Although *Prodamet* embraced only about seventeen per cent of all metallurgical plants of the empire, these plants represented seventy per cent of shareholding capital, employed thirty-three per cent of all workers in this sector and produced between seventy-four and eighty-eight per cent of the different types of metallurgical output. Even amongst the big, there were those that were bigger – only five firms predominated in *Prodamet* – they produced 40·9 per cent of all pig-iron in the empire and twenty-nine per cent of semi-finished products.[31]

Much of this regrouping activity took place under the aegis of Russian banking interests, themselves heavily penetrated by French finance, especially the Société Générale and the Banque de Paris et les Pays-Bas. Industry advanced at such a pace that it was unable to finance itself from its own recources. If steel production rose from thirty million poods in 1900 to 150 million in 1913, or if the capital of the Putilov metal works grew from twelve million roubles in 1911 to twenty-five million in 1913, and that of the capital of the Bryansk steel works from twenty-four million in 1912 to forty-one million in 1913, then clearly non-industrial sources of finance must have been available. Recourse was had to finance capital, which thus came to play a large part in the regrouping of industry.[32]

Rearmament gave economic development additional impetus. The need to re-equip the Russian fleet and army after the calamities of the Russo-Japanese war overrode the objections and misgivings of the finance minister.[33] The military budget increased from 420 million roubles in 1900 to 647 in 1910 and 861 in 1913, i.e. 21·1 per cent of all the outgoings in the national budget. Russia did not possess a specialized arms industry comparable to Vickers (Britain), Krupp (Germany) or Schneider-Creusot (France). Their place was taken by engineering and shipbuilding cartels and consortia, seeking to profit from the vast sums being poured into arms manufacture.[34]

What socio-economic influence was possessed by these conglomerates of power? This is not easy to analyse. It seems likely however, that they had a disintegrating influence in further corrupting and demoralizing the tsarist bureaucracy. An insider, V. I. Gurko, at one time assistant minister of the interior and member of the state council, avers that the integrity of the overwhelming majority of high officials was 'beyond question'. But he must also admit that private concerns engaged prominent officials at 'fabulous sums' with a view to the man's 'official connexions and his knowledge of the methods necessary to obtain governmental backing . . . particularly to secure some state concession.'[35] The line between public and private interest became more and more difficult to draw. This applied particularly to the armament industry. Take Avdakov, for example, for some years the chairman of *Produgol*, then of the Association of Industry and Trade and at the same time councillor in the ministry of industry and trade; or Lieutenant-General Brink, a former head of the department of naval construction and chief inspector of naval artillery, who became a director of the Putilov works; or Vice-Admiral Bostrem, a former commander of the Black Sea fleet, who became president of the board of the Nikolaevsk naval construction company; or General Ivanov who joined the board of the same company; or General Miller, former head of the state-owned Obukhovo works, who became director of the Tsaritzyn artillery plant.

Civilian officials similarly moved between government posts and private industry, especially if they were engaged in the ministries of finance and trade and industry. There was Timiryazev, for example, and Bark, Arandarenko, M. M. Fedorov, V. I. Kovalovsky, N. N. Pokrovsky, Langovoi, Litvinov-Falinsky – all these men moved at one time or another between their ministerial arm-chairs and an equally well-padded position in industry or an industrial association.[36]

This movement formed a military-industrial complex of some magnitude. It was accompanied by a system of bribery, regulated in accordance with a precise scale. Senators Dedulin and Neidhart conducted various enquiries into the commercial conduct of the monopolies; they found that 'a systematic and completely defined and graduated system of bribery' characterized relations between the military contractors and officials. The whole system of the distribution and acceptance of orders was such that 'it was always essential to pay and impossible not to pay.' Dedulin calculated that five to six per cent of the value of an order might be taken up in expenses on bribery. Individual bribes might amount to between one-and-a-half per cent and two per cent of the value of the order.[37]

Inevitably, the authority of the government was weakened by the fact that the monopolies, trusts, cartels and syndicates stood outside the law, constituted a law unto themselves, formed a state within a state. They have been well compared to 'economic feudalities'.[38] For all the success of the senatorial commissions of inquiry in uncovering a multitude of abuses, fraudulent deliveries and cases of curruption, the government failed to subdue the guilty parties.

The Grand Duke Alexander Mihailovitch has described graphically, if somewhat luridly, the resultant speculative atmosphere in Russian society:

During the course of the city census in St Petersburg in the spring of 1913, some 40,000 persons of both sexes registered as 'stock exchange speculators' . . .

The haughty leaders of society included stock-brokers in their visiting lists. The aristocratic officers of the imperial guard, though unable to distinguish stocks from bonds, began to discuss the imminent rise in prices on 'broad' steel. . . . Fashionable hostesses acquired a habit of featuring the presence of that marvellous genius from Odessa who has made a terrific killing in tobacco! The holy men of the church subscribed to the financial publications and the velvet-upholstered carriages of the archbishops were often observed in the neighbourhood of the stock exchange.[39]

Was this an exaggeration? Then consider the case of General Sukhomlinov. Sukhomlinov, appointed chief of the general staff (1908) and minister of war (1909–15) was eventually arrested on charges of treasonable negligence. Through backstairs influence he evaded the supreme penalty and survived to write his memoirs in Berlin. His trial showed him to possess a private fortune of some seven hundred thousand roubles. How had he acquired a sum so disproportionate to his salary? From speculations conducted on his behalf by a St Petersburg bank. It thereby hoped to secure military orders for the enterprises with which it was connected. Sukhomlinov's salary had never kept pace with the expenses incurred through his second marriage to a lady from the theatrical world of Kharkov, Kiev and Odessa – a lady 'accustomed to merry suppers in restaurants and drinking parties at home. . . . Financial difficulties became increasingly acute.' The unfortunate general had no better luck with his third wife – her particular forte, as costly as the gay dinners of her predecessor, was to patronize Parisian *haute couture*.[40]

Events at the centre of government compounded this corruption. Here *douceurs* circulated freely, to say nothing of subsidies to journalists and politicians. When Kokovtsov in January 1914 was dismissed from his position as minister of finance, the tsar held out to him a golden handshake. 'Would you be satisfied with an appropriation of two or three hundred thousand roubles?' he asked the minister. Kokovtsov, embarrassed, refused the offer.[41] But this offer could not conduce to good government.

At the end of 1910 and beginnihg of 1911 Tikhomirov, editor of *Moskovskie Vedomosti* and a former revolutionary, was using the terms 'ministerial anarchy' and '*bullum omnium contra omnes*' to describe the relations between the government, the Duma and the state council.[42]

Should the Polish language be introduced into the schools of the western provinces? In 1912 a bill to this effect illuminated Tikhomirov's lament. The bill was recommended to the state council by the chairman of the council of ministers, Kokovtsov. But N. A. Maklakov, minister of the interior, was secretly hostile. When Rodzyanko, president of the Duma, had his next audience with the tsar, he complained, with many apologies, that Russia had, in effect, no government.

'What do you mean – no government?'

'We are accustomed to think that part of the executive power of the crown is delegated to the ministers and to the nominated members of the council of the empire (i.e. state council). These latter execute the will of the government and defend it in the legislative assembly. We, the members of the lower chamber, are accustomed to think so. What do we see? During the last session we debated the bill for the admittance of the Polish language in the schools of the western provinces. It was your imperial majesty's wish that the language should be admitted in order to improve the position of the Poles by comparison with their position in Austria, and so enlist their sympathies on behalf of Russia.'

'Yes,' replied the tsar, 'that is just what I had in view.'

'So we understood it, and the bill was worked out in the Duma in that sense. Now this bill is being debated in the council of the empire, and its leading principle is defended by a representative of the government. Meanwhile, some of the nominated members of the council are absent, others vote against it, and the bill is rejected. Your majesty will agree that the members of the government either do not wish to execute your will, or do not take the trouble to understand it. The population does not know where it is. Each minister has his own opinion. The cabinet is for the most part split into two parties, the state council forma a third, the Duma a fourth, and your own will is unknown to the nation. This cannot go on, your Majesty; this is not a government, it is anarchy.'[43]

Into the quasi-vacuum created by the tsar's fumbling initiatives, governmental disunity and elements of corruption, there flowed, at first feebly, then more and more strongly, the presence of Gregory Yefimovitch Rasputin. Not the least significant item in the whole tumult of 1905 was a laconic entry in the tsar's diary: 'We have got to know a man of God – Gregory – from the Tobolsk province.'[44]

Who is this man from Tobolsk? This Gregory? He began life as a wandering pilgrim of dubious morals and in this capacity visited Jerusalem, the Balkans and Mesopotamia. After unknown adventures, he was eventually taken up by Militsa, a Montenegran princess with a taste for mysticism, and her sister, Anastasia. Through their instrumentality he was introduced to the imperial couple.

Rasputin's subsequent success in royal circles had three main features: first, his undoubted power to allay the pain consequent on the disability of the tsarevitch Alexey. After giving birth to four daughters, the empress at last gave birth to a son – but he proved to be a victim of haemophilia, transmitted through his mother, in whose family the disease was hereditary. In their despair at the inability of orthodox medicine to overcome or alleviate the disease, the imperial couple turned with relief to Rasputin; second, Rasputin's religious background and repute as a 'man of God' ensured him the sympathy of the empress. He could easily use to advantage the religious mania embodied in the hundreds of icons, triptychs, crosses, pictures of the annunciation and the madonna and child that adorned the empress's rooms. She attached physical power to objects handled by Rasputin. She sent Rasputin's stick and comb to the tsar so that he might benefit from Gregory's vigour when attending ministerial councils; lastly, Rasputin represented to the imperial couple a man of the people who would enable the tsar to overcome the barrier dividing him from his subjects.[45] Before 1909 was out Rasputin had already become to the empress her 'beloved' and 'unforgettable teacher'. 'How distraught I am without you,' she wrote. 'My soul is only at peace, I only rest, when you, my teacher, are seated beside me and I kiss your hands and lean my head on your blessed shoulders. . . . Then I only have one wish: to sleep for centuries on your shoulders, in your embraces . . .'[46]

As if an adventurer's proximity to the throne were not enough, the government had to contend with the world-wide execration provoked by the Beilis trial. This patent show-trial of a Jew, Mendel Beilis, allegedly guilty of the ritual murder of a Christian child, exposed to world-wide opprobrium and contempt the tsarist exploitation of anti-semitism as a means to diverting internal discontent.

Even an anti-semite and monarchist member of the Duma such as Shulgin could not but protest at the trial – for which he was condemned to three months' imprisonment. Beilis was acquitted in 1913, but in such circumstances that the stature of the government suffered yet further.

Even a Duma elected on the basis of the restricted franchise inaugurated in 1907 could not swallow all this – Rasputin *and* Beilis *and* governmental breakdown *and* the unending strikes. 'Compromise was impossible and had lost all sense,' Milyukov recalls. An impasse divided government and the fourth Duma.[47] On the one hand the tsar and N. A. Maklakov, minister of the interior, were tentatively planning to dissolve the Duma, impose martial law on St Petersburg and Moscow, and reduce the Duma to a consultative body. This would merely present to the tsar its majority and minority opinions for his decision and approval.[48] On the other hand, there was forming in the Duma a broadly-based political re-alignment of Kadets, Progressives and some Octobrists in an attempt to break the deadlock between the Duma and a discredited government. Guchkov, leader of an Octobrist faction, took an influential part in this re-alignment. 'We are compelled to defend the monarchy against those who are the natural defenders of the monarchic principle,' Guchkov told an Octobrist conference in November 1913, 'the church – against the ecclesiastical hierarchy, the army – against its leaders, the authority of the government – against the government itself.'[49] So fluid did the political situation become on the eve of war that Konovalov, the Moscow millionaire, Progressive deputy, and one inspirer of the new alignment, actually sought to make contact with Lenin. 'It is essential that different elements meet each other from time to time simply in order to inform each other of what is happening in the different social strata,' Konovalov, in March 1914, explained to Skvortzov-Stepanov, Lenin's Bolshevik intermediary Konovalov also confessed, it appears, that the liberals changed sides too soon in 1905; i.e. they should not have lined up behind the October Manifesto but should have pressed for further concessions. At one stage in this correspondence Konovalov was also willing to finance the forthcoming Bolshevik party congress to the tune of several thousand roubles.[50]

Nothing came of Konovalov's initiative. But his 'bloc' did bring together a number of men who would later take a prominent part in the events of 1917 either in the Petrograd Soviet or the Provisional Government – Konovalov himself, as well as Kerensky (Trudovik), Chkheidze, Skobelev (Mensheviks), Nekrasov and Tereschchenko (Kadets). Many of these men were also linked by common masonic ties.[51] At this time also different party leaders were working out the principles of 'a federal democratic republic on the basis of radical social reforms' – again of a type that emerged in February 1917.[52] This evidence of profound inner disunity, social schism and political discontent could not but influence the Russian decision in July 1914 – to fight or not to fight?

The Greater Danger

The interplay between war and the needs of internal stability was no new phenomenon in Russian society. 'Alexey Nikolayevitch, you do not know the internal condition of Russia,' Plehve had said to Kuropatkin, the Russian commander-in-chief, shortly before the Russo-Japanese war. 'In order to hold back the revolution we need a small victorious war.'[53] When tension in the Far East increased further, Plehve lost his enthusiasm and urged a moderating policy. This brought him closer to Kuropatkin himself and also to Muravyov (minister of justice). Both opposed a forward Far Eastern policy in the anticipation that it would unfavourably influence internal security. 'I wrote to the tsar,' Kuropatkin noted in his diary for 28 November 1903, 'that a war with Japan would be extremely unpopular in Russia, that the anti-governmental party will use this war in order to increase disorder, etc.'[54]

To associate war with revolution was inevitable after 1905. It recurred frequently in diplomatic interchanges between 1905 and 1914. In March 1908, for example, Bülow, the German chancellor, instructed Pourtalès, his man in St Petersburg, to warn Stolypin that 'the consequences of Russian wars had always been internal disturbances and upheavals of growing intensity'. Bülow then cited the Decembrist movement, peasant emancipation after the Crimean war, the nihilist movement after 1878, and, most recently of all, 1905. These were 'landmarks' of increasing severity, said Bülow.[55] Inevitably, the increasingly tense international atmosphere gave added point to this analysis. In 1912, for example, during the Balkan wars, certain people persuaded the tsar that 'war would bring a revolution at home', Krivoshein, minister of agriculture, reported to Marchand, Figaro correspondent. 'But in saying that to the emperor they are deceiving him,' Krivoshein continued. 'On the contrary, it is peace at any price which, in my opinion, can bring on a revolution.'[56]

The same question recurred in May 1914. 'Would war not be the signal for revolution in Russia?' Paléologue, the French ambassador, reported to his premier, Doumergue, that people in Russia were asking themselves this very question. Paléologue himself asked: 'Does the military effort of our ally risk being paralysed by a popular uprising?' This was clearly an alarming prospect for France. Happily, after assessing the prospects for revolution, Paléologue eventually felt able to give his government a reassuring answer. But to do so, he had to give heavy emphasis to the repressive powers at the disposal of the autocracy.[57]

What was evident to foreign observers was not of course lost on Russian politicians. When the Duma debated foreign affairs in May 1914 Milyukov, speaking in appropriately 'Aesopain' language, took the opportunity to warn the government against pursuing simultaneously a provocative internal *and* a provocative external policy. War must not be used either to silence discontent at home or avoided lest worse befall; and Milyukov pleaded for restraint.[58] Moreover, given Russian unreadiness, and the empire's 'accumulating internal position', Milyukov feared the probability of defeat and its incalculable consequences.[59]

The interplay of home and foreign policies came more clearly to the fore in the right wing of the Duma. An 'expansionist' and a 'conservative' trend have been identified in Russian foreign policy at this time.[60] Count Bobrinsky, of the Moderate Right, spoke for the former. He expressed Pan-Slav sympathies, vented his hostility to Germany and Austria-Hungary, and advocated the Anglo-French alignment.[61] Markov II and Purishkevich, black reactionaries and anti-semites, attacked the government most fiercely. To the former, moved particularly by hostility to Britain, 'the first duty' of Russian diplomacy was to find 'the path to a peaceful understanding with Germany'.[62] But this was not only a matter of foreign policy, for Markov II expressed alarm at what would come if war with Germany were not avoided – 'All will suffer, every state may collapse and in their place will appear Attilas, whose name is Social-Democracy and these Attilas will devour all of humanity . . .'[63] Outside the Duma, the two victors of 1905, Durnovo and Vitte, also presented Markov II's arguments. A Russo-German war would be 'mutually dangerous' to both countries, no matter who won, the former argued, '. . . there must inevitably break out in the conquered country a social revolution, which, by the very nature of things, will spread to the country of the victor.'[64] Vitte also saw the interdependence between tsarism and the continued existence of Hohenzollern and Habsburg rule.[65] Vitte continued to oppose the war, even after its outbreak, and was a sensitive party to certain peace feelers extended by Robert Mendelssohn, Vitte's German banker, in the winter of 1914–15.[66]

So much for the anti-war party. With what arguments did the war party seek to overcome the tsar's extreme reluctance to order Russian mobilization? What went on in the government *coulisses*? This does not seem to be so well documented. But one point is clear – the importance attached to the internal situation. Would war precipitate revolution, or would it rather avert revolution? This was the supremely important focus of contention. With barricades and a general strike in St Petersburg no question could be more pertinent. Maklakov, minister of the interior, for example, though confessedly well aware both of the opportunities that war would offer to the revolutionaries and of the unpopularity of war as compared with revolution, was none the less convinced that the internal situation of Russia forced his hand.[67] Sazonov, foreign minister, was more explicit in maintaining that general mobilization 'was unavoidable also for internal-political reasons'. Similarly, the Grand Dukes Nikolai Nikolayevitch and Nikolai Michailovitch told the tsar that 'Russia, if it did not mobilize, would face the greatest dangers and a peace bought with cowardice would unleash revolution at home.'[68]

Confirmation comes from the left. Trotsky and Kerensky agree with the grand dukes. They too maintain that the war interrupted the revolutionary movement.[69] Yet, as Trotsky also asserts, the price paid for this diversion was the 'extraordinary impetus' that the war gave to the revolution.[70]

13 The Storm Breaks

Herzen compared the European great powers to Genghis Khans with telegraphs. Russia too was a Genghis Khan – but it lacked the telegraphs. The right wing was not alone in recognizing Russian weakness. But what the Vittes and Durnovos feared, left-wingers welcomed. In 1904, in an article that bore the significant title *The Collapse of the Autocracy*, Parvus had already stressed 'the contradiction between war conditions and the social material of the Russian army'. Where were the national schools and political freedom needed to create a 'practical, reflective and independent soldier'? Parvus asked. How could the movement of troops and the direction of the army be reconciled with Russian 'administrative backwardness'? Or the financial demands of war and the financial resources of the country? Military defeat was the instrument chosen by history to liquidate the autocracy, Parvus concluded.[1]

If this was true in 1904, how much more true must it be in 1914? Lenin, for one, looked on the imperialist war as the opportunity for civil war. How right he was! In a mere matter of months governmental mismanagement, military incompetence, bureaucratic confusion, treachery and all manner of noxious corrupt influences, superimposed on an unviable social structure, began to dig an ever widening gulf between the government and the country. In the end all mutual confidence was lost. By February 1917 barely one rifle would fire to defend a thoroughly discredited regime.

This was by no means evident in August 1914. On the contrary, patriotism became the last refuge of the Romanovs. National feeling inspired the country to forget its divisions. Mobilization proceeded smoothly, despite some disorders in Siberia and on the Volga.[2] Down came the barricades in Petrograd (St Petersburg's war-time name) and the city gave unceasing demonstrations of loyalty.[3] 'A life for the tsar,' retained all its magical charisma. In Baku, mobilization and 'chauvinist fumes' put an abrupt end to the general strike.[4] In the Duma session of 26 July 1914 the deputies unanimously adopted a resolution declaring their readiness 'at the summons of their sovereign, to stand up in defence of their country, its honour and its possessions'. The only dissentients were the six Mensheviks, five Bolsheviks, and the Trudovik deputies. They left the session and refused to vote war-credits (though Kerensky came out in favour of a defensive war). Those were 'wonderful early August days' and Russia seemed 'completely transformed', wrote the British ambassador.[5]

From the anarchist standpoint, events fulfilled Tolstoy's grim vision. At the Uspensky Sobor (Cathedral of the Assumption) in the Kremlin, long-haired men in vestments of gold brocade prayed for victory amidst the peal of bells and the kissing of icons.[6] The high-born ladies 'getting ready to bandage those whom their husbands and brothers are setting out to kill' – these too did not lag behind. The Grand-Duchess Serge, a noted hospital worker, widow of the Grand-Duke assassinated in 1905, saw the war as a crusade, 'with all the saints of Russia ready to offer their help'.[7] Those less well born did not lag behind. Such a one was Breshko-Breshkovskaya, 'the little grand-mother of the Russian revolution', heroine of a thousand peasant riots. In remote Siberian exile she did not forget her duty to prepare lint and bandages for the wounded.[8] Other notable *révoltés* to rally round the flag were Plekhanov, Lenin's Marxist mentor, and Prince Kropotkin, the advocate of mutual aid, but now of mutual destruction.

Yet all the saints of Russia and all the enthusiasm of the populace could not compensate for Russia's geographical and economic handicaps. The empire, for example, was easily blockaded. The German navy dominated the Baltic, and Turkish hostility made the Dardanelles impassable. Only through the ports of Mrmansk and Archangel in the far north of the country, and Vladivostock in the Far East, could Allied supplies reach Russia. But all these areas had very inadequate rail contact with the interior of the country. The line from Murmansk to Petrograd was only completed during the war itself. Incredible mismanagement prevailed at Archangel. There was such a lack of storage facilities that packing cases literally sank into the soil owing to the sheer weight of the stores piled up on top of them.[9]

Russian dependence on imports of raw materials further increased the country's vulnerability to the blockade. In pre-war years the out-put of the extraction industries had failed to keep pace with the growth of manufacturing industry. The country had therefore had to import, in growing quantities, raw materials such as coal, iron, lead, petroleum, copper, zinc, wool, cotton and flax.[10] About 48·4 per cent of all these imports came via the western frontier and 38·5 per cent via the Baltic – both rendered inaccessible through the blockade. The cessation of these imports had a special relevance to the Petrograd industrial complex in that its distance from the Donetz coal-basin, where the bulk of Russian coal was mined, made it dependent on imported supplies of coal and iron. When these ceased to be available, the Ural iron works could only serve as a partial replacement, both by reason of their small production (which remained virtually static during the war), and their defective railway links with Petrograd and Moscow.[11] Coal, in particular, had to be brought to the north from the Donetz area.

This at once made the quantity of rolling stock and the extent of the railway network of prime importance. Russia in both respects was again deficient. In the years before the war, in the interests of budgetary soundness, the state had run down its expenditure on railways. The consequence of this made itself felt from the first days of the war. An overloading of the system took place, aggravated in 1915 by the German capture of the Levenstein factory at Warsaw, and the evacuation of the Russo-Baltic and Phoenix factories from Riga. South Russian manufacture could not make good these losses. By 1916 carriage production was only sixty per cent of what it had been in 1914; and there were fewer locomotives in service than there had been in 1912.[12] This coincided of course with a period when the transport of troops, foodstuffs and raw materials made unprecedented demands on the system. The quasi-breakdown further reacted on industrial production. At the end of February 1917 one of the directors of *Prodamet* reported that in fourteen important factories in the south twenty-two furnaces were no longer in operation and the other twenty-six were slowly running down – all due to a shortage of raw materials, especially coal.[13]

Agriculture suffered through the peasant's inability to obtain the most common tools or implements. Mineral fertilizers, hitherto imported from abroad, also became exceedingly scarce. For both these reasons, to say nothing of the shortage of manpower, there was a decline in the sown area and in the later stages of the war a consequent decline in food deliveries to the towns. The peasant could buy none of the necessities that he required; he had therefore little incentive to put his grain on the market. At the same time the wartime introduction of prohibition increased the supply of money in the village and thereby aggravated the problem of inflation.

Conscription accelerated industrial deterioration. By October 1917 some 15·5 million men had been called up. Manpower shortages, caused by conscripting factory workers and mine workers, had to be overcome by the employment of women, children, prisoners-of-war and refugees from the fighting areas. The consequence was a decline in productivity, that became especially acute in 1916.[14] As early as June 1915 leading industrialists were already complaining of serious manpower shortages and demanding that men be brought back from the front. Goujon, for example, the owner of an important metallurgical undertaking, cited the case of a Moscow factory that lacked sixty per cent of its working personnel.[15]

The army did not benefit from the manpower at its disposal in that it was gravely under-equipped. Even such elementary items as boots and rifles were in short supply, to say nothing of the more complex items – tanks, airplanes, shells and artillery. The losses of the army in killed, wounded and missing amounted to between 7·2 and 8·5 million men, i.e. between forty-five per cent and fifty-four per cent of all the men mobilized. This vast expenditure of life and limb did not produce commensurate results – at least so far as Russia was concerned. Despite some significant local successes, catastrophic failure marked the Russian campaigns of 1914, 1915 and 1916. For this the Russians were not themselves entirely responsible: Russian strategy was subordinated to that of the western powers. Each of the major Russian campaigns was undertaken in response to western pressure that took little or no account of Russian unreadiness – in 1914 the Russian offensive in East Prussia served to save Paris from the German attack; in 1915 the Russian offensive came in response to French pleas for a counter-blow to relieve the pressure on Verdun; and in 1916 the occasion for General Brusilov's offensive in Galicia was the parlous state of the Italian armies hard pressed by Austria-Hungary.[16] The subordination of Russian to Allied military demands continued to characterize Russian military policy even after the fall of tsarism and in its turn contributed to the fall of the Provisional Government.[17] It extended also to Russian participation in the allocation of military supplies.[18] In 1916 the French effort to secure 400,000 Russian troops for service in France, to be forwarded in successive drafts of 40,000 made clear Russia's role as a reservoir of cannon-fodder for the depleted French armies.[19]

On the home front the autocracy involved itself in a two-pronged offensive. On the one hand it came to grips with the Bolsheviks and suppressed all manifestations of revolutionary activity, so far as it was able. In those early months the party acted in the spirit of Lenin's theses that denounced 'tsarist-monarchist chauvinism' and agitated for the transformation of the imperialist war into civil war. The five Bolshevik deputies in the Duma were justifiably arrested at the end of 1914 on charges of subversion and sentenced to Siberian exile.[20] Similarly, the regime pursued a policy of the utmost hostility to labour, prohibiting trade unions and punishing with exile any workers who agitated for improved conditions. This policy undoubtedly had much success in disintegrating organized Bolshevik activity.

It merged with the other prong of the regime's home front offensive – its hostility to the need to associate all classes in the waging of war. This the structure of the indivisible autocracy could not permit.

The rationale of the government's attitude was evident enough. The prosecution of the war inevitably and necessarily required the emergence of a mass democracy similar to that in the other belligerent powers (except perhaps in Austria-Hungary). The requirements of mass warfare in respect of manpower and factory hands could only be satisfied by reconciling the masses to their sacrifices through concessions or apparent concessions of an economic or political character – a working-class party say, with its representatives in the cabinet or on governmental organizations, some token that working-class aspirations were not entirely unheeded, that due recognition was being given to the sacrifices exacted, that there existed at least the prospect of some post-war amelioration. In France, Germany, Britain, one or other of these phenomena characterized the socio-political scene – but not in Russia.

Opposition to the idea of associating labour, officially, and in some quasi-independent capacity, with the war-industrial effort was but one example of the struggle between a *soi-disant* indivisible autocracy and all manifestations of independent initiative. The very structure of the indivisible autocracy could not be reconciled with the emergence of independent social organizations. The zemstvos in 1904, during the Russo-Japanese war, had had to face this situation. In 1914 this conflict was multiplied a thousandfold. It spread to the war-industrial committees, to municipal dumas, and to all manner of permanent and *ad hoc* associations, formed to further the war effort. The autocracy contradicted the need for national mobilization. Expressed in Russian terms, the state could not belong both to society and to the tsar. One or the other had to go. Krivoshein, minister of agriculture, squarely put the position to the council of ministers in August 1915: 'There are but two ways out of the difficulty – either a strong military dictatorship, if a strong person can be found, or reconciliation with the public.'[21] But no dictator came forward; and nothing but the most grudging steps were taken towards an understanding with the public. To the bitter end the tsar would not yield one iota of his autocratic prerogatives – that they might be inherited by a sickly son.

The consistency of this attitude can be gauged from the government's treatment of the Duma provisional committee formed under the chairmanship of the Duma's president, Rodzyanko. It included leading representatives of all the important parties and concerned itself mainly with matters of first aid, relief for the wounded and army supplies. This was no easy task: the first 18,000 wounded from the battles of Lodz and the Berezina were simply transported in goods trains to the Warsaw-Vienna railway station at Warsaw and left on the platforms, 'in the cold rain and mud without as much as straw litter'. Their cries and groans 'filled the air'. Their only attention came from some Polish nurses and doctors.[22] But to attempt to organize a conference to discuss the needs of the army, especially an improvement in the supply of boots, incurred the accusation of subversion. This was precisely Rodzyanko's fate, when he raised the boot question. N. A. Maklakov, minister of the interior, charged him with wishing to discuss 'the political position of the country and demand a constitution'.[23]

Rodzyanko did eventually manage to organize his conference; and in general the zemstvos were permitted to take an indispensable part in welfare activity of the most multifarious kind. But this first clash constituted a notable symptom of the division between the government and society. Within a matter of months of the outbreak of war there would be talk in the Tsar's entourage of how best to clip the Duma's rights and reduce it to a purely consultative body.[24]

Military defeat in 1915 weakened the government's intransigence and further discredited the tsar and his ministers. In the spring and summer of that year a German break-through in the Carpathians, the loss of Libau and Galicia, the loss of the Polish fortresses, the evacuation of Warsaw, the occupation of Lithuania, the loss of Kovno, Grodno and Vilna, the entry of the German fleet into the gulf of Riga – all this shattered the precarious stability of the Russian home front.

One of the most awful concomitants of defeat was a great wave of refugees from the fighting areas driven into the interior by the Russian high command. 'Curses, diseases, grief and poverty are spreading all over Russia,' Krivoshein, minister of agriculture, told the council of ministers at the end of July.

Hungry and destitute people are bringing panic everywhere, and extinguished all the vestiges of the enthusiasm of the first months of the war. (Refugees) move in a solid mass, they tread down the fields, destroy the meadows and woods. . . . The railway lines are congested; even movements of military trains and shipments of food will soon become impossible. I do not know what is going on in the areas that fall into the hands of the enemy, but I do know that not only the immediate rear of our army but the remote rear as well are devastated, ruined . . . it is in my competence to declare, as a member of the council of ministers, that the second great migration of peoples, staged by general headquarters, will bring Russia to the abyss, to revolution and to ruin.

The army was no longer 'retreating but simply fleeing', Polivanov, minister for war, told the council. 'Confidence in its strength is completely destroyed. . . . Headquarters has completely lost its head. Contradictory orders, wavering hither and thither, feverish changes of commanding officers, and general confusion unnerve even the most courageous men. . . . The confusion at headquarters is no longer a secret and still further demoralizes the army.'[25]

The growing power of Rasputin over the tsarina and her own growing intervention in military and political matters compounded the effects of defeat. 'Lovy, I am here,' she wrote to Nicholas on 22 August 1915, 'don't laugh at silly old wifey, but she has "trousers" on unseen . . .'[26] In the early part of 1915 the tsarina's dependence on Rasputin was more and more bringing the imperial family into disrepute. Paléologue asked himself, only half-seriously, whether it might not be worth the Allies' while to bribe Rasputin and thus direct his 'inspirations instead of being incessantly inconvenienced, hampered and paralysed by them'.[27] In the latter years of the war Rasputin's influence extended from the nomination of prima donnas to food supply, from administrative and judicial matters (e.g. the suspension of Sukhomlinov's trial) to the government of the Church. He must also be kept informed of forthcoming offensives so that his prayers might decide the issue.

Not all his interventions were as frivolous as this. In 1915, one of the most fateful moves of Rasputin and the tsarina was to persuade the tsar to take the place of the Grand Duke Nikolai Nikolayevich as commander-in-chief of the Russian armies. There was already bad blood between Rasputin and the grand duke. But this move had a primarily dynastic reason: it formed part of the tsarina's campaign to preserve the autocracy intact. The grand duke was popular, despite Russian military failure, and she feared that he might supplant the tsar in popular acclaim or even attempt to seize the throne himself.[28]] Nikolai Nikolayevitch was therefore removed to the Caucasus as viceroy. The tsar himself, even if only nominally, assumed command of the Russian armies.

This action provoked the greatest alarm in Duma, Allied and governmental circles. 'If you, sire, should take over the direct leadership of our glorious army,' Rodzyanko warned the tsar, 'you, sire, the last refuge of your people – who will then execute judgement in case of failure or defeat? Is it not clear, sire, that you will then voluntarily have surrendered your inviolable person to the judgement of the people and that is fatal to Russia.'[29] Eight ministers addressed the tsar in similar terms and offered their resignation: 'Your decision . . . threatens Russia, yourself and your dynasty with heavy consequences.'[30] The tsar refused to accept the resignations, went ahead with his plans and the worst fears of his advisers and ministers were realized. Not only did all the odium of future defeats fall on the tsar himself; also, his absence at Stavka (General Headquarters) at Mogilev in western Russia, left the way clear for the virtually unhindered rule at home of the tsarina and Rasputin. Nicholas II had effectively abdicated. From the latter part of 1915 onwards a succession of nonentities, chosen for their acceptability to Rasputin, occupied ministerial positions. Not since Caligula made his horse a consul had so many strange appointments been made, said the wits of Petrograd. Albert Thomas, the French minister of munitions, came to Russia on an official visit in May 1916. He was provoked to exclaim: 'How rich and self-confident Russia must be! It could permit itself the luxury of a government in which the premier was "a disaster" and the minister of war "a catastrophe".'[31]

Governmental weakness and military defeat also activated opposition in the Duma, amongst those very forces that had first emerged in the immediate pre-war years. The Duma came more and more to occupy the central place in the struggle for a national war effort, so much so that in the spring of 1915 its pressure did force the tsar to dismiss four of the most obstructive and incapable ministers – Maklakov (interior), Sukhomlinov (war), Shcheglovitov (justice) and Sabler (procurator of the holy synod). Moreover, the tsar eventually had to authorize the establishment of a special council of national defence. It was formed under the presidency of the new minister of war (Polivanov) and included representatives of the Duma, state council, trade and industry as well as ministerial representatives. Five more specialized councils also came into existence, formed on the same model – army supply, fuel supply, foodstuffs, transport regulation and refugees. At a lower level war-industry committees were formed consisting of industrialists and (despite Bolshevik opposition) elected representatives of labour. All these had as object the adaptation of the existing industrial base to the manufacture of military and naval supplies. By the end of 1915, twenty-eight such committees existed in all the principal industrial centres.

But to many industrialists it was already clear that these councils and committees were a mere tinkering with the problem of waging a modern war within the political context of an unyielding regime. It was characteristic, for instance, of the continuing distrust between government and public that such prominent industrialists as Guchkov and Konovalov had to intercede with ministers on behalf of the workers' right freely to elect their representatives to the committees.[32] Ministers feared that the workers' leaders would 'use the opportunity to develop agitation beneath the pretext of elections'.[33] This was certainly true of the Bolsheviks.

Their new position of power gave the industrialists no comfort. On the contrary, it merely revealed the full extent of the task that had to be undertaken. Putilov, as early as June 1915, argued that nothing less than a complete reform of the whole administrative machine would suffice. One night in June 1915, over cigars and champagne, he gave full vent to the blackest pressimism. 'The days of tsarism are numbered,' he told Paléologue '. . . the revolution is now inevitable. It only awaits its opportunity.'[34] Other industrialists – Guchkov, Konovalov, Ryabushinsky – were, if not quite so pessimistic, at least every whit as oppressed by their utter lack of confidence in the tsar and the desperate position of the empire. So inept was the government, Ryabushinsky complained in August 1915, that it would be necessary in due course 'to enter on the path of a complete seizure of executive and legislative power . . .'[35]

The political expression of this disposition to change and a rehabilitated war effort was the formation of the Progressive bloc in the Duma. This had its origin in June 1915 when the Kadets, representatives of the zemstvos and municipalities and members of the industry-orientated Progressive party all advocated the formation of a ministry 'enjoying the confidence of the public'. They also urged that war-industrial committees be established to take over the manufacture of military supplies and equipment.[36]

This latter part of the programme was soon realized. In the late summer the Progressive bloc itself also came into existence in the Duma as a political force. It ranged all the way from the moderate Nationalists and Octobrists to the Kadets and had a clear majority in the Duma – 241 votes of a total of 407. 'Since 1915 we patriots had almost become Kadets because the Kadets had almost become patriots' – this was how Sulgin, a Nationalist deputy, put it.[37] In the more conservative-minded upper house, the state council, it only had eighty-nine votes out of a total of 196. 'Only a strong, firm and active authority can lead the fatherland to victory,' declared the bloc's first manifesto. Such an authority 'can only be that which rests upon popular confidence and is capable of organizing the active cooperation of all citizens'. The manifesto then outlined a programme calculated to achieve this end – *inter alia*, an amnesty for political criminals, the acknowledgement of certain national rights for Poles, Finns, Jews, Galicians, restoration of the rights of trade unions and of the labour press, legislation to give the peasants equal rights and bills to further the purposes of national defence, military supplies, welfare of refugees and the wounded, etc.[38]

Milyukov looked on his role in the Progressive bloc as the 'culminating point' of his political career.[39] This is a revealing assessment – the bloc accomplished very little. True, both in the Duma and outside the members of the bloc and its sympathizers attacked the government, often with great violence; true, it drew up a portfolio of ministers – Rodzyanko (premier), Milyukov (foreign affairs), Guchkov (interior);[40] true, a delegation of the bloc had quasi-negotiations with a number of sympathetic ministers to discuss details of their programme.[41] But all this amounted to very little.

This inertness revealed yet again the lack of self-confidence of the Russian bourgeoisie and its fear of the masses. In October 1905 it had already begun to withdraw from alignment with the mass movement. In 1915, amidst a war of shattering dimensions, Kadet and right-wing leaders (with some exceptions) were certainly not going to undertake a direct struggle for power of a type that would infallibly draw in the participation of the masses. 'Not to support the government now,' Milyukov warned the Kadets in June 1915, 'would be to play with fire. . . . All Russia now is a continuous inflamed wound. On the one hand, the greatest unprecedented ordeal on the battlefield, on the other the greatest ordeals in life at home. . . . Here tension has reached its ultimate limit, so that here, in this situation, a carelessly thrown match would set alight a terrible fire.'[42] Their programme 'must not have the character of an ultimatum . . .,' said Prince Lvov (of the Centre party) in August 1915. 'We will not enter on the path of a parliamentary struggle in war-time. We hope that this bloc will be so strong that it will convince the government to take a fresh course. Otherwise there is an abyss before us, into which we will not enter, and there will be no bloc.'[43]

But the bloc was never strong enough for this purpose; and the government never weakened to the point of yielding. As early as September 1915 not only did the bloc accept the precipitate closure of the Duma but its supporters outside, such as Chelnokov, the Kadet mayor of Moscow, actually denounced a strike declared in protest at this very closure. Following Chelnokov, the Moscow municipality limited itself to an appeal for 'the earliest possible resumption of the work of the legislative chambers and the inclusion in the government of persons enjoying the confidence of the country'.[44] Similarly, it did not escape the attention of the director of the Police Department that the strike outbreak had acted 'in a chilling manner' on the tactics of the Kadets.[45] Sazonov (minister of foreign affairs) did not err when he contemptuously told his fellow-ministers that if the Kadets were offered 'a loophole' they would be the first to come to an agreement with the government. 'Milyukov is the greatest bourgeois of all and fears a social revolution more than anything else,' he continued. 'Yes, and the majority of the Kadets are trembling for their investments.'[46] If only Sazonov had trembled for *his* investments . . .

Shulgin defined the bloc's aim in purely static terms – as an attempt 'to calm the masses'. The Duma would speak in their place and act as a buffer between, on the one hand, the street and the army and, on the other, the government. It took the only legitimate path, that of the parliamentary struggle and not that of the barricades. By standing firm, the Duma would 'not let the mob break throuth'.[47]

There was, to be sure, a left wing amongst the Kadets – men such as Mandelstamm, Obninsky and Kizevetter.[48] They disagreed with Milyukov's policy; they argued against his alignment with the right-wing parties and sought a leftwards alignment with the Mensheviks and Trudoviks. At a Kadet conference in October 1916, Prince Dolgorukov made the distinction clear:

Milyukov sees the centre of gravity of the struggle in the *parliamentary* fight with the government, (whereas) 'the provincials' (i.e. the left-wing Kadets) consider it essential to transfer the centre of gravity into the organization of the masses, into a *rapprochement* with political groups on the left, into a more decisive struggle with the government not only on parliamentary ground but also by means of all possible public organizations.[49]

Similar in this respect to the left-wing Kadets, certain industrialists also criticized the Kadet leadership. In October 1916, Konovalov, for example, reproached the latter for their 'inertia, doctrinairism and academicism' – and most of all for their 'alienation' and 'fear' of democratic forces.[50]

The Kadet dilemma – to see the need for action, yet to fear to act – was well illuminated in V. A. Maklakov's famous article *A Tragic Situation*. He compared Russia to an automobile entrusted to a chauffeur, so incapable that he is taking the vehicle to inevitable disaster. Those in the vehicle who are able to drive dare not interfere – not for one second must the car be left without a driver or else it will fly into the abyss. The chauffeur knows this and that is why he can make merry over the alarm and impotence of his passengers.[51]

The bloc, therefore, petrified by fear lest it inadvertently admit the masses to its private quarrel with the tsar, spent its time in discussion that did not lead to action. Like so many Oblomovs, it discussed, negatively and positively, the growing despair in the country, the fear of revolution, the need for another 11 March, the railway crisis, the fuel crisis. . . .[52] In retrospect, Milyukov identified the autumn of 1915 as 'the precise moment' when the revolution became inevitable.[53]

Would the Kadets have been more successful had they attempted to form some alignment with the left, inside and outside the Duma? Would they have been 'playing with fire', as Milyukov accused the Mandelstamms of wishing to do? Any answer can only be conjecture. But two things are certain; first, that the inaction of the Kadets and of most of their associates in the bloc enabled the government to persist in flouting Duma wishes; second, that there was indeed unchallenge-able risk in extending the anti-governmental struggle beyond the walls of the Duma.

The rationale of the bloc's moderation and passivity was to be found in growing restiveness on the home front. The workers' movement paralleled and accompanied that of the bloc. How much longer could it be possible in Shulgin's words, 'to calm the masses', to prevent 'the mob' from breaking through?

During the war the government took extensive powers to repress the labour movement and labour parties. Repeated arrests systematically decimated the ranks of both; it extended martial law to most large enterprises; it exiled strikers or sent them to the front; it banned the labour press and trade unions. In March 1916 the military commandant of Petrograd actually ordered factory-owners to close their factories if striking workers refused to resume work on the conditions offered by their employer.[54]

In most of 1915 the labour movement took the form of strikes for economic causes. Most of these succeeded and the workers in those industries favoured by war conditions – metallurgy, leather and chemicals – were able to maintain the purchasing power of their wages.[55] This was not a bloodless movement by any means. In the summer violent encounters between strikers and police at Kostroma and Ivanovo-Vosnesensk produced thirteen killed and wounded at the first and between twenty and thirty casualties at the second. Moreover, so sensitive was the state of labour relations that the report of these incidents sparked off an outbreak of major, politically inspired strikes in August and September 1915. In August 27,000 workers went on strike in Petrograd alone with demands for the release of the five exiled Bolshevik deputies as well as miscellaneous political demands – freedom of the press, suffrage at eighteen, withdrawal of the Cossacks guarding factories. The closing of the Duma in September and the arrest of some Putilov workers stimulated the unrest; early in that month Petrograd had 64,000 workers out on strike from thirty-four factories.[56] Altogether in 1915, in factories supervized by the inspectorate, 928 strikes took place, of which 715 had economic objectives and 213 political and non-economic objectives.[57]

There was no relaxation in 1916. The number of strikes rose to 1,410 (1,167 economic, 243 political and non-economic). The first predominated in the earlier part of the year and the latter towards its end. The commemoration of Bloody Sunday in January 1916 brought out 67,000 men in Petrograd from fifty-five factories.[58] From every point of view the movement had gained momentum; the average number of strikers involved in each strike rose from 581 (1915) to 711 (1916); and the duration of each strike lengthened from 4·17 to 4·71 days.[59] The metal-workers of Petrograd had always been prominent in the movement and this phase culminated in the vast Petrograd strike of 145,000 workers on 9 January 1917, to commemorate the twelfth anniversary of Bloody Sunday.[60] In Russia as a whole the number of strikes in January and February 1917 totalled 1,330 and involved 676,286 workers.[61]

To what degree did this movement have party-political objectives? It is hardly possible to be precise. To be sure, the Petrograd Bolsheviks tried to give the movement a political character and direction, 'to use every conflict to prepare mass revolutionary demonstrations for the conquest of political power . . .'; or to teach the workers that the enemy 'was in their own country'.[62] But the evidence does not suggest that this effort had much success. This is not surprising – even the mammoth Putilov works with their 20,000 employees counted only 150 Bolsheviks by February 1917; in the working-class and factory suburb of Vyborg there were no more than about 500 Bolsheviks.[63]

On the other hand, the strike movement benefited to some extent from German subsidies. This formed part of the German policy of exacerbating social and national tensions within the Russian empire. It played on disaffected groupings from the Baltic to the Caucasus.[64] As early as March 1915 the Germans began to give financial support to Russian revolutionary propaganda.[65] The money was channelled through Parvus who had in the meantime become an unofficial adviser to the German foreign office on Russian internal affairs. The source of this finance was already suspected, if not evident, in the Petrograd strikes of September 1915.[66] It seems that the Petrograd strikes of January 1916 and a concurrent strike at the naval yard of Nikolayev in south Russia also derived their financial backing, in the form of payment to the strikers, from the same source.[67]

In June 1916 Chkhenkeli, a Georgian Menshevik, issued a clear warning from the tribune of the Duma; 'Gentlemen, the European war that has already been raging for two years . . . must and will be liquidated not by those who began it but by quite other people,' he declared. 'You understand very well whom I understand by these "others". Gentlemen, the hour is not perhaps very distant when, in all its fullness the question will arise before the proletariat of all the belligerent countries, before democracy – when will this reign of hell and death come to an end? . . . The period of external crises must give way to a period of internal crises.'[68]

In the late summer and autumn of 1916 two factors of prime economic importance combined to produce 'the period of internal crises'. For the first time since the outbreak of war real wages began to fall behind the rising cost of living;[69] second, food shortages began to add to urban hardship. Whereas the harvest of 1914 and 1915 had equalled or surpassed pre-war levels, cereal production in 1916 fell twenty per cent below the pre-war average. Flour mills, owing to fuel shortage, were operating in December 1916 at only forty per cent of their normal capacity.[70] In the streets of the capital observers noted 'long queues of ill-clad men and garrulous women, waiting for the bread that never came'.[71]

What were they thinking, those ill-clad men? And what were they talking about, those garrulous women? They are 'on the verge of despair', the secret police report in October 1916. The slightest pretext will lead to 'elemental riots'. The incessant rise in the cost of living, the failure of wages to keep pace with the rise in prices, the shortage of food and vital necessities, the lack of fuel and firewood to heat damp unhygienic lodgings – 'all these conditions have created such a situation that the mass of industrial workers are quite ready to let themselves go to the wildest excesses of a hunger riot.' Then there were the workers' legal and political disabilities – the prohibition of meetings, the suspension of trade unions and the labour press, the ban on moving from one factory to another –

The working masses, led in their actions and sympathies by the more conscious and already revolutionary-minded elements, are violently hostile to the authorities and protest with all means and devices against a continuation of the war. . . . Thus, left-wing – revolutionary – circles are firmly convinced that a revolution will begin very soon, that its undoubted forerunners have already appeared and that the government will at once show itself powerless in the struggle with the revolutionary masses, who will be all the more dangerous because they consist two-thirds of former or present soldiers . . . the internal course of Russian state life is at present threatened by the unrelenting approach of a grave shock.[72]

In the winter of 1916–17 army morale also began to reveal disquieting symptoms. These were by no means general but they sufficed to cause alarm amongst politicians and commanders. The demoralization of the army had already begun before February 1917, Milkyukov wrote, citing the many letters he received from soldiers at the front.[73] Protopopov, last tsarist minister of interior (September 1916–February 1917) received 'horrifying' reports of the troops' morale at this time.[74] It could hardly be otherwise: at the end of 1916 there emerged the prospect of a third year's fighting, a third winter in the trenches. Moreover, as General Ruzsky on the susceptible northern front pointed out, the army must necessarily reflect 'the moods, ideas and aspirations' of the home front.[75] Other generals found that those reserves which reached the front at the end of the summer of 1916 'were from the point of view of morale far worse than all their predecessors', that their minds were 'poisoned by propaganda'. On the other hand, discipline is still said to have been 'excellent'.[76] It seems that only isolated cases of an actual refusal to obey orders occurred. One such case concerned a number of companies of the 223rd Odoevsky Regiment which in January 1917 dismantled their rifles and refused to leave their mud-huts. The corps must be transferred, the men said; the tsar had many regiments and this was the corps' second year in that sector. But in this instance discipline had undoubtedly been unfavourably influenced by 'poor unprepared reinforcements', composed in part of 'harmful elements'. One infantry company consisted of political exiles under sentence who had to be escorted to their positions by an armed guard of eighty men.[77]

In Petrograd, in the meantime, the strike movement, hunger, military defeat, governmental chaos, incipient industrial breakdown, administrative confusion – all combined to create a truly revolutionary situation. Pleas, warnings, threats assailed the tsar. 'Unrest grows; even the monarchist principle is beginning to totter . . .,' wrote Grand Duke Alexander Mihailovich. 'I repeat once more – it is impossible to rule the country without paying attention to the voice of the people, without meeting their needs. . . .' When Buchanan had his last audience with the tsar in January 1917 he warned him that he had come to 'the parting of the ways. . . . The one will lead you to victory and a glorious peace, the other to revolution and disaster. . . .' When Sir Henry Wilson was in Petrograd early in February 1917 he found it 'as certain as anything can be that the emperor and empress are riding for a fall. Everyone – officers, merchants, ladies – talk openly of the absolute necessity of doing away with them.' When General Krymov spoke to a meeting of Duma members he told them that the army would joyfully welcome 'the news of a *coup d'état*. . . . A revolution is imminent and we at the front feel it to be so. If you decide on such an extreme step, we will support you. Clearly there is no other way. . . .'[78] In the Duma itself the members of the Progressive Bloc remained hopelessly divided and inactive. The Octobrists and Kadets continued to recommend 'legal, parliamentary means' of struggle; this the Progressives rejected as 'condemned to failure'. They argued that 'the response to action on the part of the state must be action on the part of society'.[79] But what action? We do not know. Never were there more reluctant revolutionaries. Even Milyukov's thunderous denunciation of the government in November 1916 in the Duma had the limited purpose of securing a change in personnel and administration – not in the system of government.[80]

To all such talk the tsar remained impervious. Be Peter the Great, Ivan the Terrible, Tsar Paul, the tsarina exhorted her consort. 'Now don't you laugh, naughty one – but I long to see you so with all those men who try to govern you.'[81] In this spirit, apparently, the tsar turned down all pleas that he grant a constitution or even permit a ministry of confidence to take office. 'What you ask is impossible,' he reiterated to Grand Duke Paul Alexandrovitch in December 1916. 'The day of my coronation I took my oath to the absolute power. I must leave this oath intact to my son.'[82]

The only new feature of the winter of 1916–17 was the emergence of sundry plots and manoeuvres to seize the tsar and/or the tsarina, replace them on the throne by the Tsarevich Alexis and appoint as regent Grand Duke Michael Alexandrovitch, the tsar's brother.[83] But all that happened was the bizarre assassination of Rasputin. This caused great jubilation; strangers embraced each other in the street; candles were lit in the Cathedral of Our Lady of Kazan; the food queues amidst the snows and icy winds of Petrograd talked of nothing else.[84] But this was not even an *ersatz* revolution. It did nothing to break the deadlock between an increasingly bitter urban populace, an unyielding tsar and a petrified Duma.

In the end, a mass movement gave the *ancien régime* its death-blow. What the Duma most feared, now happened – the 'street' moved into action.

As so often in the past, the constitution of the Petrograd work-force was vital. The growth of war industry entailed a commensurate growth in the number of workers to almost 400,000. About two-thirds were men and one-third women. Their concentration proceeded apace. The bulk of the workers, 248,000, were employed in factories employing more than one thousand workers. No less than one-fifth of the total was employed in five mammoth plants each employing more than ten thousand workers.[85] Given the common experience of repression, the common endurance of the hardships of war, the common lack of food and fuel, it is easy to comprehend the homogeneous action of the Vyborg side – the industrial area of Petrograd.

The authorities were not unprepared. In January and February 1917, Protopopov reinforced the garrison of the capital with supposedly reliable troops and police. He also ordered the arrest of the Menshevik members of the war industries committee and, somewhat later, the members of the much depleted Bolshevik Petrograd committee.

The time when such measures could prove adequate was long past. Disorders began in a small way on 13 February, with rumours of demonstrations. Crowds of up to five hundred marched through the streets, broke shop windows, sang the *Marseillaise*, shouted 'Down with the war! Down with the police! Shoot the speculators!' Similar scenes were repeated on 14 February along the Nevsky Prospekt. Bolshevik influence was evident in some of the slogans.[86]

On 22 and 23 February hunger drove larger and larger crowds of striking workers on to the streets. But again the red flag was unfurled and some of the crowd made minor attacks on troops with bottles, hand grenades and revolvers.[87] Tsarism entered on its last steep slope. Most significant of all, the regime found it could no longer rely on troops, Cossacks and police. In the streets by the Nevsky Prospekt a Bolshevik workman and demonstrator saw the front ranks of the crowd, pressed forward by those behind, come closer and closer to a cordon of soldiers:

... the tips of the bayonets were touching the breasts of the first row of demonstrators. Behind could be heard the singing of revolutionary songs, in front there was confusion. Women, with tears in their eyes, were crying out to the soldiers, 'Comrades, take away your bayonets, join us!' The soldiers were moved. They threw swift glances at their own comrades. The next moment one bayonet is slowly raised, is slowly lifted above the shoulders of the approaching demonstrators. There is thunderous applause. The triumphant crowd greeted their brothers clothed in the grey cloaks of the soldiery. The soldiers mixed freely with the demonstrators.[88]

This did not, of course, happen everywhere at once. On 25 February the tsar ordered General Khabalov, commandant of the Petrograd military garrison, to suppress the demonstrations by force; and there was indeed shooting that day and on the morning of the 26th. But that night the reserve battalions of the Volynsky Regiment mutinied. In the morning of the 27th they killed their commanding officer and marched on to the streets. They made common cause with the demonstrators. '. . . I cannot fulfil the command to re-establish order in the capital,' Khabalov had to confess on the evening of the 27th. 'Most of the units one by one have betrayed their duty, refusing to fight the rioters.'[89] The mutiny spread with unbelievable rapidity. On 26 February there were a mere six hundred mutineers; three days later the whole Petrograd garrison of 170,000 was refusing to obey orders.[90]

On 26 February, when the mutinies first broke out, Rodzyanko wired the tsar: 'Anarchy in the capital, government paralysed . . . shooting in the streets . . . supplies of food and fuel completely disrupted . . . universal dissatisfaction growing . . . there must be no delay in forming a new government enjoying the confidence of the country. Any hesitation would mean death. I pray to God that in this hour no responsibility falls on the monarch.'[91] The tsar's reply was short – he prorogued the Duma.

What should the members do? They discussed the matter on 27 February. Do they obey? Or do they put themselves at the head of the popular movement? Petrograd, after all, had seen food-riots, strikes and demonstrations before. They had blown over. Would these be different? The Duma was left on its own, increasingly exposed. 'I do not want to revolt,' exclaimed Rodzyanko to all and sundry.

I am no rebel, I have made no revolution and do not intend to make one. . . . I am no revolutionary. I will not rise up against the supreme power. I do not want to. But there is no government any longer. Everything falls to me. . . . All the phones are ringing. Everybody asks me what to do. What shall I say? Shall I step aside? Wash my hands in innocence? Leave Russia without a government? After all, it is *Russia*! Have we not a duty to our country? What shall I do? Tell me, what?[92]

In the end, Rodzyanko, typically, sent a second telegram to the tsar: 'Situation worsening. Immediate steps are necessary, for tomorrow it will be too late. The last hour has come in which the fate of the country and the dynasty is being decided.'[93] The tsar was unimpressed. How often had people cried 'Wolf' before? 'That fat Rodzyanko has again sent me some nonsense to which I will not even reply,' he commented to Count Fredericks, minister of the court.[94]

The majority of Duma members eventually decided to disobey the tsar and not to disperse, but only to meet in an unofficial capacity. All deputies were ordered to remain at their posts. The pressure did not relax – a delegation to the Tauride Palace from 25,000 mutinous soldiers spoke of other possibilities, should the Duma refuse the power that was being thrust upon it.

This was precisely the situation that the Duma had all along sought to evade. Its leaders made one last attempt to foil the revolution. They tried to persuade Grand Duke Michael Alexandrovitch, bother of the tsar, to impose a military dictatorship in Petrograd, force the government to resign and demand of the tsar a responsible ministry. Michael did not act with sufficient alacrity. He wasted time in negotiating with the tsar – who refused to fall in with his brother's plans. 'The favourable moment was lost,' lamented Rodzyanko.[95] There remained no choice, were the Duma not to be eliminated entirely, but to attempt, in Milyukov's words, 'to direct into a peaceful channel the transfer of power which it had preferred to receive, not from below, but from above.'[96] Nothing remained for the Duma but 'to take power into its own hands and try to curb the growing anarchy . . .,' wrote Rodzyanko.[97]

At midnight on 27 February, the party leaders turned themselves into a provisional committee of the Duma. The next day, Milyukov declared to a group of soldiers that they must all be 'organized, united and subordinated to one authority' – the provisional committee. 'It is necessary to submit to it and to no other authority for dual authority is dangerous and threatens to split and divide our forces.'[98] Even so, it took the best part of three days before the provisional committee nominated a Provisional Government. Prince George Lvov became premier in a cabinet consisting mainly of Kadets and Octobrists. Its most important personalities were Milyukov (foreign affairs) and Guchkov (war). Kerensky, as minister of justice, represented the left wing of the old Duma. Many of these men and their colleagues were linked by common ties of masonry – e.g. Lvov, Kerensky, Tereshchenko and Nekrasov.[99]

The Provisional Government took as its first principles an immediate amnesty, freedom of speech, press and assembly, the abolition of all restrictions based on class, religion and nationality, the convocation of a freely elected constituent assembly, the creation of a people's militia to replace the police and a promise not to victimize the Petrograd troops. The abdication of the tsar marked a noteworthy break with the old regime. He yielded with no reluctance to the arguments of two emissaries of the provisional committee – Guchkov and Shulgin.

Now it was all over. That night, to quote the tsar's diary, the last of the Romanovs 'read a great deal about Julius Caesar' and slept 'long and deeply'.[100] Milyukov and Guchkov still hoped to save the dynasty by persuading Michael to take the vacant throne. He would rule as a constitutional monarch pending the convocation of a constituent assembly. But the grand duke refused.[101]

The first cabinet of the Provisional Government had no monopoly of power. From the outset it had to rule in concert with a very different body – a revived Petrograd Soviet.

Left-wingers in Petrograd in February 1917 were as surprised as anyone else by the suddenness of the overthrow. 'We were caught napping, like the foolish virgins of the Bible,' recalled Mstislavsky, a left-wing Socialist-Revolutionary (and later Bolshevik).[102] At a gathering of left-wingers at Kerensky's apartment on the night of 26 February the mood remained indecisive, if not pessimistic. Yurenev, a Bolshevik participant, still called for 'systematic propaganda . . . in preparation for better days'.[103] But the next morning it was clear that in 1917 spring had come earlier than expected; and in the afternoon of 27 February a group of some thirty to forty left-wingers, of all shades of opinion, came together to form a Temporary Executive Committee of the Soviet of Workers' Deputies. Through Kerensky's mediation with Rodzyanko they met in Room 12 of the Tauride Palace, the very building where the Duma also held its sessions.[104] An appeal was hastily drawn up and the populace of Petrograd called on to elect its deputies to the Soviet – one man for every one thousand workers per factory, one man for each factory with less than one thousand workers and one soldier for every company. When the Soviet held its first meeting on the evening of the 27th there were about 250 people present.[105]

From now on the Duma resounded louder than ever to the tramp of workmen's and soldiers' boots and of socialist and democratic intellectuals. At round-the-clock sessions there was no order, no agenda and no programme. Amongst the first acts of the Executive Committee was to organize companies of revolutionary soldiers should there be any hostility from troops outside the capital still loyal to the tsar; and in its famous Order No. 1 the Soviet established its authority over the soldiers of the capital. Committees were to be formed in all military units from company upwards, subordinated to the Soviet; the orders of the military commission of the Provisional Government might only be obeyed if they did not conflict with the orders of the Soviet; the elected committees must control all arms and not issue them to officers.

The Soviet also formed a contact commission 'to keep the Soviet informed regarding the intentions and acts of the government; to keep the latter, in turn, informed regarding the demands of the revolutionary people; to exert influence upon the government for the purpose of satisfying these demands; and to exercise constant control over its actions.'[106] No need existed to claim further power or to introduce any element of friction between the Soviet and the Provisional Government. On the contrary, both Socialist-Revolutionaries and Mensheviks, who dominated the Soviet, gave support to the government in so far as it accepted an immediate amnesty, freedom of press, speech, assembly, etc., and equality of rights for the army; abolished all restrictions based on nationality, class or religion; organized a citizen militia (to replace the police); made immediate preparations to summon a constituent assembly; rejected any victimization of the Petrograd garrison; and committed itself to hold democratic elections to organs of local self-government.[107] Milyukov made a last-ditch attempt to preserve the Romanov dynasty by installing Alexey as tsar and Michael as regent. The Soviet spokesmen refused to accept this item and declared that the Soviet would undertake to struggle for a democratic republic. Milyukov had to acquiesce. He was however 'pleasantly surprised' by the Soviet's position on the matter of power – 'he did not even think of concealing his gratification . . .,' noted Sukhanov, one of the Soviet negotiators, and the great diarist of 1917.[108]

These were still the halcyon days of the revolution. Not only did Russia have to contend with problems that far transcended the issues of civil liberties and a constituent assembly; not only had Lenin not yet shown his hand; there could in addition be no lasting harmony between a Soviet responsive to the war-weary masses and a government dedicated to the more efficient prosecution of the war. Milyukov might well be surprised at the moderation of the Soviet leaders. He would still have to reckon with the accumulated problems of tsarist misrule. Lenin saw this more clearly than any of his opponents (though the fear of the Duma at even a palace revolution was negative testimony to the same insight). Russia was 'seething', Lenin remarked on his return from exile. 'Millions and tens of millions of people, who had been politically dormant for ten years and politically crushed . . . *have awakened and taken eagerly* to politics.'[109] Who would dominate these millions? How would these millions move? This was the crucial question of the revolution from the outset.

Part 3

14 The Honeymoon of Revolution

The honeymoon of the revolution lasted for about a month. Five per cent of the garrison troops in Petrograd were given short leave to carry the glad tidings to the villages. In Petrograd itself the days were picturesque and full of colour. Every morning regiments on their way to the Duma to take a new oath of allegiance filled the streets with activity. Flags flew, bands played, revolutionary songs were intoned. Pedestrians cheered and blessed the men, waved handkerchiefs, lifted their hats, threw cigarettes. In a contagion of enthusiasm onlookers would fall in alongside the troops and join in the singing of the *Marseillaise*. Army trucks dashing up and down the streets, filled with armed soldiers, red flags tied to their bayonets, added further gaiety to the scene.[1]

The same spontaneity also showed itself in the formation of a multiplicity of bodies of all kinds. These were the embodiment of Lenin's 'seething' Russia. The thwarted urge to organize and associate, suddenly released, produced an overnight growth of political bodies, trade unions, cultural societies and cooperatives. The most important were soviets of workers, soldiers and peasants, works councils and factory committees. As in 1905 the soviets, dominated by Mensheviks and Socialist-Revolutionaries, were a spontaneous creation of workers, peasants and soldiers. They were, apart from the factory committees, the only mass representative institutions. They took the place that might otherwise have been taken by trade unions or political parties. For this reason the relationship between the soviets and the organs of state so rapidly became the key question of the whole revolution. The revolution spread throughout Russia with the soviets as its bearers and its defenders. They were its characteristic embodiment. The movement spread first to the large provincial towns, industrial centres and garrison towns, and thence to smaller centres of population down to village level. Everywhere the soviets had similar characteristics – the direct election of representatives with frequent re-elections to express changing opinions. There were many important variations in detail – the proportion of electors to representatives, for example, or whether soviets of workers and soldiers should meet jointly or separately. As in the case of the factory committees, the soviets also developed a rapid tendency to form territorial groupings.

In March the first provincial soviets met; at the end of March and beginning of April, the first All-Russian conference of soviets took place. This network of soviets covering the whole country has been most vividly termed 'the backbone of the revolution'.[2]

Dominating this network and at its centre stood the largest soviet of all – that of Petrograd, once the capital of tsarism, now the capital of revolution. The utmost confusion prevailed in the Tauride Palace, where the Duma also met and where the Provisional Government had its seat. The Executive Committee of the Soviet worked almost without interruption, stopping only for a few hours in the early morning, when life came to a standstill, even in the Tauride Palace. The large halls were transformed into shelters for lonely soldiers without barracks and a place of rest for the sentries. At a typical meeting in the early days the visitor would find cigarette ends scattered on the floor, men sitting in their caps and fur coats, a glimpse of a rifle and other military equipment, a flood of grey army greatcoats swamping civilians, no peasant representatives but many intellectuals. Deputies sat on chairs and benches, so densely packed that movement was difficult if not impossible. 'The assembly finally took on the appearance of a mass-meeting in a riding school,' wrote Sukhanov.[3] Until 3 March, the activities of the Executive Committee had a chaotic character; no records were kept of the decisions taken, the orders given, the appointments made. Volunteers alone staffed the Committee's technical apparatus.

Soldiers predominated in the Soviet, both in Petrograd and most other localities. Their grey army cloth obscured every other colour. The workers had only one delegate for every thousand, whereas every company of soldiers might have one or even two delegates. Amidst this confused representation and lack of organization the Soviet in its early days resembled nothing so much as a mass meeting of soldiers and workers in more or less permanent session. Gradually a certain amount of order was brought about. The Executive Committee retained its predominance but in the latter part of March and April it established a number of autonomous sections to deal with current business within a specified area of jurisdiction. It also set up a bureau of seven members to prepare all business for the plenary sessions and to conduct all current business subject to the confirmation of the Executive Committee.[4]

From the first the Petrograd Soviet was a political body of a type distinct from the other soviets. It was dominated by party-political intellectuals as specific party representatives, and these were in the main Mensheviks or Socialist-Revolutionaries. Both these parties had acquired a fame denied to the Bolsheviks. Formerly apolitical and non-political strata, now aroused to public activity, were drawn inevitably to the ranks of the Socialist-Revolutionaries whose ambiguous and unshapen character required little commitment beyond a general allegiance to the revolution and hostility to the bourgeoisie. Victor Chernov, leader of the Socialist-Revolutionaries, more than once described his followers as 'a herd'. A vote for Bolshevism, on the other hand, required far more of a commitment. The effect showed only too clearly in the derisory Bolshevik representation in the Soviet – forty out of a total of some 1,500–1,600 deputies.[5]

What was happening outside Petrograd? A survey of public opinion from twenty-seven provinces, from Archangel to the Crimea, from Kiev to Penza, broadly suggested the problems facing the government. First to be noticed was the capricious rate at which news of the February revolution travelled throughout the Empire; it reached Pskov, only three hundred versts from the capital, two weeks later than it reached Nikolayevsk, some eight thousand versts distant. In most provinces, it seems, the old authorities were smoothly displaced, especially in the towns. The clergy was most vocal in regretting the *ancien régime* and least active in proclaiming the new. The names of the tsar's ministers meant nothing to the people, whereas the names of Kerensky and Milyukov were everywhere known. But the new institutions made little impact – the government, at least in the early days, was not distinguished from the Duma. 'They did not know where the Duma ends and the government begins.' The Soviet enjoyed 'great popularity', although it was looked on as 'a rather anonymous and cloudy, amorphous force'. The peasants conceived the future in terms of a democratic republic. The ruler would be comparable to a village elder, elected for three years. 'If he were successful, he would stay; if not, he would get it in the neck.' What then of the projected constituent assembly? A 'confused impression' prevailed. 'It will be like the Duma only much larger – it will come from the whole people,' the peasants said.

In the majority of cases they do not think at all about the constituent assembly and cannot imagine it, in some places they have never heard of it, especially the peasant women. The peasants in general tell them nothing and the larger half of the agricultural population remains therefore quite uninformed of what is facing it . . .

Any informational effort would be confronted by peasant illiteracy.

The peasant only understands when he is talking himself and asking questions, but not when he hears what others are saying without directly turning to him – Ivan, Peter, Sidor. And it is necessary to make haste with these talks, otherwise it is already possible to hear a careful whisper: who do we vote for, the tsar or the students . . . ?

Five features distinguished the land situation, according to this survey: a shortage of land in the central provinces, the demand that all land be transferred to the working peasantry without compensation, isolated excesses and seizure (as a consequence of lack of information or acute shortage of land), hostility to private ownership and its continuance; lastly, the absence of any awareness by the peasants of the complexity of the land question or of the shortage of land for distribution within the limits of their canton. Disorders had already broken out, especially in Nizhegorod and Penza.

These were not the only disruptive characteristics of village life. There was a refusal to pay taxes, there was illegal distilling of spirits to consume the grain that the peasants were unwilling to sell at government prices, there was a complete cessation of legal activity. . . . Most ominous of all was the food question. The operation of the government's grain monopoly greatly reduced the supply of grain to the towns – the peasant had no incentive to sell his produce, given the inadequate supply of manufactured goods. The natural result was a shortage of food supplies and a rise in the cost of living, creating 'universal discontent'. The consuming, non-producing provinces, such as Vladimir, were worst hit. Incipient economic anarchy began to take the form of requisitioning, food searches, unilateral raising of prices by local food committees and an attempt to fix the prices of town-made products, e.g. nails and calico cloth. The prohibition on the export of grain from one government to another caused further distress. In Pavlovo, in Nizhegorod province, for example, which employed 20,000 workers in defence factories, there was no grain in May. It could be bought, but at a higher price than the fixed rate and only in a neighbouring province. The latter's governor prohibited its export. 'Outbursts of a riotous character take place,' the survey reported. Grain was sometimes bought in one province at one price, requisitioned, and then sold in another province at a higher price.

Peasant ignorance and illiteracy added to the government's difficulties. Again, the absence of the younger and more literate villagers was a disadvantage. The great thirst for information could not be slaked – and even if some attempt were made then it might easily cause further confusion. The peasants, for example, thought that printed matter could contain nothing but the truth; but the introduction of newspapers of conflicting views could hardly be reconciled with this naïveté.

As for the peasant attitudes to the war – this was left to the end of the survey. This had almost a symbolic meaning, the authors commented: the war had receded to 'a secondary level'. In the capital and large cities it remained the theme of disputes and resolutions. But in the countryside, the war was 'all but forgotten'. A significant transition in attitude was noted:

At the beginning of the (February) revolution the majority of the resolutions passed in the localities about the war, spoke of a war to final victory, later they gradually revealed a tendency to continue the war without annexationist aims, for a peace without annexations and indemnities, but it is impossible to avoid hearing such things as: 'We'll wait till autumn, then we'll see what happens, and then we'll go home.' These conversations make one think.[6]

The village, for the most part, was calm in the first few weeks that followed February. During the war the peasantry had taken advantage of the scarcity of labour to rent land on advantageous terms of tenure; by the spring of 1917 they were actually cultivating an area close to the limit of their resources. But what they still lacked of course was legal title to the land they cultivated. 'All revolutionary spirit seemed to be in the towns and in the army,' Breshkovskaya noted on her return from Siberian exile to European Russia. 'The peasants calmly gazed at their boundless fields thickly covered with wheat. At last the land was theirs. They quietly waited for the legal sanction.'[7] Peasant uncertainty of the true decay of governmental authority seems to have been one reason for this patience. The absence of the younger men in the army must also have helped. The relative prosperity of the countryside was another pacifying factor. The war undoubtedly bore heavily on the poor peasant. The number of peasant households without seed-corn and draught-animals increased in many areas of the country between 1910–12 and 1917.[8] To compensate for this, mobilization removed much of the surplus manpower from the countryside; unpaid prisoner-of-war labour was available in quantity; if Russia could not export agricultural produce on a pre-war scale, then this only signified that more remained at home for peasant consumption; the area devoted to vegetable and stock raising increased at the expense of cereal production – another index of peasant prosperity; the rise in the price of foodstuffs put additional cash into the peasants' hands (though the benefit of this must be qualified by the paucity of manufactured goods in the countryside). The peasants, despite significant exception, benefited from the war.[9]

This may or may not account in full for early peasant passivity. But of the fact of the matter there is no doubt. It seems that in March, throughout the whole country, no more than thirty-four districts were affected by peasant disorders. Moreover, these were small, isolated incidents – incendiarism, pillaging, the intimidation of day-labourers and the like.[10] Government policy gave no indication that anything more might be expected, or that the land question might become urgent. True, a statement of 19 March made much of the paramount need for land reform and foresaw its presence on the agenda of the constituent assembly. It also warned against any attempt to solve the land question by 'robbery and violence'. But it gave most stress to 'the collection of materials, the registration of land reserves, [the determination of] the distribution of landed property, and the conditions and forms of land utilisation. . . .' A land committee was envisaged in order to carry out this preparatory work.[11] In March, likewise, the policy of none of the political parties suggested that the land question would rapidly cease to be a matter of statistical inquiry but a matter of peasant revolution.

The workmen in the towns, no less than the peasants in the country-side, developed their own representative organs, specifically proletarian. This was the meaning of the factory committees or works councils.

These were swiftly and spontaneously formed in the earliest days of the February revolution, on the model of 1905. On 5 March the Petrograd Soviet ordered the resumption of work; at the same time it summoned the workers to form 'factory and shop committees for the control of factory and shop administration, for the proper organization of work . . .'[12] By the end of the month this factory-based movement had spread to almost every factory of any size throughout the empire.[13]

In these early days, little was heard of political demands, except perhaps for the arrest of the deposed tsar. The committees pressed far more vigorously for the eight-hour day and for official recognition by management of their representative status.[14] They achieved a major success on 10 March when an agreement was concluded between the Petrograd Soviet and the Petrograd Society of Manufacturers and Factory Owners. This legalized the eight-hour day in the capital, gave official status to the committees, and established arbitration boards between workers and management. The committees' principal function was to represent the workers in respect of working conditions, worker-management relations and wages; the arbitration boards concerned themselves with all misunderstandings that arose between the two sides of industry.[15] In Petrograd the eight-hour day had perforce to be accepted. In Moscow, the Donetz Basin and the Urals it provoked employer opposition.[16]

The newly recognized factory committees soon began to form themselves into groupings, particularly in Petrograd. At the first conference of such groupings, on 13 March, certain delegates demanded that workers' control over the activities of management be introduced. This far exceeded the powers of any factory committee as hitherto envisaged. At a similar conference in April, delegates reiterated this demand with somewhat stronger overtones. As a placatory gesture the government introduced a decree on 23 April which legalized the factory committees throughout the Empire. (This complemented the agreement made on 10 March between the Petrograd Soviet and the Petrograd manufacturers.) But this new agreement did not go significantly beyond its forerunner.[17]

The slogan 'workers' control' did not yet mean the expropriation of the factories. Rather, writes a former official of the ministry of Labour in the Provisional Government, it meant 'converting the workers' committees into an organ of authority in the mill, an organ of authority the scope of which, to be sure, remained diffused. . . .'[18] Until April Mensheviks and Socialist-Revolutionaries dominated the committees, it seems.[19] Thenceforward Bolshevik influence began to make its presence felt. In that month, for example, the workers at the trend-setting Putilov plant elected six Bolsheviks and seven non-party sympathizers to the committee of twenty-two members.[20]

This was an *avant-goût* of the future. The factory committees gave the Bolsheviks their entrée to the battlefield between capital and labour; here they acquired their first firm foothold in the struggle for power. Could it be otherwise, given the constant fall in the real value of wages, the ever-present shortage of food, the unimpeded disruption of life? Was this why the tsar had been overthrown?

An essentially weak government faced these accumulating problems in town and countryside. 'The old (governmental machine) had disappeared; the new was not yet established,' writes Kerensky.[21] The government enjoyed little confidence amongst the masses; and many of its members were largely unknown to the new Russia that had burst upon the political scene. Its most forceful ministers, Kerensky and Milyukov, were mutually antipathetic. An intimate has described its premier, Prince Lvov, as 'a religious and liberal Utopian, a mixture of Tolstoyan internationalism with Slavophil patriotism'.[22]

What is more, within a matter of two months this weak government had completed the bulk of its legislative programme.[23] It had introduced the eight-hour day (partially at least) and carried through a political amnesty; it had abolished capital punishment and exile, instituted trial by jury for all offences, put an end to all discrimination based on religious, class or national criteria, created an independent judiciary, introduced the full liberty of conscience, the press, worship and association, separated church and state, revised the military code so as to give civilian rights to the soldier, and introduced industrial arbitration and rural self-government. These measures closely corresponded to the aspirations of the immediate pre-war years. When Lenin returned from exile at the beginning of April he called Russia 'the freest country in the world', and justifiably so. The degree of freedom was not only remarkable by comparison with tsarist absolutism; it contrasted markedly with the fact that Russia was still at war.

Who will deny the achievements of such a government? Equally, who will deny that these achievements did not relate to the solution of a manifold host of problems mainly inherited from the tsarist regime – how to wage an increasingly unpopular war, how to supply food to the towns, how to satisfy the peasant thirst for land, how to avert embryonic industrial breakdown, how to divert anarcho-syndicalist strivings into an orderly channel. Barely had the government completed its programme – by the end of April, say – than it confronted its first major crisis. From then on it had its back to the wall. At this precise time Prince Lvov confessed that events had carried the government much further than it wished to go. He compared himself and his colleagues to 'corks borne along at the arbitrary wish of the revolutionary wave'. The revolution had overtaken and ruined their plans. If only Michael had had the courage to accept the throne, sighed Vladimir Nabokov! 'Then there would have been no disruption and anarchy.'[24]

Given this narrow basis of rule, why did the government not seek to remove that dangerous epithet 'provisional' from its title? Why, in other words, did it not press ahead with the convocation of a constituent assembly to which it was committed by the terms of its first pronouncement (3 March)? Almost a year passed before the assembly met. By then it had lost so much of its original impetus that the Bolsheviks easily put it to flight.

This delay was primarily the work of Kadet influences. From the first Milyukov concealed neither his aversion to allowing the soldiers to vote nor his efforts to evade any 'precise commitment' regarding the date of elections to the assembly.[25] Milyukov's attempt to preserve some sort of governmental continuity by appointing the Grand Duke Michael as regent for the tsarevitch Alexey likewise served the need to undercut the basis of the projected assembly.[26] Delegates at the March congress of the Kadet party even proposed that elections be postponed until the end of the war, in the interests of those Russians living in German-occupied territory and of Russian prisoners-or-war. Kadet policy as a whole was enuciated by Kokoshkin who did indeed greet the Assembly but dwelt on the obstacles to its swift convocation. Although he rejected the argument that it might have to be delayed till the conclusion of hostilities, he did assert that military operations could not but influence the timing of the elections, i.e. they would have to await a military lull and would certainly be 'absolutely impracticable' in two to three months. On the contrary, the burden of Kokoshkin's speech was the 'fairly prolonged period' that the preparation of an electoral law would require, the problems attendant on the military vote, the problems involved in the creation of organs able to compile electoral registers, the need for an interval to check the registers and a further interval for electoral activity. For all these reasons he could only envisage the end of the summer or early autumn as the earliest date for the elections. Nor could he agree that the need for the Constituent Assembly was so great as to allow of the omission of certain of these safeguards.[27] 'How was it possible to organize elections in a Russia, shaken from top to bottom by an upheaval,' rhetorically demanded Vladimir Nabokov, a Kadet jurist, 'in a Russia not yet having any democratic self-government, or a legally ordered local administrative apparatus? Or to have elections in the army. . . . ? Even if some sort of authority could be maintained up till the constituent assembly, then its convocation would undoubtedly be the beginning of anarchy.'[28]

'Immediate' preparations for the assembly moved therefore at a leisurely pace. On 30 March the government established a special council to which it appointed thirteen specialists in constitutional law, to draft an electoral law for the assembly. Political and public leaders from the main central and national-minority groups were also invited to participate in the drafting.[29] The membership of the council soon swelled to an unwieldy eighty, 'ill-adapted to rapid practical work', in the words of one member.[30] On 25 May, the members held their first meeting. This delay of almost three months since the constituent assembly had first been officially mooted followed from the 'conviction' of the first Provisional Government that the army would not be able to vote until the late-autumn lull in military operations.[31] There was therefore no need to hurry.

In the interim, what gave the Provisional Government such mass support as it enjoyed was the Petrograd Soviet. Despite the ill-defined nature of the Soviet Executive, despite its chaotic manner of working (at least in the early days), despite the ambiguous commitment it enjoyed on the part of some of its supporters – despite all this, the Soviet was popular power incarnate. The Soviet brought the general strike in Petrograd to an end; the Soviet, by virtue of its Order No. 1, controlled the Petrograd garrison; the Soviet led the struggle for the introduction of the eight-hour day. 'The Provisional Government has no real force at its disposal,' Guchkov, the minister for war, wrote to General Alexeyev, as early as 9 March, and its decrees are carried out only to the extent that is permitted by the Soviet of Workers' and Soldiers' Deputies which has in its hands the most important elements of real power, such as the army, the railways, the post and telegraphs. It is possible to say flatly that the Provisional Government exists only as long as is allowed by the Soviet of Workers' and Soldiers' Deputies. In particular, it is now possible to give only these orders which do not radically conflict with the orders of the above-named Soviet.[32]

During the war the Duma had watched with concern, but inactively, the gradual weakening of tsarist authority. It had failed to act, rightly or wrongly. Only mass action put an end to an increasingly intolerable situation. In a remarkable confession in May 1917 the right-wing Kadet, V. Maklakov, condemned himself and his colleagues for failing to fulfil the duty of 'saving Russia from a revolution from below by means of a palace revolution from above. . . . If posterity curses this revolution, then it will also curse those who did not understand the methods which could have forestalled it.'[33] History did not give the Maklakovs a second chance. But it did enable them to linger yet awhile on the stage in that it allotted to the Provisional Government the part of second fiddle in the system of dual power. The Petrograd Soviet came to the aid of the Provisional Government and shared the power that it held in abundance – but was reluctant to exercise. The Soviet gave an immeasurably broader base to the Provisional Government.

Why should the Mensheviks and Socialist-Revolutionaries in the Soviet come to aid the Kadets? They did so not without reservations and misgivings, and yet with some alacrity. Why should this have been so? There were many reasons. It was the line of least resistance; it accorded with the Menshevik view that in a bourgeois revolution the bourgeoisie must take the leading role; there was a lack of unity in the Soviet camp; the Soviet leaders had no experience of government, were needed to cope with the influx of the masses, and their best brains were still in exile; the Duma leaders, on the other hand, though they had certainly cut a sorry figure in relation to the tsar and Rasputin, were at least well organized and experienced at the lower levels of administration; there was a real sense of the burden of power – 'The leap from the remote Siberian village or the Genevan colony of exiles straight to the seats of government was like being transferred to a different planet,' wrote Chernov, the Socialist-Revolutionary. Furthermore, to cite the argument of Steklov, a Menshevik (and later Bolshevik) at the time when the agreement to support the Provisional Government was concluded, there could be no certainty of the success of the revolution; the democratic forces could only take power into their own hands in the event of the bankruptcy of moderate liberalism

Steklov also argued; then again, there was an instinctive aversion to power *tel quel* – the intellectual left looked on power as something unclean and to share power with a bourgeois administration would not only have departed from socialist tradition and teaching, but would also have raised the question of policy *vis-à-vis* the army and the war, to neither of which did any answer exist.[34] Abundant reasons assuredly explained the Soviet's restraint.

It would not be long before this restraint, that had so agreeably surprised Milyukov, would lead to such a degree of accommodation to the government's sympathy, as to inspire positive Soviet concessions, lest that sympathy be jeopardized.

An ill-matched couple thus took the place of tsarism in February–March 1917: on the one hand stood a Provisional Government born of a Duma elected on the highly limited franchise introduced in 1907. To a man the members of this government were revolutionaries *à contre-coeur*. By their side stood the Soviet, the reluctant recipient of a power thrust upon it, a power of which it strove to disembarrass itself with all possible speed. This could not be a stable relationship. From the outset a strange and complex tension enveloped the relationship of Soviet to Government. Neither could exist without the other; the Soviet had 'power without authority', the government 'authority without power', said premier Lvov.[35] It was also impossible for either party to rest content with the *status quo*, given the pressures to which each was subjected. Despite everything, the Soviet remained an acknowledged and respected mouthpiece for all the accumulated grievances and sufferings of the workmen and soldiers and peasants. The factory committees agitating for greater control over production, the soldiers disoriented, disaffected, engaged in an unpopular war, the peasants already stirring in the provinces, were beginning, in March and April, to make demands both on the Soviet and the government which far transcended the limits of the policies hitherto pursued by either. It was for this reason that the Bolsheviks would later make this uneasy, vulnerable and fluctuating relationship their main target. When Lenin arrived in Petrograd at the beginning of April the potentialities of this inherently unstable situation were exploited to the full. Lenin's appearance inaugurated a period of the most intense and unscrupulous political in-fighting. Lenin and Milyukov confronted each other, as 'serious representatives of the basic classes of society', writes Trotsky.[36] Both were leaders of minorities.

15 Lenin Arrives

On 25 March 1917, the Volynsky Regiment organized a concert at the Maryinsky theatre in aid of the victims of the revolution. Here, where Karsavina and Kshessinskaya had once danced, a most moving ceremony of homage was paid to some thirty heroes and heroines of the underground, now present in triumph: there was Vera Zasulich who had shot and wounded General Trepov in 1877; Lopatin, a friend of Marx and Engels, arrested in 1884, and sentenced to twenty years' imprisonment; Vera Figner, an accomplice in the assassination of Alexander II in 1881; Morozov of the underground *Narodnaya Volya*, Catherine Izmailovitch ... and a host of others. Vera Figner dominated the ceremony with a recital of the names of those who had endured tsarist prison, exile and execution. She was no longer the anarchist of her youth but a distinguished elderly lady: '... she comes from a good family, connected with the nobility,' Paléologue, that incorrigible snob, cannot forbear to add. Her mere recital of the victims' names made the audience weep.[1] Yet, for all their heroism, Vera Figner and her companions belonged to the past.

The future belonged to Lenin. Lenin was 'a great link' in the chain of objective historic forces, wrote Trotsky. 'The party could fulfil its mission only after understanding it. For that Lenin was needed.'[2] Curious links forged this alleged chain. Lenin's frantic desire to quit his war-time exile in Zurich for the scene of the upheaval coincided with the requirements of German political warfare.

The outbreak of the February revolution gave tremendous impetus to the German policy of weakening the Russian home front. Milyukov, the first foreign minister in the Provisional Government, did, it is true, emphasize from the first Russia's unchanged loyalty to the allied cause. Even so, to see tsarism overthrown could not but arouse confident German doubt in any future Russian war-effort. How could this success be best reinforced? The answer again came from Parvus. In the new favourable circumstances created by the February overturn, it seems to have been Parvus who took the initiative in suggesting that Lenin be enabled to return to Russia. The idea gained rapid adherents in the German foreign office, Reichstag and High Command. Parvus sought a revolution in Russia, whereas his collaborators sought a means of so weakening the new Russian regime as to force it to sign a separate peace. Even so, there was sufficient common ground between the two parties to justify common action. 'Germany must create in Russia as much chaos as possible,' wrote Brockdorff-Rantzau, the German ambassador in Copenhagen and confidant of Parvus, to the German foreign office. Overt intervention in the course of the revolution must be avoided. 'On the other hand, we should in my opinion do our utmost unobtrusively to deepen the conflicts between the moderate and the extreme parties,' Rantzau continued, 'for we have the greatest interest in the latter gaining the upper hand, because then an upheaval will be inevitable and take forms which must shatter the stability of the Russian empire.'[3]

Lenin was not of course privy to these dispatches but they would have been sweet music to his ears. He was as surprised as anyone else at the outbreak of the February revolution. No sooner had it taken place, however, than he was all agog to return, consumed with frustration in what Trotsky called his 'Zurich bird-cage'. His nostrils twitched with the scent of power. Thus it was that the famous sealed train left Zurich railway station at 3.10 on the afternoon of 27 March/9 April. It carried thirty-three passengers, of whom nineteen were Bolsheviks. It arrived at the Finland Station in Petrograd on the evening of 3/16 April after an uneventful journey. During the last stage, from the Finnish border to Petrograd, an English officer accompanied Lenin and his party.[4] In May and June more than four hundred other *émigrés*, likewise of all nuances of political opinion, returned to Russia under German auspices.[5]

To the British and pro-Allied forces in Russia, to Balfour and Milyukov for example, the indiscriminate return of political exiles was highly unwelcome.[6] Prince Lvov did not carry his 'Tolstoyan internationalism' *that* far: he found the German move 'extremely disturbing'.[7] A selective process operated; and suspect characters figured on Allied black lists. The criterion was based on the exile's attitude to the war. If he were favourable to its continuance, then he could count on British support for his return. Plekhanov, for example, the grand old man of Russian Marxism and Lenin's one-time mentor, but a Germanophobe defencist since 1914, was shipped back to Russia in a British armoured cruiser, accompanied by six pro-war French and British socialists.[8] Trotsky, on the other hand, a noted opponent of the war, was for a time detained by the British in Halifax on his return to Russia from New York. In Lenin's case there was 'a hectic moment' when the Allied ministers in Stockholm at first considered whether, with the aid of the Swedish authorities, they might not prevent Lenin from continuing his journey. But it was finally felt that this might worsen the situation. 'Indeed, so far had the revolution gone in Russia by that time,' wrote the British minister in Stockholm, 'that it appeared wiser to let things take their course rather than interfere in matters of which we were then practically ignorant.'[9] Buchanan and Paléologue had to content themselves with feeding material to the foreign ministry in Petrograd that could be used against Lenin in the press.[10]

This attention did not exaggerate Lenin's importance. At a meeting in March of the Provisional Government, when ministers were discussing Bolshevik agitation, Kerensky hysterically exclaimed: 'Just wait, Lenin himself is coming. Then the real thing will start.'[11] Events justified this fearsome anticipation. The 'real thing' did indeed start with Lenin's arrival at the Finland station in Petrograd.

Like Plekhanov a few days earlier, Lenin too had his thunderous welcome, a bouquet, a tumultuous crowd, an escort of supporters, a reception in the former imperial waiting room, embraces, and a speech of welcome from Chkheidz, Menshevik chairman of the Petrograd Soviet. With fine impartiality the same committee welcomed the pro-war Plekhanov and the anti-war Lenin.[12] There the similarity ended.

From the earliest days of the war Lenin had seen in it 'the eve of the socialist revolution'. The events of February 1917 gave substantial justification to this view. But they were only the first stage. Lenin's conviction of the need to intensify the revolution marked him off from the leaders of the Soviet, and even from the Bolsheviks inside Russia. The Bolsheviks had hitherto played little part in the shaping of events. Theoretically also, they had not yet elaborated a policy towards the Soviet and the Provisional Government. Certain isolated groups and personalities argued in favour of the Soviet declaring itself a provisional government; others condemned this as leading to the isolation of the Bolsheviks; yet others sought contact with the Mensheviks.[13] Not until Lenin returned to Russia were these ideological and tactical differences harmonized. It was a long process, never completely carried through.

Lenin brought with him a set of views that represented a synthesis between the influence of war-time developments on his thought and the situation of dual power that had arisen in Russia. He saw the possibility that Russia, although a peasant country and the most backward country in Europe, might yet undergo a revolution such as would act as prologue to a socialist world revolution. Second, Lenin made a decisive break with social-patriots, defencists and pacifists, both inside and outside Russia. This removed in advance any possibility of cooperation with Mensheviks and Socialist-Revolutionaries so long as they adhered to their policy of giving support, however circumscribed, to the Russian war effort; third, Lenin drew a line of continuity between the Paris Commune of 1871, the St Petersburg Soviet of 1905 and the existing Petrograd Soviet of Workers' and Soldiers' Deputies. This latter he called 'the germ cell of a workers' government'. He assigned to the soviets throughout Russia the task of organizing insurrection and of serving as organs of revolutionary state power. This insight delineated one of the main axes of advance towards the new Bolshevik policy that Lenin was in process of working out.

The Bolsheviks had requisitioned the villa of the prima ballerina Kshessinskaya, favourite of the ex-tsar. It stood by the Peter and Paul fortress. These sumptuous rooms, whence all movable furniture had been removed, became what Trotsky truly called 'the laboratory' of history. On the very evening of his arrival, Lenin spoke for two hours to an impromptu conference of Bolsheviks. 'I declare that no one had expected anything similar,' noted Sukhanov. 'It seemed as though all the elements had risen from their lair, and that the spirit of universal destruction, seeing neither hindrances nor doubts, neither human difficulties nor human calculations, was hovering above the heads of the enthralled disciples.'[14]

The next day, Lenin formally summarized his new position in the celebrated 'April Theses'. Their proclamation marked a landmark in the development of the February overturn. Lenin first denounced any support for the Russian war effort. Since the government remained capitalist, the war remained as 'predatory' as before. Furthermore, since war and capitalism were inseparably connected, the war could only be brought to an end through the overthrow of capitalism. This view must be propagated amongst the army, and fraternization encouraged. Second, Lenin argued that the present state of Russia was characterized by the transition from the first stage of the revolution to the second stage 'which must place power in the hands of the proletariat and the poorest sections of the peasantry'. This entailed the utmost hostility to the Provisional Government on the one hand, combined with work amongst the soviets, on the other – enlightening the masses to the fact that 'the soviets of workers' deputies represent the *only possible* form of revolutionary government'; and therefore, as long as that government lay under capitalist influence the task of the Bolsheviks could only be a systematic explanation to the masses of 'the errors of their tactics'.

'So long as we are in the minority we carry on the work of criticizing and exposing errors and at the same time we preach the necessity of transferring the entire state power to the soviets of workers' deputies. . . .' Such a government, Lenin continued, would represent a higher stage than a parliamentary republic.

In agrarian matters Lenin advocated the expropriation of all large landed estates, the nationalization of the whole land of the empire, with the right of land disposal to be transferred to local peasant soviets. He did not propose to introduce socialism as the main task 'but only to bring social production and the distribution of products at once under the *control* of the soviets of workers' deputies'. Lenin ended with a dual call to form a revolutionary International and to change the name of the party from 'social-democratic' to 'communist'.[15]

Why should Lenin advocate the transference of power to soviets dominated by his Menshevik and Socialist-Revolutionary opponents? Because, in Trotsky's words, such a transference would 'have opened before the Bolsheviks a complete opportunity to become a majority in the soviet' and no armed insurrection would be necessary.[16] Power would fall 'to determined revolutionary groups further to the left'.[17] It was this emphasis on the potentialities inherent in the transformation of the first stage of the revolution that brought Lenin close to the theory of permanent revolution. Partly for this reason also, Lenin's programme aroused consternation amongst the more staid of the Bolsheviks. Criticism centred on two points, argued most persuasively by Kamenev. Lenin's general scheme was 'unacceptable', he said, in so far as it assumed that the bourgeois revolution was completed and in so far as it counted on 'the immediate transformation of this revolution into a socialist revolution'; second, Kamenev and his supporters condemned Lenin's explicit tendency to isolate the Bolsheviks and cut them off from the other left-wing parties. Lenin's opponents wanted the Bolsheviks to remain 'the party of the revolutionary masses of the proletariat' and not become 'a group of communist propagandists', Kamenev declared.[18]

In those early April days, Lenin was all but isolated in the party. The Petrograd committee rejected the theses by thirteen votes to two (with one abstention). Lenin met the same defeat in Moscow. But at the All-Russian party conference at the end of April an overwhelming majority of the 151 delegates adopted resolutions that condemned the Provisional Government for its collaboration with counter-revolution and its participation in an imperialist war, and demanded 'the rapid transfer of all state power into the hands of the soviets of workers' and soldiers' deputies or of other organs directly expressing the will of the majority of the people'. The conference had disquiet only when it came to specifying the possibility of a transition to the socialist stage of the revolution.[19]

By the end of April, then, the Bolsheviks found themselves committed, under Lenin's tutelage and inspiration, to a war on the Provisional Government and its foreign policy, to capturing the soviets from the Mensheviks and Socialist-Revolutionaries as a means to seizing state power, to encouraging the peasants to take the land in an organized way, and to propagating the view that the war could only be terminated when state power in at least several of the belligerent countries had passed into the hands of the proletariat.

This was a highly dynamic policy that took full account of the restiveness amongst the army, the factory workers and the peasantry. Lenin and Trotsky invented none of this but they were fully alive to what the latter calls 'the yet chaotic voice of the awakening mass'. Lenin, Trotsky writes, saw how 'everything simmered and bubbled' beneath a superficial legality. 'Hatred towards the police, the district inspector, the police commissar, the registrars, the manufacturers, those who lived on their incomes, property-holders, towards the parasites, the white-handed, the reviler and the assailant, prepared the greatest revolutionary overturn in history.' Trotsky imagines Lenin exclaiming,

You fools, babblers, and idiots, do you believe that history is made in the salons, where high-born democrats fraternize with titled liberals, where miserable provincial advocates of yesterday very soon learn to kiss illustrious little hands? . . . History is made in the trenches where under the foolish pressure of war-madness the soldier thrusts his bayonet into the officer's body and escapes to his home village to set fire to the manor house. Doesn't this barbarity please you? Don't get excited, history answers you: just put up with it all. Those are merely the consequences of all that has gone before.[20]

This dynamic demagogic appeal and understanding contrasted most markedly with the demands of the situation as seen by Axelrod, a representative Menshevik:

The expropriation of large landholdings in favour of the peasant masses, the conclusion of a democratic peace and as a necessary presupposition both for the full and consistent realization of these demands and for the affirmation and consolidation of all the conquests of the revolution – ensuring the convocation of a constituent assembly.[21]

Such a programme could never set the Neva on fire – all the more so as the Mensheviks and Social-Revolutionaries, through their support of the Provisional Government and their later coalition with the Kadets, failed to bring about a democratic peace (or any other sort of peace for that matter), tried to stem the peasant movement and connived at the repeated postponement of the constituent assembly.

16 The First Crisis

How did the government deal with the problems it had inherited? It prolonged the war and trod in the tsar's footsteps. To continue tsarist foreign policy and combine it with an adventurous military offensive would, it was hoped, divert attention from the problems of the home front. In Chernov's words – 'The propertied classes regarded a military victory and its concomitant chauvinism as the only way to avoid aggravation of the social revolution.'[1]

Max Weber established the connexion between war and revolution in a remarkable article published on 23 April 1917. All that had hither-to happened in Russia was the 'elimination' of an incapable monarch, and not a revolution, Weber argued. The former ruling class remained dominant, thus condemning the socialists to the role of 'hangers-on', despicable but necessary, in so far as they gave to the masses the illusion of a really 'revolutionary' government. But in order to main-tain this precarious *status quo* it was necessary to maintain the army in being and to justify this by the prolongation of the war. This served the dual purpose of preventing the peasant masses from participating in any generalized land seizure and of enabling the regime to acquire some sort of stability. The generals, officials, landowners, therefore, '*in order to keep the peasants far from their homes*, unconditionally support the continuation of the war *for its own sake*, even if it is com-pletely hopeless.' 'The rulers need the war on account of their position of power,' Weber concluded.[2]

A leading Menshevik, Theodore Dan, explains how the war dominated the course of the revolution:

> The defence of the country whilst awaiting a general democratic peace made it necessary to keep a multi-million army in fighting con-dition and to take care to avoid anything that might disorganize this army. From this there then followed the consequence that the agrarian reform was postponed until the summoning of a constituent assembly, for a revolutionary expropriation of the land and the division of the estates would have inevitably entailed the desertion of millions of peasant soldiers from the front who wanted to be on the spot when the

land was divided. Only a carefully elaborated and well organized agrarian reform could prevent this disorderly flight from the front by giving to everyone the assurance that his rights would be preserved. The maintenance of the front further demanded an enormous manufacturing effort to ensure supplies of food, clothing, shoes, arms, etc. But industry as well as the railways was in a miserable condition at the end of the third year of the war. With all the radicalism of the first period of the revolution (eight-hour day, social insurance, etc.) efforts had to be made so that industry and transport would function without friction, that the flow of grain from the villages, at a standstill because of the beginning of depreciation of paper money, would be resumed, and that the state financial system, in the grip of a violent crisis, did not finally collapse. Lastly, efforts had to be made to avoid fresh upheavals, in particular to prevent a civil war which must disorganize the whole economic life of the empire and bring about the collapse of the front.

The continuation of the war, even if only for defensive purposes, was, in the last resort, the reason for the 'timidity' of the first phase of the revolution, its fear of violent social upheavals, its inclination to remove all crises by a compromise solution.[3]

Therefore, for right wingers it was natural to proclaim the need for all to rally round the Provisional Government and discard internal differences. 'Citizens,' proclaimed Rodzyanko, 'to work! Leave aside all disputes, the country is in danger!'[4] Guchkov sharply condemned the left-wing slogan – 'Peace on the front and war at home'. It was 'pernicious', he declared, and must be 'drowned by the imperative call of the great Russian nation, "war on the front, peace at home"'.[5] Simple patriotism coincided most happily with the requirements of social stability. The support of the Mensheviks for bourgeois leadership drew them along the same belligerent path (though not without reservations and only after passing through an initial internationalist phase). The only important division between the parties in the post-February situation was that between supporters and opponents of the war. This antithesis determined the issue – 'If the revolution did not finish the war, then the war would strangle the revolution,' said Sukhanov.[6]

In the first phase after February the personification of Russian beligerence was Paul Milyukov. To a natural pro-western orientation he happily added belief in the stabilizing power of war. When Vladimir Nabokov, a leading Kadet and head of chancellery in the Provisional Government, once argued that war-weariness was one of the causes of the February revolution, Milyukov in essence replied: 'Who knows, perhaps it is thanks to the war that everything still hangs together somehow, and without the war everything would collapse more quickly.'[7] Milyukov also expected that hardship and perennial crises inseparable from the war would so discredit the regime that there would take place 'a natural passage of confidence to the more moderate parties, in particular the Kadets'.[8]

This was a gamble – but a gamble that had to be taken. The only other choice was to allow greater play to the socio-economic ferment. But this was incompatible with the maintenance of the *status quo*, than which no aim stood higher in Kadet thinking.

In his first declaration on foreign affairs therefore, Milyukov stressed the Provisional Government's loyalty to 'the international obligations contracted by the fallen regime' and Russia's resolve 'to fight the common foe to the end. . . .'[9] In the most explicit terms possible, Milyukov assured Paléologue of 'every guarantee' that the new Russia would consider itself bound by the oath of the former tsar.[10] The Provisional Government thus committed itself to the secret treaties assuring Russia of Constantinople and the Straits, portions of Asiatic Turkey, spheres of expansion in China, and the freedom to determine at its own discretion Russia's western frontiers. On 6 March the government 'sacredly' affirmed the alliances binding Russia to the other powers and its commitment 'unswervingly (to) carry out the agreements entered into by the Allies'.[11] New Russia and the former tsar marched hand in hand.

On the strength of these assurances – sweet music to Allied ears – the Entente formally extended its recognition to the Provisional Government. This took place on 11/24 March. (The United States government had extended its recognition two days earlier.) Russia would fight 'till her last drop of blood', Milyukov proclaimed to the assembled Allied ambassadors. These words made the British military attaché, the percipient General Knox, wonder to himself: 'I have no doubt that Milyukov would, but can he answer for Russia?'[12]

In order to make good Milyukov's claim, the Allied governments exerted the most intense pressure on Russia. This needs no explanation. There was considerable anxiety in western circles at what Balfour, British foreign secretary, called 'a predominance in the soviets of extreme elements hostile to the war'.[13] The February revolution with all its eloquent implications for the prolongation of the Russian war effort, could hardly have taken place at a worse time for the Allies – what with the mutinies in the French army, the desperate British shipping position and the virtual Italian retirement from the struggle after the Caporetto disaster.

Allied pressure took the most varied forms. If it was in the German interest to transport Lenin to Russia and thereby implant a thorn in the side of the Soviet and Provisional Government, it was correspondingly in the Allied interest to attempt to remove that thorn or at least render it harmless. At one point, therefore, the British came close to taking a leaf from the German book and envisaged an attempt to bribe

Lenin. 'Anything could be done in Russia, Turkey or Greece by bribery,' ran a memorandum that Milner passed to Lloyd George in May 1917.[14] In the early part of the year, however, the Allied governments – and these included the United States – contented themselves with less unorthodox methods of diplomacy.

An early example was the pressure brought to bear on Alexeyev, the Russian chief-of-staff by Nivelle, commander-in-chief of the French northern and north-eastern armies. Over-riding Alexeyev's references to a state of 'disrupted' morale in all the Russian reserve units and to the poor supply of horses, Nivelle forcefully insisted on the Russian fulfilment of an undertaking entered into by the tsarist regime to open an offensive on the eastern front in 1917, that would coincide with the Anglo-French offensive in the west.[15]

Encouraging noises came from across the Channel and the Atlantic. Lloyd George sent to Prince Lvov a message welcoming Russia into the ranks of those nations 'which base their institutions upon responsible government'.[16] Greetings came in similar terms from the House of Commons and the French Chamber of Deputies. In Washington, Wilson's presidential war message of 20 March/2 April greeted 'the heartening things that have been happening within the last few weeks in Russia'. He spoke warmly of 'the great, generous Russian people (who) have been added in all their native majesty and might to the forces that are fighting for freedom in the world, for justice and for peace. Here is a fit partner for a League of Honor.'[17]

This 'partner' had however, to be kept in order. The future of Russia's military capacity gave no less alarm to Washington than to London and Paris. Alexander Onou, the Russian chargé d'affaires in Washington, reported to Milyukov on 16 April that the American government was 'alarmed at the freedom of action' enjoyed in Russia by opponents of the war and by rumours of a breakdown in discipline.[18] This alarm was translated into the most intense American financial pressure on the Provisional Government. Lansing, secretary of state, informed Francis, the US ambassador in Petrograd, that press reports of a Russian government

influenced by extreme Socialist parties that aim at a separate peace for which Germany yearns so intensely, are doing much damage to the Russian interests here; and if these communications do not cease they might prevent Russia from obtaining her share of the loan assigned to the Allies. As far as propriety allows, please widely inform the Russian leaders of this and insist that measures be taken in order to redress the unfortunate bad impression produced on the American people.

If the new Russian government were able to maintain order and carry on the war, Lansing continued, it would open vast possibilities for

Russia's post-war developments. A separate peace, on the other hand, 'would preclude the possibility of any kind of assistance on the part of America.'[19]

The Allied powers, in their attempt to influence Russian foreign policy, added ideological to financial, diplomatic and military pressure. This took the form of despatching to Russia French and British pro-war socialists who would stiffen the Russian war effort. Sir George Buchanan, it seems, initiated this programme, in his alarm at the possibility of growing anti-war feeling in Russia.[20] Britain sent two Labour Members of Parliament – Will Thorne and James O'Grady, and William Sanders, secretary of the Fabian Society. Arthur Henderson, minister of labour, also went. France sent three socialist deputies – Moutet, Lafont and Cachin.

The most impressive mission came from the United States. It was led by Elihu Root, a former secretary of state, and followed a suggestion made by Lansing. He called Wilson's attention to the fact that it was necessary to 'prevent the socialistic element in Russia from carrying out any plan which would destroy the efficiency of the Allied powers'.[21] The only result of Root's mission was a scheme for a $5 million campaign to provide the Russians with what Root called 'kindergarten material' and strengthen, if not create, a pro-allied public opinion in Russia.[22]

Patriotism, labour solidarity, the danger of peace talk, national unity, the need for final victory over German despotism – these were the themes of the innumerable harangues made by the visiting socialists to soviets at the front and in the rear, to the Executive Committee in Petrograd, to soldiers' meetings, to government ministers. It can all be summed up as an exercise in 'the moral preparation of the offensive' – a phrase used to General Alexeyev by Vandervelde, a social-patriot from Belgium who also visited Russia at this time.[23] But the experiment of left talking to left had little success. Even a Menshevik, such as Sukhanov, could identify the visiting western socialists as 'agents of Anglo-French capital and imperialism'.[24]

This hostile reception helps to explain the initial divergence of outlook between the soviets and the Provisional Government. In the first fortnight or so of the revolution, the latter could go its way unimpeded. The first attempted break with tsarist foreign policy did not come until mid-March and then it caused the first profound crack in the February regime. A voice different from that of Milyukov came to represent Russia to the world. It was the voice of the Soviet and on 14 March it issued a call to the peoples of the world 'to take into their own hands the decision of the question of war and peace'. To the workers of Germany and Austria the Soviet made a special appeal:

Throw off the yoke of your semi-autocratic rule, as the Russian people have shaken off the tsar's autocracy; refuse to serve as an instrument of conquest and violence in the hands of kings, landowners and bankers – and then by our united efforts, we will stop the horrible butchery which is disgracing humanity . . .

It went no further than this and coupled its appeal to the German workers with the proclaimed determination not 'to retreat before the bayonets of conquerors and not (to) allow itself to be crushed by foreign military force'.[25] Chkheidze, the Menshevik chairman of the Soviet, gave special emphasis to the fact that

in addressing the Germans we do not let the rifles out of our hands. And before speaking of peace we are suggesting that the Germans follow our example and overthrow Wilhelm. . . . If the Germans pay no attention to our appeal then we will fight for our freedom till the last drop of blood. We are making this proposal with guns in our hands. The slogan for the revolution is 'Down with Wilhelm'.[26]

This slogan and policy enjoyed the unanimous approval of the Soviet; also, apart from certain nuances of phraseology and a certain wavering, the support of those few Bolsheviks in Petrograd at this time, of Martov's group of Menshevik-Internationalists and the Unity group of Plekhanov.[27] Almost the only opposition came from Lenin, still in his Zurich 'bird's-cage'. The slogan – 'The Germans must overthrow Wilhelm' – he rejected as too narrow. 'Why not add: the English, the Italians, etc., must overthrow their kings; and the Russians their monarchists Lvov and Guchkov?' The Provisional Government's refusal to publish the secret treaties proved that the government was endeavouring to represent the war as defensive while in fact continuing to pursue the aggressive war aims of tsarism, Lenin argued. To such a war the Bolsheviks would be 'most resolutely opposed'.[28]

The Soviet followed its manifesto to the world with a denunciation of secret diplomacy and a precise demarcation of the difference between its own attitude to the war and that of the bourgeoisie. To the one hand there stood the Soviet: 'We do not aspire to conquer foreign lands. We want to guarantee liberty to the peoples and, first of all, liberty to the peoples inhabiting Russia. We shall fight, arms in hand, against everything that stands in the way of this liberty.' To the other hand there stood the bourgeoisie: in Russia it sought the Dardanelles, Constantinople, Galicia, Armenia and the recovery of liberated Poland; in Britain it aspired to seize the German colonies and Mesopotamia; in France it demanded Alsace-Lorraine, parts of Germany up to the Rhine, Syria, parts of Asia Minor; in Italy it demanded the Tyrol and the Trentino and territories in the Balkans.

'It is obvious that our attitude towards the war is quite different from that of the bourgeoisie,' the Soviet concluded.[29]

Indeed it was. The freedom that the Soviet enjoyed made it into the voice of all those war-weary elements in the belligerent countries in the spring of 1917 – the mutineers in the French army, the suppressed Slav minorities in Austria-Hungary, the newly-formed Independent Social-Democrats in Germany. For all the contradictions and ambiguities in its analysis, the Soviet's policy shone, almost, like a good deed in a naughty world.

The Soviet followed up its challenge to the Provisional Government's foreign policy by pressing the government to revise that policy and to renounce Russia's annexationist aims.[30] Milyukov fiercely resisted. But in the cabinet he was outnumbered. Kerensky thought the dispute between the Soviet and the government 'casuistical' and deplored 'endless discussions' which upset and irritated public morale. But he was quite willing to advise Milyukov 'to change entirely the language of all our diplomatic notes and declarations'.[31] The premier, Prince Lvov, also had a certain sympathy for the Soviet in that the latter's internationalism coincided with what Milyukov terms Lvov's 'idealistic Slavophile anticipations'.[32]

The Soviet eventually extracted from the Provisional Government a compromise document. It had three main points. 'The liberation of our country from the invading enemy constitute(s) the foremost and most urgent task of our fighters defending the nation's liberty.' The government next declared that the aim of free Russia 'was not domination over other nations, or seizure of their national possessions, or forcible occupation of foreign territories, but the establishment of a stable peace on the basis of the self-determination of peoples'. Lastly, the government re-affirmed its continued adherence to 'all obligations assumed towards our Allies'.[33] The negotiating parties had the document ready on 27 March; it was made public the following day.

Milyukov agreed to it, though very much *à contre coeur* – 'not in terms of a diplomatic note but in terms of a summons to citizens'. Moreover, he added, it was couched in such terms as 'did not exclude the possibility of his previous understanding of the tasks of foreign policy and did not demand from him any changes in the pursuit of this policy'.[34]

This was not an official diplomatic communication. It was designed for home consumption, and it did exert for a time a certain appeasing influence. But it by no means stilled the Soviet's agitation for a definition of war aims, and on 30 March the first All-Russian Conference of Soviets urged the government 'to enter into negotiations with its allies for the purpose of working out a general agreement along the lines indicated' (i.e. an agreement whereby the Allies would also join in the renunciation of annexations and indemnities). This resolution was adopted by the overwhelming majority of 325 to fifty-seven.[35]

Further dissension followed between the government and the Soviet. The Soviet insisted that the declaration of 27 March be turned into a diplomatic document. Milyukov understood only too well that such a move – tantamount to asking France, for example, to renounce its war aims – was impossible. Once again he had to compromise with the Soviet: he would send to Russia's Allies the declaration of the 27th but accompany it by a note.[36] This note, despatched on 18 April, precipitated the first crisis of the Provisional Government, forced Milyukov's resignation and led to a wholesale reshuffle of the government.

The ostensible reason for the communication of the document of the 27th, together with an accompanying note, was to deny rumours that Russia sought a separate peace. But the denial included in the note far exceeded this limited aim; it referred to 'a decisive victory', to the government's commitment to observe to the full Russia's obligations towards its Allies, and to those (post-war) 'guarantees and sanctions which are required to prevent new bloody encounters in the future'.[37]

This document was published on 20 April. It provoked in Petrograd an immediate storm of protest. The government hastily issued an expository note, reiterating Russia's absence of territorial ambitions and interpreting 'guarantees and sanctions' to signify the limitation of armaments, international tribunals, and the like. The Soviet accepted this explanation and did its utmost to calm the crowds. It urged citizens 'to let no one disturb the run of peaceable life in free Russia'; and it ordered soldiers not to appear on the streets armed, unless called out by the Executive Committee.[38]

But the damage was done. The note caused all the more inflammation in that 18 April (1 May in the west) was celebrated in Russia as May Day. For the first time in Russian history, the holiday could be *openly* celebrated. Petrograd, therefore, was all the more prone to react with violence. On 21 and 22 April the streets filled with demonstrators and counter-demonstrators, crowds, political gatherings, armed workers and soldiers. Clashes and spasmodic street fighting took place between the different groups. 'Down with Milyukov', 'Milyukov must go', were slogans borne by some of the demonstrating soldiers and workers.[39]

The Bolsheviks themselves took no part in initiating the demonstrations.[40] But they certainly spurred them on. The crowds, especially the soldiers, seem largely to have been motivated by a will for peace (though not a separate peace) and by hostility to a man who could only think in terms of a decisive victory'. Milyukov was the target rather than the Provisional Government.[41] No matter, the agitation *per se* was all grist to the Bolsheviks' mill. Their Central Committee seized the occasion to castigate a Provisional Government 'bound hand and foot to Anglo-French and Russian capital', intent on an annexationist policy despite all its peaceful protestations – a policy moreover, which the dominant soviet parties were powerless to influence. The petty-bourgeois masses must therefore vacillate between the capitalists and the workers. The only salvation lay in their decisive move over to the workers' cause in preparation for the moment when 'the revolutionary proletariat and the revolutionary soldiers, supported by the majority of the population, assume state power through the Soviet of Workers' and Soldiers' Deputies. . . .'[42] This theme of fluctuating class-alignments also dominated Lenin's hasty assessment of the situation. He saw the crisis precipitated by the swing of the masses 'away from the capitalists *toward the side* of the revolutionary workers'. The lesson for the party was clear: it must devote its whole strength to rallying support for the Soviets and advocating revolution as the sole means to end the war.[43]

Milyukov bore the brunt of the crowd's animus. It was not he alone who suffered; the position of the government also took a toss. In the words of Kerensky, the crisis revealed 'the contradiction between the composition of the government and the disposition of forces in the country. . . .'[44] This was certainly true. It may indeed be said perhaps that the April demonstrations marked not only a rift between the Soviet and the Provisional Government but also between the Soviet leaders and their followers. Into this rift the Bolsheviks could make their way.

17 The Government's Answer

The government's first reaction, in the face of the crisis over foreign policy, was to seek to broaden its base. A reference to the threat of 'civil war and anarchy' played its part in a bid for the cooperation of 'those active creative forces of the country' which had not previously taken part in the government.[1] Prince Lvov and Kerensky also made direct personal approaches to the Soviet.

Here opinions were divided. The threat of civil war, displayed by the government, evidently played its part. Not only did it not induce in the Soviet, according to Tseretelli, the Menshevik leader, the urge to pit itself 'against the government. On the contrary, it aroused a feeling of responsibility and the wish to put an end to the crisis whose development, as felt by all, might become fatal not only to the government but also to the destiny of the entire revolution.'[2] This by no means signified a willingness to allow representatives from the Soviet actually to serve in the government. Many of those sympathetic to the government's position yet shrank back from openly sharing power with the bourgeoisie. Any such cooperation would arouse hopes that could not be fulfilled, it was feared, and thus promote disillusion amongst supporters of the Soviet. The discussion, to some extent, cut across party lines, and there were others again, especially Socialist-Revolutionaries, who argued in favour of peasant representation. Only Kamenev, the Bolshevik spokesman, forthrightly denounced any support for the government. On the contrary, the Bolsheviks were 'directing all their efforts towards preparing the transition of all power into the hands of the soviets,' Kamenev declared. But his speech met with mockery.[3] The eventual vote gave extremely close figures. By a majority of twenty-three to twenty-two with eight absentions, the Executive Committee refused to allow its representatives to take part in forming a coalition government.

On 1 May, Guchkov, minister of war and navy and former Octobrist, unexpectedly resigned. Conditions in the army and the fleet made it impossible any longer for him conscientiously to fulfil his duties, 'conditions which I am powerless to alter and which threaten the defence, freedom and even the existence of Russia with fatal consequences.'[4] In the eyes of leading ministers – Lvov, Kerensky and Tereshchenko (finance) – this not only made it more imperative than ever to associate the Soviet with the government; it also offered an opportunity 'of putting an end to the anomaly of a dual government . . .'[5]

Simultaneously, Guchkov's resignation also put the Executive Committee of the Soviet into a new position in so far as it threatened a complete governmental breakdown. To the Soviet's moderate members at least, it was clear that 'a new rejection by the Executive Committee of a coalition could only lead to a collective withdrawal of the government and a sharpening of the crisis'. In these circumstances, 'all waverings must be abandoned and a decision taken in favour of a coalition.' This was true *par excellence* of the Mensheviks. In the last resort only the Bolsheviks, three Menshevik-Internationalists and four Left Socialist-Revolutionaries voted against the acceptance of the government's invitation. These mustered only nineteen whereas the majority totalled forty-four. There were two abstentions.[6]

The crisis was still far from resolution. The next four days were spent in virtually continuous negotiations between delegations from the Soviet and the government. The climax came in the night of 5 May:

Questions were not even discussed any more; everyone was simply speaking – or, to be precise, shouting – from his corner. Chernov, unkempt and furious, was attacking little Peshekhonov, squeezed into a corner. Gvozdev was uttering some final words in anger at the confusion of everything that was going on. . . . Even Tseretelli lost his balance, and in spite of my fiery appeals for calm, was shouting, it seems, at Chkheidze . . . when all of a sudden Kerensky rushed in and announced that a solution had been found.[7]

The solution entailed the removal of Milyukov from the cabinet and his replacement by Tereshchenko as foreign minister. Lvov remained premier, Kerensky became minister of army and navy, and five other socialists entered the cabinet. They included Chernov (Socialist-Revolutionary, agriculture), Skobelev and Tseretelli (Mensheviks, respectively labour, and posts and telegraphs), and 'little Peshekhonov' (Popular Socialist, food).

The Mensheviks supported, and the Bolsheviks opposed, the coalition. In Lenin's eyes the Socialist-Revolutionary and Menshevik leaders had committed 'a grave and fatal mistake'.[8] They had placed themselves beyond the pale of revolutionary Social Democracy. The two parties were moving ever further apart. The Mensheviks and the Socialist-Revolutionaries, alarmed by the spectre of civil war, misled by an erroneous analysis, fearful of exercising power in their own right, and the victims of patriotic propaganda, were now entering into a coalition with the Kadets, continuing to tread the same path that had led them in February to support the Provisional Government. Events would progressively reveal the error made in succumbing to the aristocratic embrace of the Kadets.

The Bolsheviks had as yet little power to make good their hostility. But they gained a strong ally in the person of Trotsky who arrived in Petrograd from New York, by way of Halifax, at the very time when the coalition was being formed. He entered the hall of the Soviet's deliberations on the day that the Executive Committee commended the coalition to the members of the Soviet. Chkheidze, the chairman, made no move to greet the distinguished revolutionary, returning after an absence of twelve years to the scene of his triumph of 1905. But the 'familiar penetrating eyes, the familiar wavy hair, and an unfamiliar little beard' were soon recognized. The hall resounded to the cries of 'Trotsky! We want comrade Trotsky!' Trotsky by no means pleased his audience, and positively infuriated the socialist ministers present. He spoke in cautious terms, yet he none the less condemned the coalition as 'a capture of the Soviet by the bourgeoisie'. The coalition was fruitless and mistaken, he maintained – although not a very serious mistake. Trotsky enunciated three revolutionary articles of faith: 'Do not trust the bourgeoisie; control the leaders; rely on your own force.' These remarks made an unfavourable impression. Trotsky left the hall to far less applause than had greeted his entrance.[9] None the less, his evident rapproachement with the Bolsheviks, his later accession to the party, together with that of a small group of his intellectual following (the Mezhrayontsi), gave powerful support to those forces opposed to the coalition policy.

The coalition government was finally formed on 5 May. It denoted a momentous step in Russia's political evolution in so far as it necessarily brought the government the support of the left-wing parties. 'Thanks to this, dual power has disappeared . . .,' Tereshchenko proudly claimed, '. . . the ministry is supported by Kadets, Popular-Socialists, SR's and Mensheviks. Only the Bolsheviks oppose the government . . .'[10]

It based its programme on the demand for peace 'in the preservation of full unity with the Allies, on the basis of the self-determination of peoples without annexations on either side, which excludes the realization of the plans of German imperialism', the re-organization of the army 'and preparedness to attack', the regulation of economic life 'on the model of the other belligerent states', the preparation of the organized transfer of land to the peasants, the creation of a local government system and a strong authority at the centre.[11]

In the crucial matter of foreign policy all this connoted no change. When the Soviet allowed its representatives to serve with bourgeois ministers in the cabinet, 'it accepted simultaneously the war and the power,' writes an intimate of Kerensky.[12] Tereshchenko, however, took more cognizance of public opinion than had Milyukov. Under Tereshchenko's direction, 'Allied diplomats knew that the "democratic" terminology of his despatches was a forced concession to the demands of the moment – and they looked on it patronizingly as long as they could reckon that they would gain in substance for concessions in form,' Milyukov wrote of his successor in office.[13]

Those Allied diplomats were right. Tereshchenko talked one language in public and another in private. He told the Russian press in May that he would 'apply every effort' to accelerate an agreement with the Allies on war aims.[14] But in May and again in July, he informed Russian envoys abroad that he had hitherto 'not approached any country through diplomatic channels with an invitation to take part in the conference' (on war aims). This was perfectly understandable in view of Russian military weakness and internal distruption. Any encounter with the Allies could only work out to Russia's disadvantage. In Tereshchenko's view the appropriate moment could not come until 'the present efforts of the Provisional Government to restore the situation at the front are crowned with success'.[15]

In the meantime, of course, Tereshchenko insisted that the secret treaties remain secret, and not subject to discussion or revision. Their publication would be tantamount to 'a rupture with the Allies', would lead to the 'isolation of Russia' and 'the beginning of a separate peace'.[16]

But Tereshchenko also had left-wing colleagues, Tseretelli, Chernov and Skobelev. How would they react to the contents of Russia's annexationist aims and tsarist commitments? Their possible reaction gave Buchanan some alarm. 'The new socialist ministers will naturally be apprised of the contents of Russia's secret agreements,' Buchanan wrote to the foreign office, 'and if the Russian soldiers are told that they must go on fighting till the objects of these agreements have been realized they will demand a separate peace.'[17]

Sir George need not have worried. Tseretelli, the Menshevik, fully concurred with Tereshchenko, the Kadet. Russia had no right to publish the agreements without the consent of the Allied powers, was his first argument. Second, Tseretelli asked the Soviet to consider how the publication would be used by the neighbouring countries.

Do you know what national chauvinism would arise (directed) against the Russian Provisional Government acting under our pressure . . . ? We would risk antagonizing the imperialist circles as well as the national masses, who would not understand what it is that we are demanding and what it is that their governments must do.[18]

For the same reason Tseretelli was also reluctant to press the Allied governments too hard even for any re-examination of the secret treaties – 'we could not leave out of account our international circumstances and the state of public opinion in the Allied countries.' Only a gradual approach could save Russia from the danger of 'a breach with the Allies and the inevitable consequence of this breach – a separate peace with Germany . . .'[19]

It was left to the Bolsheviks to publish the treaties, after the October coup. Until then Tereshchenko continued to direct Russian foreign policy, throughout all the subsequent coalition governments. Under his aegis the Provisional government *and* the Soviet fought for tsarist war-aims. This was a truth that only the Bolsheviks could reveal.

The failure of the Mensheviks and Socialist-Revolutionaries to enforce an alternative foreign policy, even on a government in which they themselves participated, was paralleled by their failure to secure any conference of international labour to discuss war aims. The two failures were of course interdependent.

The Soviet at first welcomed enthusiastically a Dutch–Danish–German proposal for a socialist conference at Stockholm. 'Not a single faction of the proletariat should refuse to participate in the general struggle for peace . . . ,' declared a Soviet appeal of 2 May to the socialists of all countries. 'A united stand by the proletariat international will be the first victory of the toilers over the imperialist international.'[20]

The growth of intimacy between the Soviet and the Provisional Government perceptibly limited this internationalism. At the first All-Russian Congress of Soviets in June, the resolution on the war straddled two positions, that could be reconciled only with difficulty. It called for an early end to the war but it rejected categorically a separate peace; it then reiterated the need for an international conference 'to make out definite peace terms and means to put them into force'; it called for a re-examination of war aims in conjunction with the Allies; but in its final clause the resolution declared that

until the war is brought to an end by the efforts of the international democracy, the Russian revolutionary democracy is obliged to keep its army in condition to take either the offensive or defensive. The destruction of the Russian front means defeat for the Russian revolution and a heavy blow to the cause of international democracy. The question whether to take the offensive should be decided from the purely military and strategic point of view.[21]

This marked a definite retreat from the universalism of the March appeal. Moreover, the attempt to talk of peace and war in the same breath made it easy for Lenin to seize the initiative and to attack the whole contradictory policy embodied in the resolution.[22]

The Allied powers put further difficulties in the way of the proposed congress. The American government refused passports to intending American socialist delegates; the French and Italian governments followed suit. In their different ways and, of course, for different reasons, both Lloyd George and Lenin also helped to kill the conference. After some early sympathy, prompted by Britain's desperate position in the spring of 1917 from which an international conference might provide some relief, Lloyd George executed a complete volte-face. He secured and publicized the opinion of the attorney-general condemning the illegality of intercourse with the enemy in time of war without government permission; the government would therefor refuse the necessary passports for intending delegates to Stockholm. Second, he forced Arthur Henderson, the foremost Labour supporter of Stockholm, out of the cabinet on this very issue. Lloyd George further undermined the pro-Stockholm forces in the Labour Party by publishing a dispatch that Tereshchenko had sent to Constantine Nabokov, the Russian envoy in London. This authorized Nabokov to inform the foreign office that 'although the Russian Government does not deem it possible to prevent Russian delegates from taking part in the Stockholm conference, they regard this conference as a party concern and its decision in no wise binding upon the liberty of action of the government'. By making this document available for publication Nabokov was 'proud' to contribute to averting what would otherwise have been the 'international catastrophe' of Stockholm.[23]

Lenin welcomed this defeat. He had always feared that an international socialist peace conference, combined with the growing sympathy for peace in governmental quarters, might produce what he called 'an imperialist peace'. This would pacify the masses at the cost of a few concessions and thus bring the war to an inglorious end – prematurely, before it had served its full revolutionary purpose.[24] He thus opposed any revival of the influence of the Second International.

The Stockholm failure discredited those socialist parties in Russia, primarily the Mensheviks, who had set the greatest store by an international socialist conference. It correspondingly enhanced the prestige of the Bolsheviks. From the start they had decried the possibility of any fruitful results emerging from the ruins of the Second International or even the Zimmerwald movement.[25] As for the soldiers, the last hope of peace that had sustained them while the conference was in preparation, produced further disillusion with the moderate Soviet parties and a corresponding swing in sympathy towards the Bolsheviks.[26] The tsar's oath to the Allies had already cost his own regime its life; that same oath was rapidly bringing its successor of February to the same pass. The preparation of an offensive at the front accelerated this process most powerfully.

18 The Revolution Gathers Strength

On the morrow of the February revolution certain Allied quarters were wont to assume that the free subjects of a democratic regime would fight for their new-won freedom more vigorously than the dragooned subjects of an autocrat. This argument, sometimes based on an analogy with the French revolutionary armies, overlooked a difference, so well put by Namier – in Russia, the revolution broke out in the third year of war; in France, the war broke out in the third year of revolution. It was precisely the French ambassador who needed to be reminded of this.

'Do not deceive yourself,' Paléologue was told in April by some highly-placed fellow guests at dinner one evening, 'despite all the fine phrases in official speeches, the war is dead. Only a miracle can bring it back to life.' The country would not accept a separate peace, they said, but it was 'totally uninterested' in the war. Nobody, except Milyukov, and then only because he was a historian, gave a thought to Constantinople, Saint-Sophia, the Golden Horn. As for the army, the garrisons in the rear were given over to indiscipline, idleness, vagabondage and desertion.[1]

Every account of military morale confirms this view. Those pre-February symptoms of disintegration rapidly multiplied a thousand-fold in the following few months. One spectacular phenomenon was a vast increase in the number of deserters. By October 1917 it had reached a total of more than two million. It is not possible to chart this movement in chronological detail but there is no doubt that the bulk of this self-demobilization took place between February and October.[2] The total number of registered deserters (as distinct from the far larger but unknown total of unregistered deserters) from the outbreak of war to February 1917, was 195,130 or 3,423 per fortnight. But from the beginning of the revolution to 15 May the total was 85,921 or 17,185 per fortnight. Thenceforward this figure did not fluctuate much either way, apart from a rise to 23,864 in the period 1 July–15 July, i.e. the period of the unsuccessful summer offensive.[3]

Those troops who did remain with their units were subject to progressive demoralization. 'The Army is sick,' declared a representative report on morale in mid-March. 'To establish normal relations between officers and men will require probably not less than two or three months. The spirit of the officers is now low, the troops are restless, and cases of desertion are numerous. The fighting capacity of the army has diminished, and one can hardly count on it for an advance.' According to General Selivachev, 'the sole preoccupation' of the soldiers was to receive additional grants of land – 'this is their chief desire.' Social composition was important here: infantry units were worst affected (i.e. the untrained peasant masses); slightly less so the cavalry; and the artillery least of all.[4] By April and May deterioration had made yet further progress. Soldiers interpreted the slogan, 'Peace without annexations and indemnities', to mean that there was no longer any reason why a man should sacrifice his life; a thirst for peace was all-pervasive; when reinforcements arrived at the front they refused to take their rifles – 'What for?' they asked, 'we are not going to fight'; mutual confidence between officers and men had all but disappeared; reinforcements refused to relieve front-line units; fraternization with the Germans was on the increase and German peace agitation widely heeded: the Bolshevik journal *Pravda* enjoyed a wide circulation; the Soviet was more highly regarded than the ministers and decrees of the Provisional Government.[5]

The Bolsheviks bent great efforts to intensifying this state of affairs, in particular by interposing elected committees between officers and men. They also published a journal, *Soldatskaya Pravda*, and broadsheets aimed specifically at the troops. This policy pursued the dual purpose of depriving the bourgeoisie of any military backing and of accelerating the coming of peace with all its revolutionary implications.[6] From Lenin's point of view, as advanced in the April Theses, the war could only be brought to an end by overthrowing the Provisional Government. So long therefore, as the war continued, so long as the army continued to obey the government and not rise up against it, a very powerful counter-action nullified Lenin's aspirations. This is to say nothing, of course, of the hopes that Lenin placed in any transmission of Russian pacifist defeatism to the other belligerent powers.

In propagating this doctrine Lenin had to tread most carefully. However demoralized the army might be, or the public, neither was yet ready to think in terms of a separate peace or to fall victim to anything that smacked of a German-inspired policy. Precisely how widespread this attitude was may be judged from a parade that passed along the Nevsky Prospekt on 17 April. It consisted of the armless, the legless, and the blinded, led by their nurses. 'The country is in danger', 'Without victory no liberty', 'Down with Lenin', their banners proclaimed. This pathetic cortege lasted about an hour.[7]

However, such manifestations did not mean that the army as a whole was not resistant to the spread of democratization, although disruptive of the normal canons of obedience. Committees abounded – by May the whole army was ' "committeefied" ' from top to bottom, noted Stankevich, a close observer of military conditions, '. . . it was necessary either to destroy the army or to destroy the committees. But in practice it was impossible to do either the one or the other.'[8]

The number of committees specifically under Bolshevik influence does not seem to have been so large. Even as late as the second half of June, a conference of Bolshevik military organizations brought together 107 delegates representing only 26,000 members.[9] But it is also true that the dynamism of the Bolshevik message to the soldiers could well canalize their undoubted war-weariness. On 15 June 1917, for example, the regimental committees of the 169th Infantry Division jointly discussed the home and foreign policy of the Provisional Government. They condemned it as 'harmful to revolutionary democratic Russia' and demanded the immediate convocation of army representatives (to be elected by equal and secret ballot) who would, in concert with the soviets of workers' and peasants' deputies, take power into their own hands. 'At the present time,' the resolution continued, 'given the existence of treaties concluded by the old government with the imperialistic governments of the Allies, an offensive by the revolutionary Russian army would be a betrayal of the slogans proclaimed by our revolutionary democracy.' At the same time, in view of the incomplete organization of the army and its inadequate democratization, an offensive could only entail the transfer of power into the hands of counter-revolutionary forces, 'therefore, at the present time there can be no offensive.'[10] Bolsheviks were acting in accordance with Trotsky's dictum – that 'the first task' of every insurrection is to bring the army over to its side.[11]

Unrest in the army was matched by the growth of the Bolshevik party and Bolshevik influence at home. In February the party had 20,000 members; in April nearly 80,000; at the end of July more than 200,000. It seems to have been strongest, in the spring and summer, in the provinces of Petrograd, the Urals, Moscow, the Donetz Basin and the oil centres of the Caucasus.[12] To be sure, the Bolsheviks were still comparatively weak in the peasant world; of more than 1,100 delegates to the first All-Russian Congress of Peasant Deputies in the first half of May, only 103 were Mensheviks and Bolsheviks combined; at the first All-Russian Congress of Soviets of Workers' and Soldiers' Deputies in June, 105 Bolsheviks confronted 533 Socialist-Revolutionaries and Mensheviks. The new Central Executive Committee elected by the congress contained only thirty-five Bolsheviks as against 104 Mensheviks and ninety-nine Socialist-Revolutionaries. In the trade unions the Bolsheviks were slightly better placed; here, at the third All-Russian Conference of trade unions, eighty Bolsheviks faced a combined total of 120 Mensheviks, Socialist-Revolutionaries and sympathizers. In the Executive Committee of the Central Council of trade unions the two Social-Democratic parties were almost equally balanced – five Mensheviks faced four Bolsheviks. The conference became an arena of clashing policies. To Menshevik spokesmen the revolution was still in its bourgeois stage, the proletariat was still weak and unprepared for power; in the meantime, therefore, it must continue to lean on the bourgeoisie. The Bolsheviks, by contrast, saw the imminence of the socialist revolution, denounced any talk of agreement with the bourgeoisie and advocated the most rigorous class struggle.[13]

The most fertile source of Bolshevik power in the spring and summer months lay in such relatively amorphous bodies as the factory committees. At the end of May the Bolsheviks made a true breakthrough at the first conference of Petrograd factory committees. 'At present there is no occasion to speak of unemployment,' the minister of labour, Skobelev, a Menshevik, confidently told the conference. He stressed the continuing presence of the bourgeois phase of the revolution, condemned the transfer of factories to the workers, and asserted that the control of industry could not be the concern of one class alone but must be that of the state. This was no way to calm the hungry workers of Petrograd, especially as the Bolsheviks were represented by three of their best orators, Lenin, Sverdlov and Zinoviev.

The main conference resolution, drafted by Lenin and Zinoviev and adopted by the overwhelming majority of 297 votes to twenty-one (with forty-four abstentions), urged 'genuine workers' control'. Confiscate profits, the resolution urged; introduce a two-thirds majority of workers' organizations into the conduct of factories and financial undertakings; admit workers to the inspection of all trading and bank books; give workers the right to regulate the production and distribution of goods. Politically, the Lenin–Sverdlov resolution demanded an immediate end to the war and the seizure of power by the soviets.[14]

This was not *per se* an important conference. But it had great significance as a symptom of the spreading tendency for local bodies to seize local power, or to be encouraged to do so. Soviets at Tsaritsyn, Ekaterinodar and Krasnoyarsk, for example, proclaimed their independence of the central government and assumed sole authority in their respective areas pending the convocation of the first Congress of Soviets or the constituent assembly.[15] The most famous such incident took place at the naval base and fortress of Kronstadt in the Gulf of Finland. 'The sole power in Kronstadt is the soviet of workers' and soldiers' deputies,' the sailors proclaimed on 13 May. Bolshevik influence was strong but not paramount.[16] The government never fully succeeded in bringing the Kronstadt situation under control and the sailors remained a centre of extremist action.

All such manifestations, whether Bolshevik-inspired or not, were grist to Lenin's mill and conformed excellently to the main theme of Bolshevik agitation – 'all power to the soviets'. Menshevik and Socialist-Revolutionary demagogy was limited to talk of defending a revolution that had so soon run out of steam, of preaching the necessity, if not the virtues of bourgeois rule, and of achieving peace by resuscitating a dead war. The Bolsheviks, on the other hand – especially Lenin and Trotsky – were fully alive to the need, either to reinforce mass discontent or to provoke it, by a policy of demonstrations. The Bolsheviks used continuous probing tactics, seeking to exploit every weakness in the policy of the majority parties. Inevitably, given the swift swelling of the Bolshevik ranks by newcomers to its discipline, the party became more and more difficult to control. Lenin had now to restrain his more hot-headed supporters, now to goad laggards into action.

In April, the Bolsheviks had taken part in demonstrations directed against Milyukov and his foreign policy, as a means, according to Lenin, of carrying out 'a peaceful reconnoitring of the enemy's forces; we did not want to give battle'.[17] The next Bolshevik move came in June. The party at first intended to exploit the hostility of the Petrograd garrison to the government's preparations for the imminent offensive and the delay in convoking the constituent assembly. On 9 June, party workers, aided by Kronstadt sailors, covered the city with posters calling on all workers and soldiers to demonstrate peaceably the following day against counter-revolution. The imperialist war and capitalists' profits were responsible for the workers' economic distress; millionaire bankers were prolonging the war in order to crush freedom. No effective steps had been taken to improve the food situation – 'On to the streets, comrades! Down with the Duma! Down with the ten capitalist ministers! All power to the soviets! BREAD, PEACE, FREEDOM!!' This was the message of the posters.[18]

That same day the Executive Committee of the Petrograd Soviet and the All-Russian Congress of Soviets banned all demonstrations for three days. The Bolsheviks had perforce to yield. Tseretelli defended the prohibition on the grounds that the proposed demonstration concealed a Bolshevik plot and would have provoked counter-revolution, with threat of bloodshed. 'By striking at anarchy, we will kill the counter-revolution,' he said.[19]

A week later the Bolsheviks had their revenge. The Soviet itself called for a peaceful demonstration as a token of the support it enjoyed. Tseretelli crowed in anticipation of his triumph. 'Now we shall all see whom the majority follow, you or us,' he boasted to Kamenev, the Bolshevik spokesman in the Soviet.[20]

And whom did the majority follow? Tseretelli's confidence was misplaced. Bolshevik slogans dominated the procession: 'All power to the Soviets', 'Down with the ten capitalist ministers', 'Peace for the hovals, war for the palaces'.[21] The day was a Bolshevik triumph. With this sweet music resounding in his ears Lenin left Petrograd on 29 June for a short holiday in Finland. He needed to recover from indisposition caused by overstrain.

Lenin could also take with him the thought that the Bolsheviks' projected demonstration had perceptibly thwarted Kadet hopes for the postponement of the constituent assembly.

The special council to draft an electoral law was already a political *place d'armes*. What, for example, should the voting age be? The Bolsheviks suggested eighteen, the main Soviet parties twenty and the Kadets twenty-one. The voting age was eventually fixed at twenty for the general population and eighteen for the army. Were deserters (of whom there were more than one million) entitled to vote? This was not a juridical crime, argued the Bolshevik delegates; it flowed from a political attitude towards the war. The council rejected this view. Were members of the Romanov dynasty entitled to vote? On what grounds could individuals be deprived of their electoral rights, argued the right-wing Kadet jurists on the council, such as Maklakov and Kokoshkin? Besides, was not a return to the monarchy theoretically possible? Only the constituent assembly itself would and could decide the future form of the state. The council, in the absence, it seems, of its left-wing members, accepted this view but the government stepped in and reversed this decision.[22]

When should elections to the assembly be held? This was the most contentious matter. Political considerations were again paramount. The announcement in June of the Bolshevik demonstration forced the cabinet into action. It met on 14 June and hastily appointed 17 September as election day, with the assembly actually to be convoked on 30 September. This, the cabinet hoped, would 'remove from Bolshevik agitation its sting . . . paralyse the action of its demogogic poison . . . distract the masses from sympathy for the Bolsheviks and avert the success of the street demonstration.'[23] Kokoshkin vainly endeavoured to push the electoral date forward to 1 December. There was insufficient interval between the formation of new organs of local self-government and the scheduled election, he argued. Shingarev and other Kadet ministers supported this line for a time. Nabokov suggested that the Kadets might boycott the election; to no avail.[24] The election would take place in September – at least, assuming there were no further politically-imposed delay.

The storm in the countryside burst in April. Statistics, necessarily incomplete, show an unmistakeable and sudden upsurge. In March the number of districts affected by peasant disorders had been thirty-four; in April it was 174; in May 236; in June 280; and in July 325.[25] Why should there be this quick change? Perhaps many factors combined. A government decree of 28 March that requisitioned all surplus grain reserves and established a grain monopoly at fixed prices seemed to presage, quite erroneously, a general confiscation of the land; fixed cereal prices aggravated the small peasant; there was famine in certain areas of Belorussia, the north-west Ukraine and the upper Volga; lastly, governmental authority in the countryside had almost disappeared. A Tambov report speaks eloquently of the difference between March and April:

The old people, invalids and women who remained in the village met the (February) overturn calmly and explained it as a consequence of the irrational government of the country by the tsar. It was possible to expect that the demand for a social overturn would not penetrate quickly into the countryside and would initially remain a demand of the army and the workers.

The report continues:

However, the replacement of local government, the destruction of the police, of all the usual authorities in the countryside, the amnesty for criminals, accelerated the process of revolution. The approaching revolution from outside the village did not find here any state institutions.[26]

Prince Volkonsky, from his estate in Borisoglebsk, noted that there was not a single arrest in the first three weeks of the revolution. Trouble only began in the second month, 'and gradually all restraints were broken.' All his complaints of the felling of trees, of the damage done to the fields by the peasants' cattle that Volkonsky made to the local zemstvo chairman had no effect – 'and when I saw him he said there were no means of counter-acting these acts.'[27] In quite a number of provinces, Bolshevik soldiers, either demobilized or deserters, were amongst the most active peasant leaders, e.g. in Kaluga, Mogilev, Smolensk and Yaroslav.[28]

As in previous agrarian upheavals stricken landowners appealed to the government. 'I implore you to save the life of my manager Zarin who has been arrested by the peasants despite the decree of the local committee,' wired Molostvova, a landowner in Kazan, to premier Lvov on 7 April. 'They are threatening him with trial although he has been declared innocent by the Spassk security committee. The position is serious, the peasants have sent away all agricultural workers, they do not allow sowing to take place and are also not sowing themselves.'[29] No troops or police answered Molostvova's call, for the first time in centuries. If they did come, they might make common cause with the peasants. In one district in Kazan, the militia not only refused to help the landowners but demanded of them that they comply with the requests of the peasant committees.[30]

Henceforward government agrarian policy followed a threefold path of coercion, conciliation and obstruction. On 8 April, Prince Lvov authorized provincial authorities to use troops to suppress any manifestations of disorder.[31] On 21 April, with its other arm, the government established the chief land committee to collect and process all the information required for the projected land reform. It also called into existence local land committees at provincial, district and cantonal level. Their principal duties were to collect information for the chief committee, to execute the decisions of the governmental authorities relating to agrarian matters and to settle 'disputes and misunderstandings' arising in these matters 'within the limits of existing statues and laws of the Provisional Government'.[32] Peasant committees, frequently inspired by Socialist-Revolutionaries, were already fast springing into existence with far more radical aims than those envisaged by the government. The soviet of peasant deputies of Kazan province, for example, demanded the expropriation of all privately owned lands, cattle, etc., and their distribution to peasant committees.[33]

The decree of 21 April can therefore be understood in part as an attempt to curb this radicalism by placing the peasant committees under the aegis of the government, and diverting their impetus into provisionally harmless, long-term research projects. How, for example, could a body of some sixty members, such as was the chief land committee, representing every nuance of political opinion – Socialist-Revolutionary, Popular Socialist, Bolshevik, Menshevik, Kadet, Progressive, Octobrist, Nationalist, to say nothing of the Peasant Cooperative Union, the Soviet, the Duma and sundry government departments – how could such a body ever attain a united outlook? Even a sympathizer had to describe it as 'very cumbersome and at times (it) seemed incapable of real work'.[34] In fact, in the crucial months of 1917 – between February and July – the full committee met only *twice*. Moreover, its chairman, the noted agricultural expert, Professor Postnikov, had no confidence in his colleagues – 'Get rid of them all,' he once exclaimed in an exasperated moment. He wanted intelligent and cultured people who had enjoyed economic and juridical training and higher education.[35]

The need to await the deliberations of the constituent assembly imposed a further obstacle to quick decision; likewise the need to undertake no steps of a nature likely to disturb the already shaken allegiance of the peasant armies. This was obliquely recognized in the preamble to the decree of 21 April: 'Let our valiant soldiers . . . be calm. Let them rest assured that no one in their native land will start to settle the land question in their absence and without their participation.'[36] Given the already existing state of disintegration in the army any officially sanctioned land partition could not but have led to further disintegration. Even illicit seizure of land had irresistible attractions. When rumours to this effect reached the army, 'soldiers from many parts of the front began to desert to their homes. There appeared a possibility of mass desertions.'[37] This illustrates the interdependence of the *status quo* at home and war abroad. In the short run, the prolongation of the war helped to take some of the heat off the home front; conversely, the longer the stability, however relative, of the home front, the more it became possible to maintain the army (and the war) in being.

No serious challenge came to this policy from the Socialist-Revolutionaries. In May the first All-Russian Congress of Peasant Soviets, dominated by this party, reiterated the conviction that the land would cease to be private property, without compensation. It also condemned 'lawless seizures'. The congress invited the peasantry 'to remain peaceful but to work with determination and steadfastness for the realization in a legal manner of the cherished thoughts and hopes of the agricultural labourer. . . .' But it was not clear how the demand of the congress for land nationalization could be reconciled with its demand that the land be handed over to local peasant committees.[38] The third congress of the Socialist-Revolutionaries reached no very different conclusion; neither did the first All-Russian Congress of Soviets of Workers' and Soldiers' Deputies.[39]

The sole dissentient voice came from the Bolsheviks. Lenin's April Theses had already demanded the immediate passage of the land into the hands of the peasantry organized in peasant soviets. Thenceforward, the party had striven to increase its influence in the countryside. But to no great avail. In May Lenin submitted a resolution to the Congress of Peasant Soviets calling for the transfer of all privately owned lands to the peasants, and the abolition of all private property in land; and he encouraged the peasantry to take over all the land immediately, in an organized manner, through their soviets of peasant deputies.[40] This resolution received a derisory number of votes. Lenin could console himself with the thought that the constituent assembly would yield a majority of peasants more radical than the Socialist-Revolutionary deputies to the congress.

19 Unquiet on the Eastern Front

In the spring of 1917 all was quiet on the eastern front – 'a virtual armistice' prevailed, Prince Lvov complained.[1] 'There was neither the crack of machine guns nor the exchange of artillery fire,' Kerensky noted on returning from Galicia. 'The trenches were deserted. All preparatory work for offensive operations had been abandoned. With their uniforms in ludicrous disorder, thousands of troops were devoting their time to interminable meetings.' Most of the officers were completely confused. The local Galician population looked on in surprise and amusement.[2]

This eastern quiescence was not fortuitous. It formed part of a German campaign expressly intended to encourage Russian defeatism, promote fraternization and thus subserve the aim of a separate Russo-German peace.[3] With the Bolsheviks inside Russia also actively fostering revolutionary defeatism and fraternization, the German campaign undoubtedly had considerable success. To such good effect that a separate peace, Tereshchenko said, might well have come about 'under the pressure of spontaneous forces by a simple cessation of all military action at the front. . . .'[4] Precisely for this reason, as early as 12 April, Kerensky openly expressed the hope that the Germans would attack – 'Once the fighting began, the army would pull itself together,' he predicted.[5] A month later, *Izvestiya*, official organ of the Soviet, took the argument a stage further and propounded the necessity of the possibility of a Russian offensive 'to stop the process of disintegration which is beginning in our army'.[6]

Once only was the truce broken. At the end of March the Germans attacked a Russian bridgehead over the River Stokhod. The attack succeeded and the surprisingly large number of prisoners testified to the low state of Russian morale, Ludendorff thought. But military success signified political failure for, according to Tseretelli, the German attack 'reinforced defencist moods'.[7] The Germans accordingly made as little as possible of their success.[8]

This German strategy made the Provisional Government choose either a separate peace or to reactivate the front; in Kerensky's words, Russia had either 'to accept the consequences of the virtual demobilization of the Russian army and capitulate to Germany, or to assume the initiative in military operations'.[9] The first meant an enormous aggravation of the already disrupted home front; the second, an offensive. Precisely the same circumstances that persuaded Lenin of the need to stimulate defeatism and fraternization, persuaded his opponents to resort to a revived belligerence. Kerensky justifiably claimed that no insistence by the Allies on a renewed Russian offensive would have been of avail had it not been for

the inner development of events in Russia. For no army can remain in indefinite idleness. An army may not always be in a position to fight, but the expectancy, at all times, of impending action constitutes the fundamental condition of its existence. To say to an army in the midst of war that under no circumstances would it be compelled to fight is tantamount to transforming the troops into a meaningless mob, useless, restless, irritable and therefore capable of all sorts of excesses. For this reason and to preserve the interior of the country from the grave wave of anarchy threatening from the front it was incumbent upon us . . . to make of it once more an army, i.e. to bring it back to the psychology of action, or of impending action.[10]

There were still some nine million men under arms – mainly of course the younger and more active men. The addition of these 'restless, irritable' men, many influenced by Bolshevik ideas and virtually all obsessed with the future agrarian order, to the increasingly disturbed home front makes sense of the government's policy to use the war as an instrument of stabilization – as it also makes sense of Lenin's attempt to use peace as an instrument of upheaval.

This assessment of the situation prevailed in military as much as in political circles. At Stavka the generals had hopes according to Denikin, that a successful offensive would encompass the defeat of the revolution altogether. 'In its passive condition, deprived of impulse and stimulating causes to military action, the Russian army would undoubtedly have quickly and completely disintegrated,' Denikin writes.

An offensive, however, accompanied by success, might raise and purify its morale, if not with an outburst of patriotism then with an intoxicating, overwhelming feeling of great victory. This feeling could destroy all international dogmas sown by the enemy on the receptive soil of the defeatist moods of the socialist parties. A victory would give external peace and some possibility of internal peace also. A defeat would open before the state a bottomless abyss. A risk was unavoidable and was justified by the end – the salvation of the country.[11]

Diplomats and revolutionaries, Mensheviks and Bolsheviks – all sang the same tune, some with hope, some with dismay. Listen to Buchanan: '... the sooner the fighting begins, the better it will be for the internal situation.' Listen to Root, his United States colleague: 'A victory at the front and the reinforcement of the position of the government – these are two sides of the one task.' Listen to the Menshevik, Tsereteli; he saw in a successful offensive 'the reinforcement of the democratic regime, the approach of peace and the collapse of all the hopes of the Bolsheviks for the conquest of power'. Lenin, the Bolshevik, expressed a negative evaluation but attached precisely the same significance to the offensive. 'The offensive will be a turning point in the whole policy of the Russian revolution,' Lenin told the first Congress of Soviets on 4 June, 'that is, it will be a transition from waiting, from paving the way for peace by means of a revolutionary uprising from below, to the resumption of the war.'[12]

Only Lenin and the Bolsheviks could explain to the troops that they were being used in a stabilizing endeavour. In the pages of *Pravda* Lenin expounded his case against the generals and Kerensky, and in favour of the 'virtual truce'. He protested against further killing and maiming; he argued that fraternization on one front could not but lead to fraternization on all fronts; he argued that to force an offensive on Germany would be to hold back the incipient revolution in Germany. 'The Russian people have two programmes to choose from,' Lenin concluded.

One is the programme of the capitalists, adopted by the Chernovs and the Tseretellis. This is the programme of the offensive ... dragging out the carnage.

The other programme is that of the world's revolutionary workers, advocated in Russia by our party. This programme says: stimulate fraternization ... ; thereby hastening the proletarian revolution in all countries ... ; hasten thereby the conclusion of a really just, really universal peace, in the interests of the working people, and not in the interests of the capitalists.[13]

In the meantime, about the middle of May, envoys of the Provisional Government had already been taking the first step towards activating the south-western and Rumanian fronts and counter-acting Bolshevik influence.[14]

Kerensky, for his part, undertook a vast public-relations tour of the fronts, in order to raise the morale of the men and galvanize them into an offensive. This 'little Joan of Arc', as he was known to some of the generals, now had his finest hour. Kerensky's visit to the front was the Soviet's last throw, said his colleague Tereshchenko.[15] Kerensky's oratory rose to appropriate heights; patriotic clichés burst from his lips:

Warriors! officers, soldiers and sailors . . . the hard but glorious duty of defending revolutionary Russia. . . . Not a single drop of blood will be shed in a wrong cause. . . . Free sons of Russia, you will move forward, in ranks. . . . On the points of your bayonets you will bring peace right, truth and justice . . . your duty is hard . . . your names will be sacred . . . the enemy threatens . . . liberty has increased out might . . . Russia gives you its blessing . . . red banners of the revolution . . .[16]

All this was for public consumption. Privately, Kerensky spoke a very different language and after a first failure on the South-Western Front confessed to General Brusilov that he had no belief in the success of the offensive.[17]

The officers also tried to do their bit in this vast public-relations enterprise. But they were ill-equipped for the task. Besides, the soldiers had an irrefutable answer when asked to participate in a defensive attack. 'The enemy here is fine and has told us that he will not attack, if we do not attack,' they said to Brusilov. 'What we want is to return home and enjoy freedom and land. Why should we go on being wounded?'[18]

In the rear, both the Soviet and the right wing made encouraging noises. The phraseology was inevitably different. The Soviet gave its blessing in revolutionary terms – 'To you, who are shedding your blood on the field of battle in the cause of the revolution and universal peace. . . . Our thoughts are with you, sons of the revolutionary army.' The right wing spoke of 'giving a helping hand to our allies . . . the solemn oath to do one's duty and to die for free Russia'.[19] But it came to the same thing in the end.

The offensive began on 18 June, and demonstrators marched in unison along the Nevsky Prospekt. They carried portraits of Kerensky and sang patriotic airs. But what was happening at the front? Were the troops singing patriotic airs?

Most decidedly not. The sons of the revolutionary army showed great reluctance to advance. Perhaps they had shed enough blood already. The Russian troops were at this time superior in numbers, guns and aeroplanes to the enemy.[20] Even so, they only managed to achieve short-lived local success. Some divisions were 'in a state bordering on mutiny'. Some regiments showed only 'perfunctory obedience'. To the very last moment 'the officers did not know whether the soldiers would follow them in the attack'.[21]

To a German counter-attack on the south-western front the Russian response was retreat, desertion and disintegration. Orders went unheeded. The men abandoned their posts at the first shot of the enemy. In some instances units deserted in a body and flocked to the rear 'with or without guns, able-bodied, bold, shameless and fearless of consequences'.[22] It was the same story on the northern, western and Rumanian fronts.[23] The Russian army had been 'irretrievably ruined' as a fighting organization, concluded General Knox, the British military attaché.[24] The government's 'last throw', the offensive that would either stabilize or destroy the post-February situation, had failed. The consequences soon made themselves felt in the rear.

July was perhaps the cruellest month. The failure of the June offensive led to no talk of peace. No member of the Soviet's Central Executive Committee at its plenary meeting on 19 July even raised the topic. 'They had *forgotten* peace for more important matters,' lamented Sukhanov.[1] Yet peace, no less than all the other demands of internal policy, could not be for ever denied; and in the summer of 1917 they came home to the government and the Soviet in a more violent and exasperated form than ever before.

The month began with a sudden crisis similar to that which had precipitated the projected Bolshevik demonstration at the beginning of June.[2] Certain regiments in the capital were once again preparing to launch armed street demonstrations against the government. Some encouragement came from the Bolshevik military committee in Kshessinskaya's villa.[3] 'In July we made enough mistakes,' said Lenin.[4] Did one Bolshevik hand know what the other was doing? Sukhanov wondered.[5]

From the evening of 3 July, and until the morning of the 5th, armed soldiers, later joined by sailors from Kronstadt and delegations of factory workers from all the major plants, streamed into the central areas of Petrograd. They aimed at the Tauride Palace, seat of the Soviet Executive Committee. They ignored the Mariinsky Palace where the government had its seat. This was natural – the whole intent of the demonstrators, and some of their Bolshevik mentors, was to force the Soviet to take power – a demand all the more vociferous in that the Kadets had resigned from the government on the eve of the demonstration. 'It is probable,' Trotsky admitted, 'that certain purely military actions during the July days were taken on the initiative of certain comrades who were sincerely of the opinion that their standpoint did not deviate from Lenin's assessment of the situation.'[6]

And what was Lenin's assessment of the situation? He had none; he was still in Finland, recovering from overstrain. He knew nothing of happenings in Petrograd until 6 a.m. on 4 July when Savelov, an emissary of the Central Committee, hotfoot from Petrograd, woke him up. Savelov's suggestion that 'serious events' might be afoot, Lenin rejected as 'absolutely untimely'. His first reaction on the train back to the capital was that the movement must be quelled and perhaps brought to an immediate halt. In the press he read of the attacks on the Bolsheviks and feared that these might presage an open counter-revolution capable of inflicting temporary harm on the party. In Petrograd, therefore, when Lenin spoke from Kshessinskaya's balcony to some 20,000 Bolshevik-minded Kronstadt sailors his tone was distinctly muted. In effect he did no more than say that 'our slogan, "all power to the soviets" must win and would win despite all the zig-zags on the path of history'.[7]

The Bolshevik Central Committee, meanwhile, tried to prevent the demonstration, and then, when this proved impossible, to give it as peaceful and as organized a character as possible.[8] It was felt that the Petrograd vanguard had run far ahead of the movement as a whole.[9] This is not the whole story. The fact is that the excited mood of the sailors caught the Bolshevik leadership unprepared. Something was indeed being planned but not for execution at the beginning of July. Bolshevik policy, it seems, was to hold fire and wait until the failure of the offensive had thoroughly discredited the ruling parties. 'It was clear to the Central Committee,' said Stalin, its spokesman,

that the bourgeoisie as well as the Black Hundreds would have liked to provoke us into action in order to have the possibility of saddling us with responsibility for the recklessness and the offensive. We had decided to await the offensive at the front and to let the offensive finally compromise itself in the eyes of the masses, not to succumb to provocation and, so long as the offensive lasted, in no circumstances to move into action, to wait and to give the Provisional Government time to exhaust itself.[10]

These Bolshevik aspirations were of course anathema to the majority parties in the Soviet. In response to Zinoviev's urging that the Soviet take power, Tseretelli once again referred to the danger of civil war. The authority of the Provisional Government outside Petrograd was much greater than was usually thought inside the capital, he also argued.[11] The Soviet went further and denounced all those soldiers and workers who refused to disperse as 'traitors and enemies of the revolution'.[12] In the end, deprived of any sort of support, the demonstrators dispersed to their barracks and homes, after some three days of confused and aimless activity.

This anti-climax to the July Days did not mean that they were inconclusive. On the contrary, they made a definite contribution to the history of 1917. The Bolsheviks learned, in Trotsky's view – and here he quotes the appreciation of his fellow-historian and arch-enemy, Milyukov – 'with what elements they had to deal, how to organize these elements and finally what resistance could be put up by the government, the soviet and the military units. . . .'[13] July was in some measure a rehearsal for October.

In the short term, however, the July Days had the most catastrophic effect on the party's fortunes. In the night of 4–5 July the Government published documents, partly forged and partly intercepted from the channels linking Parvus and the Bolsheviks. These purported to show that Lenin was a German agent 'commissioned to use every means in his power to undermine the confidence of the Russian people in the Provisional Government' and to agitate for the speediest possible conclusion of a separate peace with Germany.[14] This material enabled the government to withdraw from their passive or active support of the July demonstration those regiments that had hitherto been sympathetic or neutral to the Bolsheviks. Government emissaries raided and closed down *Pravda*, the Bolshevik journal, ransacked the party's headquarters in Kshessinskaya's villa, forced Lenin and other party leaders into hiding and thrust the party itself into a semi-legal limbo. Anti-Bolshevik sentiment spread throughout wide areas of the country.[15]

Buchanan lamented, in concert with Tereshchenko, that the government was 'too weak' in its campaign against the Bolsheviks.[16] Why did it not go further? Because repressive measures for political crimes, as even Tseretelli had to admit, were too closely identified with 'the arbitrary violence of autocratic power'. But political motives were also at work. The Soviet had moved so close to right-wing forces that it could not at the same time entirely disavow the left wing, lest it lose all authority and credit. It had to balance concessions to the one by concessions to the other.[17]

Even so, the new cabinet that emerged from the prolonged crisis of July connoted a swing to the right. True, eleven socialists confronted seven non-socialists. But Milyukov was well justified in asserting that '. . . the real preponderance in the cabinet unconditionally belonged to the adherents of bourgeois democracy.' This 'first step' in emancipating Kerensky from the soviets would lead to further desirable changes in the cabinet, Milyukov hoped.[18]

The new coalition cabinet assumed powers to suppress publications advocating disobedience to military orders or containing appeals to violence; it prohibited all processions and street meetings in Petrograd; it condemned all attempts by the peasantry to seize the land; it called on all elective organs of urban and rural administration to assist government commissars in the execution of their duties; it acquired the right to close all meetings constituting a danger to the security of the state or to the war effort; it instituted measures for administrative arrest and deportation; and it threatened to punish with hard labour 'a person guilty of an act of violence designed to change the existing state structure in Russia, or to sever from Russia any of its parts, or to remove organs of the supreme power in the state or to deprive them of the possibility of exercising such power . . .'[19]

The Kadets joined the cabinet in the enjoyment of a veto on all legislation by virtue of the conditions they imposed; the government must limit itself to safeguarding the conquests of the revolution and not undertake measures that might lead to civil strife: 'therefore the carrying out of all basic social reforms and the determination of all questions relating to the form of government are to be left absolutely to the constituent assembly.'[20]

And what of the constituent assembly itself? This too the Kadets succeeded in postponing, by their insistence that the requisite elections be conducted

in the observance of all guarantees indispensable to the expression of a genuine national will, with the assignment of supervision for the conduct of the elections to correctly elected organs of local self-government and institutions formed with their participation, and with the guarantee of freedom of pre-electoral campaigning.[21]

In effect, the Kadets were demanding the postponement of the elections, for such conditions could not possibly obtain in the Russia of 1917. Their demand was, however, granted as part of the price that the soviet parties had to pay if the Kadets were to share power with them in a new coalition.[22] The new electoral date now became 12 November with the opening of the assembly fixed for 28 November. Milyukov, making great play with the difficulty in the timely preparation of electoral rolls, hailed this postponement as a rectification of 'the political sin' of the first coalition.[23] But of course, between September and November, the Bolshevik *coup* took place.

The Kadet sense of self-preservation dictated their obstructionist policy. The peasants in their millions would clearly determine the outcome of the election. Milyukov denied that they would necessarily vote Socialist-Revolutionary although he had an overwhelming fear that the influence of local peasant soviets would incline them to do so. What more natural than that the Kadets should drag their feet? They would thus gain time, at least to try to make their own party as well known to Ivan, Peter and Sidor as were the other parties.[24] Moreover, the longer the delay, the greater the hope that a turn in political evolution might render nugatory the whole idea of a constituent assembly. In July, there was already talk in Kadet circles of a strong man, able to erect a 'bourgeois military dictatorship'.[25]

Kadet stalling tactics, for all their Micawberish air, had a politico-realistic basis for there was no relationship between Kadet influence in the government and Kadet influence in the countryside. But the effect of the tactics was to leave the government increasingly deprived of support in the country. This was all the more dangerous in that its problems continuously multiplied. Moreover, the Soviet's regular submission to the government further alienated much Menshevik and Socialist-Revolutionary support.

This danger did not immediately reveal itself, for the government's anti-Bolshevik campaign all but emasculated the party. Lenin had gone underground. Trotsky was imprisoned for a time and the party's legal standing jeopardized. Both the Executive Committee of the Soviet and the Executive Committee of Peasant Soviets had denounced the Bolsheviks as traitors to the revolution. They were cut off from the corridors of power.[26]

This situation made a tactical *volte face* essential. Lenin gave out the new line. He dropped the slogan – 'All power to the soviets.' Now, for the first time, there came mention of a direct struggle for power. 'All hopes for a peaceful development of the Russian revolution have vanished for good,' Lenin declared. He saw no middle way between a military dictatorship or 'victory for the workers' armed uprising which is only possible when the insurrection coincides with a deep mass upheaval against the government and the bourgeoisie caused by economic disruption and the prolongation of the war'. He called on the party 'without abandoning legal activity but never for a moment over-rating it' to combine legal and illegal work. He flayed the Soviet leaders as 'puppets' without real power; they had turned the soviets into 'a fig leaf of counter-revolution'. How, then, could it be anything but mockery to talk of a transfer of power into such hands? Objectively this slogan would mean 'deceiving the people'. The misleading slogan must yield to a new demand – 'The transfer of power into the hands of the proletariat supported by the poor peasantry to put into execution the programme of our party.'[27] The soviets, in Trotsky's words, suddenly became 'wholly subordinate to the question of the struggle of the proletariat and the semi-proletarian masses of the city, the army and the country, for political power, for a revolutionary dictatorship'.[28]

The party gave a mixed reception to the new policy. Stalin put it forward at the second conference of the Petrograd branch. It was opposed by those members who argued that the class character of the revolution had not changed since July, and feared the isolation of the Bolsheviks. In some cases there was a revival of the arguments advanced earlier in the year against Lenin's April Theses.

This feature also distinguished the sixth Bolshevik Party Congress held in semi-legality at the end of July. Before the 175 delegates Stalin again argued that the 'dual power' had disappeared and that the soviets no longer represented any real force.[29]

However, in deference to the opposition, the resolutions of the congress had a somewhat compromise nature. On the one hand, it reiterated disbelief in the possibility of a painless transfer of power from the 'counter-revolutionary bourgeoisie'. On the other, it limited itself to calling on the party 'to take on the role of advance-guard against counter-revolution', to defend the soviets, factory committees, etc., against the counter-revolution and to acquire influence in these organizations.[30]

The time to pass from the conquest of influence in and over the soviets to the overthrow of bourgeois rule had not yet come. Meanwhile, the party was exhorted not to yield 'to the provocations of the bourgeoisie who at the present time most fervently wish to incite it to a premature battle'. During the whole of August, and especially in the latter half, party leaders repeatedly warned workers and soldiers – 'Do not go into the streets.'[31]

There was in fact no need for the Bolsheviks to go into the 'streets'. The 'streets' began to come to the Bolsheviks. The background to the political radicalization of both left- and right-wing forces in the late summer of 1917 was a marked deterioration of living conditions. This made itself most evident in the larger cities and industrial areas, whence of course the Bolsheviks were already attracting most of their supporters. In Moscow, for example, no improvement in food supplies took place between March and June. The city remained subject to shortages of the most essential foodstuffs – bread, meat, potatoes and grain. Scuffles outside bakeries, empty-handed food queues, complaints from the hungry crowds were an everyday occurrence.[32] The prices of such food as was available far outstripped any rise in wages. Whereas the latter rose by fifty-three per cent between February and July 1917, the prices of prime necessities increased by an average of 112 per cent – rye bread 150 per cent, potatoes 175 per cent, clothing and shoes 170 per cent.[33]

The trade unions were unable to combat this situation. No sooner was a wage agreement made than rising prices sharply reduced any advantage that might otherwise have accrued to the workers. The consequence was growing tension between capital and labour that found its embodiment in increasing activity by factory committees. Sometimes this even took the form of physical attacks on unpopular employers and managers. Sporadically also, as the spring and summer progressed, factory committees took over control of their enterprise from the owners and technicians and attempted to run them themselves. In less extreme cases the committees would establish control commissions to examine a firm's books, or probe the reasons for dismissal of staff or ascertain whether a closure was justified on economic grounds and did not perhaps constitute a means of political pressure.

Capital experienced this onslaught in the form of reduced gross profits, caused of course not only by the activities of factory committees but also by general economic distruption and the shortage of supplies. Taking 1913 = 100, the profits of 345 firms had risen to 136 in 1914, 283 in 1915 and to 390 in the palmy year of 1916. But in 1917 they shrank to 289, i.e. only seventy-four per cent of the previous year.[34]

Management first reacted to the hostility from labour with proposals for a general lock-out. But these were rejected on account of 'the detriment' that a lock-out would cause to the moral position of industry. In its stead employers decided that 'an object lesson' would be provided by life itself 'without an organized "demonstration" bound up for the employers with a tremendous responsibility'. Factories would close down 'inevitably and gradually, so to speak, one by one, which was in fact soon observed.'[35] Between March and July 568 firms employing just over 100,000 workers closed down. The reasons given were shortage of materials, excessive demands by the workers, lack of orders and shortage of fuel.[36] Ryabushinsky, the Moscow tycoon, added his own gloss to the programme of lock-outs. At a Congress of Trade and Industry early in August he threatened the workers with 'the bony hand of hunger'.

At a less extreme level employers tried to curb or even eliminate altogether the factory committees. The government gave them such support as it could. The Menshevik minister of labour, Skobelev, issued two circulars on 23 and 28 August which reserved to management the right to engage and dismiss workers (if no agreement existed to the contrary with workers' representatives) and limited factory committee meetings to non-working hours. 'The task of every worker before the country and the revolution is to devote all his strength to intensive labour and not lose a minute of working time,' ran the second circular.[37]

This advice was hardly realistic in conditions of food shortage and unemployment. When the second conference of factory committees took place in Petrograd on 7 August, its leadership was solidly Bolshevik.[38] This was as it should be: these committees, in Lenin's words, 'must become the organs of insurrection'.[39]

Precisely at this time the peasant movement entered a phase of mass eruption. A crescendo of explosions in May, June and the beginning of July followed the first explosion in April. It was not everywhere uniform, of course. In April and May the provinces worst affected were the old storm-centres of the central agricultural and middle Volga regions – Kursk, Tula, Ryazan, Tambov, Penza and Simbirsk. Thence the movement spread southwards to Voronezh and north-eastwards to Kazan. The provinces in the Ukraine and Belorussia were also powerfully affected. By the summer of 1917 there was no important area of rural Russia that was not in a state of upheaval.[40] Almost half the number of disturbances (43·7 per cent) came from the central agricultural and middle Volga regions.[41] The western Russian provinces of Minsk, Pskov and Mogilev formed a third important centre. To the north, east and south of these areas the intensity of the upheaval gradually fell away.[42]

What were the peasants actually doing? What form did the agrarian movement take? Spontaneously formed peasant committees took command. In June a governmental commissar in Kovno province complained that the powers of the committee far eclipsed his own.

Never once was it said that they (i.e. the peasants) should turn to the district commissar for any explanation and all the decisions of the cantonal committees were put into effect without any participation at all of the district commissars. . . . Relying on the protocol of the peasant assembly in Disna of 4 June, the cantonal and village committees removed the landowners, disposed of privately owned meadows, woods, pastures, etc., as if they were their own property. They take away the workers, issue decrees regarding the pasturing of cattle on meadows, on clover or other arable land, both to private individuals and to military units and organizations. When the commissar tried to restrain the peasants from land seizures they shouted to him: 'We elected you and if you don't go with us then we'll throw you out.'[43]

There were other areas, Tambov for example, where cantonal committees similarly encouraged the distribution of landowners' timber, livestock and implements.[44]

The province of Voronezh in May, yields perhaps the clearest picture of the agrarian revolution. Everywhere the peasants hindered the further conduct of private farming. They seized estates either wholly or in part. They pastured stock upon private land. They trespassed on corn, hayfields and young forest plantations. They drove away servants and labourers, removed prisoners-of-war, prevented the sale of live- and dead-stock, and fixed very low rents for leases, which they made payable not to the landowner but to the cantonal committee. They fixed inappropriately high wages and forbade the employment of labour from other cantons. They levied communal dues, and prevented the legal cutting of timber, even for defence purposes. They appropriated monastic and church lands and treasury timber-estates. 'All these actions are carried out, frequently in accordance with cantonal resolutions, or with the approval of cantonal committees.' Searches and arrests in accordance with resolutions of communal organizations, or on private initiative, were a frequent event. There were also some cases where officials of the former government, priests and private citizens were violently expelled from their localities.[45]

As these accounts suggest, the peasants emphasized first and foremost the expropriation of land and property. The incidence of *jacquerie*, terror, incendiarism and murder was very low. Until the early autumn the percentage of incidents involving the sacking of estates, as distinct from lesser forms of violence, remained very small: it was in March eight per cent, April three per cent, May three per cent, June two per cent, July one per cent, August five per cent. But in September the percentage took a sudden leap to thirty-six and in the first twenty days of October to forty-two.[46]

This situation corresponded to the increasing procrastination of the government. This, in its turn, followed the growth of Kadet influence and the failure of the Socialist-Revolutionaries led by Chernov.

In May 1917 he became minister of agriculture in the first coalition cabinet and soon afterwards made public his intention of acting in accordance with the principle – 'all the land to all the labouring people'. This would not usurp the authority of the constituent assembly, Chernov claimed.[47] Together with the minister of justice he next issued an administrative order which prohibited legal offices from registering any changes in the status of land-holdings throughout the country.[48] This affected the buying, selling, leasing and mortgaging of land. Its purpose was to preserve unimpaired the land fund at the disposal of the state and to protect it from decrease through, for example, sales to foreigners or the distribution of estates among members of the same family, or by selling off particularly valuable parts of an estate, e.g. woodland.

In effect, however, Chernov's policy was directed towards creating a *fait accompli*. Although the constituent assembly would decide the ownership of the land – and it was scarcely conceivable that it would pronounce any verdict that did not bring about expropriation with compensation – in the meantime the owner should certainly be deprived of the fruits of ownership. Similarly, Chernov issued circulars that supported the actions of the local land committees in reducing the rents of land leased by the peasants, seizing untilled fields for peasant use and commandeering prisoner-of-war labour from private landowners. Legislation must 'not always lag behind reality . . . (but must) hastily dig a new channel for its irresistable current,' Chernov argued.[49]

This policy provoked the most violent hostility inside the government. Prince Lvov led the opposition. He accused Chernov of going behind the back of the government and he prevailed on the ministry of justice to challenge the legality of Chernov's circulars. The cabinet split wide open. While Menshevik ministers sought to reconcile the two men, Lvov expressed his fear of anarchy in the countryside, defended the right of the landowner to dispose freely of his property and accused Chernov of wishing to abrogate the rights of the constituent assembly.[50] Support came to Lvov from the Union of Landowners which argued that any solution to the land problem must necessarily be 'a lengthy process'. Many years would be required for 'delimitation, allotment, resettlement and migration'. 'What would a landless or semi-landless peasant do after getting a plot of fifteen to twenty dessyatins when he has neither livestock nor agricultural implements?' the Union's chairman asked.[51] In the end it came to the question: Lvov or Chernov? Lvov went first; he resigned on 7 July. He accused Chernov of destroying respect for law, pursuing a partisan not a national policy, justifying anarchy, and placing the constituent assembly before a *fait accompli*.[52]

Chernov's victory was hollow. The prolonged governmental crisis that accompanied Lvov's resignation could only be resolved at the price of accepting a Kadet veto on 'all basic social reforms', pending the convocation of the constituent assembly. And with any luck the latter might never meet – a 'strong man' was already waiting in the wings.

21 The Men on Horseback Fail

Petrograd burned while the Kadets fiddled. It took most of July for the second coalition cabinet to be formed. When the coalition did come about, it was as rootless as its predecessor – 'hanging in the air' was Sukhanov's verdict.[1] Governmental weakness was as pronounced as ever. 'The central government does not know what is happening in the outlying districts, and in the localities they don't know what is happening in the central government,' Avksentiev, the new minister of the interior, confessed. 'I will say more,' he continued, 'the provincial commissars do not know what the cantonal commissars are doing, and *vice versa*. Every canton pursues its own policy, works for itself, and thinks that this expresses the highest idea of democracy.'[2]

In an attempt to overcome this remoteness and impotence the government summoned a state conference. But it was never anything more than an *ersatz* constituent assembly.

The original decision was taken on 12 July and a month later the conference met – not in revolutionary Petrograd, but in the Bolshoi Theatre, in comparatively quiescent Moscow.

The stage was set for the *Queen of Spades*. This was not the only odd thing about the proceedings. Can the Bolshoi ever have housed a more disparate audience? A thousand participants were expected – about 2,500 actually attended. Terrorist veterans, judges, priests, generals, financiers, peasants, trade-unionists, members of the four Dumas, spokesmen of the minorities – the whole spectrum of Russian life displayed itself on the rising tiers of seats – with one exception perhaps. 'One gains the general impression that morning coats, frock coats and starched shirts dominated over blouses . . .,' commented *Izvestiya*.[3]

The Bolsheviks were excluded from the conference.[4] Their Central Committee denounced it as a 'conspiracy of the counter-revolution against workers who are threatened with lock-outs and unemployment, against peasants to whom land "is not given", against soldiers who are deprived of the freedom obtained in the days of the revolution. . . .' The party called for protest meetings but it also warned against street demonstrations lest they be construed as provocation.[5]

Did the conference deserve such attention? Did it amount to anything more than a succession of eighty speakers, day and night, holding forth for forty-eight hours, to quote an irreverent French diplomat?[6] Was it more than a succession of theatrical gestures? That celebrated handshake, for example, on the stage of the Bolshoi between Tseretelli of the left and Bublikov of the right, a Moscow industrialist and financier? On the third day of the conference some delegates were absent, some dozing, and some attending the opening of the All-Russian Church Convocation.[7] Kerensky had clearly failed in his endeavour to broaden the basis of the government and provide a substitute for the missing constituent assembly.

Only the presence of General Kornilov redeemed the conference from oblivion. Kornilov commanded the Petrograd military district at the outbreak of the revolution. Dismayed by the breakdown in discipline and bitterly hostile to the influence of the Soviet, he sought a command at the front. He was given the Eighth Army which achieved comparative success in the June–July offensive. He was rewarded with command of the entire south-western front. This he accepted on condition that the offensive be at once halted to give time for the reorganization of the army by means of 'strict discipline'. First and foremost he demanded the reintroduction of the death penalty, and of field courts-martial in the theatre of operations.[8] Kerensky accepted this demand on 12 July. On 16 July Kornilov was then appointed commander-in-chief in place of General Brusilov. Kornilov imposed three conditions before he accepted the appointment: he must be responsible to his own conscience and to the *whole* nation; he must enjoy full operational freedom; the front-line measures recently introduced (i.e. the death penalty) must be extended to those areas in the rear where reserves were stationed.[9]

Kornilov's rapid rise made him suspect to the Soviet.[10] It might well do so. Kornilov became an early focus for all counter-revolutionary forces. His programme was simplicity itself. 'The time has come to hang the German agents and spies, headed by Lenin,' he told his aide-de-camp, 'to disperse the Soviet of Workers' and Soldiers' Deputies so that it can never reassemble.'[11] Similar sentiments animated the Union of Cossack regiments, the Union of Officers of the Army and Navy, and the Union of Georgian Cavalrymen. They all passed resolutions of support and confidence in Kornilov.[12] He also enjoyed the support of a private committee of banking and insurance interests organized in April 1917 at the initiative of A. I. Putilov. Guchkov (the first minister of war in the Provisional Government) was connected with the committee. Its aim was to collect funds 'for supporting moderate bourgeois candidates for the constituent assembly and for combating the influence of socialists at the front'. The committee later decided to place its 'large funds' at the disposal of General Kornilov 'for the purpose of organizing an armed struggle against the soviets'.[13] Leading Kadets and right-wing politicians, such as Milyukov, Rodzyanko and Ryabushinsky all expressed sympathy for Kornilov and his intention to disperse the Soviet (though the Kadets took care not to compromise themselves in public for fear of popular wrath).[14]

Not until Kornilov, in his role of commander-in-chief, addressed the state conference in Moscow did his programme reach a wider audience. Prolonged applause from the right contrasted with silence from the left. Amidst cheers and interruptions Kornilov demanded the crushing of anarchy in the army, the restoration of iron discipline, the enhancement of the status of the officers, the curbing of soldiers' soviets and the application of these measures to the rear also: .' . . I believe that there should be no difference between the front and the rear in terms of the severity of those measures necessary to save the country.'[15]

Kornilov was a confused man. On the one hand, he refused to have any truck with Guchkov's plan for a restoration of the Romanovs, the Grand Duke Dmitry Pavlovitch perhaps.[16] On the other, his military programme and his intention to disperse the Soviet and hang Lenin amounted to the installation of a military dictatorship. One observer noted the first '*frisson*' of civil war in the whole Kornilov affair.[17]

Kornilov's programme attracted some Allied support and sympathy. In the case of Britain, this extended to finance and the use of a British squadron of armoured cars.[18] This alignment of forces again prefigured the intervention. A leading Petrograd banker, a friend of the ambassador, made Buchanan privy to the maturing plot at the end of August. Buchanan decided not to denounce the plot and wisely urged the plotters to renounce an enterprise that was not only doomed to failure but so easily exploitable by the Bolsheviks. 'If General Kornilov were wise,' Buchanan told his banker friend, 'he would wait for the Bolsheviks to make the first move and then come and put them down.'[19]

This, of course, was precisely what the Bolsheviks were determined not to do. Lenin and Trotsky were no less alive than the ambassador to the political balance of forces. Why should they stick their necks out first and thereby give Kornilov the excuse he needed?

In the event, for reasons that are still not clear, it was Kornilov who acted first, thereby precipitating a pro-Bolshevik swing. On 26 August Kerensky abruptly dismissed Kornilov from his position as supreme commander on the grounds of his demand for 'all civil and military powers . . . and the re-establishment in the country of a regime opposed to the conquests of the revolution. . . .' Kornilov refused to yield, and, melodramatically, said that he preferred death to giving up his post.[20] In the meantime, despite attempts by Milyukov and General Alexeyev to mediate between Kornilov and Kerensky, the latter ordered resistance to Kornilov's advancing cavalrymen and called for the general's arrest.

This galvanized the Petrograd Soviet into action; at once the workers were organized into armed defence squads. Railwaymen diverted trains, blocked the lines and removed the rails. Others went as agitators to Kornilovite cavalrymen and dissuaded them from moving on to the capital. A special 'Committee for Struggle with Counter-Revolution' formed of Bolsheviks, Mensheviks, peasant deputies and Socialist-Revolutionaries coordinated all these measures. The political section of this committee, on which the Bolsheviks were in a minority, prevented any conciliation between the government and Kornilov. 'We declared that there could be no hesitation, that the government has but one way before it – that of a merciless struggle against Kornilov,' said a Menshevik, Bogdanov, the committee's *rapporteur* to the Soviet. 'Under our influence the government stopped all negotiations and refused to accept any of Kornilov's offers . . .'[21]

General Krymov, who led the advance-guard against the Soviet, committed suicide. His fellow-conspirators – Kornilov himself, Lukomsky, his aide-de-camp, and Kaledin, *ataman* of the Don Cossacks – were all taken prisoner, but not harshly treated.[22] After the Bolshevik *coup* in October they all fled southwards where they formed some of the first centres of civil war activity on the Don. 'There seemed no longer any hope for the regeneration of Russia,' sighed Meriel Buchanan, the ambassador's daughter.[23]

The men on horseback had failed. The Kornilov movement, such as it was, ended in a fiasco, without bloodshed. The very completeness of this defeat disclosed the basic error in Lenin's analysis of the post-July Soviet. Not only did the Soviet nullify the idea of a military dictatorship; more important, the Soviet, supposedly a fig-leaf for counter-revolution, actually turned itself into a shield against counter-revolution, even if it also be true that this was only because the latter revealed itself in too flagrant and transparent a guise.

Lenin's error did not mar his sense of timing. Kerensky himself had asked the Bolsheviks 'to influence the soldiers to come to the defence of the revolution'.[24] This the Bolsheviks most willingly did. But they were not defending Kerensky, or the Provisional Government or even the revolution – far from it, they were fostering Bolshevism. 'We shall not overthrow Kerensky right now,' Lenin said, 'we shall approach the task of struggling against him *in a different way*, namely, we shall point out to the people (who are fighting against Kornilov) Kerensky's *weakness and vacillation*. This has been done in the past as well. Now, however, it has become *the all-important thing. . . .*'[25] 'Use Kerensky as a gun-rest to shoot Kornilov,' was the pithy way the sailors put it.[26] The part taken by the Bolsheviks in the struggle against Kornilov helped to turn them, in popular eyes, from traitors to the revolution into its most ardent defenders. 'The army that rose against Kornilov was the army-to-be of the October revolution,' Trotsky claimed, not altogether unjustifiably.[27]

The Soviet, meanwhile, followed the defeat of Kornilov with a summons to all democratic organizations to participate in a conference 'to determine the conditions guaranteeing the existence of a strong revolutionary authority. . . .'[28] This democratic conference, as it was known, by no means connoted a turn to the left. Eighty-five leading Mensheviks published an open letter in which they warned that

a homogeneously bourgeois government as well as a homogeneously socialist government would . . . throw Russia into the abyss of a new civil war . . .

Outside a coalition government, there is no salvation for a Russia torn by class hatred and class egotism.[29]

Similarly, a group of leading Kadets, such as Nabokov, Baron Nolde, and Vinaver hoped to form a majority with the moderate socialists to support Kerensky against the Bolsheviks.[30]

However, when the democratic conference met on 14 September the coalition question did in fact dominate every other issue. Should the Mensheviks and Socialist-Revolutionaries continue to rule in concert with the Kadets? The conference voted by a majority of 766 to 688 (with thirty-eight absentions) for a coalition – the first time this principle had been challenged on such a scale. But the conference also voted by a majority of 798 to 139 (with 196 abstentions) to exclude from a coalition those Kadet elements involved in the Kornilov plot. Then the conference voted by 595 to 493 (with seventy-two abstentions) to exclude from the coalition the Kadet Party. Finally, the conference accepted the resolution as a whole by a majority of 813 to 183 (with eighty abstentions).[31]

What an imbroglio! A forty-minute break followed to enable the presidium to sort out the conclusion. When Tseretelli, the presidium's spokesman, returned he had to confess that there was 'no agreement, no unity of will which could be translated into reality by the forces of the whole democracy or by its greater majority'.[32] For the moment the upshot was the formation, on 25 September, of the last coalition cabinet. It consisted of right Socialist-Revolutionaries, Mensheviks, Kadets, non-affiliated socialists and non-party men. Kerensky remained premier. This was no solution at all. Equally impotent as a means to filling the governmental vacuum was a Council of the Republic, formed from the democratic conference and intended to serve as an advisory body to the government.[33] The whole episode testified unerringly to the final bankruptcy of the coalition policy, such as had been followed since February. Not only that – the failure to construct any viable regime made it all the easier for the Bolsheviks to strike ahead on their own, in opposition to the Mensheviks and Socialist-Revolutionaries. Trotsky made this quite clear in his demonstrative withdrawal from the Pre-Parliament. He came out with the full-throated Bolshevik roar for workers' control of industry, the transfer of all land to the peasant committees, denunciation of the secret treaties, an immediate peace, the arming of the workers, organization of a Red guard, and self-determination for the nationalities of Russia. 'We . . . Bolsheviks,' thundered Trotsky, 'declare that with this traitorous government we have nothing in common.'[34]

What was happening outside Petrograd? In September and October a virtual breakdown of all authority was at hand if it had not already set in. Governmental impotence and paralysis was matched by arbitrary action in the localities. Banditry, arson, pillaging, riots, murder, mutiny made this manifest. During these months the Russian torment reached unprecedented depth. In Zhitomir women rioted over a rise in bread prices. In Kharkov, a wine store was looted and the drunken mob, joined by soldiers from the local garrison, paraded through the streets. Shops were wrecked, and private dwellings searched. Jews were molested and even killed. In Azov, in the Crimea, disorders broke out over the high price of bread and flour. A crowd marched to the city hall, broke into the food department and attacked government employees. When Makarovsky, a member of the municipal government, attempted to pacify the crowd, he was thrown down the stairs from the second floor, after which books, orders and papers found in the department were flung about. Only members of the local soviet pacified the disorderly crowd. In Astrakhan, when the bread ration was reduced, crowds crossed the Volga to the office of the local food committee, broke into the commissariat, wounded the commissar and threw him into the street. In Petrovsk, disorderly crowds broke into jails and detention centres, releasing the prisoners. In Bugulma, in the province of Samara, wine stores, pharmacies and shops were looted. In villages near Kazan and Ekaterinburg opponents of the government grain monopoly attacked local food officials and tortured and killed them. In Kutais, near Tiflis, disturbances began with the ransacking of some wine cellars. 'The drunken rioters, joined by ever-increasing crowds began to break into grocery and other shops and also into private quarters: in many places they started fires: the local chemical plant was burned and the freight station was robbed.' Order was not restored until troops arrived from Tiflis. In Tashkent

a number of soldiers decided to arrest the food manager . . . and his two assistants. It was decided to transfer the business of provisions into the hands of the soldiers and workers and not to permit the shipment of manufactured goods to Bokhara. For this purpose a special guard was sent to the station. At the same time it was decided to conduct a general search through the entire city. On 25 September at a meeting attended by thousands of soldiers and workers the resignation of the Executive Committee of the Soviet of Deputies was demanded. Speakers proclaimed Bolshevik slogans. A provisional revolutionary committee of fourteen was elected . . . [35]

The army was in no less parlous a state. Basically, this stemmed from the effort of the state to maintain some nine to ten million men under arms when it had provisions for only seven million. In September the fronts received only twenty-six per cent of their requirements in flour and forty-eight per cent in grain forage. Meat supplies were fifty per cent in deficit. In the rear the Moscow military district lived on a hand-to-mouth basis – it often had to resort to force of arms to obtain supplies. Shortages of footwear and warm clothing were also evident. There were no less than two million estimated deserters. Two hundred thousand had been rounded up but when these were returned to the front they only accelerated the process of disintegration.

From the northern front at the end of September intelligence reports described 'a complete lack of confidence in the officers and the higher commanding personnel. . . . The influence of Bolshevik ideas is spreading very rapidly. To this must be added a general weariness, an irritability and a desire for peace at any price.' Malingering was widespread. In the Twelfth Army 'an intensive agitation is being conducted in favour of an immediate cessation of military operations on all fronts. Whenever a whole regiment or battalion refuses to carry out a military order, the fact is immediately made known to other parts of the army through special agitators.' On the western front,

because of general war-weariness, bad nourishment, mistrust of officers, etc., there has developed an intense defeatist agitation accompanied by refusals to carry out orders, threats to the commanding personnel, and attempts to fraternize with Germans. Everywhere one hears voices calling for immediate peace, because, they say, no one will stay in the trenches during the winter. . . . Among the phenomena indicative of tendencies in the life in the rear of the western front are the recent disturbances at the replacement depot in Gomel. On 1 October, over eight thousand soldiers who were to be transferred to the front demanded to be sent home instead. . . . Incited by agitators they stormed the armoury, took some 1,500 suits of winter equipment and assaulted the assistant commissar and a member of the front committee.

On the south-western front, the reports say,

the Bolshevik wave is growing steadily, owing to general disintegration in the rear, the absence of strong power and the lack of supplies and equipment. The dominant theme of conversation is peace at any price and under any conditions. Every order, no matter what its source, is met with hostility. . . . The position of the commanding personnel is very difficult. There have been instances of officers committing suicide. . . . The soldiers are engaging in organizing armed invasion of the surrounding country estates, plundering provisions . . . of which there is a scarcity in the army.

In the rear of the front, Helsingfors reported the shooting of four officers by sailors, the seizure of three generals and one colonel suspected of participating in the Kornilov affair; they were then thrown from a bridge into the water. 'After that a number of other regimental commanders and officers were attacked and thrown into the water. Those who tried to save themselves were killed. In all, about fifteen officers were killed. . . .' In Berdichev, a mob of soldiers surrounded the building where Generals Denikin, Elsner and Markov were kept. They demanded that the prisoners go to the station on foot.

To avoid complications the soldiers' demand was satisfied but to safeguard the prisoners the commander-in-chief of the south-western front, General Volodchenko, walked all the way to the station beside the prisoners. . . . At the station the soldiers demanded that the generals be placed in a prisoners' car instead of a second-class railway car. As no prisoners' car was available, a freight car had to be used instead. . .

In Podolsk province the soldiers were seizing bread, fodder, horses and oxen from the large estates. They stormed and set on fire wine distilleries. In Balashev, the garrison rebelled and seized the post and telegraph installations. Soldiers travelling on the railroad between Ryazan and Uralsk pillaged flour and other foodstuffs. Theodosia, in the Crimea, was declared to be in a state of siege because of the riotous conduct of the troops. In Irkutsk, soldiers, led by agitators, seized rifles from the arsenal and refused to obey their commander.[36]

The distintegration of the army had reached such dimensions that General Verkhovsky, the new minister of war, could see no alternative to concluding a separate peace and thereby cutting the ground from under the feet of 'the noxious and corrupting influences'.[37] The comparatively mild treatment of the Kornilovite generals gave added bitterness. When it was seen that discipline and capital punishment were for soldiers, not for generals, 'the front swelled with anger and turned black like the sea before a tempest. The Bolsheviks had only to catch the favouring wind and fill their sails.'[38] Kerensky became 'one of the most hated men in the army', recalled Woytinsky, government commissar on the northern front.[39]

This wind blew not only from the front-line trenches, from the reserve depots, from the barracks and the garrison towns – it blew also from the villages. As in 1905 peasant disorders had reached their first peak towards the middle of the year. A slight lull followed, lasting from the end of July until the beginning of September.[40] This is to be attributed to the need to bring the harvest in during these months, to undertake autumn sowing and thus remove the threat of immediate hunger in certain areas; second, to the fact that the peasants in the earlier part of the year had achieved the first phase of their demands, i.e. the seizure of meadows and pastureland, the withdrawal of prisoner-of-war labour, the distribution of property and the reduction or re-negotiation of terms of tenure. Hitherto also, there was always the hope that the land itself might be acquired peacefully. But it seems that by the end of August the peasantry were at last losing patience. A representative of the ministry of agriculture spoke to a meeting of the land committee in the Odessa district on 21 August: 'very stern opposition' confronted him. 'A dull dissatisfaction prevailed amongst the peasantry. More and more loudly, voices were saying, "We're sick of waiting. In Petrograd they talk and talk, but we must plough. In winter you can't plough. We must help ourselves."'[41]

The second phase of the peasant movement after August was therefore more largely composed of land seizure and of purposeless, anarchic destruction intended to drive the landowners from their estates. This was particularly true of the central black earth and Volga areas to the south and south-east of Moscow. On 8 and 9 September the first manor houses were destroyed in the Kozlov district of Tambov province. Within three days another twenty-four disappeared. The peasants were saying: 'If the land isn't taken by 20 September, then it's too late.' At Balashov (Saratov province) the land authorities reported on 11 September to the Provisional Government: '. . . the peasants are destroying the manor houses, driving out and beating the owners and employees, and burning the buildings.' In October a wave of violence swept over Ryazan province, especially the districts of Ranenburg and Skopin. In the first half of the month between three and five manor houses were destroyed every day.

Some disappeared entirely, even the foundations of the houses are carried away; elsewhere houses stand without windows and doors, with smashed hearths. The character of the destruction is now different from what it was in 1905-6. Then the peasants did not in general prevent the landlords from removing their possessions – furniture, crockery, silver, household goods and so forth. Now the picture has changed. The possessions of the landlords are removed to the last item and distributed per head of family. It cannot be said that the peasants as a whole take part in these depredations. Often the village assembly decides, before the destruction, to keep the landlord's house for peasant use – as a school, for example – but words and actions differ and so the movement of the peasants towards the estate generally ends with incendiarism and destruction. There are rarely acts of violence of any sort against those living in the manor houses. Only some cases of beating by the crowd are to be noted.

On 2 October, the central government was warned that 'if measures are not taken to quell disturbances, mob rule, hunger and civil war would occur'. In Orel province 'anarchy was assuming the character of a public catastrophe'.[42]

This upheaval was not of course uniform throughout the country. As in the earlier part of the year, it was concentrated in the central agricultural and Volga provinces of Ryazan, Orel, Voronezh, Penza and Tambov; and in the White Russian provinces of Minsk, Mogilev and Vitebsk. None the less, even allowing for these limitations, the destruction of what remained of the landowning class and the destruction of the government's authority in the countryside was sufficiently widespread to remove yet one further obstacle to the fuller development of the revolution.

'All purely economic indications pointed to the failure of the October revolution,' wrote Pokrovsky, '. . . in a purely economic perspective . . . it was impossible to predict what actually happened, that we would force our way to socialism through all the laws, despite narrow economic laws.'[1] No, it was not economic laws that formed the setting for the Bolshevik *coup* but conditions of near-anarchy over significant areas of the countryside, a breakdown of law and order in the towns, governmental paralysis, a disintegrating army. There was a popular Bolshevism at work – made up, Sukhanov noted, of 'hatred for "Kerenskyism", fatigue, rage and a thirst for peace, bread and land . . .'[2] This did not by any means give the Bolsheviks a conscious majority but it persuaded wide circles to look with indifference at Bolshevik activity. The party and its context fitted most aptly together. 'October was unavoidable, as a natural necessity,' writes one historian of 1917, Isaac Steinberg, deeply involved in the events of the year.

October was accomplished, it is true, apparently by the actions of a definite party but it was at the same time prepared by all the unfolding events hitherto. Its success speaks of this better than anything else. The army, exhausted by a desperate thirst for peace and anticipating all the horrors of a new winter campaign, was looking for a decisive change in policy. The peasantry, yearning for freed land and fearing to lose it in incomprehensible delays, was also waiting for this change. The proletariat, having seen lock-outs, unemployment and the collapse of industry and dreaming of a new social order, which must be born of the revolutionary storm, of which it was the vanguard, awaited this change. And finally, vast innumerable circles of the population, 'the men in the street', stifled by the atmosphere of political and military uncertainty, were also awaiting the easing of this atmosphere. It was not purely socialist ideas alone that inspired all those who were awaiting and preparing the October storm; the demand for the satisfaction of the elementary *democratic* presuppositions of the revolution (the conclusion of peace, the transfer of the land, control of industry) multiplied to an incommensurable degree the mass of those sympathetic to an imminent upheaval. . . . As in 1905, so in March 1917, Petrograd in October expressed the hidden thoughts and hopes of every Russian town and village.[3]

This last is an undoubted exaggeration. But even to the extent that it is true, Petrograd in October was not a self-propelling event; it required human direction. This came largely from Lenin. Rarely had he displayed to better advantage his sense of timing, his ability to see one jump ahead of his opponents. He had spurred his men on in April, May and June; he had held them back in July and August; now, after the Kornilov fiasco, he once again spurred them on. As Engels wrote to Vera Zasulich in 1885, Russia was 'one of the exceptional cases where it is possible for a handful of people to make a revolution . . . if ever Blanquism – the fantasy of overturning an entire society through the action of a small conspiracy – had a certain justification for its existence, that is certainly in Petersburg.'[4]

No sooner did the Soviet make manifest its hostility to Kornilov, than Lenin abruptly revised his own contempt for the Soviet. He revived the slogan – 'All power to the soviets', i.e. a government formed of Mensheviks and Socialist-Revolutionaries. This would be responsible to the soviets, although the Bolsheviks would retain full liberty of manoeuvre. They could not themselves participate in such a government owing to the absence of the conditions necessary for the dictatorship of the proletariat and the poor peasantry.

No reponse came to this proposal. This was not surprising, for it was intended as a tactical feint. On the one hand, it would demonstrate to the Bolsheviks that the leading soviet parties were not intending to cut loose from the coalition policy, still less thinking in terms of revolution; second, Lenin's proposal was designed to make of such a government, should it in fact come about, 'a transmission mechanism' to carry the power from the bourgeoisie to the proletariat.[5] Rather than engage themselves on this path to Bolshevism, the Soviet leaders preferred to call the deomocratic conference, which, of course, amidst unexampled confusion, finally supported a policy of coalition.[6]

Lenin's proposal was a mere prelude to the opportunity opened up by Kornilov. Still in hiding, Lenin was at this time (August/September) concerned with the writing of *The State and the Revolution*. He made his watchword the need for 'boundless audacity in destroying the old state machine entirely . . . for the purpose of *overthrowing the bourgeoisie, destroying bourgeois* parliamentarism, for a democratic republic after the type of the Commune, or a republic of soviets of workers' and soldiers' deputies, for the revolutionary dictatorship of the proletariat.'[7]

This meant that Kornilov's failure must be exploited to the uttermost. Confront Kerensky with 'partial demands', urged Lenin: for example, 'Arrest Milyukov; arm the Petrograd workers: summon the Kronstadt, Vyborg and Helsingfors troops to Petrograd; dissolve the Duma; arrest Rodzyanko; legalize the transfer of the landowners' land to the peasants; introduce workers' control over grain and factories, etc., etc.' These demands were not really addressed to Kerensky, Lenin emphasized; Lenin's true aim was to maintain and intensify the popular hostility to Kornilov, to whip up yet further the emotions of those workers, soldiers and peasants who had been 'carried away' in the course of the anti-Kornilov struggle.

Keep up their enthusiasm; encourage them to deal with the generals and officers who have declared for Kornilov; urge them to demand the immediate transfer of the land to the peasants; suggest to them that it is necessary to arrest Rodzyanko and Milyukov, dissolve the Duma. . , . The 'Left' S. R.'s must be especially urged on in this direction.

Draw the masses into the struggle against Kornilov, arouse them, inflame them – this was the burden of Lenin's cry.[8]

At the heart of this campaign there was rooted Lenin's conviction that the tide was turning and must be taken at the flood. What made up this tide? Lenin was looking in part to the immediate movement of opinion; in part, he sensed its unfolding. In August, September and October manifold indications disclosed the growing popularity of Bolshevism. Amongst the first institutions to rally to the Bolsheviks were the factory committees. By June/July the Petrograd committees were already under Bolshevik control; and at the third All-Russian Conference of Factory Committees (17–22 October) more than half the 167 voting delegates were Bolsheviks who also enjoyed the support of the twenty-four Socialist-Revolutionary delegates. The opposition consisted only of seven Mensheviks and thirteen Anarcho-Syndicalists. This was indeed, as Trotsky proudly claimed, 'the most direct and indubitable representation of the proletariat in the whole country.'[9]

The local elections in Moscow at the end of September told a similar story. In round figures, the Bolshevik vote, as compared with the June elections, jumped from 75,000 to 198,000 (fifty-one per cent of the total); that of the Mensheviks declined from 76,000 to 16,000 (four per cent); that of the Socialist-Revolutionaries from 375,000 to 54,000 (fourteen per cent); and that of the Kadets from 109,000 to 101,000 (twenty-six per cent).[10] For the first time the Bolsheviks had won an absolute majority in a large urban centre. Petrograd local elections showed the same trend, though not to quite the same degree as Moscow. Between August and November the Bolshevik vote rose from 184,000 to 424,000, the Socialist-Revolutionary vote fell from 206,000 to 152,000 and the Kadet rose from 114,000 to 247,000 and the Menshevik from 24,000 to 29,000.[11] Even in the trade unions, which had initially been a Menshevik stronghold, the Bolsheviks won much ground. In the Kronstadt soviet, which functioned as a semi-autonomous body, new elections emphasized the predominance of the left; one hundred Bolsheviks, seventy-five Left Socialist-Revolutionaries and twelve Menshevik-Internationalists, held sway. They were supported by some ninety non-party men not one of whom dared openly acknowledge any moderate sympathies.[12] Kronstadt's strategic position *vis-à-vis* Petrograd made this victory all the more important. It was a characteristic of the September and October situation that Bolshevism was influential not only in the areas to the north and west of the capital, but also in the adjacent army and naval units. At the Finland Congress of Soviets, for example, on 15 September, sixty-nine Bolsheviks and forty-eight Left Socialist-Revolutionaries represented 150,000 sailors, soldiers and workers.[13]

The Petrograd Soviet underwent the most dramatic change of all. Under the fresh impact of the Kornilov movement the Soviet accepted by 279 to 115 votes, with fifty-one abstentions, a Bolshevik resolution expressing lack of confidence in the Provisional Government. Attendance was manifestly small on this occasion. These figures were dramatically eclipsed on 9 September. The Bolsheviks presented to the thousand-odd deputies a resolution on the method of electing the presidium of the Soviet. The ostensibly procedural matter was in fact a matter of substance. The meeting proceeded 'in the utmost imaginable tension. . .', Trotsky recalled.

All understood that they were deciding the question of power – of the war – of the fate of the revolution. . . . In every corner of the hall an impassioned although whispered agitation now began. The old presidium or the new? The coalition or the Soviet power? . . . The arms of an unseen scale were oscillating. The presidium, hardly able to control its excitement, remained throughout the whole hour upon the platform.

At last the figures came – for the presidium and the coalition 414 votes, against 519, abstainers sixty-seven. 'The new majority applauded like a storm, ecstatically, furiously.'[14] The Bolshevik, Trotsky, took the place of the Menshevik, Chkheidze. Moscow went the same way.

Many regional congresses of soviets paralleled this evolution – at Ekaterinburg, Saratov, Irkutsk, Kiev, Minsk, for example. A certain amount of pro-Bolshevik impetus came from the decision of the Petrograd Soviet, at Bolshevik insistence, to summon a second All-Russian Congress of Soviets.[15] The moderate socialists, hitherto dominant in Petrograd, had hesitated to take this step, lest the

Congress reflect growing Bolshevik strength and, in addition, hamper the work of the imminent constituent assembly.

But there still remained many towns and districts where Mensheviks and Socialist-Revolutionaries retained the upper hand in the soviets – in Tiflis, Rostov-on-Don, Vitebk, Novgorod, Nishni Novgorod, Voronezh, Orel, Tambov, Perm and Simbirsk. The Socialist-Revolutionaries also dominated the overwhelming majority of peasant soviets at all levels. On the other hand, the pro-Bolshevik left-wing branch of the party was making strong headway.[16]

A general map of the forces throughout the empire would show Bolshevik emphasis in the key areas of the industrial centres and the garrison towns – Petrograd, Finland, the fleet, the northern armies, the Moscow industrial area and the Urals. The Socialist-Revolutionaries were dominant in the peasant soviets and amongst the front-line troops. But a strong Left Socialist-revolutionary party in the making was already cooperating with the Bolsheviks. The moderate Socialist-Revolutionaries were strongest in the black earth and central Volga region; in the Ukraine, where they shared power with the national Ukrainian socialist parties; and on the west, south-west and Rumanian fronts. The Mensheviks, with the exception of the Caucasus (especially Georgia), had everywhere lost the leading position in the soviets that they had occupied in the first months of the revolution.[17]

This was the disposition of forces when Lenin, on 13 September, demanded of the Bolshevik Central Committee that it make immediate preparations for an armed uprising: 'Having obtained a majority in the Soviets of Workers' and Soldiers' Deputies in both capitals, the Bolsheviks can and *must* take state power into their own hands.' It would be 'naïve' to wait for a 'formal' majority on the side of the Bolsheviks. 'No revolution ever waits for that.' This was historically true. 'History will not forgive us if we do not assume power now.'[18]

Lenin toyed at the same time with various plans for the seizure of power in either Petrograd or Moscow. 'Distribute our forces,' he ordered the Central Committee, 'move the reliable regiments to the most important points; surround the Alexandrinsky Theatre; occupy the Peter and Paul fortress; arrest the general staff and the government; . . . mobilze the armed workers and call them to fight the last desperate fight. . . .'[19] Lenin also put forward a plan for a three-pronged attack – in Moscow, Petrograd and the Baltic fleet – against the government. 'To refrain from taking power now . . . is to doom the revolution to failure.'[20] Common to all these plans, fanciful or realistic, was Lenin's conviction that insurrection must be treated as a technique; a technique that the party must put into practice at once. It was now – or never.

To the Central Committee these demands came as a violent blow. The members rejected the proposal of 13 September to prepare an armed uprising; they burnt Lenin's letter. Almost a month passed before the committee could bring itself, or be brought, to share Lenin's sense of urgency. At one point Lenin had to threaten to resign from the committee and free himself to carry his agitation into the rank and file of the party.

The first check to Lenin came over his proposed boycott of the council of the republic. A vote in the Central Committee and the Bolshevik faction to the democratic conference rejected this proposal by seventy-seven votes to fifty. This conflict once again revived the disagreements of April and initiated others yet to come – in Trotsky's words, 'whether the party should accommodate its tasks to the development of a bourgeois republic or should really set itself the goal of conquering the power.'[21]

In the Central Committee Zinoviev and Kamenev confronted the absent presence of Lenin. They denounced an armed uprising as a gamble with the future of the Bolshevik party and also the future of the Russian and international revolution. Far better, they argued, to count on Bolshevik victory in the constituent assembly. This, together with the soviets, would then form 'that combined type of state institution towards which we are going'. The two men also denied that the party was supported either by the majority of the people of Russia or of the international proletariat. It must therefore limit itself to a 'defensive position'. In the constituent assembly, on the other hand,

we shall be such a strong opposition party that in a country of universal suffrage our opponents will be compelled to make concessions to us at every step, or we will form, together with the Left Socialist-Revolutionaries, non-party peasants, etc., a ruling bloc which will fundamentally have to carry out our programme.

Zinoviev and Kamenev ultimately looked forward to the development of the Bolshevik party into a nucleus around which the soviets of 'all proletarian and semi-proletarian organizations' would consolidate themselves. 'Such a connexion is in any case a preliminary condition for the actual carrying out of the slogan "All power to the Soviets!",' they concluded.[22] This was essentially a plea for a democratic dictatorship of the workers and peasantry, reached by way of a workers' and peasants' republic. In the meantime more and more support would flow to the Bolsheviks. The Zinoviev–Kamenev argument stood in marked contrast to Lenin's programme of a one-party seizure of power in the name of a minority that identified itself with what it took to be the best interests of the majority.

Zinoviev and Kamenev sent their letter of protest to wide Bolshevik committees in Petrograd, Moscow and to the Bolshevik group in the Central Executive Committee of the Congress of Soviets and in the Congress of Soviets of the northern region. The letter was also published in Gorky's newspaper. It made no significant impact. Lenin was quite undeterred by the possibility – indeed the probability – of preparing a revolution with but minority support.

The final decision to prepare an armed insurrection was taken on 10 October. The Central Committee met in Sukhanov's flat in Petrograd whence the anti-Bolshevik diarist had been diverted by his pro-Bolshevik wife.[23]

This meeting still did not determine the *date* of the insurrection. A dispute on this matter brought Lenin and Trotsky at loggerheads. Trotsky fully concurred with Lenin as to the necessity for an immediate insurrection; but he differed in the matter of timing. Trotsky, perhaps because of his closer contact with the Petrograd atmosphere (whereas Lenin still dared make only fleeting and surreptitious visits to the capital) took more cognizance of the need to time the uprising so as to coincide with the assembly of the second Congress of Soviets. This would give an aura of Soviet authority to a *party* insurrection.

This consideration had particular relevance to the mood of the soldiers. There were certainly many units, both in the army and the Baltic fleet, who had Bolshevik sympathies and supported such Bolshevik policies as the end of the coalition government, workers' control over production, the publication of the secret treaties, all power to the Soviets, the immediate conclusion of peace and the abolition of capital punishment.[24]

But Trotsky also understood that the soldiers 'only knew the party through the (Soviet) Congress'. Therefore, if the projected rising were to take place 'behind the back of the Congress, without connexion with it, without being covered by its authority,' the soldiers of the Petrograd garrison might succumb to 'dangerous confusion'.[25]

A deception had to be practised. It was one thing to organize an armed insurrection 'under the bare slogan of the seizure of power by a party,' Trotsky wrote. But to prepare and then execute an uprising under the slogan of defending the rights of the Congress of Soviets was 'something quite different'. However, even if the seizure of power were timed to coincide with the second Congress of Soviets, this still did not suggest any naïve hopes that the Congress could itself decide the question of power. 'Such a fetishism of soviet forms was completely alien to us. . . . Whilst moving forward all along the line, we maintained an appearance of defensiveness.'[26]

Three groups formed inside the Central Committee – those who opposed the seizure of power; Lenin, who demanded immediate action; and those who wished to associate the revolt with the scheduled opening of the Congress of Soviets. In the end an approximate date of 15 October was decided on.[27] Trotsky justified his recourse to the anticipatory method of insurrection by arguing that although a referendum on the question of insurrection could have given only 'extremely contradictory and uncertain results', a genuine majority in favour of insurrection none the less actually existed. The differing outlook of the people would be 'overcome in action'. Leading cadres would inspire waverers and isolate opponents. The Bolsheviks would not count up their majority but win it over.[28]

'At the decisive moment, at the decisive point, an overwhelming superiority of force . . .' – this was Lenin's prescription for success. This was what the Bolsheviks now needed. As late as 24 October, Lenin implored party leaders to understand that everything 'now hangs by a thread', that there were matters on hand that

> could not be solved by conferences, or congresses (not even by congresses of soviets) but exclusively by peoples, by the masses, by the struggle of the armed people. . . . We must not wait! We may lose everything!! . . . The people have the right and are in duty bound to decide such questions not by a vote but by force.[29]

Trotsky organized and deployed this force. A change in the mood of the Petrograd garrison came to his aid. Not until September, following the Kornilov revolt, did its distrust of the Bolsheviks turn to sympathy or a watchful neutrality. This process gained impetus from the government's attempt, after the loss of the Gulf of Riga to the Germans early in October, to redeploy troops from the Petrograd garrison. But even in the middle of October a majority of the troops continued to support either the Provisional Government or the Soviet.[30] This was the situation that made sense of Trotsky's need for a *ruse de guerre*, his need to pull the wool over the garrison's eyes and insinuate that an anti-Soviet move was in fact a pro-Soviet move.

The Mensheviks unwittingly played into Trotsky's hands. On 9 October their deputies in the Petrograd Soviet proposed the formation of a committee of revolutionary defence. It had the purpose of defending the capital with workers' cooperation. The Bolsheviks in the Soviet seized on this idea; it offered a welcome opportunity to evade the danger of calling a revolt in the name of one party alone, a means to overcome the difficulty of reconciling an instrument of insurrection with a Soviet in which anti-Bolshevik parties were also represented.[31]

Despite Menshevik protests the Bolshevik leaders of the Executive Committee of the Soviet therefore turned the committee into the military revolutionary committee. Ostensibly it had a defensive purpose; but in reality it was to act as the instrument of an armed uprising.[32]

Some Mensheviks and Socialist-Revolutionaries, with Dan and Martov prominent, underwent a deathbed conversion to the Bolshevik programme. On 25 October the Council of the Republic passed a resolution (123 for, 102 against, twenty-six abstentions) demanding of the Provisional Government that it invite the Allies to stop fighting and open negotiations for a general peace; that it issue orders authorizing the transfer of land to the peasant communities; and that the date of the constituent assembly be advanced. (The same motive may also account for Nabokov's dramatic appeal in support of the Constituent Assembly. He had once abhorred it as the forerunner of anarchy; after the Bolshevik *coup* it became the institution 'on which the whole country is henceforth setting its hopes'.)[33] But this was precisely Lenin's platform. It was far, far too late to dish the Bolsheviks – now, at the twenty-fifth hour.

In any case, the Provisional Government moved with an equanimity that is only surprising in retrospect. It was no secret that in Bolshevik headquarters at Smolny some sort of *coup* was in preparation.[34] But it gave rise to no special fear in Kerensky, for example. On the contrary, he almost looked forward to a Bolshevik uprising. It would justify government intervention to deal the Bolsheviks a *coup de grace*. 'I only wish that they would come out,' he told Buchanan, 'and I will then put them down.' Buchanan hoped that he, Kerensky, would make a better job of it than he had done in July.[35] Polkovnikov, commandant of the Petrograd military district, merely warned the public that the government had prohibited demonstrations in the capital and ordered the garrison not to allow itself to be involved in any 'actions'.[36]

This was altogether inadequate to prevent the leaders of the military revolutionary committee from securing control of sufficient members of the garrison or from neutralizing its hostile elements. The committee used the pretext that the garrison was about to be sent to the front, that Petrograd must be defended against counter-revolution, that the second congress of Soviets was threatened. This was again a tactical *ruse de guerre* designed to secure the allegiance of the garrison and to gear it to the insurrectionary activity of the proletariat.[37] Similarly, the Bolshevik sailors on the cruiser *Aurora* were ordered by Trotsky to broadcast the fallacious message 'that the counter-revolution had taken the offensive'.[38]

On this ground the final breach between the Soviet or, more precisely, its Bolshevik element, and the Provisional Government, took place. In the night of 21–2 October relations were broken off between the military revolutionary committee and the Petrograd military district. On 24 October Colonel Polkovnikov ordered all units of the army to remove the commissars appointed by the Soviet. At the same time the government under Kerensky summoned loyal troops to occupy strategic points in the city and to depose the committee. Cadets patrolled the Winter Palace, seat of the government; they occupied the electric power station, railway stations, and government institutions. They patrolled and picketed the streets. That same day Kerensky proclaimed Petrograd to be in a state of insurrection and at first demanded and then revoked the arrest of the committee. The committee, meanwhile, repeated its claim to defend solely the interests of the garrison and democracy against counter-revolution and pogroms. Pro-Bolshevik troops and the Red Guard of armed factory workers went into action during the night of 24-5 October.

Petrograd's *dolce vita* was not interrupted. Guards officers clicked their spurs and engaged in gay adventures. The sound of wild parties burst from the private salons of elegant restaurants. The electric current was switched off at midnight but heavy gambling continued by candle-light.[39]

When dawn broke the gamblers and the diners and the guards officers were in a different world. Almost without bloodshed the forces of the military revolutionary committee occupied all the strategic points of the city – railway stations, telephone exchange, State Bank. There only remained the Winter Palace to be taken. That morning our man in Petrograd walked along the Neva quay to the square in front of the Palace and saw one of the government buildings being surrounded. The quay itself had a more or less normal appearance, save for groups of armed soldiers stationed near the bridges.[40]

'The situation in Petrograd is menacing,' Polkovinkov informed Stavka on the morning of the 25th. There were no street disorders but Bolshevik troops were systematically seizing government buildings and railway stations. 'None of my orders is obeyed,' he continued. Cadets surrendered their posts almost without resistance. Cossacks rejected repeated orders to come to the defence of the government. 'The Provisional Government is in danger.'[41]

It was not only in danger – it was already deposed: 'In the name of the military revolutionary committee I announce that the Provisional Government no longer exists,' Trotsky proudly proclaimed to the Petrograd Soviet in the afternoon. This was not quite true; the Winter Palace would hold out until early the next morning. But it was true enough: mate in two moves, in Trotsky's apt phrase.[42] While non-Bolsheviks tried to form a committee of public safety and Kerensky tried in vain to find troops loyal to the government, the Bolsheviks were making themselves masters of the capital. When the long awaited second Congress of Soviets eventually assembled in the night of 25-6 October, its will, in Trotsky's words, had already been predetermined by the colossal fact of the insurrection of the Petrograd workers and soldiers'.[43]

This was not how the congress saw it. It was less representative than its forerunner. There were some 650 delegates, of whom the Bolsheviks had not quite a majority. The Left Socialist-Revolutionaries were the second strongest party. The Right Socialist-Revolutionaries and Mensheviks, once the dominant groups, could count on less than a hundred votes.[44] While these delegates were still assembling, scattered skirmishing continued in the city. Martov, leader of the Menshevik-Internationalists, proposed a commission to discuss the formation of a common socialist government. This the Bolsheviks agreed to, for tactical reasons. Then the Mensheviks and Right Socialist-Revolutionaries read a protest resolution against the uprising and left the hall. Together with certain peasant organizations, trade unions and members of the Council of the Republic, they formed a committee to save the country and the revolution. This put itself in the place of the Provisional Government and denounced the Bolshevik seizure of power as a *coup d'état*.[45] This demonstrative action served as a pretext for Trotsky to denounce Martov's earlier compromise proposal and to consign his enemies to 'the dustbin of history'. This withdrawal 'completely united the hands of the Bolsheviks . . . leaving to them the whole arena of the revolution,' Sukhanov regretfully noted.[46]

About 6 a.m. the session ended. 'A grey and cold autumn morning was dawning over the city,' Trotsky recalled. 'The hot spots of the camp fires were fading out in the gradually lightening streets. The greying faces of the soldiers and the workers with rifles were concentrated and unusual. If there were astrologers in Petrograd, they must have observed portentous signs in the heavens.'[47]

What were those signs? The Congress opened its session that night at 9 o'clock. The newly elected Central Executive Committee, dominated by Bolsheviks, confirmed in office the all-Bolshevik Council of People's Commissars, headed by Lenin; and Lenin issued Bolshevik decrees declaring an armistice and abolishing private property in land.

This was just as well, perhaps. Lenin headed a minority government and needed all the help he could get. In the view of the well-informed Sukhanov, no more than five hundred good troops could have dispersed the Bolsheviks.[48] A month later the elections of 25 November to the constituent assembly gave the Bolsheviks just under twenty-four per cent of the total votes cast. This entitled them to 168 seats compared with the 299 seats won by the Socialist-Revolutionaries (*excluding* the eighty-one seats of the Ukrainian Socialist-Revolutionaries, and the thirty-nine of the Left Socialist-Revolutionaries). The Mensheviks had a bare eighteen seats and the Kadets an even barer fifteen. Sundry national groupings won seventy-seven seats.

The elections also disclosed the stronghold of each party. The Socialist-Revolutionaries were dominant in the north, north-west, central black earth, south-eastern Volga, in the north Caucasus, Siberia, most of the Ukraine and amongst the soldiers of the south-western and Rumanian fronts, and the sailors of the Black Sea fleet. The Bolsheviks, on the other hand, held sway in White Russia, in most of the central provinces, and in Petrograd and Moscow. They also dominated the armies on the northern and western fronts and the Baltic fleet. The Mensheviks were virtually limited to Transcaucasia, and the Kadets to the metropolitan centres of Moscow and Petrograd where, in any case, they took second place to the Bolsheviks.[49] Bolshevik allegiance had its essential base in the larger towns, the industrial centres and the garrisons in the rear. The Bolsheviks had their greatest backing in the centre of the country, whereas their opponents were dominant on the periphery.

This disposition of support had immediate relevance to Lenin's principal problem in the autumn of 1917 – the winning of support in the country and the intimation of civil war. This latter had hitherto been masked through the repeated concessions made by the leading soviet parties to the Kadets and their allies, but it grew *pari passu* with the assertion of Bolshevism. In February/March fear of civil war had helped to deter the Menshevik and Socialist-Revolutionary leaders from taking power themselves and encouraged them rather to support the Provisional Government. In May and July the same fear had persuaded the Mensheviks to give further support to the February regime by entering into coalition governments with the Kadets. Even in September, at the time of the democratic conference, when the bankruptcy of the coalition principle stood revealed, the Mensheviks still clung to its necessity as the supposed alternative to civil war.

The Bolsheviks of course rapidly broke with this tradition and asserted a claim to the monopoly of power. For the first time since February a genuine *political* challenge to the old order broke through, though as yet only partially. The sequel could not but be an immediate impetus to the type of policy embodied in the Kornilov movement. The formation of a Bolshevik Council of People's Commissars and the outbreak of civil war were two sides of the same coin. The first centre of anti-Bolshevik resistance developed in the region of the Don where General Kaledin assumed power in his capacity as *ataman* of the Don Cossack armies.[50] General Alexeyev, former chief of staff, and Generals Denikin, Lukomsky and Kornilov soon joined him. The latter were all in flight from the prison at Bykov where they had been held since August. It was not long before a mixed military and civilian council was formed to give some cohesion and direction to these efforts. In addition to the generals, it included Milyukov and Struve (of the Kadets), representatives of Moscow commercial circles and Cossack leaders. It was also proposed to include certain Social-Democrats and Socialist-Revolutionaries.[51] The Volunteer Army, as it came to be known, had as its aims the struggle against anarchy, the struggle against the Bolsheviks and Germans, and the defence of civil liberties such as would enable the Russian people to express its will through the constituent assembly, to whose authority the Volunteer Army would submit.[52]

But this was a period of extreme political fluidity. In the spring of 1918 Milyukov joined forces with certain right-wing groupings that sought German aid for the expulsion of the Bolsheviks as a preliminary to the establishment of a constitutional monarchy under an acceptable Romanov. Other Kadets and Socialist-Revolutionaries sought aid from the Allies as a means to expel the Bolsheviks.[53]

One of the first acts of the Council of People's Commissars was to declare war on the Cossack chiefs. 'The revolution is in danger,' cried the Bolshevik declaration of war on Kaledin and the Kadets. Expeditionary forces were sent against Kaledin from the north and northwest. Simultaneously, the sailors of the Black Sea fleet were ordered to enter the sea of Azov and support the proletarian Red Guards of the industrial and mining centres of the Don Basin. The local populations were forbidden to give any support to the Volunteer Army.[54]

When the Bolsheviks seized power not only did the threat of civil war begin to become reality; the revolution also became internationalized. Again an implicit situation became explicit. German support for the Bolsheviks, and British support for Kornilov were indications enough.

Allied diplomats in Petrograd watched the Bolshevik *coup* with indifference. Russia had in any case become well-nigh useless as an ally. Instinctive dislike of the Bolsheviks was mitigated by the belief that they were much too weak to last long. When they inevitably collapsed, the way would be clear for a revival of pro-Allied forces.[55]

To accelerate this process British and French financial support and military missions began to flow towards the Volunteer Army. At the end of December 1917 an Anglo-French convention determined spheres of responsibility for each power. The British would operate in the Cossack territories, the Caucasus, Armenia, Georgia and Kurdistan; the French in Bessarabia, the Ukraine and the Crimea. French operations would take place north of the Black Sea, against the Germans and Austrians; the British would move against the Turks, south of the Black Sea.[56]

Lenin's response to this was predetermined. He had a twofold task: he had, first, to hold the fort in Russia, and second, propagate that revolution in Europe and the world that alone could enable the revolution in Russia to survive and take root. Hence the publicity given by the Bolsheviks to the peace decree of 26 October, the disclosure of the secret treaties, and Bolshevik delaying tactics at the Brest-Litovsk negotiations with the Germans.

These attempts were all unsuccessful of course. Yet they proved to have an importance that far transcended the time-conditioned situation of their emergence – in a small way Lenin made himself into a rival of President Wilson.

In its early months the Petrograd Soviet had envisaged the Russian revolution of February as not only national but also international.[57] The Soviet's continued commitment to the war soon diluted this universalistic appeal. Lenin revived it however, in tones that blended well with Wilson's ideology of pacifism and liberalism. There existed, to be sure, no identity of ultimate interest between the two viewpoints. Yet the terminology of Lenin's peace decree had resonant Wilsonian echoes: 'a just and democratic peace . . . without annexations and without indemnities,' the abolition of secret diplomacy, the commitment 'to conduct all negotiations absolutely openly before the entire people'. And when the decree referred to the workers of England, France and Germany, it did so in circuitous terms, merely asserting that 'these workers by their resolute and vigorous activity will help us to bring to a successful end the cause of peace . . .'[58]

Would the Bolsheviks steal Wilson's ideological thunder? Would Lenin dish Wilson in this contest for the allegiance of the war-weary masses of Europe? At the beginning of December Wilson was already apprehensive lest his ideals fall under the wrong patronage.[59] A month later he feared that 'if the appeal of the Bolsheviki was allowed to go unanswered, if nothing were done to counteract it, the effect would be great and would increase'.[60] The enunciation of the Fourteen Points constituted Wilson's effort to avert this danger.[61]

The long-range dialogue between Wilson and Lenin ceased at the end of 1918. The growth of intervention made any pretence as to the identity of aim between the two men increasingly untenable. Yet not only did its inception and impact testify to the world-weight of embattled Bolshevism, it also served as harbinger of the future. However insecure Lenin's position at home, however incomplete the revolution, Bolshevism had already transcended the boundaries of Russia.

The economic impact took longer to show itself. We began with Vitte and we end with Lenin. This is not fortuitous. The community of interests that links these two men, without straining a parallel, reintroduces the revolution into the continuity of Russian history. Both shared a concern with the modernization of the country; both sought to avert its degeneration into a colony of the western powers; both planned industry, primarily heavy industry, from the top, with an eye to the construction of a military–industrial base. Lenin, to be sure, had little time to make these considerations explicit (he died in 1924). Stalin made good this lack with the introduction of the first Five Year Plan. He recalled on this occasion how 'Peter the Great, having to deal with the more developed countries of the west, feverishly built factories and workshops to supply the army and strengthen the defences of the country'.

But Peter the Great's successors failed to maintain the momentum, with consequences that made themselves only too apparent in the nineteenth and early twentieth century – the Napoleonic invasion, defeat in the Crimea, in the Russo-Japanese war and in the first World War, Vitte's attempt to turn the balance in the Russian favour by creating the requisite of strength through industrialization came too late to affect this sequence. Moreover, those efforts that he did make only created greater tension between an economy in the process of industrialization and a politico–administrative structure marked by inefficiency and corruption and much overt hostility to industrialization. It is no matter for wonder that this structure, in 1914–17, proved unable to carry the additional burden of an active foreign policy, in the form of actual belligerence.

In this light Bolshevik policy and the meaning of the Bolshevik revolution are to be understood as attempts to make up for the deficiencies of the tsars. The revolution was a symptom of backwardness, or rather, of an attempt to overcome backwardness, of the need to drag Russia into the twentieth century by the most brutal means.

In so doing the Bolsheviks reverted to the traditional pattern of Russia's industrialization – squeezing the home consumer, particularly the peasant, a policy of state-directed capital investment and the institution of a national plan, together with the development of an ideology that justified the sacrifice of the individual to the state. This was a brutal process. The degree of naked coercion exceeded that implemented by Vitte and was fully comparable to the early stages of the industrial revolution in Britain. But the effort succeeded and this has given to Soviet Russia its standing, not as *the* model for under-developed countries, but certainly as one pattern whereby the penalties of backwardness may be overcome.

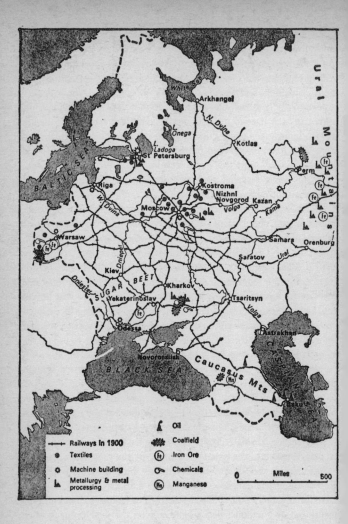

Legend:

- ━━━ Railways in 1900
- ● Textiles
- ✿ Machine building
- ⚒ Metallurgy & metal processing
- ⛽ Oil
- ✦ Coalfield
- (fe) Iron Ore
- ⚷ Chemicals
- (Mn) Manganese

0 ———— Miles ———— 500

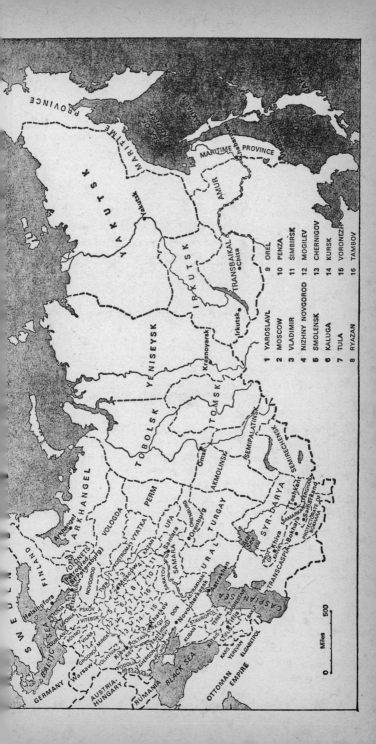

1 YAROSLAVL
2 MOSCOW
3 VLADIMIR
4 NIZHNY NOVGOROD
5 SMOLENSK
6 KALUGA
7 TULA
8 RYAZAN
9 OREL
10 PENZA
11 SIMBIRSK
12 MOGILEV
13 CHERNIGOV
14 KURSK
15 VORONEZH
16 TAMBOV

Abbreviations

ARR	Arkhiv Russkoi Revolyutsii
ASEER	American Slavic and East European Review
BDOW	British Documents on the Origins of the War, 1898-1914
DDF	Documents Diplomatiques Français
DGP	Die grosse Politik der Europäischen Kabinette
FZOG	Forschungen zur osteuropäischen Geschichte
JFGO	Jahrbücher für die Geschichte Osteuropas
KA	Krasny Arkhiv
SEER	Slavonic and East European Review

Chapter References

PREFACE

1. BÜLOW, PRINCE B. (1931), *Denkwürdigkeiten*, 4 vols., Berlin, IV, 573. (Marx died in 1883.)
2. cf. 'In general there is a revolution when the pressure of a horizontal formation creates a tension such that the monopoly of power is broken. Thenceforward the latter is no longer exerted by the institutions of power (army, gendarmerie, police, law courts) but also by specific organizations that have emerged from the social formation in revolt (passive resistance, terrorist cells, sabotage units, armed crowds, groups militarily constituted).' JANNE, H. (1960), *Un modèle théorique du phénomène révolutionnaire? Annales*, XV, 2, 1,147.
3. ECKSTEIN, HARRY (1965), On the Etiology of Internal Wars (*History and Theory*), IV, 2, 143–4.

INTRODUCTION

1. GIRAULT, R. (1963), La révolution russe de 1905 d'après quelques témoignages français *Revue Historique*, 230, 99–100.
2. NICOLSON, H. (1930), *Lord Carnock*, 221, 223.
3. WEBER, MAX (1906), *Zur Lage der Bürgerlichen Demokratie in Russland*, Beilage, *Archiv für Sozialwissenschaft und Sozialpolitik*, 12, 63.
4. POKROVSKY, M. N. (1929), *Oktyabrskaya Revolyutsia*, Moscow, 88–9.
5. VITTE, S. Y. (1924), *Vospominaniya III, Detstvo*, 2nd ed., Leningrad, 338.
6. RASHIN, A. G. (1956), *Naselenie Rossii za 100 Let*, Moscow, Tables 20 and 21, 46–8. There is considerable disparity in the estimates of the Russian population at this period. But in no case are the proportional magnitudes disputed.
7. ibid., Table 54, 93.
8. GOLDSMITH, R. W. (1960–61), Economic growth of tsarist Russia 1860–1913, *Economic Development and Cultural Change*, IX, 442.
9. VITTE, S. Y. (1912), *Konspekt Lektsii*, 2nd ed., St Petersburg, 127.
10. MOSOLOV, A. A. (1935), *At the Court of the Last Tsar*, Engl. trans., London, 12.
11. BUCHANAN, SIR GEORGE (1923), *My Mission to Russia*, 2 vols. London, II, 46; see also Mossolov, op. cit., 131.
12. For some account of Pobedonostzev's policy see THADEN, E. C. (1964), *Conservative Nationalism in Nineteenth Century Russia*, Seattle, 198 ff.; see also below, 51.
13. LAUE, TH. VON (1956), *Die Revolution von aussen als erste Phase der russischen Revolution 1917*, JFGO, IV, 2, 139. Other articles on the same theme by this author include *Problems of Modernization in Russian Foreign Policy*,

ed. I. LEDERER (1962), Yale, and Of The Crises in the Russian Polity in *Essays in Russian and Soviet History*, ed. J. S. CURTISS (1963), Leiden. To all these the present writer is deeply indebted.

14. The term is used in the sense adumbrated by Eckstein in the article referred to above, Preface, note 3.

15. ROSEN, BARON R. (1922), *Forty Years of Diplomacy*, 2 vols. (London), II, 240; cf. also the reaction of Dr Dillon, the *Daily Telegraph* correspondent in Russia, to the events of 1905: '(they) convinced me that any democratic revolution, however peacefully effected, would throw open the gates wide to the forces of anarchism and break up the empire. And a glance at the mere mechanical juxtaposition – it could not be called union – of elements so conflicting among themselves as were the ethnic, social and religious sections and divisions of the tsar's subjects would have brought home this obvious truth to the mind of any unbiassed and observant student of politics.' (DILLON, E. J. (1918), *The Eclipse of Russia*, New York, 378).

16. LOUIS, GEORGES (1967), *Les Carnets*, 2 vols., Paris, I, 230.

PART I

CHAPTER I

1. For an amusing picture of an old-time Russian merchant with his get-rich-quick ethics see POLUNIN, V. (1957), *Three Generations*, Engl. trans., London, 347–8.

2. PORTAL, R. (1954), *Das Problem einer industriellen Revolution in Russland*, FZOG, I, 209 ff.

3. The policies of the three ministers of finance are discussed in CRISP, O. (1953–4), Russian Financial Policy and the Gold Standard at the end of the Nineteenth Century, *Economic History Review*, 2nd s. VI, No. 2.

4. AMES, E. (1947), *A Century of Russian Railway Construction 1837–1936*, ASEER, VI, Nos. 18–19.

5. VITTE, *Konspekt Lektsii*, 60.

6. Vitte's memorandum is reprinted in SIDOROV, A. L. (ed.) (1959), *Materiali po Istorii SSSR*, VI, Moscow, 173 ff.

7. ibid., 179, 183–4.

8. *Dokladnaya Zapiska Vitte Nikolayu II*, Istorik-Marksist 2–3, 1935, 133.

9. ibid., 137–9

10. VITTE, *Konspekt Lektsii*, 343–4.

11. KHROMOV, P. A. (1950), *Ekonomicheskoe Razvitie Rossii v 19–20 vekakh*, Moscow, 211.

12. MIGULIN, P. P. (1904), *Russkii Gosudarstvennii Kredit*, Kharkov, III, 1, 148–9.

13. LYASHCHENKO, P. I. (1949), *History of the National Economy of Russia*, Engl. trans., New York, 560.

14. LAUE, TH. VON, The State and the Economy, in BLACK C. E. (ed.) (1960) *The Transformation of Russian Society*, Cambridge, Mass., 217, n. 16.

15. IZVOLSKY, A. (1920), *Memoirs*, Engl. trans., London, 118.

16. WALLACE, SIR D. M. (1912), *Russia*, revised ed., London, 666.

17. VITTE, *Vospominaniya III, Detstvo*, 336.

18. DILLON, E. J., op. cit., 275.

19. SCOTT, J. B. (ed.) (1917), *Reports to the Hague Conferences of 1899 and 1907*, Carnegie, Oxford, 1–2.

20. FORD, T. K. (1936), Genesis of the First Hague Peace Conference, *Political Science Quarterly*, LI, No. 3, 363.

21. GERSHENKRON, A. (1947), The Rate of Industrial Growth in Russia since 1885, *Journal of Economic History*, VII (Supplement), 146, 150.

22. MOTYLEV, V. E. (1955), *Ob Osobennostyakh Promyshlennovo Razvitiya Rossii v Kontze XIX – Nachale XX Veka*, *Voprosy Istorii*, No. 7, 18.

23. KHROMOV, op. cit., Appendices, Tables 8, 4.

24. ibid. 217.

25. MOTYLEV, op. cit., 20.

26. These points are dealt with in greater detail below, 40.

27. GERSCHENKRON, op. cit., 146.

28. The general impact of the crisis is described in YAKOVLEV, A. (1955), *Ekonomicheskie Krizisy v Rossii*, Moscow, 250 ff.

29. Quoted MENDEL, A. P. (1961), *Dilemmas of Progress in Tsarist Russia*, Harvard, 55.

30. POKROVSKY, M. (1922), *Dnevnik Kuropatkina*, KA, II, 17; (1923) *Dnevnik Polovtsova*, ibid., III, 164.

31. LENIN, V. I. (1960–), *Collected Works*, Engl. trans., Moscow, Vol. 13, 442.

32. Quoted GINDIN, I. F. (1963), *Russkaya Burzhuaziya v period kapitalizma*, *Istoriya SSSR*, VII, No. 2, 74, n. 45.

33. The theme of this argument is further developed in ROSTOW, W. W. (1960), *Industrialization and Economic Growth*, First International Conference of Economic History, The Hague; and in OLSON JR., M. (1963), Rapid Growth as a Destabilizing Force, *Journal of Economic History*, XXIII, No. 4.

CHAPTER 2

1. LYASHCHENKO, op. cit., 538–9.

2. LIVSHITZ, R. C. (1955), *Razmeshchenie Promyshlennosti v Dorevolyutsionnoi Rossii*, Moscow, 200.

3. EASON, W. W., *Population Changes* in BLACK op. cit., 82.

4. RASHIN, A. G. (1958), *Formirovanie Rabochevo Klassa Rossii*, Moscow, 208; see also LENIN, V. I. (1956), *The Development of Capitalism in Russia*, Engl. trans., London, 573.

5. ibid., 540.

6. ibid., 560 ff.

7. RASHIN, op. cit., 171, Table 50.

8. PAZHITNOV, K. (1955), *Polozhenie Rabochevo Klassa v Rossii Nakanune Revolyutsii 1905–6*, *Voprosy Ekonomii*, No. 5, 35.

9. See PANKRATOVA, A. M. (1955), *Proletarizatziya Krestyanstva*, *Istoricheskie Zapiski*, No. 54, especially Table 1, 201.

10. GOEBEL, O. (1920), *Entwicklungsgang der russischen Industriearbeiter bis zur ersten Revolution*, Leipzig/Berlin, 13; see also the data cited in RASHIN, op. cit., Ch. 8.

11. LYASHCHENKO, op. cit., 545.

12. IVANOV, L. M. (ed.) (1961), *Rabochee Dvizhenie v Rossii v XIX Veke*; IV, Pt. I, Leningrad, IX.

13. PAZHITNOV, K. A. (1906), *Polozhenie Rabochevo Klassa v Rossii*, St Petersburg, 200–203.

14. ibid., 129–30.

15. ibid., 210–11.

16. LAUE, TH. VON (1964), Russian Labour between Field and Factory, *California Slavic Studies*, III, 62 ff.

17. GOEBEL, op. cit., 39–40.

18. PAZHITNOV, K., op. cit., 38.

19. VITTE, *Dokladnaya Zapiska Nikolayu II*, 134.

20. GERSHENKRON, A., *The Early Phases of Industrialization in Russia*, in ROSTOW, W. W. (ed.) (1963), *The Economics of Take-Off into Sustained Growth*, London, 154.

21. OZEROV, I. KH. (1906), *Politika po rabochemu voprosu v Rossii za posledniye gody*, Moscow, 24–5.

22. PANKRATOVA, A. M. (ed.) (1950), *Rabochee Dvizhenie v Rossii v 19 veke 1875–84*, Moscow, II, Pt. II, No. 34, 641.

23. LENIN, *Collected Works*, Vol. 2, 122. After 1900 the reports were once again passed for publication.

24. ibid., 110.

25. See the data cited in VON LAUE, T. (1961), Russian Peasants in the Factory 1892–1904, *Journal of Economic History*, XXI, No. 1, 75–6, and RIMLINGER, G. V. (1960), Autocracy and the Factory Order in Early Russian Industrialization ibid., XX, No. 1, 81–2.

26. PATKIN, A. L. (1947), *The Origins of the Russian-Jewish Labour Movement*, Melbourne, 132–3.

27. The full significance of the St Petersburg strikes in Russian labour history is evaluated in SVYATLOVSKY, V. (1907), *Professionalnoye Dvizhenie v Rossii*, St Petersburg, 18 ff.

28. PANKRATOVA (1963), op. cit., IV, Pt. II, Moscow, No. 51, 208–10. (Italics in the original.)

29. ibid., No. 134, 421–3.

30. ibid., No. 152, 483–4.

31. OZEROV, op. cit., 26–7.

32. ibid., 161.

33. PETROV, V. (1950), Tsarskaya Armiya v Borbe s massovym Revolyutsionnym Dvizheniem v nachale XX Veka, *Istoricheskie Zapiski*, No. 34, 324–5.

34. SYROMATNYKOVA, M. (1936), *Rabochee Dvizhenie na zavodakh Peterburga v Mae 1901 g.*, KA, 3 (LXXVI).

35. ibid., 52 ff.

36. PANKRATOVA, op. cit., II, Pt. 2, No. 29, 635.

37. TATAROV, I. (1927), K. Istorii 'Politseiskovo Sotsializma', *Proletarskaya Revolyutsiya*, 5, (64) 115.

38. ZASLAVSKY, D. (1918), Zubatov i Marya Vilbushevich, Byloe, No. 9 (3), 110 ff.

39. OZEROV, op. cit., 200.

40. Further reference is made to this strike below, 66.

CHAPTER 3

1. DEBAGORY-MOKRIEVICH, V. (1904), *Vospominaniya*, 3rd ed., St Petersburg, 136 ff.

2. MILYUKOV, P. (1962), *Russia and its Crisis*, Collier Books, New York, 295.

3. Quoted GORN, V. (1909–14), Krestyanskoe Dvizhenie in *Obshchestvennoe Dvizhenie v Rossii*, ed. MARTOV, J., MASLOV, P., and POTRESOV, A., 4 vols., St Petersburg, I, 235.

4. ibid., 241–2.

5. DUBROVSKY, S. (1930), Iz Istorii Borby s Agrarnym Dvizheniem 1905–6 gg., KA, 2 (XXXIX), 87, 92.

6. MAKLAKOV, V. (1923–4), The Peasant Question and the Russian Revolution, SEER, II, No. 5, 226.

7. MILYUKOV, op. cit., 250.
8. loc. cit.; see also NOVIKOV, A. (1906), *Das Dorf* in MELNIK, J. (ed.), *Russen über Russland*, Frankfurt, 82.
9. PAVLOVSKY, G. (1930), *Agricultural Russia on the Eve of the Revolution*, London, 84 ff.
10. See Professor Khodsky's calculations in BRUTSKUS, B. (1925), *Agrarentwicklung und Agrarrevolution in Russland*, Berlin, 58.
11. KHROMOV, op. cit., Table 25b, 498–9; GERSCHENKRON, A. (1965), Agrarian Policies and Industrialization: Russia 1861–1917, *Cambridge Economic History*, VI, Pt. 2, 778.
12. CARSON JR., G. B., *The State and Economic Development: Russia, 1890–1939* in AITKEN, H. (ed.) (1959), *The State and Economic Growth*, New York, 118.
13. GERSCHENKRON, *The Rate of Industrial Growth in Russia since 1885*, 149, n. 9.
14. CARSON, op. cit., 121.
15. KROPOTKIN, P. (1885), *Paroles d'un Révolté*, ed. RECLUS, E., Paris, 101.
16. ROBINSON, G. T. (1932), *Rural Russia under the Old Régime*, London, 291, n. 42. A greater disparity is given by GERSCHENKRON, *Agrarian Policies*, 776; SINZHEIMER, G. P. G. (1965), Reflections on Gerschenkron, Russian Backwardness and Economic Development, *Soviet Studies*, XVII, 2, 220.
17. RASHIN, *Naselenie Rossii*, Table 170, 221–2.
18. PREYER, W. D. (1914), *Die Russische Agrarreform*, Jena, 96–7.
19. ibid., 99; see also GERSCHENKRON, op. cit., 729–30.
20. BRUTSKUS, op. cit., 62–3.
21. PAVLOVSKY, op. cit., 94.
22. KHROMOV, op. cit., 161.
23. BRUTSKUS, op. cit., 140, n. 1; for absolute estimates see KERBLAY, B. (1962) L'Evolution de l'alimentation rurale en Russie 1896–1960, *Annales*, No. 5.
24. See, for example, the description of peasant households by KENNARD, H. P. (1907) (an English doctor who worked for some years in Russia) in his *The Russian Peasant*, London, 23–42.
25. *Dnevnik Kuropatkina*, KA, II (1922), 26.
26. COQUIN, F.-X. (1964), Faim et Migrations Paysannes en Russie au XIXe Siècle, *Revue d'Histoire Moderne et Contemporaine*, XI.
27. MASLOV, P. *Krestyanskoe Dvizhenie* in *Obshchestvennoe Dvizhenie*, II, Pt. 2, 204.
28. DUBROVSKY, S. (1925), *Krestyanskoe Dvizhenie v 1905 g.*, KA, 2 (IX), 68–9.
29. DUBROVSKY, *Iz Istorii Borby*, loc. cit.
30. STEPNIAK (1888), *The Russian Peasantry*, 2 vols., London, I, 121; ANDERSON, C. A. (1956), A Footnote to the Social History of Modern Russia – The Literacy and Education Census of 1897, *Genus*, XII, Nos. 1–4.
31. BONCH-BRUYEVITCH, V. (ed.) (1908), *Materialy K Istorii i Izucheniu Russkovo Sektanstva i Raskola*, Vypusk Pervii, St Petersburg, 231 ff.
32. STEPNIAK, op. cit., 120.

CHAPTER 4

1. See below, 164 ff.
2. *Dnevnik Polovtzova*, KA, III (1923), 99.
3. IZVOLSKY, op. cit., 118; GWYNN, S. (1929), *The Letters and Friendships of Sir Cecil Spring Rice*, 2 vols., London, I, 425.
4. HARDINGE, VISCOUNT (1947), *The Old Diplomacy*, London, 78–9.

5. IZVOLSKY, op. cit., 277.

6. WILLIAMS, H. (1923–4), *Petrograd*, SEER, II, No. 4, 20; see also VIROU-BOVA, ANNA (1923), *Memories of the Russian Court*, London, 27.

7. CHERNAVIN, T. (1938–9), *The Home of the Last Tsar*, SEER, XVII, No. 51.

8. MOSSOLOV, op. cit., 31.

9. Quoted PETROV, op. cit., 326.

10. BING, E. J. (ed.) (1937), *The Letters of Tsar Nicholas and Empress Marie*, London, 207.

11. KONSTANTINOV, M. (1925), *Nikolai II v 1905 godu*, KA, 4–5, (XI–XII), 437.

12. The tsar's attitude is amply documented in the preface to BYKOV, P. M. (1930), *The Last Days of Tsardom*, Engl. trans., London.

13. *Perepiska N.A. Romanova i P. A. Stolypina*, KA, V (1924), 105.

14. See below, 95.

15. BING, op. cit., 190–91.

16. MOSSOLOV, op. cit., 131.

17. SCHWEINITZ, H. L. V. (1927), *Denkwürdigkeiten*, 2 vols., Berlin, II, 223.

18. See POBEDONOSTZEV, K. (1898), *Reflections of a Russian Statesman*, Engl. trans., London; useful expositions of Pobedonostzev's ideas are to be found in BYRNES, R. F. (1951), Pobedonostzev's Conception of the Good Society, *Review of Politics*, XIII, 2; ADAMS, A. E. (1952), Pobedonostzev's Thought Control, *Russian Review*, XI, 4; ADAMS, A. E. (1953), *Pobedonostzev and the Rule of Firmness*, SEER XXXII, No. 78.

19. PARES, B. (1931), *My Russian Memoirs* London 184.

20. VITTE, S. Y. (1908), *Samoderzhavie i Zemstvo*, St Petersburg, 208–9.

21. LEONTYEV, K. (1912), *Srednyi Evropeetz*, in *Sobranei Sochinenii*, Moscow, VI, 51. (Italics in the original.)

22. HERZEN, A. I. (1919), *Polnoe Sobranii Sochinenii i Pisem*, ed. M. Lemke, Petrograd, VIII, 151. Further reference is made to this speech below, 139.

23. PORTAL, R. (1963), Industriels Moscovites, *Cahiers du Monde Russe et Soviétique*, IV, 9–10.

24. BRUNNER, O., Europäisches und Russisches Bürgertum, *Vierteljahrshefte für Sozial – und Wirtschaftsgeschichte*, XL, 1, 3.

25. EASON, op. cit., 82–4.

26. VITTE, *Vospominaniya III, Detstvo*, 318–19; NEMIROVITCH-DAN-CHENKO, V. (1937), *My Life in the Russian Theatre*, Engl. trans., 131–2.

27. BRUTSKUS, B. (1934), Die historischen Eigentümlichkeiten der wirt-schaftlichen und sozialen Entwicklung Russlands, *Jahrbücher für Kultur und Geschichte der Slawen*, 87.

28. LIVSHIN, YA. I. (1959), 'Predstavitelniye' Organizatsii Krupnoi Burz-huazii, *Istoriya SSSR*, III, 2, 97.

29. POKROVSKY, M. (1927), Russkaya Burzhuaziya in *Bolshaya Sovetskaya Entziklopedia*, VIII, 187.

30. For all the above see ERMANSKY, A. *Krupnaya Burzhuaziya do 1905 g.* in *Obshchestvennoe Dvizhenie*, I, 313 ff.; see also CHERMENSKY, E. (1939), *Burzhuaziya i Tsarizm v Revolyutsii 1905–7*, Moscow/Leningrad, 18.

31. Quoted ERMANSKY, op. cit., 317–18.

32. See below, 139 ff.

CHAPTER 5

1. CHERNOV, V. (1934), *Rozhdenie Revolyutsionnoi Rossii*, Prague, 238–9.

2. MASLOV, P. P., Narodnicheskaya Partiya in *Obshchestvennoe Dvizhenie*, III, Pt. 5, 98.

3. ZENZINOV, V. (1919), *Iz Zhizni Revolyutsionera*, Paris, 24–5.

4. See below, 68.

5. Quoted WALLACE, *Russia*, 685.

6. STEINBERG, I. (1935), *Spiridonova*, Engl. trans., London, 41.

7. SAVINKOV, B. (1931), *Memoirs of a Terrorist*, New York, 112 ff.

8. MILYUKOV, op. cit., 169.

9. WEBER, MAX, *Zur Lage der bürgrelichen Demokratie in Russland*, 244.

10. RODICHEV, F. (1923), *The Liberal Movement*, SEER, II, No. 5, 254. The Union's lack of homogeneity is further stressed by another supporter who writes that it 'could by no means be termed a political party. It was rather a kind of war coalition of diverse groups, monarchists and republicans, liberals and socialists, temporarily united to carry on a guerilla fight against the common enemy – autocracy.' (TYRKOVA-WILLIAMS, A. (1953), The Cadet Party, *Russian Review*, XII, 3, 173.)

11. LENIN, V. (1963), *What is to be done?* ed. and trans. S. UTECHIN, Oxford, 63, 140, 156, 160.

12. These remarks by Axelrod and Martov respectively are quoted from GEYER, D. (1962), *Lenin in der russischen Sozialdemokratie*, Cologne/Graz, 400–401; see Martov's account of the debate in MARTOV, J. and DAN, TH. (1926), *Geschichte der Russischen Sozial-Demokratie*, Berlin, 84–97.

13. See DANIEL, R. V. (1957), Lenin and the Russian Revolutionary Tradition, *Harvard Slavic Studies*, IV, The Hague.

14. WEBER, MAX, op. cit., 167.

15. All the above is based on data assembled and analysed in LANE, D. S. (1964), *Social and organisational differences between Bolsheviks and Mensheviks, 1903 to 1907*, Discussion Papers Series Rc/C, No. 1, Centre for Russian and East European Studies, University of Birmingham.

PART II

CHAPTER 6

1. ORLOV, V. (1936), *Studencheskoe Dvizhenie v 1901 g.*, KA, 2 (LXXV). There were no universities in the Caucasus. Students from these territories attended either Odessa or Kiev.

2. VITTE, *Vospominaniya*, I, 177.

3. GORN, op. cit., 245 ff.

4. PETROV, op. cit., 324–5.

5. CHAADAYEVA, O. (1938), *K Istorii Vsyeobschchei Stachki na Yuge Rossii v 1903 g.*, KA, 3 (LXXXVIII), 80 ff.

6. ibid. 101.

7. NABOKOV, V., *Das aussergerichtliche Strafverfahren*, in Melnik, op. cit., 298; GURKO, V. I. (1939), *Features and Figures of the Past*, Stanford, 319.

8. Nikolai II i Samoderzhavie v 1903 g., *Byloe*, No. 1 (29), January 1918, 191.

9. VITTE, Vosponinaniya, I, 239; DILLON, op. cit., 132.

10. *Dnevnik Kuropatkina*, 83, 90.

11. POKROVSKY, M. N. (1933), *Brief History of Russia*, Engl. trans., 2 vols., London, II, 101.

12. DILLON, op. cit., 133; ULAR, ALEXANDER (1905), *Russia from Within*, Engl. trans., London, 10–15.

13. SHIPOV, D. N. (1918), *Vospominaniya i Dumy o Perezhitom*, Moscow, 240.

14. GURKO, op. cit., 299. More details are given of this conference below, 70.

15. ibid., 304.

16. MILYUKOV, op. cit., 382.

17. FISCHER, G. (1958), *Russian Liberalism*, Cambridge, Mass., 193–4.

18. SHIPOV, op. cit., 267.
19. ibid., 586–7. (Italics in the original.)
20. GURKO, op. cit., 317.

CHAPTER 7

1. LENIN, op. cit., Vol. 8, 21.
2. Lascelles to Lansdowne, 28 December 1904, *BDOW*, III, No. 65, 57.
3. ALEXEYEV, V. (1925), *Pismo Gapona*, KA, 2 (IX), 294 ff.
4. RUTENBERG'S account of the secret Socialist-Revolutionary trial, condemnation and execution of Gapon is related in his *Ubiistvo Gapona*, Leningrad, 1925. This was first published in *Byloe*, XI–XII, 1909.
5. NEVSKY, V. (1922), Yanvzrskie Dni v Peterburge v 1905 g., *Krasnaya Letopis*, I, 31.
6. KRUPSKAYA, N. (1935), *Memories of Lenin*, Engl. trans., 2 vols., London, 3rd ed., I, 123–4, 130.
7. ROMANOV, B. (1925), *9 Yanvarya 1905 g. – Doklady V.N. Kokovtsova Nikolayu II*, KA, 4 (XI), 14; BUCHBINDER, N. A. (1922), K Istorii 'Sobraniya Russkikh Fabrichno-Zavodskikh Rabochikh St P.', *Krasnaya Letopis*, I, 299.
8. GAPON, FATHER G. (1905), *The Story of My Life*, Engl. trans., London, 104.
9. The first figure is given in PANKRATOVA, A. M. (1951), *Pervaya Russkaya Revolyutsia*, Moscow, 56–7; and the second in GUERASSIMOV, GENERAL (1934), *Tsarisme et Terrorisme*, French trans., Paris, 33.
10. KUZNETZOVA, L. C. (1955), Stachechnaya Borba Rabochikh Peterburga v 1905 g., *Voprosy Istorii*, No. 1, 16; see also NEVSKY, op. cit., 29.
11. GAPON, op. cit., 142–3.
12. PANKRATOVA, A. (ed.) (1955), *Revolyutsia 1905–1907 gg. v Rossii – Nachalo Pervoi Russkoi Revolyutsii*, Moscow, No. 61, 99.
13. GAPON, op. cit., 158.
14. ibid., 153; KUZNETZOVA, op. cit., 15; Tretii Syezd RSDRP, Protokolli (1959 ed.), Moscow, 545.
15. ibid., 17–18, 23.
16. GAPON, op. cit., 168.
17. PANKRATOVA, op. cit., Nos. 15 and 22, 19–20, 31–3; see also NEVSKY, op. cit., GUERASSIMOV, op. cit., 36–7, and BONCHBRUYEVICH, V. (1929), Devyatoe Yanvarya, *Proletarskaya Revolyutsia*, No. 1 (84), 97 ff.
18. NEVSKY, op. cit., 31.
19. GAPON, op. cit., 163–4.
20. NEVSKY, op. cit., 39.
21. ibid., 21; GORKI'S deposition on his activities is contained in *Istoricheskii Arkhiv*, No. 1, 1955, 96–8; see also the *Daily Telegraph*, 10/23 January, 1905.
22. SVERCHKOV, D. (1925), *Na Zare Revolyutsii*, 3rd ed., Leningrad, 96.
23. GUERRASSIMOV, op. cit., 36; HARDINGE, op. cit., 113.
24. WILLIAMS, H., op. cit., 19.
25. GAPON, op. cit., 181–2.
26. HARDINGE, op. cit., 114–14.
27. NEVSKY, loc. cit., 56, estimates the number of casualties at about 1,000; BONCH-BRUYEVICH, loc. cit., at not less than 4,000.
28. GAPON, op. cit., 193 ff.; PANKRATOVA, op. cit., No. 39, 55–7.
29. ASKEW, W. C. (1952), An American View of Bloody Sunday, *Russian Review*, XI, 1, 43.

30. BING, op. cit., 217–20.

31. LENIN, op. cit., Vol. 8, 97.

32. BUCHBINDER, N. A. (1922), Yevreiskoe Rabochee Dvizhenie i 9-e Yan-varya, *Krasnaya Letopis*, No. 1, 87.

33. MAYEVSKY, E., Massovoe Dvizhenie s 1904 ro 1907 gg., in *Obshchest-vennoe Dvizhenie*, II, Pt. 1, 36–7.

34. KUZNETZOVA, op. cit., 23–4; see also the report of the senior factory inspector in ROMANOV, B., op. cit., 24–5.

35. LUXEMBURG, R. (1963), *Die Russische Revolution*, ed. FLECHTHEIM, O. K., Frankfurt, 31.

36. AMALRIK, A. S. (1955), K Voprosu o chislennosti i geographicheskom Razmeshchenii stachechnikov v Evropeiskoi Rossii v 1905 g., *Istoricheskie Zapiski*, 52, 184–5. GIRAULT, op. cit., 102 ff., gives a lively description of events in the provinces, based on French consular reports.

37. See below, 86.

38. WOYTINSKY, W. (1961), *Stormy Passage*, New York, 13–14.

39. GALAI, S. (1965), The Impact of the Russo-Japanese War on the Russian liberals, 1904–5, *Government and Opposition*, I, 1, 101.

40. POKROVSKY, *Brief History*, II, 152, 315.

41. PANKRATOVA, op. cit., No. 292, 464.

42. The content of the Bolshevik slogans in 1905 is enumerated and analysed in LANE, D. S., *The 'Social Eidos' of the Bolsheviks in the 1905 Revolution*, Discussion Papers RC/C No. 2, Centre for Russian and East European Studies, University of Birmingham.

43. PANKRATOVA, op. cit., No. 458, 774.

44. ibid., No. 438, 677.

45. KOLTZOV, D., Rabochie v 1905–7 in *Obshchestvennoe Dvizhenie*, II, Pt. 1, 225–6.

46. *Zapiski A.S. Yermolova*, KA 1, (VIII), 1925, 52.

47. TATAROV, I. (1927), *Trepovsky Proekt Rechi Nikolaya II k rabochim posle 9 yanvarya 1905 g.*, KA, 1 (XX), 240 ff.; the selection of the workers is described in GAPON, op. cit., 216 ff.

48. *Doklady Kokovtsova*, 22.

49. *Zapiski A.S. Yermolova*, especially 54, 65–6.

50. LANE, D. S. (1964), The Russian Social Democratic Labour Party in St Petersburg, Tver and Ashkhabad, 1903–5, *Soviet Studies*, XV, 3, 335.

51. The work of the commission is described in ANWEILER, O. (1958), *Die Rätebewegung in Russland*, Leyden, 43–5; for the educational influence of the commission see DAN, T. (1964), *The Origins of Bolshevism*, Engl. trans., London, 354, and *Pisma P.B. Axelroda i J. O. Martova 1901–1916*, Berlin, 1924, 127.

52. GURKO, op. cit., 369–72.

53. ROMANOV, B. (1928), *Konets Russkoy-Yaponskoy Voiny*, KA, 3 (XXVIII), 201.

54. The Polish side of 1905 is described in DZIEWANOWSKI, M. K. (1957), The Polish Revolutionary Movement and Russia 1904–7, *Harvard Slavic Studies*, IV.

55. Quoted POKROVSKY, op. cit., II, 134–5.

56. But not without much heart-searching and reluctance on the part of a minority. The mood of the May Congress is described in SHIPOV, op. cit., 317 ff.

57. See LEONTOVITSCH, V. (1957), *Geschichte des Liberalismus in Russland*, Frankfurt, 318–19; FISCHER, op. cit., 189–91.

58. Quoted LENIN, op. cit., Vol. 9, 174–5.

59. See DUBROVSKY, S. and GRAVE, V. (1925), *Agrarnoe Dvizhenie v 1905–7 gg.*, Moscow/Leningrad, 233, 264, 332, 442, 457, 567.
60. DUBROVSKY, S. (1925), *Krestyanskoe Dvizhenie 1905 goda*, K.A, 2, (IX), 68 ff.; MASLOV, P., Krestyanskoe Dvizhenie in *Obshchestvennoe Dvizhenie*, II, Pt. 2, 229 ff.
61. ibid., 236.
62. ibid., 237; ROBINSON, op. cit., 160 ff.

CHAPTER 8

1. PANKRATOVA, A. (ed.) (1955), *Vsyerossisskaya politicheskaya stachka v Oktyabre 1905 g.*, 2 vols., Moscow/Leningrad, I, No. 30, 48.
2. GRINEVITCH, V. (1908), *Professionalnoye dvizhenie rabochikh v Rossii*, St Petersburg, 40.
3. PANKRATOVA, op. cit., No. 144, 217–20.
4. ibid., No. 136, 203 ff.; No. 52, 76–7; No. 108, 157 ff.; II, No. 528, 17; No. 592, 96.
5. MARTYNOV, A., Konstitutzionno–Demokraticheskaya Partiya in *Obshchestvennoe Dvizhenie*, III, Bk. 5, 13. But see also note 16 below.
6. ANWEILER, O. (1955), *Russische Revolution 1905*, JFGO, III.
7. VITTE, *Vospominaniya I, Tsarstvovaniye*, 455–6.
8. BING, op. cit., 202–3.
9. GIRAULT, op. cit., 107.
10. VITTE, op. cit., 450–51, 453.
11. Vitte's reports and memoranda of this period are reprinted in TATAROV, I. (1925), *Manifest 17 Oktyabrya*, KA, 4 (XI), 46 ff.; see also VUICH, N. I., and OBOLENSKY, N. D., *K Istorii Manifesta 17-ovo Oktyabrya*, ARR, II.
12. BING, op. cit., 188.
13. TATAROV, op. cit., 99–105.
14. ERMANSKY, A., Krupnaya Burzhuaziya in *Obshchestvennoe Dvizhenie*, II, Pt. 2, 54.
15. DAN, F., and TCHEREVANIN, N., Soyuz 17 Oktyabrya in ibid., III, Pt. 5, 171.
16. CHERMENSKY, op. cit., 148–55; see also KIZEVETTER, A. A. (1929), *Na Rubezhe Dvukh Stoletii*, Prague, 406–8; GRAVE, B. (1931), *Kadety v 1905–6 gg.*, KA, 3 (XLVI), 53; PETRUNKEVITCH, I. I., *Iz Zapisok Obshchestvennovo Deyatelya*, ARR, XXI, 393.
17. SHIPOV, op. cit., 339 ff.; see also DAN and TCHEREVANIN, loc. cit.
18. DUBNOW, S. M. (1920), *History of the Jews in Russia and Poland*, 3 vols., Engl. trans., Philadelphia, III, 127 ff.; see also PETRUNKEVITCH, op. cit., 405.
19. A point made by POKROVSKY, op. cit., II, 171.
20. GURKO, op. cit., 383.
21. ROGGER, H. (1964), Formation of the Russian Right, *California Slavic Studies*, III, 78 ff.
22. GUERASSIMOV, op. cit., Ch. 24, describes the official protection and financial aid extended to the Union.
23. LENIN, op. cit., Vol. 9, 394–5.
24. KUZNETZOV, I. (1936), *Agrarnoe Dvizhenie v Smolenskoi Gubernii v 1905–6 gg.*, KA, 1 (LXXIV), 105, 112.
25. ZENZINOV, op. cit., 18.
26. See above, 84.
27. LENIN, op. cit., Vol. 9. 78.

28. MARTOV in *Arbeiter-Zeitung* (Vienna), 11/24 August 1905, quoted LENIN, ibid., 224–5.
29. MARTOV and DAN, op. cit., 146.
30. LENIN, op. cit., Vol. 10, 19–28.
31. ibid., 81.
32. TROTSKY, L. (1930), *My Life*, London, 154.
33. Quoted PETROVA, L. F. (1955), Peterburgski Soviet Rabochikh Deputatov v 1905 g., *Voprosy Istorii*, No. 11, 26.
34. These details are taken from ANWEILER, *Die Rätebewegung*, 56 ff., 65 ff.
35. NEVINSON, H. W. (1906), *The Dawn in Russia*, London, 26 ff.
36. For evidence of Bolshevik hostility to the soviet concept see MARTOV and DAN, op. cit., 144 ff.
37. GUERASSIMOV, op. cit., 67.
38. MAYEVSKY, E., op. cit., 113; see also KIZEVETTER, op. cit., 398.
39. GURKO, op. cit., 443–4.
40. ibid., 444.
41. NEVINSON, op. cit., 146 ff.
42. LEMBERGSKAYA, V. L. (1925), *Dvizhenie v Voiskakh na Dalnem Vostoke*, KA, 5 (XII), 289 ff.
43. A. S., *Pribaltiiskii Krai v 1905 g.*, ibid., 282.
44. GIRAULT, op. cit., 108.
45. BING, op. cit., 212.
46. Graf Vitte v Borbe s Revolyutsiei, *Byloe*, No. 3, March 1918, 4.
47. ibid., 7, 8.
48. ibid., 6.
49. DUBROVSKY, S. (1925), *Agrarnoe Dvizhenie v 1905 g. po otchetam Dubassova i Panteleeva*, KA, 4 (XI), 188.
50. KUZNETZOV, I., op. cit., 110–11; see also MASLOV, op. cit., 225.
51. ROBINSON, op. cit., 172 ff.
52. DUBROVSKY, S., (1929) Die *Bauernbewegung*, in Russland, Berlin, 41.
53. BRESHKO-BRESHKOVSKAYA, K. (1931), *The Hidden Springs of the Russian Revolution*, Stanford, 285–8.
54. DUBROVSKY, op. cit., 101.
55. LURYE, M. L. (1936), *K Istorii Borby Samoderzhaviya s Agrarnym Dvizheniem v 1905–7 gg.*, KA, 5 (LXXVIII), 153.

CHAPTER 9

1. BING, op. cit., 201.
2. See the data cited in KEEP, J. L. H. (1955–6), *Russian Social-Democracy and the First State Duma*, SEER, XXXIV, 181.
3. TCHULOSHNIKOV, A. (1926), *K Istorii Manifesta 6 Augusta 1905 g.*, KA, I, (XIV), 269.
4. BING, loc. cit.
5. VITTE, *Vospominaniya, Tsarstvovanie*, II, 237.
6. MILYUKOV, P., SEIGNOBOS, CH., EISENMANN, L. (1933), *Histoire de Russie*, 3 vols., Paris, III, 1, 123–4.
7. ROMANOV, B. (1925), *K. Peregovoram Kokovtsova o zaime v 1905–6 gg.*, KA, 3 (X), 3–4.
8. KOKOVTSOV, op. cit., 70–71.
9. ibid., 83 ff.; see also SIDOROV, A. L. (1955), Finansovoe Polozhenie Tsarskovo Samoderzhaviya v Peryod Russko-Yaponskoi Voiny, *Istoricheskii Arkhiv*, No. 2.

10. KOKOVTSOV, op. cit., 90, 94; see also Vitte to Kokovtsov, 22 December 1905/4 January 1906, ROMANOV, op. cit., 14.

11. VITTE, op. cit., 194.

12. ibid., 198; the full circumstances in which the loan was concluded, and its foreign-political implications are analysed in CRISP, OLGA (1961), The Russian Liberals and the 1906 Anglo-French loan to Russia, SEER, XXXIX, No. 93; see also GIRAULT, R. (1961), Sur quelques Aspects Financiers de l'Alliance Franco-Russe, Revue d'Histoire Moderne et Contemporaine, VIII.

13. GURKO, op. cit., 454.

14. See the analyses in WALSH, W. B. (1950), Political Parties in the Russian Dumas, Journal of Modern History, XXII, 2, and in GOLDENWEISER, E. A. (1915), The Russian Duma, Political Science Quarterly, XXIX.

15. KOKOVTSOV, op. cit., 148, 149.

16. ibid., 131, 141–3.

17. ibid., 129–30; GURKO, op. cit., 470.

18. KOKOVTSOV, op. cit., 130–31.

19. MAKLAKOV, V. A. (1939), Pervaya Gosudarstvennaya Duma, Paris, 49.

20. BARING, M. (1907), A Year in Russia, London, 191–2, 202.

21. BOMPARD, M. (1937), Mon ambassade en Russie, Paris, 213–14.

22. This is further discussed below, 120.

23. MAKLAKOV op. cit., 197. (Italics in original.)

24. ibid., 216.

25. KOKOVTSOV, op. cit., 153–4.

26. ibid., 155; MAKLAKOV, op. cit., 224.

27. Quoted GOKHLERNER, V. M. (1955), Krestyanskoe Dvizhenie v Saratovskoi Gubernii, Istoricheskie Zapiski, No. 52, 198.

28. PARES, B. (1913), Conversations with Stolypin, Russian Review, II, 1, 106.

29. Stolypin's land policy is discussed separately below, 124 ff.

30. SHIPOV, op. cit., 461–71.

31. GURKO, op. cit., 491–3.

32. STRAKHOVSKY, L. I. (1956), The Statesmanship of Peter Stolypin, SEER, XXXVII, No. 89, 356; LEVIN, A. (1940), The Second Duma, New Haven, 21, n. 28.

33. PARES, op. cit., 101.

34. SYROMATNIKOV, S. (1912), Reminiscences of Stolypin, Russian Review, I, 2, 78–9.

35. TOKMAKOFF, G. (1965), Stolypin's Assassin, Slavic Review, XXIV, 2.

36. BING, op. cit., 265–6.

37. DREZEN, A. K. (ed.) (1936), Tsarism v Borbe s revolyutsiei 1905–7 gg., Moscow, 82.

38. KUCHEROV, S. (1953), Courts, Lawyers and Trials under the last three Tsars, New York, 206, 211; see also ROBINSON, op. cit., 198.

39. LEVIN, op. cit., 262.

40. HARPER, S. (1912), Exceptional Measures in Russia, Russian Review, I, 4, 105.

41. KOKOVTSOV, op. cit., 165–6.

42. MAKLAKOV, V. A., Vtoraya gosudarstvennaya Duma, Paris (n.d.), 50–51.

43. KRYZHANOVSKY, S. E. (1938), Vospominaniya, Berlin, 153 ff.

44. LEVIN, op. cit., 71.

45. All the above data is taken from WALSH, op. cit.

46. LEVIN, op. cit., 68, 71.

47. LENIN, op. cit., Vol. 12, 114–15.

48. MAKLAKOV, op. cit., 98.

49. *Gosudarstvennaya Duma: Sozyv II, Sessiya 2, Stenographichcheskii Otchet*, 120–29.
50. These differences are discussed in MARTOV and DAN, op. cit., 210–11; see also LEVIN, A. (1939), The Fifth Social-Democratic Congress and the Duma, *Journal of Modern History*, XI, 4.
51. MAKLAKOV, op. cit., 85, 102.
52. PARES, B. (1923–4), *The Second Duma*, SEER II, 48–9
53. *Gosudarstvennaya Duma:* ibid., 1482–6.
54. Quoted ROSEN, BARON (1922), *Forty Years of Diplomacy*, 2 vols., London, II, 240.
55. WILLIAMS, HAROLD (1914), *Russia of the Russians*, London, 92.
56. BING, op. cit., 229.
57. *Perepiska N. A. Romanova i P. A. Stolypina*, KA, V (1924), 110. Golovin was the chairman of the second Duma.
58. GURKO, op. cit., 510–11; KOKOVTSOV, op. cit., 178–9; see also LEVIN, A., *June 3, 1907: Action and Reaction* in FERGUSON, A. D. and LEVIN, A. (eds.) (1964), *Essays in Russian History*, Hawden, Connecticut.
59. LEVIN, A. (1963), *Russian Bureaucratic Opinion in 1905*, JFGO, XI, I, 10–11.
60. ibid., 8, n. 29.

CHAPTER 10: 1. The Wager on the Strong

1. VITTE, *Vospominaniya II, Tsarstvovanie*, 314, 316.
2. See above, 103.
3. See e.g. VITTE'S argument in *Dnevnik Polovtzova*, 165.
4. PAVLOVSKY, op. cit., 118 ff.
5. GAISTER, A. (1926), *K Istorii Agrarnoi Reformy Stolypina*, KA, 4 (XVII), 84–5.
6. See GOREMYKIN'S speech of 13 May 1906 (*Gosudarstvennaya Duma, Sozyv I, Sessiya 1, Stenographicheskii Otchet*, 321 ff.).
7. ibid., *Sozyv III Sessiya 2*, 2279 ff.
8. PAVLOVSKY, op. cit., 132.
9. Quoted YANEY, G. L. (1961), *The Imperial Government and the Stolypin Land Reform*, Ph.D. Thesis (unpublished), Princeton, 126.
10. DIETZE, C. (1920) Stolypinsche Agrarreform und Feldgemeinschaft Leipzig/Berlin, 10 ff.
11. See the data cited in DUBROVSKY, S. (1963), *Stolypinskaya Zemelnyaya Reforma*, Moscow, 194 ff.
12. For the specific experiences of a land captain see Zapiski Zemskovo Nachalnika, *Russkaya Mysl*, XXXVIII (1917), 7–8.
13. PERSHIN, P. N. (1922), *Uchastkovoe Zemlepolzovanie v Rossii*, Moscow, 8.
14. ibid., 18–19.
15. ibid., Map 6, 20.
16. ibid., 22; PAVLOVSKY, op. cit., 136, 139.
17. OWEN, L. A. (1937), *The Russian Peasant Movement 1906–17*, London, 87.
18. PERSHIN, op. cit., 33. Less optimistic views are given in DUBROVSKY, *Bauernbewegung*, 31 ff., and in ROBINSON, op. cit., 237–8.
19. ibid., 231.
20. PERSHIN, op. cit., 7.
21. OWEN, op. cit., 78 ff.
22. YAKOVLEV, op. cit., 367.
23. ibid., 366.
24. DUBROVSKY, *Stolypinskaya Zemelnyaya Reforma*, 518.
25. BRUTSKUS, op. cit., 133–4.

26. ibid., 135; see also TYUMENEV, A. (1925), *Ot Revolyutsii k Revolyutsii*, Leningrad, Ch. VIII, *passim*.
27. A similar pessimistic evaluation is reached in MOSSE, W. E. (1965), *Stolypin's Villages*, SEER, XLIII, No. 101.

2. Theories of Revolution

1. There is an analysis of the positions of the two factions in LEVIN, A. (1939), The Fifth Social Democratic Congress and the Duma, *Journal of Modern History*, XI, 4.
2. LENIN, op. cit., Vol. 10, 448.
3. LENIN, op. cit., Vol. 13, 243, 422–3, 424.
4. ibid., 425, 426.
5. ibid., Vol. 12, 143–4.
6. LENIN, op. cit., Vol. 10, 2.
7. ibid., 8, 282.
8. ibid., 284.
9. ibid., 9, 94. (Italics in the original.)
10. MARTOV and DAN, op. cit., 128–30.
11. LENIN, op. cit., 9, 82.
12. See e.g. DAN, T. (1964), *The Origins of Bolshevism*, Engl. trans., London, 379–80.
13. LENIN, op. cit. Vol. 8, 539; ibid., 9, 17.
14. ibid., 52.
15. ibid., 28.
16. ibid., 98.
17. ibid., 10, 91.
18. ibid., 92; see also 9, 412.
19. TROTSKY, L. (1962), *The Permanent Revolution*, London, 25.
20. HERZEN, op. cit., 151. (Italics in the original.)
21. TROTSKY, *My Life*, 147. For a succinct outline of Parvus' career see SCHURER, H. (1959), Alexander Helphand-Parvus, *Russian Review*, October.
22. TROTSKY, loc. cit., 164.
23. PARVUS, A. (1906), *Rossiya i Revolyutsia*, St Petersburg, 83. This work reprints articles written by Parvus in 1904 and 1905.
24. ibid., 95; see also ibid., 108–9, 123.
25. TROTSKY, L. (1947), *Stalin*, London, 430.
26. PARVUS, op. cit., 179.
27. TROTSKY, op. cit., 430.
28. LENIN, op. cit., Vol. 8, 291.
29. TROTSKY, *Permanent Revolution*, 168.
30. ibid., 171 ff.
31. ibid., 183, 198. (Italics in the original.)
32. ibid., 8.
33. ibid., 237. (Italics in the original.)

CHAPTER II

1. ADORNO, T. (1963), *Prismen*, Munich, 67.
2. See above, Ch. 140.
3. STEPUN, F. (1948–9), *Vergangenes und Unvergängliches*, 3 vols., Munich, I, 348–9.
4. LENIN, op. cit., Vol. 19, 328–31.

5. LEROY-BEAULIEU, A. (1897), *L'Empire des Tsars et les Russes*, 3 vols., Paris, 4th ed., I, 375.

6. ISGOYEV, A. S. (1909), Ob Intelligentnoi Molodezhi in GERSHENZON, M. O. (ed.) *Vekhi*, 3rd ed., Moscow, 97 ff., and *Russkoe Obshchestvo i Revolyutsia*, St Petersburg, 1909, 197 ff.; see also CHERNOV, V. (1934), *Rozhdenie Revolyutsionnoi Rossii*, Prague, 32.

7. KISS, G. (1963), *Die gesellschaftspolitische Rolle der Studentenbewegung im vorrevolutionären Russland*, Munich, 97–8.

8. TRUBETSKOY, E., *Die Universitätsfrage*, in MELNIK, op. cit., 45, 51–2.

9. BACHTIN, N. (1963), *Lectures and Essays*, Birmingham, 47.

10. STEPUN, op. cit., 224.

CHAPTER 12

1. GRINEVITCH, V. (1927), *Die Gewerkschaftsbewegung in Russland I (1905–14)*, Berlin, 237.

2. See the data cited in GLIKSMAN, J., *The Russian Urban Worker*, in BLACK, op. cit., 314.

3. LIVSHIN, YA. (1957), K voprosu o voenno – promyshlennikh monopoliyakh v Rossii v nachale XX veka, *Voprosy Istorii*, No. 7, 63.

4. This point is discussed in COQUIN, F.-X. (1960), Apercus sur l'economie tsariste avant 1914, *Revue d'Histoire Moderne*, No. 7, 67.

5. GRINEVITCH, V. (1908), *Professionalnoye Dvizhenie v Rossii*, St Petersburg, 278–9.

6. TURIN, S. P. (1935), *From Peter the Great to Lenin*, London, 115–16.

7. LURYE, M. (1963), *Tsarizm v Borbe s Rabochim Dvizheniem v Gody Podyema*, KA, 1 (LXXIV), 61.

8. M.L.L. (1937), *Lensky Rasstrel 1912 g.*, KA, 2 (LXXXI), 154–5.

9. LURYE, loc. cit.

10. Quoted TURIN, loc. cit.

11. LURYE, loc. cit.

12. ibid., 53.

13. ibid., 61–2.

14. ibid., 41, 51, 54.

15. GRINEVITCH, *Die Gewerkschaftsbewegung*, 289.

16. KORBUT, M. (1926), *Uchet Departmentom Politzii Opyta 1905 goda*, KA, 5 (XVIII), 221 ff.

17. LYASHCHENKO, op. cit., 692.

18. *Rabochee Dvizhenie v Petrograde v 1912–1917 gg.*, Leningrad, 1958, No. 102, 209.

19. ibid., No. 104, 214–15.

20. ibid., No. 114, 231–2.

21. Yulskie Volneniya 1914 g. v. Peterburge, *Proletarskaya Revolyutsia*, No. 7 (30), 1924, 203.

22. For a general view of July 1914 from the viewpoint of a Bolshevik Duma deputy, see BADAYEV, A. (1933), *The Bolsheviks in the Tsarist Duma*, Engl. trans., London, ch. XIX; see also HAIMSON, L. (1964), The Problem of Social Stability in Urban Russia 1907–17, I, *Slavic Review*, XXIII, No. 4.

23. YAKOVLEV, *Ekonomicheskie Krizisi*, 353, 364–5. Between 1910 and 1913 the average unnual rate of production increase was 7.5 per cent (GERSCHENKRON, *Rate of Industrial Growth in Russia since 1885*, 153).

24. DAN, T., op. cit., 389; CHERNOV, V. (1953), *Pered buryei*, New York, 284.

25. LIVSHIN, YA. (1959), 'Predstavitelniye' Organizatzii, 112–13.

26. ROOSA, R., *Russian Industrialists look to the future 1906–17*, in CURTISS, op. cit., 198–218.
27. PARES, B. (1939), *The Fall of the Russian Monarchy*, London, 116.
28. Quoted ERMANSKY, op. cit., 89; see also LIVSHIN, op. cit., 111, 115, where other spokesmen are quoted to the same effect.
29. e.g. by SCHUMPETER, J. (1955), *Imperialism and Social Classes*, Meridian ed., New York, 79.
30. BOYVKIN, V. I., GINDIN, I. F., TARNOVSKY, K. H. (1959), Gosudarstvennii monopolisticheskii Kapitalizm v Rossii, *Istoriya SSSR*, No. 3, 92.
31. LYASHCHENKO, P. (1946), Iz istorii monopolii v Rossii, *Istoricheskie Zapiski*, No. 20, 155. This article also gives the text of the agreement made between *Prodamet* and the Goujon metal factories in Moscow, loc. cit., 175–88).
32. COQUIN, op. cit., 63.
33. KOKOVTSOV, op. cit., 239 ff.
34. LIVSHIN, *K Voprosu*, 55.
35 GURKO, op. cit., 199–200.
36. LIVSHIN, '*Predstavitelniye*' *Organizatzii*, 115.
37. LIVSHIN, *K Voprosu*, 64–5.
38. COQUIN, op. cit., 68.
39. MIHAILOVITCH, ALEXANDER (1932), *Once a Grand Duke*, New York, 248–9.
40. GURKO, op. cit., 552 ff.
41. KOKOVTSOV, op. cit., 425.
42. *Iz Dnevnika Lva Tikhomirova*, KA, 1 (LXXIV), 1936, 183, 189.
43. RODZYANKO, M. V., *Krushenie Imperii*, ARR, XVII, 72–3; see also KOKOVTSOV, op. cit., 349 ff.
44. SPIRIDOVITCH, A. (1935), *Raspoutine*, French trans., Paris, 53.
45. PARES, *Fall*, 140 ff.; MOSSOLOV, op. cit., 148; CHERNAVIN, op. cit., 664 ff.; SPIRIDOVITCH, A. (1928), *Les dernières années de la cour de Tsarskoye Selo*, 2 vols., Paris, II, 46 ff.
46. ILIODOR (1917), *Svyatoi Chort-Zaspiski o Rasputine*, Moscow, 31–2.
47. MILYUKOV, P. (1955), *Vospominaniya*, 2 vols., New York, II, 156; for the influence of the Beilis trial see ibid., 165. HAIMSON, L. (1965), The Problem of Social Stability in Urban Russia 1905–17, II, *Slavic Review*, XXIV, 1, deals at length with the relations between the government and public life in the immediate pre-war years.
48. SEMENNIKOV, V. P. (1927), *Monarkhiya Pered Krusheniem*, Moscow/Leningrad, 92.
49. This speech is reported in *Russian Review*, III, No. 1, 1914, 158 ff.; see also PIOTROW, F. (1962), *Paul Milyukov and the Constitutional-Democratic Party*, unpublished Ph.D. thesis, Oxford, 274 ff.
50. Pismo, I. I. Skvortzova-Stepanova N.I. Leninu, *Istoricheskii Arkhiv*, No. 2, 1959, 14–17, and LENIN's reply, loc. cit., 13.
51. HAIMSON, op. cit., II, 14.
52. KERENSKY, A. F. (1934), *The Crucifixion of Liberty*, London, 164.
53. See above, 67.
54. *Dnevnik Kuropatkina*, KA, II (1922), 83, 90.
55. BULOW to POURTALES, 3 March 1908, *DGP* XXV, 2 No. 8734 348.
56. LOUIS, GEORGES (1926), *Les Carnets*, 2 vols., Paris, II, 48.
57. PALEOLOGUE to DOUMERGUE, 21 May 1914, *DDF* 1871–1914, 3rd series, X, No. 267.
58. *Gosudarstvennaya Duma, Sozyv IV, Sessiya 2, Stenographicheskii Otchet*, 377–8.

59. MILYUKOV, op. cit., II, 174.
60. TARLE, E. (1958), *Sochineniya*, XI, Moscow, 503 ff.
61. *Gosudarstvennaya Duma*, ibid., 378 ff.
62. ibid., 419 ff.
63. ibid., 431–2.
64. GOLDER, F. (ed.) (1927), *Documents of Russian History*, New York, 19.
65. PALEOLOGUE, M. (1922), *La Russie des Tsars*, 3 vols., Paris, I, 120–21; see also BUCHANAN, op. cit., I, 182, 220; and MARYE, G. T. (1929), *Nearing the End in Imperial Russia*, Philadelphia, 109–10.
66. SCHERER, A., and GRUNEWALD, J. (eds.) (1962), *L'Allemagne et les Problemes de la Paix pendant la première guerre mondiale*, Paris, I, Nos. 25–7, 37–9.
67. POURTALES, GRAF (1919), *Am Scheidewege zwischen Krieg und Frieden*, Berlin, 71; DOBROROLSKI, GENERAL SERGE (1922), *Die Mobilmachung der russischen Armee 1914*, Berlin, 25.
68. *Graf Fredericks und die russische Mobilmachung 1914*, Berliner Monatshefte, IX, 9, 1931, 869–72.
69. TROTSKY, L., *Uroki Oktyabrya*, n.d., 12; KERENSKY, A. F. (1927), *The Catastrophe*, London/New York, 77, 81.
70. TROTSKY, loc. cit.

CHAPTER 13

1. PARVUS, op. cit., 110.
2. LUKOMSKY, GENERAL A. S. (1922), *Vospominaniya*, 2 vols., Berlin, I, 53 ff.
3. RODZYANKO, op. cit., 79; see also KERENSKY, *Crucifixion*, 175.
4. ARUTYUNOV, G. A. (1959), Vsyeobshchaya Stachka Bakinskikh Rabochikh v 1914 godu, *Istoriya SSSR*, No. 3, 138–9.
5. BUCHANAN, op. cit., I, 213.
6. ibid., 214–15.
7. ALMEDINGEN, E. M. (1964), *Unbroken Unity, A Memoir of Grand-Duchess Serge of Russia*, London, 83 ff.
8. CHERNOV, op. cit., 316.
9. RODZYANKO, op. cit., 100.
10. cf. the data cited in ZAGORSKY, S. O. (1928), *State Control of Industry in Russia during the war*, New Haven, 14 ff.
11. LABRY, R. (1919), *L'Industrie russe et la Revolution*, Paris, 43.
12. ibid., 48–9; see also ZAGORSKY, op. cit., 50.
13. LABRY, op. cit., 55–8.
14. ZAGORSKY, op. cit., 54 ff.
15. GRAVE, B. B. (ed.) (1927), *Burzhuaziya Nakanune Fevralskoi Revolyutsii*, Moscow/Leningrad, No. 4, 11.
16. For Allied pressure on Russia see, inter alia, PALEOLOGUE, op. cit., I, 97 ff.; BUCHANAN, op. cit., I, 216 ff., II, 1–2; SEMENNIKOV, V. P. (ed.) (1927), *Monarkhiya pered krusheniyem*, Moscow/Leningrad, 252 ff.
17. See below, 216, 242.
18. SIDOROV, A. L. (1945), Otnosheniya Rossii s Soyuznikami i snostranniye Postavki vo Vremya Pervoi Mirovoi Voiny, *Istoricheskie Zapiski*, No. 15.
19. PALEOLOGUE, op. cit., II, 260.
20. BADAYEV, op. cit., 214 ff. Kerensky was one of the Bolsheviks' defence counsels (KERENSKY, op. cit., 222) and in August 1915, during the negotiations between the Progressive Bloc and ministers, he intervened with A. A. Khvostov (minister of justice) to secure the release of the exiles.

Milyukov seems to have supported this initiative (LAPIN, N. (1932), *Progressivnyi Blok v 1915–17 gg.*, KA, Nos. 1–2 (L–LI), 147–8).

21. YAKHONTOV, A. N., *Tyzahelie Dni*, ARR XVIII, 84.

22. RODZYANKO, op. cit., 84.

23. ibid., 86.

24. SEMENNIKOV, op. cit., 95–6; see also BUCHANAN, op. cit., II, 46, for the tsar's suspicion of the zemstvos' political aspirations.

25. YAKHONTOV, op. cit., 37, 52.

26. PARES B. (ed.) (1923), *Letters of the Tsaritsa to the Tsar 1914–16*, London, 114. The next day these trousers had become 'immortal' (loc. cit., 119). The imperial couple corresponded in a sort of pidgin English.

27. PALEOLOGUE, op. cit., I, 364.

28. GOLDER, op. cit., 239; MARYE, op. cit., 240; DANILOV, YU. N. (1930), *Velikyi Knyaz Nikolai Nikolayevich*, Paris, 264 ff.

29. SEMENNIKOV, V. P. (1926), *Politika Romanovykh Nakanune Revolyutsii*, Moscow/Leningrad, 84–5.

30. ibid., 87–8.

31. RODZYANKO, op. cit., 125. (The ministers were respectively Stürmer and Shuvayev.)

32. GOLDER, op. cit., 126 ff.

33. YAKHONTOV, op. cit., 101.

34. PALEOLOGUE, op. cit., I, 370.

35. GRAVE, op. cit., Nos. 9–10, 20 ff. and No. 13, 29 ff.; see also GRAVE, B. (1926), *K Istorii Klassovoi Borby v Rossii*, Moscow/Leningrad, 272.

36. See the report of the Kadet congress of June 1915 in LAPIN, N. (1933), *Kadety v dni Galitsiiskovo Razgroma*, KA, 4 (LIX), 117–22.

37. SHULGIN, V. V. (1928), *Tage*, German trans., Berlin, 198.

38. GOLDER, op. cit., 134–6.

39. MILYUKOV, *Vospominaniya*, II, 207.

40. GRAVE, *Burzhuaziya*, No. 9, 21.

41. LAPIN, N. (1932), *Progressivnyi Blok v 1915–17 gg.*, KA, 1–2 (L–LI), 145 ff.

42. GRAVE, op. cit., No. 26, 62.

43. LAPIN, op. cit., 144. (Italics in original.)

44. Shcherbatov (minister of the interior) to Nicholas II, 16 September 1915, SEMENNIKOV, op. cit., 97–8; see also GRAVE, op. cit., No. 18, 40 ff.

45. ibid., No. 17, 40.

46. YAKHONTOV, op. cit., 114.

47. SHULGIN, op. cit., 120–21.

48. GRAVE, *K Istorii*, 310 ff.

49. GRAVE, *Burzhaziya*, No. 62, 146 (italics in the original); see also Nos. 28 and 29, 66–9.

50. ibid., No. 60, 141–4.

51. ibid., No. 27, 65.

52. LAPIN, N. (1932), *Progressivnyi Blok v 1915–17 gg.* (continuation), KA, 3 (LII). 11 March 1801 was the date of the tsar Paul's assassination in a palace *coup d'état*.

53. MILYUKOV, P. N. (1925), *Russlands Zusammenbruch*, 2 vols., German trans., Berlin, I, 18; see also SEMENNIKOV, op. cit., 72 ff.

54. *Rabochee Dvizhenie v Petrograde v 1912–17 gg.*, Leningrad, 1958, 635, n. 175.

55. GRAVE, *K Istorii*, 56, 74.

56. *Rabochee Dvizhenie*, Nos. 189–94, 199, 325 ff.

57. MELLER, V. L., and PANKRATOVA, A. M. (eds.) (1926), *Rabochee Dvizhenie v 1917 g.*, Moscow/Leningrad, 16–17. By the beginning of 1917 the

factory inspectorate supervised 12,392 institutions employing some two million workers, i.e. forty per cent and seventy per cent of the respective totals (loc. cit., 13, n. 2). Therefore the official data relating to the number of strikes and strikers must necessarily give an incomplete picture.

58. *Rabochee Dvizhenie*, No. 241, 398–401.

59. MELLER and PANKRATOVA, op. cit., 16–17, 20.

60. *Rabochee Dvizhenie*, No. 349, 523 ff.; see also GRAVE, *K Istorii*, 71.

61. MELLER and PANKRATOVA, op. cit., 20 ff.

62. *Rabochee Dvizhenie*, No. 310, 485, and No. 312, 489.

63. WARD, B. (1964), Wild Socialism in Russia: The Origins, *California Slavic Studies*, III, 136; KUTUZOV, V. V. (ed.) (1957), *Velikaya Oktyabrskaya Sotsialisticheskaya Revolyutsia – Khronika Sobytii*, Moscow, I, 5.

64. This policy is best described in FISCHER, FRITZ (1964), *Griff nach der Weltmacht*, Hanover, 155 ff.

65. ZEMAN, Z. A. B. (1958), *Germany and the Revolution in Russia*, No. 3, 3; see also ZEMAN, Z. A. B., and SCHARLAU, W. (1965), *The Merchant of Revolution*, Oxford, 152.

66. *Rabochee Dvizhenie*, No. 201, 345.

67. ZEMAN and SCHARLAU, op. cit., 187 ff.

68. *Gosudarstvennaya Duma, Sozyv IV, Sessiya 4, Stenographicheskii Otchet*, 4, 814.

69. WARD, op. cit., 130 ff.; see also GRAVE, *K Istorii*, 56.

70. STRUVE, P. B. (1930), *Food Supply in Russia during the World War*, New Haven, 311 ff.; see also RODZYANKO, M. V., *Gosudarstvennaya Duma i Fevralskaya 1917 goda Revolyutsia*, ARR, VI, 53.

71. LOCKHART, R. B. (1937 ed.), *Memoirs of a British Agent*, London, 160.

72. POKROVSKY, M. N., *Politicheskoe Polozhenie Rossii Nakanune Fevralskoi Revolyutsii*, KA, 4 (XVII), 1926.

73. MILYUKOV, P. N. (1920), *Bolshevism: An International Danger*, London, 68; RODZYANKO, op. cit., 41.

74. SHCHEGOLEV, P. (ed.) (1924–6), *Padenie Tsarskevo Rezhima, Stenographiches Kie Otchety*, Leningrad, I, 149.

75. GELIS, I. (1926), *Revolyutsionnaya Propaganda v Armii v 1916–17 gg.*, KA, 4 (XVII), 50.

76. LUKOMSKY, op. cit., I, 105; BRUSILOV, A. A. (1930), *A Soldier's Notebook*, Engl. trans., London, 282.

77. BILYK, P. (1937), *V Tsarskoi Armii Nakanune Fevralskoi Burzhuazno-Demokraticheskoi Revolyutsii*, KA, 2 (LXXXI), 106, 110.

78. For all the above see GOLDER, op. cit., 251; BUCHANAN, op. cit., II, 49; CALLWELL, MAJOR-GENERAL SIR C. E. (1927), *Field-Marshal Sir Henry Wilson: His Life and Diaries*, 2 vols., London, I, 319.

79. GRAVE, *Burzhuaziya*, No. 73, 166; for further reports of Kadet divisions between activists and passivists see ibid., No. 78, 176–8.

80. RODZYANKO, *Duma*, 52.

81. PARES, op. cit., 455.

82. PALEY, PRINCESS (1924), *Memoirs of Russia (1916–19)*, London, 26.

83. There is some description of these plans in the Introduction to *The Russian Provisional Government 1917 – Documents*, 3 vols., Stanford, 1961, ed. BROWDER, R. P., and KERENSKY, A. F., I, 18 ff. (This work is hereinafter referred to as *B. and K.*); see also RODZYANKO, *Krushenie*, 159, and MELGUNOV, S. P. (1931), *Na Putyakh k dvortzovomu perevorotu* Paris, *passim*.

84. PALEOLOGUE, op. cit., III, 131–2.

85. SHLYAPNIKOV, A. *1917 god*, I, Moscow, n.d. 7-12; see also RASHIN, *Formirovanie*, 82 ff.
86. GRAVE, *K Istorii*, 206.
87. *Padenie*, I, 183.
88. *Illustrated History of the Russian Revolution*, Engl. trans., London, 1928, 71-2.
89. *Fevralskaya Revolyutsiya 1917 Goda*, KA, 2 (XXI), 1927, 15-16.
90. KUTUZOV, V. V. (ed.) (1957), *Velikaya: Oktyabrskaya Sotsialisticheskaya Revolyutsia – Khronika Sobytii*, Moscow, I, 23.
91. RODZYANKO, *Duma*, 59.
92. SHULGIN, op. cit., 157.
93. RODZYANKO, loc. cit.
94. *Padenie V*, 38.
95. RODZYANKO, op. cit., 57.
96. MILYUKOV, P. N. (1921), *Istoriya Vtoroi Russkoi Revolyutsii*, Sofia, I, 1, 37.
97. RODZYANKO, op. cit., 58
98. *B. and K.*, I, 51.
99. GESSEN, I. V., *V Dvukh Vekakh*, ARR, XXII, 217.
100. *Dnevnik Nikolaiya Romanova*, KA, 1 (XX), 1927, 137.
101. MILYUKOV, op. cit., 53 ff.
102. Quoted TROTSKY, L. (1934), *History of the Russian Revolution*, Engl. trans., London, 162.
103. KERENSKY, op. cit., 236-7.
104. ibid., 244.
105. *B. and K.*, I, 71-2; for a detailed presentation of these events see FERRO, MARC (1960), *Les Debuts du Soviet de Petrograd*, *Revue Historique*, 223.
106. GOLDER, op. cit., 310-11.
107. MILYUKOV, op. cit., 47.
108. SUKHANOV, N. (1922), *Zapiski o Revolyutsii*, 7 vols., Berlin, I, 283.
109. LENIN, op. cit., Vol. 24, 61. (Italics in the original.)

PART III -

CHAPTER 14

1. See GOLDER, F. et al., (1918), *The Russian Revolution*, 73-4.
2. ANWEILER, *Rätebewegung*, 144.
3. SUKHANOV, op. cit., I, 190.
4. GOLDER, op. cit., 288-9.
5. SHLYAPNIKOV, op. cit., II, 175.
6. All the above is taken from YAKOVLEV, YA. (1926), *Mart-Mai 1917 g.*, KA, 2 (XV), 30-60.
7. BRESHKOVSKAYA, op. cit., 298.
8. DUBROWSKI, S. M., *Bauernbewegung*, 58.
9. See the data cited in SORLIN, P. (1964), *Lénine et le problème paysan en 1917*, *Annales*, XIX, No. 1, 254 ff.; see also ANTSIFEROV, A. N. et al. (1930), *Russian Agriculture during the War*, New Haven, 294-6.
10. OWEN, op. cit., 145 ff.
11. *B. and K.*, II, 524-5.
12. *B. and K.*, II, 710.
13. AVRICH, PAUL (1963), *Russian Factory Committees in 1917*, JFGO, XI, No. 2, 162.
14. MELLER, V. L., and PANKRATOVA, A. M. (eds.) (1926), *Rabochee Dvizhenie v 1917 g.*, Moscow/Leningrad, 47-56.

15. *B. and K.*, II, 712–13.
16. SHLYAPNIKOV, op. cit., II, 131–2.
17. For text see *B. and K.*, II, 718–20.
18. SCHWARZ, S. M., quoted *B. and K.*, II, 724–7.
19. AVRICH, op. cit., 165–6.
20. ANWEILER, op. cit., 156.
21. KERENSKY, op. cit., 258.
22. ONOU, A. (1933), The Provisional Government of Russia in 1917, *Contemporary Review*, October, 447.
23. KERENSKY, op. cit., 262.
24. *Iz Dnevnika A. N. Kuropatkina*, 1927, KA, 1 (XX), 66–7.
25. PALEOLOGUE, op. cit., III, 245; right-wing hostility to the idea of a constituent assembly is discussed in MELGUNOV, S. P. (1961), *Martovskie Dni*, Paris, 440 ff.
26. A point made by TSERETELLI, I. G. (1963), *Vospominaniya o Fevralskoi Revolyutsii*, 2 vols., The Hauge, I, 474.
27. VISHNYAK, M. (1932), *Vserossiisskoe Uchreditelnoye Sobranie*, Paris, 72; KOKOSHKIN, F. F. (1917), *Uchreditelnoye Sobranie*, Petrograd, 4 ff.
28. NABOKOV, V. D., *Vremennoye Pravitelstvo*, ARR, I, 72.
29. *B. and K.*, I, 434–5.
30. TSERETELLI, op. cit., I, 476.
31. MILYUKOV, op. cit., I, 1, 68–9.
32. SHLYAPNIKOV, op. cit., II, 235–7.
33. *B. and K.*, III, 1276.
34. For the above, see: CHERNOV, V. (1936), *The Great Russian Revolution*, Engl. trans., New Haven, 117 ff.; STEKLOV in *B. and K.*, III, 1233–1224; STANKEVITCH, V. B. (1920), *Vospominaniya*, Berlin, 91 ff.
35. BUCHANAN, op. cit., II, 127.
36. TROTSKY, *History*, 845; see ibid., 204, for Trotsky's appreciation of Milyukov.

CHAPTER 15

1. PALEOLOGUE, op. cit., III, 291 ff.; BUCHANAN, op. cit., II, 113.
2. TROTSKY, op. cit., 343.
3. HAHLWEG, W. (1957), *Lenins Rückkehr nach Russland 1917*, Leyden, No. 8, 48.
4. V. Romberg to Bethmann Hollweg, 13/26 April 1917, HAHLWEG, op. cit., No. 71, 107.
5. HAHLWEG, W. (1957), Lenins Reise durch Deutschland in April 1917, *Vierteljahrshefte für Zeitgeschichte*, V, 4, 333.
6. WARTH, R. (1954), *The Allies and the Russian Revolution*, Durham, North Carolina, 37 ff.; see also POPOV, A. (1927), *Diplomatiya Vremennovo Pravitelstva v Borbe s Revolyutsiei*, KA, 1 (XX), 8 ff.
7. Romberg to the German foreign office, 3/16 April 1917, HAHLWEG, *Lenins Rückkehr*, No. 13, 56.
8. TSERETELLI, op. cit., I, 171; PLATTEN, F. (1924), *Die Reise Lenins in plombierten Wagen durch Deutschland*, Berlin, 16.
9. HOWARD OF PENRITH, LORD ESME (1936), *Theatre of Life*, II (1905–16), London, 264.
10. cf. documents in RUBINSTEIN, N. L. (1929), K Priezdu Lenina v Rossiyu v 1917 g., *Proletarskaya Revolyutsiya*, No. 4, 222–5.
11. NABOKOV, V. D., op. cit., 75.

12. See RASKOLNIKOV's description in *Illustrated History . . .*, 121 ff.; ANET, C. (1917), *La Révolution Russe*, I, Paris, 176.
13. ANWEILER, op. cit., 182 ff.
14. SUKHANOV, op. cit., III, 27.
15. LENIN, op. cit., Vol. 24, 21-6.
16. TROTSKY, op. cit., 816.
17. SUKHANOV, op. cit., IV, 515.
18. KAMENEV published his views in an article in *Pravda*, 8 April 1917, re-published in LENIN, op. cit., 50 ff.
19. *KPSS v Rezolyutsiakh*, I, Moscow, 1953, 353.
20. TROTSKY, L. (1962), *Lenin*, Capricorn Books, New York, 81-4.
21. AXELROD, P. (1932), *Die russische Revolution und die sozialistische International*, Jena, 133. This was written shortly after the Bolshevik *coup*.

CHAPTER 16

1. CHERNOV, op. cit., 300.
2. WEBER, MAX (1921), *Russlands Ubergang zur Scheindemokratie* in *Gesammelte Politische Schriften*, Munich, 120, 117, 124. (Italics in original.)
3. MARTOV and DAN, op. cit., 298-9.
4. HELLMAN, M. (ed.) (1964), *Die Russische Revolution 1917*, Munich, 191.
5. *B. and K.*, III, 1261.
6. SUKHANOV, op. cit., II, 413.
7. NABOKOV, V., op. cit., 41.
8. ZALESSKAYA, F. (1927), Yunskaya Demonstratsiya 1917 goda, *Proletarskaya Revolyutsiya*, 6 (65), 128-9.
9. *B. and K.*, II, 1042.
10. PALEOLOGUE, op. cit., III, 246.
11. GOLDER, op. cit., 312.
12. KNOX, MAJOR-GENERAL SIR ALFRED (1921), *With the Russian Army 1914-17*, 2 vols., London, II, 585.
13. Quoted GOLOVANOV, N. I. (1960), O Roli Imperialistov S.Sh.A. i Antanti v Yunskom Nastuplenii Russkoi Armii v 1917 g., *Istoriya SSSR*, 4, 130.
14. GOLLIN, A. M. (1964), *Proconsul in Politics, A Study of Lord Milner*, London, 531-2.
15. SHLYAPNIKOV, op. cit., II, 234-5; *B. and K.*, II, 927 ff.
16. LLOYD GEORGE, D. (1938), *War Memoirs*, 2 vols., London, I, 970-71.
17. Quoted WARTH, R., op. cit., 48.
18. GOLOVANOV, op. cit., 130.
19. Lansing to Francis, 8/21 April 1917, POPOV, A. (1927), *Inostranniye Diplomati o revolyutsiei 1917 g.*, KA, 5 (XXIV), 132.
20. LLOYD GEORGE, op. cit., II, 1117-18.
21. Quoted WARTH, op. cit., 96.
22. ibid., 104.
23. VANDERVELDE, E. (1918), *Three Aspects of the Russian Revolution*, Engl. trans., London, 113.
24. SUKHANOV, op. cit., II, 404 ff. See also LOCKHART, R. B. (1937), *Memoirs of a British Agent*, London, 183 ff.; HAMILTON, M. (1938), *Arthur Henderson*, London, Ch. VII; *Fevralskaya Revolyutsia i Evropeiskie Sotsialisti*, KA, 2 (XV), 1926, 61-85.
25. GOLDER, op. cit., 325-6.
26. *B. and K.*, II, 1077.
27. GEYER, D. (1957), Die russischen Räte und die Friedensfrage, *Vierteljahrshefte für Zeitgeschichte*, V, 3, 224-5.

28. LENIN, op. cit., Vol. 23, 369.
29. *B. and K.*, II, 1079 ff.
30. An account of these discussions can be found in TSERETELLI, op. cit., I, 62 ff.
31. KERENSKY, *Catastrophe*, 130–31.
32. MILYUKOV, op. cit., I, Pt. I, 85.
33. *B. and K.*, II, 1045–6.
34. MILYUKOV, op. cit., 86; see also Milyukov's speech to a private conference of Duma members (*B. and K.*, III, 1273).
35. ibid., II, 1083–4.
36. MILYUKOV, op. cit., 92.
37. *B. and K.*, II, 1098. The words 'guarantees and sanctions' were inserted at the request of Albert Thomas, the French minister of labour, who was in Russia at this time (MILYUKOV, op. cit., 93).
38. GOLDER, op. cit., 335.
39. MILYUKOV, op. cit., 94; *Illustrated History . . .*, 149 ff.
40. YUGOR, M. S. (1927), *Sovety v period pervoi Revolyutsii* in POKROVSKY, M. N. (ed.) *Ocherki po istorii Oktyabrskoi Revolyutsii*, Milyukova i Aprelskie Dni, *Proletarskaya Revolyutsiya*, 4 (63), 100.
41. TSERETELLI, op. cit., I, 93 ff.
42. *Illustrated History . . .*, 148.
43. *B. and K.*, III, 1246; LENIN, op. cit., Vol. 24, 213–16.
44. KERENSKY, op. cit., 133.

CHAPTER 17

1. *B. and K.*, III, 1249 ff.
2. TSERETELLI, op. cit., I, 79.
3. ibid., 126 ff.
4. *B. and K.*, III, 1267.
5. BUCHANAN, op. cit., II, 127.
6. TSERETELLI, op. cit., I, 136–7.
7. STANKEVITCH, op. cit., 131.
8. LENIN, op. cit., Vol. 24, 372.
9. SUKHANOV, op. cit., III, 440 ff.; TROTSKY, *History*, 377.
10. POPOV, A. (1927), *Diplomatiya Vremennovo Pravitelstva v Borbe s Revolyutsiei*, KA, I (XX), 18–19.
11. ibid., 20.
12. STANKEVITCH, op. cit., 132.
13. MILYUKOV, op. cit., 167.
14. *B. and K.*, II, I, 1104.
15. ibid., 1120–23.
16. ibid., 1104.
17. BUCHANAN, op. cit., II, 129.
18. *B. and K.*, II, 1083.
19. TSERETELLI, op. cit., I, 362.
20. GOLDER, op. cit., 340–43. The origins and course of the Stockholm negotiations are excellently analysed in MEYNELL, H. (1960), The Stockholm Conference of 1917, *International Review of Social History*, V, 1–2.
21. *B. and K.*, II, 1119–20.
22. LENIN, op. cit., Vol. 25, 29 ff.
23. NABOKOV, K. D. (1921), *The Ordeal of a Diplomat*, London, 137, 158.
24. LENIN, op. cit., Vol. 25, 265–73.

25. PHILIPS PRICE, M. (1921), *My Reminiscences of the Russian Revolution*, London, 66 ff.

26. MARTOV and DAN, op. cit., 300.

CHAPTER 18

1. PALEOLOGUE, op. cit., III, 295–6.

2. GOLOVINE, N. N. (1931), *The Russian Army in the World War*, New Haven, 124–5.

3. GOLOVINE, N. N. (1937), *Rossiiskaya Kontr-Revolyutsiya v 1917–18 gg.*, Pt. I, Bk. I, Tallinn, 132.

4. GOLOVINE, N. N., *Russian Army*, 261; see also *Iz Dnevnika A.N. Kuropatkina*, KA, 1 (XX), 1927, 73–4.

5. See the minutes of a conference between Army commanders, the Soviet and the government reprinted in DENIKIN, A. I. (1922), *Ocherki Russkoi Smuty*, Paris, I, Pt. 2, 48 ff.; see also NABOKOV, V. D., op. cit., 74, and CHAADAYEVA, O. (1937), *Armiya v Period Podgotovki i Provedeniya Velikoi Oktyabrskoi Sotsialisticheskoi Revolyutsii*, KA, 5 (LXXXIV), 142–3.

6. See e.g. SHLYAPNIKOV, op. cit., II, 177.

7. SUKHANOV, op. cit., III, 111–12; ANET, op. cit., I, 207.

8. STANKEVITCH, opp. cit., 146–7.

9. BUNYAN, J., and FISHER, H. H. (eds.) (1934), *The Bolshevik Revolution 1917–18, Documents and Materials*, Stanford, 14; see also CHAADAYEVA, op. cit., 136.

10. VLADIMIROVA, V. (1933), *Bolshevizatsiya Fronta v Predyulskie Dni 1917 g.*, KA, 3 (LVIII), 88.

11. TROTSKY, *History*, 1031.

12. SCHAPIRO, L. B. (1963), *History of the Communist Party of the Soviet Union*, London, 171; see also TROTSKY, *History*, 812.

13. There is a short analytical summary of this debate in AVRICH, op. cit., 168–9.

14. *Illustrated History*, 188.

15. PHILIPS PRICE, M., op. cit., 34.

16. ibid., 41; see also TROTSKY, *History*, 440.

17. LENIN, V. I., *The April Conference*, London, n.d., 27.

18. VLADIMIROVA, V. (1924), *Revolyutsiya 1917 Goda, Khronika Sobytii*, III, Moscow/Leningrad, 268–9; see also ZALESSKAYA, F. op. cit.

19. *B. and K.*, III, 1317.

20. SUKHANOV, op. cit., IV, 336.

21. ibid., IV, 339; see also LENIN, op. cit., Vol. 25, 109–10.

22. TSERETELLI, op. cit., I, 480–82.

23. VISHNYAK, op. cit., 76; see also DREZEN, A. K. (ed.) (1932), *Burzhuaziya i Pomeshchiki v 1917 godu*, Moscow/Leningrad, 215, and TSERETELLI, op. cit., I, 483 ff.

24. ibid., 487–8.

25. KOTELNIKOV, G., and MELLER, V. L. (eds.) (1927), *Krestyanskoe dvizhenie v 1917 g.*, Moscow/Leningrad, iii.

26. MARTYNOV, M. (1926), *Agrarnoe dvizhenie v 1917 g. po dokumentam Glavnovo Zemelnovo Komiteta*, KA, 1 (XIV), 191–2.

27. WOLKONSKY, PRINCE S., *Reminiscences*, 2 vols., London, n.d., II, 163.

28. CHAADAYEVA, O. (1927), *Soyuz Zemelnykh Sobstvennikov v 1917 godu*, KA 2 (XXI) 102, 103, 107, 108.

29. M.R. (1936), *Borba za Zemlyu v 1917 g.*, KA, 5 (LXXVIII), 87.

30. CHAADAYEVA, op. cit., 103.
31. *B. and K.*, II, 584-5.
32. ibid., 528-32.
33. M.R., op. cit., 78-9.
34. CHERNOV, op. cit., 234.
35. See Postnikov's remarks quoted SEMENOV TYAN-SHANSKY, V. P., *Glavny Zemelny Komitet*, ARR, XII, 292.
36. *B. and K.*, II, 528.
37. From a lecture given by Chernov in Moscow on 30 April 1917, quoted OWEN op. cit., 160.
38. GOLDER, op. cit., 375-8.
39. See the description of the Congress in RADKEY, O. H. (1958), *The Agrarian Foes of Bolshevism*, New York, 213 ff.; and the resolution passed at the Soviet Congress in *B. and K.*, II, 604-5.
40. *B. and K.*, II, 603; LENIN, op. cit., Vol. 24, 483.

CHAPTER 19

1. Prince Lvov to *Rech*, 7 May 1917, *B. and K.*, II, 1102.
2. KERENSKY, op. cit., 193.
3. LUDENDORFF, E. (1919), *Meine Kriegsaerinnerungen*, Berlin, 343.
4. *B. and K.*, II, 1139.
5. BUCHANAN, op. cit., II, 117.
6. *B. and K.*, II, 938.
7. TSERETELLI, op. cit., II, 292.
8. LUDENDORFF, loc. cit.
9. KERENSKY, op. cit., 209.
10. KERENSKY, op. cit., 207 ff., cf. also this dialogue between Samuel Harper, the American Russian expert, and Kerensky – 'Some years later I asked Kerensky in Chicago if the ill-fated Russian offensive of July 1917 was the result of this hopeful pressure from the Allies and particularly from America or whether it was dictated by internal policies – the desire to stop, by military action, the internal disintegration which was progressing rapidly. I have always been comforted by Kerensky's answer: "Both factors." ' (HARPER, S. N. (1945), *The Russia I Believe In*, Chicago, 108.)
11. DENIKIN, op. cit., I, Pt. 1, 178.
12. For all the above see LLOYD GEORGE, op. cit., II, 1520; *Novoye Vremya*, 14 June 1917, quoted GOLOVANOV, op. cit., 130; TSERETELLI, op. cit., II, 292; LENIN, op. cit., Vol. 23, 25.
13. ibid., 24, 375-7.
14. STANKEVITCH, op. cit., 133.
15. GURKO, B. (1918), *Russia 1914-17*, London, 320; (1927) *Iz Dnevnika A.N., Kuropatkina*, KA, 1 (XX), 72.
16. These phrases from Kerensky's speeches are taken from *B. and K.*, II, 935 ff.
17. DENIKIN, op. cit., I, Pt. 2, 160.
18. TSERETELLI, op. cit., I, 404.
19. GOLDER, op. cit., 427-8; *B. and K.*, II, 937-8.
20. KNOX, op. cit., II, 641.
21. KERENSKY, op. cit., 218-19.
22. GOLDER, op. cit., 428-9.
23. GOLOVINE, op. cit., 272 ff.
24. KNOX, op. cit., II, 648.

CHAPTER 20

1. SUKHANOV, op. cit., V, 75–6. (Italics in original.)
2. See above, 234.
3. See *Yulskie Dni v Petrograde*, KA, 5 (XXIV), 1927, 20 ff.
4. TROTSKY, L., *Uroki Oktyabrya*, n.d., 24.
5. SUKHANOV, op. cit., IV, 413.
6. TROTSKY, loc. cit.
7. BONCH-BRUYEVICH, V. D. (1963), *Vospominaniya o V.I. Lenine 1917–24*, *Izbranniye Sochineniya*, III, Moscow, 54–5.
8. LIDAK, O. A. (1927), *Yolskie Sobyatiya 1917 goda* in POKROVSKY, op. cit.
9. ZINOVIEV, quoted MILYUKOV, op. cit., I, 1238.
10. STALIN, J. V. (1938), *Rechi Na Shestom Syezde RSDRP(b)*, 40–42.
11. *B. and K.*, III, 1349–50.
12. ibid., 1351.
13. TROTSKY, *History*, 594–5. The passage quoted from MILYUKOV is in the latter's *Istoriya*, I, 1, 1248.
14. *B. and K.*, III, 1365; the most judicious assessments of this contentious question are to be found in CARSTEN, F. (1959), Was Lenin a German Agent? *Problems of Communism*, VIII, 1; and in BONNIN, G. (1965), Les Bolchéviques et l'argent allemand pendant la première guerre mondiale, *Revue Historique*, No. 233.
15. KERENSKY, op. cit., 245 ff.
16. BUCHANAN, op. cit., II, 155.
17. TSERETELLI, op. cit., II, 343; CHERNOV, op. cit., 427–8.
18. MILYUKOV, op. cit., I, 2, 44–5, 48.
19. *B. and K.*, III, 1440–41.
20. ibid., 1402; see also loc. cit., 1425, and MILYUKOV, op. cit., I, 2, 49.
21. VISHNYAK, op. cit., 77.
22. This seems to be obliquely referred to in KERENSKY, *Catastrophe*, 279.
23. MILYUKOV, op. cit., I, 2, 91.
24. DREZEN, A. K. (ed.) (1932), *Burzhuaziya i Pomeshchiki v 1917 godu*, Moscow/Leningrad, 216. Only when nemesis had already struck did the Kadets realize their error. On 22 November 1917, Nabokov issued an appeal: 'The attempt to seize power (i.e. by the Bolsheviks) has disorganized communications, created anarchy and terror and interrupted the business of the commission (i.e. electoral commission of the constituent assembly). Nevertheless it is necessary to hold the elections wherever there is the slightest possibility of doing so.' (TYRKOVA-WILLIAMS, A. (1919), *From Liberty to Brest-Litovsk*, London, 334–5.)
25. STEPUN, op. cit., II, 203.
26. VLADIMIROVA, *Khronika*, III, 178–80.
27. LENIN, op. cit., Vol. 25, 177–8, 185.
28. TROTSKY, *History*, 818.
29. STALIN, op. cit., 64–70.
30. ibid., 77–8.
31. TROTSKY, op. cit., 815.
32. *Prodovolstvennoe Polozhenie v Moskve v Marte-Yune 1917 goda*, KA, 2 (LXXXI), 1937. For a general picture of economic collapse see *Zapiski V.A. Stepanova*, KA, 3 (X), 1925, 86–94.
33. CHERNOV, op. cit., 220.
34. WARD, BENJAMIN (1964), Wild Socialism in Russia: The Origins, *California Slavic Studies*, III, Table 4, 146.

35. AVERBACH, V. A., *Revolyutsionnoe Obshchestvo po lichnym Vospominaniyam*, ARR, XIV, 34–5.
36. *Istoriya Grazhdanskoi Voiny v SSSR*, Moscow, 1935, I, 212 ff.
37. MELLER, V. L. and PANKRATOVA, A. M. (eds.) (1926), *Rabochee Dvizhenie v 1917 godu*, Moscow/Leningrad, 114–15.
38. SUKHANOV, op. cit., V, 146.
39. TROTSKY, op. cit., 818.
40. DUBROWSKI, op. cit., 66 ff.; MARTYNOV, op. cit., 196; OWEN, op. cit., 139 ff.
41. KOTELNIKOV and MELLER, op. cit., xiii.
42. MARTYNOV, op. cit., 184–5 and map facing ibid., 224.
43. ibid., 225–6.
44. KOTELNIKOV and MELLER, op. cit., 91.
45. ibid., 47–8.
46. SHESTAKOV, A. (1927), Yulskie Dni v Derevne, *Proletarskaya Revolyutsia*, No. 7, (66), 31.
47. GOLDER, op. cit., 374–5.
48. CHERNOV, op. cit., 236.
49. ibid, 242; see also RADKEY, op. cit., 258–9.
50. TSERETELLI, op. cit., II, 351 ff.
51. *B. and K.*, II, 609.
52. GOLDER, op. cit., 470–71.

CHAPTER 21

1. SUKHANOV, op. cit., V, 146.
2. *B. and K.*, III, 1443.
3. ibid., 1457.
4. GOLDER, op. cit., 491.
5. *B. and K.*, III, 1452 ff.
6. KOHN, RICHARD (ed.) (1963), *La Révolution russe*, Paris, 276.
7. GOLDER, op. cit., 505.
8. MILYUKOV, op. cit., I, 2, 58–9; see also *Iz Dnevnika A.N. Kuropatkina*, KA, 1 (XX), 1927, 66–7.
9. MILYUKOV, op. cit., I, 2, 69.
10. GOLDER, op. cit., 516.
11. LUKOMSKY, A. (1922), *Vospominaniya*, 2 vols., Berlin, I, 228.
12. MILYUKOV, op. cit., II, 2, 103.
13. *B. and K.*, III, 1527 ff. For a recent description of the ramifications of the plot see LAVERYCHEV, V. YA. (1964), Russkie Monopolisti i Zagovor Kornilova, *Voprosy Istorii*, No. 4.
14. LUKOMSKY, op. cit., I, 231; DENIKIN, II, 32–3, 63; MILYUKOV, op. cit., II, 2, 251.
15. *B. and K.*, III, 1474 ff.
16. MELGUNOV, S. P. (1951), *Sudba Imperatora Nikolaya II Posle Otrecheniya*, Paris, 186.
17. OSSIP-LOURIE (1918), *La Russie en 1914–17*, Paris, 241.
18. Evidence to this effect is summarized in WARTH, op. cit., 123 ff.
19. BUCHANAN, op. cit., II, 175–6.
20. GOLDER, op. cit., 520, 522. The precise degree of Kerensky's cognizance of, and involvement in, Kornilov's intentions is not clear. Two recent analyses may be consulted: ASCHER, A. (1953), The Kornilov Affair, *Russian Review*, XII, 4, and STRAKHOVSKY, L. (1955), *Was there a Kornilov Rebellion?* SEER, XXXIII.

21. Quoted MILYUKOV, op. cit., I, 2, 269–70. This report is also referred to in TROTSKY, op. cit., 728.
22. LUKOMSKY, op. cit., I, 258.
23. BUCHANAN, MERIEL (1932), *The Dissolution of an Empire*, London, 241.
24. TROTSKY, op. cit., 738, 740.
25. LENIN, op. cit., Vol. 25, 286. (Italics in the original.)
26. TROTSKY, op. cit., 739.
27. TROTSKY, *My Life*, 273.
28. *B. and K.*, III, 1671.
29. ibid., 1670–71.
30. PIOTROW, F. J. (1962), *Paul Milyukov and the Constitutional Democratic Party*, unpublished Ph.D. Thesis (Oxford), 392.
31. *B. and K.*, III, 1684–6.
32. ibid., 1686.
33. BARON, B. E. NOLDE (1930), *Dalyekoe i Blizkoye*, Paris, 159–60.
34. GOLDER, op. cit., 566.
35. All these data are taken from BUNYAN, K., and FISHER, H. H. (1934), *The Bolshevik Revolution 1918–17, Documents and Materials*, Stanford, 29 ff.
36. ibid., 24 ff.; *B. and K.*, III, 1735 ff.
37. ibid., 1738–9.
38. CHERNOV, op. cit., 380–81.
39. WOYTINSKY, op. cit., 357.
40. See the chart in DUBROWSKI, *Bauernbewegung*, 87.
41. ibid., 69.
42. ibid., 69 ff.; BUNYAN and FISHER, op. cit., 31 ff.; KOTELNIKOV and MELLER, op. cit., 321.

CHAPTER 22

1. Quoted BOVYKIN, V. I., GINDIN, I. F., TARNOVSKY, K. H. (1959), Gosudarstvenno-Monopolisticheskii Kapitalizm v Rossii, *Istoriya SSSR*, No. 3, 87.
2. SUKHANOV, op. cit., VII, 36–7.
3. STEINBERG, I., *Ot Fevralya po Oktyabr 1917 g.*, Berlin/Milan (n.d.), 126. (Italics in the original.)
4. MARX, KARL, and ENGELS, FRIEDRICH (1934), *Correspondence 1846–95*, London, 437.
5. TROTSKY, op. cit., 823.
6. See above, 261.
7. LENIN, V. I. (1947), *The State and Revolution*, Engl. trans., London, 139, 141. (Italics in original.)
8. LENIN, op. cit., Vol. 25, 286–9. (Italics in the original.)
9. TROTSKY, op. cit., 935.
10. MILYUKOV, op. cit., I, 3, 80.
11. RADKEY, O. (1950), *The Elections to the Russian Constituent Assembly of 1917*, Harvard, 53.
12. TROTSKY, op. cit., 801.
13. ibid., 804.
14. ibid., 804–6.
15. ibid., 935.
16. ANWEILER, *Rätebewegung*, 230.
17. ibid., 231–2.

18. LENIN, op. cit., Vol. 26, 19–21. (Italics in the original.)

19. ibid., 27. (The Alexandrinsky Theatre was the seat of the Democratic Conference.)

20. ibid., 84. (Italics in the original.)

21. TROTSKY, op. cit., 842.

22. BUNYAN, J., and FISHER, H. H. (eds.) (1934), *The Bolshevik Revolution 1917–18*, Stanford, 59 ff.

23. SUKHANOV, op. cit., VII, 33.

24. See e.g. DREZEN, A. K. (ed.) (1932), *Bolskevizatsiya Petrogradskovo Garnizona*, Leningrad, 294, and the same author's *Baltiiski Flot v Oktyabrskoi Revolyutsii i Grazhdanskoi Voine*, Moscow/Leningrad, 1932, 3 ff.

25. TROTSKY, *Lenin*, 94.

26. TROTSKY, *Uroki Oktyabrya*, 44.

27. TROTSKY, *Lenin*, 95.

28. TROTSKY, *History*, 1027–8.

29. LENIN, op. cit., Vol. 26, 235.

30. OLDENBOURG, S. (ed.) (1929), *Le Coup d'Etat Bolchévique*, Paris, 70.

31. TROTSKY, op. cit., 943, 1126–7.

32. GOLDER, op. cit., 589–90; BUNYAN and FISHER, op. cit., 68.

33. ibid., 92–3; see also *B. and K.*, III, 1778–80; for Nabokov's appeal see TYRKOVA-WILLIAMS, A. (1919), *From Liberty to Brest-Litovsk*, London, 334–5, and NOLDE, op. cit., 154.

34. See e.g. BUCHANAN, MERIEL (1918), *Petrograd, The City of Trouble*, London, 187–8.

35. BUCHANAN, op. cit., II, 196, 201; see also NABOKOV, V., op. cit., 36, and NOLDE, op. cit., 163. MELGUNOV, S. P. (1953), *Kak Bolsheviki Zakhvatili Vlast*, Paris, 48 ff., gives a picture of governmental disarray and self-confidence.

36. OLDENBOURG, op. cit., 67–8.

37. TROTSKY, *Uroki Oktyabrya*, 43; see also TROTSKY, *History*, 1055.

38. ibid., 1056.

39. ibid., 1049.

40. BUCHANAN, op. cit., II, 206.

41. BUNYAN and FISHER, op. cit., 99.

42. TROTSKY, *History*, 1139.

43. OLDENBOURG, op. cit., 171.

44. ANWEILER, op. cit., 242–3. The exact allegiance of the delegates cannot be determined; for approximate analyses see BUNYAN and FISHER, op. cit., 110, n. 65.

45. ibid., 146 ff.; MELGUNOV, op. cit., 178 ff.

46. SUKHANOV, op. cit., VII, 219–20.

47. TROTSKY, op. cit., 1163.

48. SUKHANOV, op. cit., VII, 108–9.

49. See the analysis of the voting in RADKEY, op. cit., Appendix, pp. 78–80.

50. OLDENBOURG, op. cit., 232.

51. BUNYAN and FISHER, op. cit., 411–14.

52. ibid., 414–15.

53. PIOTROW, op. cit., 395 ff.

54. BUNYAN and FISHER, op. cit., 407–9.

55. BRADLEY, J. (1964), The Allies and Russia in the light of French Archives, *Soviet Studies*, XVI, No. 2, 168.

56. The terms of this convention and the circumstances of its signature are described in ULLMAN, R. (1961), *Intervention and the War*, Princeton, 52 ff.

57. See above, 217.
58. DEGRAS, J. (ed.) (1951), *Soviet Documents on Foreign Policy*, Oxford, I, 1–3.
59. MAYER, A. (1959), *Political Origins of the New Diplomacy*, Yale, 276.
60. GWYNN, op. cit., II, 423.
61. MAYER, op. cit., 352 ff.

Bibliography

DOCUMENTS

BROWDER, R. P., and KERENSKY, A. F. (eds.) (1961), *The Russian Provisional Government 1917 – Documents*, 3 vols., Stanford.

BUNYAN, J., and FISHER, H. H. (eds.) (1934), *The Bolshevik Revolution 1917–18, Documents and Materials*, Stanford.

DEGRAS, J. (ed.) (1951), *Soviet Documents on Foreign Policy*, I, Oxford.

Documents Diplomatiques Francais, Third Series, X.

DREZEN, A. K. (ed.) (1932), *Burzhuaziya i Pomeshchiki v 1917 godu*, Moscow/Leningrad.

— (ed.) (1936), *Tsarism v Borbes revolyutsiei 1905–7 gg.*, Moscow.

DUBROVSKY, S., and GRAVE, A. (eds.) (1925), *Agrarnoe Dvizhenie v 1905–7 gg.*, Moscow/Leningrad.

GANKIN, O. H., and FISHER, H. H. (eds.) (1940), *The Bolsheviks and the World War*, Stanford.

GOLDER, F. (ed.) (1927), *Documents of Russian History*, New York.

GOOCH, G. P., and TEMPERLEY, H. W. (eds.) (1928, 1929), *British Documents on the Origins of the War*, Vols. III, IV, London.

GRAVE, B. B. (ed.) (1927), *Burzhuaziya Nakanune Fevralskoi Revolyutsii*, Moscow/Leningrad.

HAHLWEG, W. (ed.) (1957), *Lenins Rückkehr nach Russland 1917*, Leyden.

HELLMANN, M. (ed.) (1964), *Die russische Revolution 1917*, Munich.

IVANOV, L. M. (ed.) (1961), *Rabochee Dvizhenie v Rossii v XIX Veke*, IV, Pt. I, Leningrad.

KOHN, RICHARD (ed.) (1963), *La Révolution russe*, Paris.

KOTELNIKOV, G., and MELLER, V. L. (eds.) (1927), *Krestyanskoe dvizhenie v 1917 g.*, Moscow/Leningrad.

KUTUZOV, V. V. (ed.) (1957), *Velikaya Oktyabrskaya Sotsialisticheskaya Revolyutsia – Khronika Sobytii*, Moscow.

MELLER, V. L., and PANKRATOVA, A. M. (eds.) (1926), *Rabochee Dvizhenie v 1917 g.*, Moscow/Leningrad.

OLDENBOURG, S. (ed.) (1929), *Le Coup d'État Bolchévique*, Paris.

PANKRATOVA, A. M. (ed.) (1955), *Vsyerossiskaya politicheshkaya stachka v Oktyabre 1905 g.*, 2 vols., Moscow/Leningrad.

— (1955), *Revolyutsia 1905–7 gg. v Rossii – Nachalo Pervoi Russkoi Revolyutsii*, Moscow.

— (1950), *Rabochee Dvizhenie v Rossii v XIX veke 1875–84*, II, Pt. II, Leningrad; (1963), IV, Pt. II, Moscow.

Rabochee Dvizhenie v Petrograde v 1912–17 gg., Leningrad, 1958.

RUBINSTEIN, N. L. (ed.) (1929), *K Priezdu Lenina v Rossiyu v 1917 g.*, *Proletarskaya Revolyutsiya*, No. 4.

SHCHEGOLEV, P. (ed.) (1926), *Padenie Tsarskovo Rezhima*, Vols. I, V, Moscow/
Leningrad.

SCHERER, A., and GRUNEWALD, J. (eds.) (1962), *L'Allemagne et les Problèmes
de la Paix pendant le première guerre mondiale*, Paris.

SCOTT, J. B. (ed.) (1917), *Reports to The Hague Conference of 1899 and 1907*,
Carnegie, Oxford.

SEMENNIKOV, V. P. (ed.) (1926), *Politika Romanovykh nakanune Revolyutsii*,
Moscow/Leningrad.

— (1927), *Monarkhiya pered krusheniyem*, Moscow/Leningrad.

SIDOROV, A. L. (ed.) (1959), *Materiali po Istorii SSSR*, VI, Moscow.

VLADIMIROVA, V. (1924), *Revolyutsiya 1917 Goda, Khronika Sobytii*, III,
Leningrad.

ZEMAN, Z. A. B. (ed.) (1958), *Germany and the Revolution in Russia*, Oxford.

MEMOIRS, CORRESPONDENCE, BIOGRAPHIES, ETC.

ALEXEYEV, V. (1925), *Pismo Gapona*, KA, 2 (IX–X).

ALMEDINGEN, E. M. (1964), *Unbroken Unity, A Memoir of Grand-Duchess Serge
of Russia*, London.

ANET, C. (1917), *La Révolution Russe*, I, Paris.

ASKEW, W. C. (1952), An American View of Bloody Sunday, *Russian Review*,
XI, No. 1.

AVERBACH, V. A., *Revolyutsionnoe Obshchestvo po Lichnym Vospominaniyam*,
ARR, XIV.

Pisma P. B. Axelroda i J. O. Martova, 1901–16, Berlin, 1924.

BADAYEV, A. (1933), *The Bolsheviks in the Tsarist Duma*, Engl. trans., London.

BARING, M. (1906), *A Year in Russia*, London.

BING, E. J. (ed.) (1937), *The Letters of Tsar Nicholas and Empress Marie*, London.

BOMPARD, M. (1937), *Mon ambassade en Russie*, Paris.

BONCH-BRUYEVICH, V. D. (1929), Devyatoe Yanvarya, *Proletarskaya Revolyutsia*, No. 1 (84).

— (1963), Vospominaniya o V. I. Lenine 1917–24, *Izbranniye Sochineniya*, III,
Moscow.

BRESHKO-BRESHKOVSKAYA, K. (1931), *The Hidden Springs of the Russian
Revolution*, Stanford.

BRUSILOV, A. A. (1930), *A Soldier's Note-Book*, Engl. trans., London.

BUCHANAN, SIR GEORGE (1923), *My Mission to Russia*, 2 vols., London.

BUCHANAN, MERIEL (1918), *Petrograd, The City of Trouble*, London.

— (1932), *The Dissolution of an Empire*, London.

BYRNES, R. F. (1951), Pobedonostzev's Conception of the Good Society,
Review of Politics, XIII, No. 2.

CALLWELL, MAJOR-GENERAL SIR C. E. (1927), *Field-Marshal Sir Henry
Wilson: His Life and Diaries*, 2 vols., London.

CHERNAVIN, T. (1938–9), *The Home of the Last Tsar*, SEER, XVII.

CHERNOV, V. (1953), *Pered buryei*, New York.

DANILOV, YU.N. (1930), *Velikyi Knyaz Nikolai Nikolayevich*, Paris.

DEBAGORY-MOKRIEVICH, V. (1904), *Vospominaniya*, 3rd ed., St Petersburg.

DENIKIN, A. I. (1922), *Ocherki Russkoi Smuty*, Paris.

DOBROROLSKI, SERGE (1922), *Die Mobilmachung der russischen Armee 1914*,
Berlin.

Graf Fredericks und die russische Mobilmcahung 1914, *Berliner Monatshefte*,
IX, 9 (1931).

GAPON, FATHER G. (1905), *The Story of My Life*, Engl. trans., London.

GESSEN, I. V., *V dvukh vekakh*, ARR, XXII.

GIRAULT, R. (1963), La Révolution Russe de 1905 d'après quelque temoignages français, *Revue Historique*, 223.

GOLLIN, A. M. (1964), *Proconsul in Politics, A Study of Lord Milner*, London.

GUERASSIMOV, GENERAL (1934), *Tsarisme et Terrorisme*, French trans., Paris.

GURKO, B. (1918). *Russia, 1914–17*, London.

GURKO, V. I. (1939), *Features and Figures of the Past*, Stanford.

GWYNN, S. (ed.) (1929), *The Letters and Friendships of Sir Cecil Spring Rice*, 2 vols., Boston.

HAHLWEG, W. (1957), Lenins Reise durch Deutschland in April 1917, *Vierteljahrshefte für Zeitgeschichte*, V. 4.

HARDINGE, VISCOUNT (1947), *The Old Diplomacy*, London.

HAMILTON, M. (1938), *Arthur Henderson*, London.

HARPER, S. N. (1945), *The Russia I Believe In*, Chicago.

HOWARD OF PENRITH, LORD ESME (1936), *Theatre of Life (1905–16)*, London.

ILIODOR (1917), *Svyatoi Chort – Zapiski o Rasputine*, Moscow.

IZVOLSKY, A. (1920), *Memoirs*, Engl. trans., London.

KERENSKY, A. F. (1927), *The Catastrophe*, London.

— (1934), *The Crucifixion of Liberty*, London.

KIZEVETTER, A. A. (1929), *Na Rubezhe Dvukh Stoletii*, Prague.

KNOX, MAJOR-GENERAL SIR ALFRED (1921), *With the Russian Army 1914–17*, 2 vols., London.

KONSTANTINOV, M. (1925), *Nikolai II v 1905 g.*, KA, 4–5 (XI–XII).

KROPOTKIN, P. (1885), *Paroles d'un Révolté*, ed. RECLUS, E., Paris.

KRUPSKAYA, N. (1935), *Memories of Lenin*, Engl. trans., 2 vols., London, 3rd ed.

KRYZHANOVSKY, S. E. (1938), *Vospominaniya*, Berlin.

Dnevnik Kuropatkina, KA, II, 1922; I (XX), 1927.

LEROY-BEAULIEU, A. (1897), *L'Empire des Tsars et les Russes*, 3 vols., 4th ed., Paris.

LLOYD GEORGE, D. (1938), *War Memoirs*, 2 vols., London.

LOCKHART, R. B. (1937), *Memoirs of a British Agent*, London.

LOUIS, G. (1926), *Les Carnets*, 2 vols., Paris.

LUDENDORFF, E. (1919), *Meine Kriegserinnerungen*, Berlin.

LUKOMSKY, GENERAL A. S. (1922), *Vospominaniya*, 2 vols., Berlin.

MARX, K., and ENGELS, F. (1934), *Correspondence 1846–95*, London.

MARYE, G. T. (1929), *Nearing the End in Imperial Russia*, Philadelphia.

MELGUNOV, S. P. (1951), *Sudba Imperatora Nikolaya II posle Otrecheniya*, Paris.

MIHAILOVITCH, ALEXANDER (1932), *Once a Grand Duke*, New York.

MILYUKOV, P. (1955), *Vospominaniya*, 2 vols., New York.

MOSOLOV, A. A. (1935), *At the Court of the Last Tsar*, Engl. trans., London.

NABOKOV, K. D. (1921), *The Ordeal of a Diplomat*, London.

NABOKOV, V. D., *Vremennoye Pravitelstvo*, ARR, I.

NEMIROVITCH-DANCHENKO, V. (1937), *My Life in the Russian Theatre*, Engl. trans., London.

NEVINSON, H. W. (1906), *The Dawn in Russia*, London.

NEVSKY, V. (1922), *Yanvarskie Dni v Peterburge v 1905 g.*, Krasnaya Letopis, I.

NICOLSON, H. (1930), *Lord Carnock*, London.

NOLDE, BARON B. E. (1930), *Dalyekoe i Blizkoye*, Paris.

Padenie Tsarskovo Rezhima, I, Moscow, 1924.

PALÉOLOGUE, M. (1922), *La Russie des Tsars*, 3 vols., Paris.

PALEY, PRINCESS (1924), *Memoirs of Russia (1916–19)*, London.

PARES, B. (1913), *Conversations with Stolypin*, Russian Review, II, No. 1.

— (ed.) (1923), *Letters of the Tsaritsa to the Tsar 1914–16*, London.

— (1931), *My Russian Memoirs*, London.

PETRUNKEVITCH, I. I., *Iz zapisok obshchestvennovo deyatelya*, ARR, XXI.

PLATTEN, F. (1924), *Die Reise Lenins im plombierten Wagen durch Deutschland*, Berlin.

POBEDONOSTZEV, K. (1898), *Reflections of a Russian Statesman*, Engl. trans., London.

POLUNIN, V. (1957), *Three Generations*, Engl. trans., London.

POURTALES, GRAF (1919), *Am Scheidewege zwischen Krieg und Frieden*, Berlin.

PRICE, M. PHILIPS (1921), *Reminiscences of the Russian Revolution*, London.

RODZYANKO, M. V., *Krushenie Imperii*, ARR, XVII.

Dnevnik Nikolaiya Romanova, KA. I, (XX), 1927.

Perepiska N. A. Romanova i P. A. Stolypina, KA, V (1924).

ROSEN, BARON R. (1922), *Forty Years of Diplomacy*, 2 vols., London.

RUTENBERG, P. (1925), *Ubiistvo Gapona*, Leningrad.

SAVINKOV, B. (1931), *Memoirs of a Terrorist*, New York.

SCHURER, H. (1959), *Alexander Helphand-Parvus*, Russian Review, October.

V. SCHWEINITZ, H. L. (1927), *Denkwürdigkeiten*, 2 vols., Berlin.

SHIPOV, D. N. (1918), *Vospominaniya i Dumy o Perezhitom*, Moscow.

SHULGIN, V. V. (1928), *Tage*, German trans., Berlin.

Pismo I. I. Skvortzova-Stepanova N. I. Leninu, *Istoricheskii Arkhiv*, No. 2, 1959.

SPIRIDOVITCH, A. (1928), *Les dernières années de la cour de Tsarskoye Selo*, 2 vols., Paris.

— (1935), *Raspoutine*, French trans., Paris.

STANKEVICH, V. B. (1920), *Vospominaniya*, Berlin.

STEINBERG, I., *Ot Fevralya Oktyabr 1917*, Berlin-Milan (n.d.).

STEINBERG, I. (1935), *Spiridonova*, Engl. trans., London.

Zapiski V. A. Stepanova, KA, 3 (X), 1925.

STEPUN, F. (1948-9), *Vergangenes und Unvergängliches*, 3 vols., Munich.

STRAKHOVSKY, L. (1959), *The Statesmanship of Peter Stolypin*, SEER, XXXVII, No. 89.

SUKHANOV, N. (1922), *Zapiski o Revolyutsii*, 7 vols., Berlin.

SVERCHKOV, D. (1925), *Na Zare Revolyutsii*, 3rd ed., Leningrad.

SYROMATNIKOV, S. (1912), *Reminiscences of Stolypin*, Russian Review, I, 2.

TATAROV, I. (1927), *Trepovsky Proekt Rechi Nikolaya II k Rabochim posle 9 Yanvarya 1905, g.*, KA, I (XX).

Iz Dnevnika Lva Tikhomirova, KA, I (LXXIV), 1936.

TOKMAKOFF, G. (1965), Stolypin's Assassin, *Slavic Review*, XXIV, 2.

TROTSKY, L. (1930), *My Life*, London.

— (1962), *Lenin*, New York.

— (1947), *Stalin*, London.

TSERETELLI, I. S. (1963), *Vospominaniya o Fevralskoi Revolyutsii*, 2 vols., The Hague.

TYAN-SHANSKY, SEMENOV, *Glavny Zemleny Komitet*, ARR, XII.

TYRKOVA-WILLIAMS, A. (1919), *From Liberty to Brest-Litovsk*, London.

ULAR, ALEXANDER (1905), *Russia From Within*, Engl. trans., London.

VANDERVELDE, E. (1918), *Three Aspects of the Russian Revolution*, Engl. trans., London.

VIROUBOVA, ANNA (1923), *Memories of the Russian Court*, London.

VITTE, S. Y. (1924), *Vospominaniya*, 2nd ed., Leningrad.

Graf Vitte v Borbe s Revolyutsiei, Byloe, No. 3, March 1918.

WILLIAMS, H. (1914), *Russia of the Russians*, London.

WOLKONSKY, PRINCE S., *Reminiscences*, 2 vols., London (n.d.).

WOYTINSKY, W. (1961), *Stormy Passage*, New York.

YAKHONTOV, A. N., *Tyazhelie Dni*, ARR, XVIII.

Zapiski A. S. Yermolova, KA, I (VIII), 1925.

Zapiski Zemskovo Nachalnika, *Russkaya Mysl*, XXXVIII, 1917.

ZEMAN, Z. A. B., and SCHARLAU, W. (1965), *The Merchant of Revolution*, Oxford.

ZENZINOV, V. (1919), *Iz Zhini Revolyutsionera*, Paris.

SOCIAL, ECONOMIC

AMES, E. (1947), *A Century of Russian Railway Construction, 1837–1936*, ASEER, VI, Nos. 18–19.

AMALRIK, A. S. (1955), K Voprosu o Chislennosti i geographicheskom razmeshchenii stachechnikov v Evropeiskoi Rossii v 1905 g., *Istoricheskie Zapiski*, No. 52.

ANDERSON, C. A. (1956), A Footnote to the Social History of Modern Russia – The literacy and education census of 1897, *Genus*, XII, Nos. 1–4.

ARUTYUNOV, G. A. (1959), Vsyeobshchaya Stachka Bakinskikh Rabochikh v 1914 godu, *Istoriya SSSR*, No. 3.

AVRICH, PAUL (1963), *Russian Factory Committees in 1917*, JFGO XI, 2.

BILYK, P. (1937), V Tsarskoi Armii Nakanune Fevralskoi Burzhuazno-Demokraticheskoi, Revolyutsii, KA, 2 (LXXXI).

BOVYKIN, V. I., GINDIN, I. F., TARNOVSKY, K. H. (1959), Gosudarstvennii monopolisticheskii Kapitalizm v Rossii, *Istoriya SSSR*, No. 3.

BRUNNER, O., Europäisches und Russisches Bürgertum, *Vierteljahrshefte für Sozial und Wirtschaftsgeschichte*, XL, No. 1.

BRUTSKUS, B. (1925), *Agrarentwicklung und Agrarrevolution in Russland*, Berlin.

— (1934), *Die historischen Eigentümlichkeiten der wirtschaftlichen und sozialen Entwicklung Russlands*, Jahrbücher für Kultur und Geschichte der Slawen.

BUCHBINDER, N. A. (1922), K Istorii 'Sobraniya Russkikh Fabrichno-Zavodskikh Rabochikh St. P.', *Krasnaya Letopis*, I.

CARSON JR., G. B. (1959), *The State and Economic Development: Russia, 1890–1939* in AITKEN, H. (ed.), *The State and Economic Growth*, New York.

CHAADAYEVA, O. (1927), *Soyuz Zemelnykh Sobstvennikov v 1917 godu*, KA, 2 (XXI).

— (1937), *Armiya v Period Podgotovki i Provedeniya Velikoi Oktyabrskoi Sotsialisticheskoi Revolyutsii*, KA, 5 (LXXXIV).

— (1938), *K Istorii Vsyeobschei Stachki na Yuge Rossii v 1903 g.*, KA, 3 (LXXXVIII).

CHERNOV, V. (1934), *Rozhdenie Revolyutsionnoi Rossii*, Prague.

COQUIN, F.-X. (1960), Aperçus sur l'économie tsariste avant 1914, *Revue d'Histoire Moderne*, No. 7.

— (1964), Faim et Migrations Paysannes en Russie au XIX siècle, *Revue d'Histoire Moderne et Contemporaine*, XI.

CRISP, O. (1953–4), Russian Financial Policy and the Gold Standard at the end of the Nineteenth Century, *Economic History Review*, 2nd s., VI.

DANIEL, R. V. (1957), Lenin and the Russian Revolutionary Tradition, *Harvard Slavic Studies*, IV, The Hague.

DUBROVSKY, S. (1925), *Agrarnoe Dvizhenie v 1905 g. po otchetam Dubassova i Panteleeva*, KA, 4–5 (XI–XII).

— (1925), *Krestyanskoe Dvizhenie v 1905 g.*, KA, 2 (IX).

— (1929), *Die Bauernbewegung in Russland*, Berlin.

— (1930), *Iz Istorii Borby s Agrarnyn Dvizheniem 1905–6 gg.*, KA, 2 (XXXIX).

— (1963), *Stolypinskaya Zemelnaya Reforma*, Moscow.

DZIEWANOVSKI, M. K. (1957), The Polish Revolutionary Movement and Russia 1904–7, *Harvard Slavic Studies*, IV.

EASON, W. W. (1960), *Population Changes*, in BLACK, C. E. (ed.), *Transformation of Russian Society*, Cambridge, Mass.

Fevralskaya Revolyutsiya 1917 goda, (1927), KA, 2 (XXI).

FORD, T. K. (1936), Genesis of the First Hague Peace Conference, *Political Science Quarterly*, LI, No. 3.

GAISTER, A. (1926), *K Istorii Agrarnoi Reformy Stolypina*, KA, 4 (XVII).

GELIS, I. (1926), *Revolyutsionnaya Propaganda v Armii v 1916–17 gg.*, KA, 4 (XVII).

GERSHENKRON, A. (1947), The Rate of Industrial Growth in Russia since 1885, *Journal of Economic History*, VII (Supplement).

— (1963), *The Early Phases of Industrialization in Russia*, in ROSTOW, W. W. (ed.), *The Economics of Take-Off into Sustained Growth*, London.

GEYER, D. (1962), *Lenin in der russischen Sozialdemokratie*, Cologne/Graz.

GINDIN, I. F. (1963), Russkaya Burzhuaziya v period kapitalizma, razvitie i osobennosti, *Istoriya SSSR*, VII, No. 2.

GLIKSMAN, J., *The Russian Urban Worker*, in BLACK, C. E. (ed.) *The Transformation of Russian Society*.

GOEBEL, O. (1920), *Entwicklungsgang der russischen Industriearbeiter*, Leipzig/Berlin.

GOKHLERNER, V. M. (1955), Krestyanskoe Dvizhenie v Saratovskoi Gubernii, *Istoricheskie Zapiski*, No. 52.

GOLDSMITH, R. W. (1960–61), Economic Growth of Tsarist Russia 1860–1913, *Economic Development and Cultural Change*, IX.

GOLOVINE, N. N. (1931), *The Russian Army in the World War*, New Haven.

— (1937), *Rossiiskaya Kontr-Revolyutsiya v 1917–18 gg.*, Pt. I, Bk. I, Tallinn.

GRINEVITCH, V. (1908), *Professionalnoye dvizhenie rabochikh v Rossii*, St Petersburg.

— (1927), *Die Gewerkschaftsbewegung in Russland I (1905–14)*, Berlin.

HAIMSON, L. (1964), The Problem of Social Stability in Urban Russia 1907–17, *Slavic Review*, XXIII, 4; XXIV, 1, 1965.

HARPER, S. N. (1912), Exceptional Measures in Russia, *Russian Review*, I, No. 4.

IZGOYEV, A. S. (1909), *Russkoe Obshchestvo i Revolyutsia*, St Petersburg.

— (1909), Ob Intelligentnoi Molodezhi in GERSHENZON, M. O. (ed.), *Vekhi*, 3rd ed., Moscow.

KENNARD, H. P. (1907), *The Russian Peasant*, London.

KERBLAY, B. (1962), L'Evolution de l'alimentation rurale en Russie 1896–1960, *Annales*, No. 2.

KHROMOV, P. A. (1950), *Ekonomicheskoe Razvitie Rossii v 19–20 vekakh*, Moscow.

KISS, G. (1958), *Die gesellschaftspolitische Rolle der vorrevolutionären Studentenbewegung in Russland*, Munich.

KORBUT, M. (1926), *Uchet Departamentom Politzii Opyta 1905 goda*, KA, 5 (XVIII).

KUCHEROV, S. (1953), *Courts, Lawyers and Trials Under the Last Three Tsars*, New York.

KUZNETZOV, I. (1936), *Agrarnoe Dvizhenie v Smolenskoi Gubernii v 1905–6 gg.*, KA, I (LXXIV).

KUZNETZOVA, L. C. (1955), Stachechnaya Borba Rabochikh Peterburga v 1905 g., *Voprosy Istorii*, No. 1.

M.L.L. (1937), *Lensky Rasstrel 1912 g.*, KA, 2 (LXXXI).

LABRY, R. (1919), *L'Industrie russe et la Révolution*, Paris.

LANE, D. S. (1964), *Social and organisational difference between Bolsheviks and Mensheviks, 1903 to 1907*, Discussion Papers Series Rc/C, No. 1, Centre for Russian and East European Studies, University of Birmingham.

LAUE, TH. VON (1956), *Die Revolution von aussen als erste Phase der russischen, Revolution 1917*, JFGO, IV, No. 2.

— (19—), *Of the Crises in the Russian Polity* in CURTISS, J. S. (ed.) *Essays in Russian and Soviet History*, Leyden.

— *The State and the Economy*, in BLACK, C. E. (ed.) *The Transformation of Russian Society.*

— (1961), *Russian Peasants in the Factory 1892–1904*, *Journal of Economic History*, XXI, No. 1.

— (1962), *Problems of Modernization*, in LEDERER, I. (ed.), *Russian Foreign Policy*, Yale.

— (1964), *Russian Labour between Field and Factory*, *California Slavic Studies*, III.

LEMBERGSKAYA, V. L. (1925), *Dvizhenie v Voiskakh na Dalnem Vostoke*, KA, 4–5 (XI–XII).

LENIN, V. I. (1956), *The Development of Capitalism in Russia*, Engl. trans., London.

LEROY-BEAULIEU, A. (1897), *L'Empire des Tsars et les Russes*, 3 vols., Paris, 4th ed.

LIVSHIN, YA. (1957), *K voprosu o voenno – promyshlennikh monopoliyakh v Rossii v nachale XX veka*, *Voprosy Istorii*, No. 7.

— (1959), 'Predstavitelniye' Organizatsii Krupnoi Burzhuazii, *Istoriya SSSR*, III, No. 2.

LIVSHITZ, R. C. (1955), *Razmeshchenie Promyshlennosti v dorevolyutsionnoi Rossii*, Moscow.

LURYE, M. (1936), *Tsarizm v Borbe s Rabochim Dvizheniem v gody Podyema*, KA, 1 (LXXIV).

— (1936), *K Istorii Borby Samoderzhaviya s agrarnym dvizheniem v 1905–7 gg.*, KA, 5 (LXXVIII).

LYASHCHENKO, P. (1946), Iz istorii monopolii v Rossii, *Istoricheskie Zapiski*, No. 20.

— (1949), *History of the National Economy of Russia*, Engl. trans., New York.

MAKLAKOV, V. (1923–4), The Peasant Question and the Russian Revolution, *Slavonic Review*, II, No. 5.

MARTOV, J., MASLOV, P., POTRESOV, A. (eds.) (1909–14), *Obshchestvennoe Dvizhenie v Rossii*, 4 vols., St Petersburg.

MARTYNOV, M. (1926), *Agrarnoe dvizhenie v 1917 g. po dokumentam Glavnovo Zemelnovo Komiteta*, KA, 1 (XIV).

MAVOR, J. (1914), *Economic History of Russia*, 2 vols., London.

MENDEL, A. P. (1961), *Dilemmas of Progress in Tsarist Russia*, Harvard.

MIGULIN, P. P. (1904), *Russkii Gosudarstvennii Kredit*, III, Kharkov.

MILYUKOV, P. (1962), *Russia and its Crisis*, Collier Books, New York.

MOSSE, W. E. (1965), *Stolypin's Villages*, SEER, XLIII, No. 101.

MOTYLEV, V. E. (1955), Ob Osobennostyakh Promyshlennovo Razvitiya Rossii v Kontze xix – Nachale xx Veka, *Voprosy Istorii*, No. 7.

Nikolai II i Samoderzhavie v 1903 g., *Byloe*, No. 1 (29), January 1918.

NOVIKOV, A. (1906), *Das Dorf* in MELNIK, J. (ed.) *Russen über Russland*, Frankfurt-on-Main.

OLSON JR., M. (1963), Rapid Growth as a Destabilizing Force, *Journal of Economic History*, XXIII, No. 4.

ORLOV, V. (1936), *Studencheskoe Dvizhenie v 1901 g.*, KA, 2 (LXXV).

OWEN, L. L. (1937), *The Russian Peasant Movement 1906–17*, London.

OZEROV, I. K. (1906), *Politika po rabochemu voprosu v Rossii za posledniye gody*, Moscow.

PANKRATOVA, A. M. (1955), Proletarizatziya Krestyanstva, *Istoricheskie Zapiski*, No. 54.

PARVUS, A. (1906), *Rossiya i Revolyutsia*, St Petersburg.

PATKIN, A. L. (1947), *The Origins of the Russian-Jewish Labour Movement*, Melbourne.

PAVLOVSKY, G. (1930), *Agricultural Russia on the Eve of the Revolution*, London.

PAZHITNOV, K. (1955), Polozhenie Rabochevo Klassav Rossii nakanune Revolyutsii 2905–6, *Voprosy Ekonomii*, No. 5.

PAZHITNOV, K. A. (1906), *Polozhenie Rabochevo Klassa Rossii*, St Petersburg.

PERSHIN, P. N. (1922), *Uchastkovoe Zemlepolzovanie v Rossii*, Moscow.

PETROV, V. (1950), Tsarshaya Armiya v borbe s massovym Revolyutsionnym Dvizheniem v Nachale xx veka, *Istoricheskie Zapiski*, No. 34.

POKROVSKY, M. N. (1926), *Politicheskoe Polozhenie Rossii Nakanune Fevralskoi Revolyutsii*, KA, 4 (XVII).

— (1927), Russkaya Burzhuaziua in *Bolshaya Sovetskaya Entsiklopediya*, VIII.

PORTAL, R. (1954), *Das Problem einer industriellen Revolution in Russland*, FZOG, I.

— (1962), Industriels Moscovites, *Cahiers du Monde Russe et Soviétique*, IV, Nos. 1–2.

PREYER, W. D. (1914), *Die Russische Agrarreform*, Jena.

Prodovolstvennoe Polozhenie v Moskve v Marte-Yune 1917 goda., KA, 2 (LXXXI).

RADKEY, O. H. (1958), *The Agrarian Foes of Bolshevism*, New York.

RASHIN, A. G. (1956), *Naselenie Rossii za 100 let*, Moscow.

— (1958), *Formirovanie Rabochevo Klassa Rossii*, Moscow.

RIMLINGER, G. V. (1960), Autocracy and the Factory Order in Early Russian Industrialization, *Journal of Economic History*, XX, No. 1.

ROBINSON, G. T. (1932), *Rural Russia under the Old Régime*, London.

RODICHEV, F. (1923), *The Liberal Movement*, SEER, II, No. 5.

ROMANOV, B. (1925), *K Peregovoram Kokovtsova o zaime v 1905–6 gg.*, KA, 3 (X).

— (1925), *9 Yanvarya 1905 g. – Doklady V. N. Kokovtsova Nikolayu II*, KA, 4 (XI–XII).

ROOSA, R. (1963), Russian Industrialists look to the future 1906–17, in CURTISS, J. (ed.), *Essays in Russian and Soviet History*, Leyden.

ROSTOW, W. W. (1960), *Industrialization and Economic Growth*, First International Conference of Economic History, The Hague.

A.S. (1925), *Pribaltiiskii Krai v 1905 g.*, KA, 5 (XII).

SHESTAKOV, A. (1927), Yulskie Dni v Derevne, *Proletarskaya Revolyutsiya*, No. 7 (66).

SIDOROV, A. L. (1955), Finansovoe Polozhenie Tsarskovo Samoderzhaviya v Peryod Russko-Yaponskoi Voiny, *Istoricheskii Arkhiv*, No. 2.

SINZHEIMER, G. P. G. (1965), Reflections on Gerschenkron, Russian Backwardness and Economic Development, *Soviet Studies*, XVII, 2.

SORLIN, P. (1964), Lénine et le problème paysan en 1917, *Annales*, No. 2.

STEPNIAK (1888), *The Russian Peasantry*, 2 vols., London.

SVYATLOVSKY, V. (1907), *Professionalnoye Dvizhenie v Rossii*, St Petersburg.

SYROMATNYKOVA, M. (1936), *Rabochee Dvizhenie na Zavodakh Peterburga v Mae 1901 g.*, KA, 3 (LXXVI).

TATAROV, I. (1927), K Istorii 'Politskeiskovo Sotsializma', *Proletarskaya Revolyutsiya*, No. 5 (64).

TRUBETSKOY, E. (1906), Die Universitätsfrage, in MELNIK (ed.), *Russen über Russland*, Frankfurt am Main.

TURIN, S. P. (1935), *From Peter the Great to Lenin*, London.

TYRKOVA-WILLIAMS, A. (1953), The Cadet Party, *Russian Review*, XII, No. 3.

TYUMENEV, A. (1925), *Ot Revolyutsii k Revolyutsii*, Leningrad.

VITTE, S. Y. (1935), Dokladnaya Zapiska Vitte Nikolayu II, *Istorik-Marksist*, 2/3.

— (1908), *Samoderzhavie i Zemstvo*, St Petersburg.

— (1912), *Konspekt Lektsii*, 2nd ed., St Petersburg.

VLADIMIROVA, V. (1933), *Bolshevizatsiya Fronta v Predyulskie Dni 1917 g.*, KA, 3 (LVIII).

WALLACE, SIR D. M. (1912), *Russia*, revised ed., London.

WARD, B. (1964), Wild Socialism in Russia: The Origins, *California Slavic Studies*, III.

WEBER, M. (1906), Zur Lage der bürgerlichen Demokratie in Russland, *Beilage, Archiv für Sozialwissenschaft und Sozialpolitik*, XXII.

— (1921), *Gesammelte Politische Schriften*, Munich.

YAKOVLEV, A. (1955), *Ekonomicheskie Krizisy v Rossii*, Moscow.

YAKOVLEV, YA. (1926), *Mart-Mai 1917 g.*, KA, 2 (XV).

YANEY, G. L. (1961), *The Imperial Government and the Stolypin Land Reform*, Ph.D. Thesis (unpublished), Princeton.

Yulskie Volneniya 1914 g. v Peterburge, *Proletarskaya Revolyutsia*, No. 7 (30), 1924.

Zapiski Zemskovo Nachalnika, *Russkaya Mysl*, XXXVIII, Nos. 7–8, 1917.

ZASLAVSKY, D. (1918), Zubatov i Marya Vilbushevich, *Byloe*, No. 9 (3).

POLITICAL

ADAMS, A. E. (1952), Pobedonostzev's Thought Control, *Russian Review*, XI, No. 4.

— (1953), *Pobedonostzev and the Rule of Firmness*, SEER, XXXII, No. 78.

AXELROD, P. (1932), *Die russische Revolution und die sozialistische Internationale*, Jena.

BLOK, ALEXANDER, *Posledniye Dni Staravo Rezhima*, APR, IV.

CRISP, OLGA (1961), *The Russian Liberals and the 1906 Anglo-French loan to Russia*, SEER, XXXIX, No. 93.

DAN, T. (1964), *The Origins of Bolshevism*, Engl. trans., London.

FISCHER, G. (1958), *Russian Liberalism*, Cambridge, Mass.

GIRAULT, R. (1961), Sur quelques aspects financiers de l'alliance francorusse, *Revue d'Histoire Moderne et Contemporane*, VIII.

GOLDENWEISER, E. A. (1914), The Russian Duma, *Political Science Quarterly*, XXIX.

Gosudarstvennaya Duma: Stenographicheskii Otchet, Sozyv II, Sessiya 2; Sozyv III, Sessiya 2; Sozyv IV, Sessiya , 4.

GRAVE, B. (1931), *Kadety v 1905–6 gg.*, KA, 3 (XLVI).

KEEP, J. L. H. (1955–6), *Russian Social-Democracy and the First State Duma*, SEER, XXXIV.

KOKOSHKIN, F. F. (1917), *Uchreditelnoye Sobranie*, Petrograd.

KPSS v Rezolyutsiakh, I. Moscow, 1953.

LANE, D. S., *The iSocial Eidos' of the Bolsheviks in the 1905 Revolution*, Discussion Papers Rc/C No. 2, Centre for Russian and East European Studies, University of Birmingham.

— (1964), The Russian Social Democratic Labour Party in St Petersburg, Tver and Ashkhabad, *Soviet Studies*, XV, 3.

LAPIN, N. (1932), *Progressivnyi Blok v 1915–17 gg.*, KA, 1–2 (L–LI).

LAPIN, N. (1932), *Progressivnyi Blok v 1915–17 gg.* (continuation), KA, 3 (LII).
— (1933), *Kadety v dni Galitsiiskovo Razgroma,* KA, 4 (LIX).
LENIN, V. I. (1963), *What is to be done?,* ed. and trans., UTECHIN, S., Oxford.
— *The April Conference,* London (n.d.).
— (1947), *The State and Revolution,* Engl. trans., London.
— (1960–64), *Collected Works,* Engl. trans., Vols. 2, 8, 9, 10, 12, 13, 19, 23, 24, 25, 26, Moscow.
LEONTOVITSCH, V. (1957), *Geschichte des Liberalismus in Russland,* Frankfurt-on-Main.
LEVIN, A. (1939), The Fifth Social-Democratic Congress and the Duma, *Journal of Modern History,* XI, 4.
— (1940), *The Second Duma,* New Haven.
— (1963), *Russian Bureaucratic Opinion in 1905,* JFGO, XI, 1.
LUXEMBURG, R. (1963), *Die Russische Revolution,* ed. FLECHTHEIM, O. K., Frankfurt-on-Main.
MAKLAKOV, V. A. (1939), *Pervaya Gosudarstvennaya Duma,* Paris.
— *Vtoraya Gosudarstvennaya Duma,* Paris (n.d.).
MILYUKOV, P. N. (1920), *Bolshevism: An International Danger,* London.
ONOU, A. (1933), The Provisional Government of Russia in 1917, *Contemporary Review.*
PARES, B. (1923–4), *The Second Duma,* SEER, II.
PETROVA, L. F. (1955), Peterburgski Soviet Rabochikh Deputatov v 1905 g., *Voprosy Istorii,* No. 11.
PIOTROW, F. (1962), *Paul Milyukov and the Constitutional-Democratic Party,* Ph.D. Thesis (unpublished), Oxford.
RADKEY, O. (1950), *The Election to the Russian Constituent Assembly of 1917,* Harvard.
RODZYANKO, M. V., *Gosudarstvennaya Duma i Fevralskaya 1917 goda Revolyutsia,* ARR, VI.
ROGGER, H. (1964), Formation of the Russian Right, *California Slavic Studies,* III.
SCHAPIRO, L. B. (1963), *History of the Communist Party of the Soviet Union,* London.
STALIN, J. V. (1938), *Rechi na Shestom Syezde RSDRP (b).*
TCHULOZHNIKOV, A. (1926), *K Istorii Manifesta 6 Augusta 1905 g.,* KA, I (XIV).
Tretti Syezd Rsorp, Protokolli (1959 ed.), Moscow.
TROTSKY, L. *Uroki Oktyabrya* (n.d.).
— (1962), *The Permanent Revolution,* London.
VISHNYAK, M. (1932), *Vserossiiskoe Uchreditelnoye Sobranie,* Paris.
WALSH, W. B. (1950), Political Parties in the Russian Dumas, *Journal of Modern History,* XXII, 2.
ZALESSKAYA, F. (1927), Yunskaya Demonstratsiya 1917 g., *Proletarskaya Revolyutsiya,* No. 6 (65).

HISTORICAL

ANTSIFEROV, A. N. et. al. (1930), *Russian Agriculture during the War,* New Haven.
ANWEILER, O. (1955), *Russische Revolution 1905,* JFGO III.
— (1958), *Die Rätebewegung in Russland, 1901–21,* Leyden.
ASCHER, A. (1953), The Kornilov Affair, *Russian Review,* XII, 4.
BONNIN, G. (1965), Les Bolchéviques et l'argent allemand pendant la première guerre mondiale, *Revue Historique,* No. 233.

BRADLEY, J. (1964), The Allies and Russia in the light of French Archives, *Soviet Studies*, XVI, 2.

BYKOV, P. M. (1934), *The Last Days of Tsardom*, Engl. trans., London.

CARSTEN, F. (1959), Was Lenin a German Agent?, *Problems of Communism*, VIII, No. 1.

CHERMENSKY, E. D. (1939), *Burzhuaziya i Tsarism v Revolyutsii 1905-7*, Moscow/Leningrad.

CHERNOV, V. (1936), *The Great Russian Revolution*, Engl. trans., New Haven.

DILLON, E. J. (1918), *The Eclipse of Russia*, London.

DUBNOW, S. M. (1920), *History of the Jews in Russia and Poland*, III, Engl. trans., Philadelphia.

FERGUSON, A. D., and LEVIN, A. (eds.) (1964), *Essays in Russian History*, Hawden, Connecticut.

FERRO, MARC. (1960), Les Débuts du Soviet de Petrograd, *Revue Historique*, No. 223.

GALAI, S. (1965), The Impact of the Russo-Japanese War on the Russian Liberals 1905-5, *Government and Opposition*, I, 1.

GEYER, D. (1957), Die russischen Räte und die Friedensfrage, *Vierteljahrshefte für Zeitgeschichte*, V, 3.

GOLDER, F., et. al. (1918), *The Russian Revolution*, Oxford.

GOLOVANOV, N. I. (1960), O Roli Imperialistov S.Sh.A. i Antanti v Yunskom Nastuplenii Russkoi Armii v 1917 g., *Istoriya SSSR*, No. 4.

GRAVE, B. (1926), *K Istorii klassovoi borby v Rossii*, Moscow/Leningrad.

Illustrated History of the Russian Revolution, Engl. trans., London, 1928.

KAZOVSKAYA, A. (1927), Nota Milyukova i Aprelskie Dni, *Proletarskaya Revolyutsia*, No. 4 (63).

MELGUNOV, S. P. (1953), *Kak Bolsheviki Zakhvatili Vlast*, Paris.

— (1961), *Martovskie Dni*, Paris.

MEYNELL, H. (1960), The Stockholm Conference of 1917, *International Review of Social History*, V, 1-2.

MILYUKOV, P. N. (1921), *Istoriya Vtoroi Russkoi Revolyutsii*, Sofia.

— (1925), *Russlands Zusammenbruch*, 2 vols., German trans., Berlin.

PANKRATOVA, A. M. (1951), *Pervaya Russkaya Revolyutsia*, Moscow.

PARES, B. (1939), *The Fall of the Russian Monarchy*, London.

POKROVSKY, M. N. (ed.) (1927), *Ocherki po istorii Oktyabrskoi Revolyutsii*, 2 vols., Moscow.

— (1929), *Oktyabrskaya Revolyutsia*, Moscow.

— (1933), *Brief History of Russia* Engl. trans. 2 vols., London.

POPOV, A. (1927), *Diplomatiya Vremennovo Pravitelstva v Borbe s Revolyutsiei*, KA, 1 (XX).

— (1929), *Inostranniye Diplomati o revolyutsii 1917 g.*, KA 5 (XXIV).

SHLYAPNIKOV, A. (1926), *Fevralskaya Revolyutsia i Evropeiski Sotsialisti*, KA, 2 (XV).

SHLYAPNIKOV, A. (1926), *Fevralskaya Revolyutsia i Evropeiski Sotsialisti*, KA — *1917 god*, 2 vols., Moscow.

STRAKHOVSKY, L. (1955), *Was there a Kornilov Rebellion?*, SEER, XXXIII, No. 81.

STRUVE, P. B. (1930), *Food Supply in Russia during the World War*, New Haven.

TROTSKY, L. (1934), *The History of the Russian Revolution*, Engl. trans., London.

ULLMAN, R. (1961), *Intervention and the War*, Princeton.

WARTH, R. (1954), *The Allies and the Russian Revolution*, Durham, North Carolina.

Yulskie Dni v Petrograde, KA, 5 (XXIV), 1927.

ZAGORSKY, S. O. (1928), *State Control of Industry in Russia during the war*, New Haven.

MISCELLANEOUS

BACHTIN, N. (1963), *Lectures and Essays*, Birmingham.

FISCHER, FRITZ (1964), *Griff nach der Weltmacht*, Hanover.

GERSCHENZON, M. O. (ed.) (1909), *Vekhi*, 3rd ed., Moscow.

HERZEN, A. I. (1919), *Polnoe Sobranii Sochinenii i Pisem*, ed. LEMKE, M., VIII, Petrograd.

LEONTYEV, K. (1912), Srednyi Evropeetz, in *Sobranie Sochinenii*, VI, Moscow.

MAYER, A. (1959), *Political Origins of the New Diplomacy*, Yale.

SIDOROV, A. L. (1945), Otnosheniya Rossii s Soyuznikami i Inostranniye Postavki vo Vremya Pervoi Mirovoi Voiny, *Istoricheskie Zapiski*, No. 15.

TARLE, E. (1958), *Sochineniya*, XI, Moscow.

THADEN, E. C. (1964), *Conservative Nationalism in Nineteenth Century Russia*, Seattle.

WEBER, MAX (1906), Zur Lage der bürgerlichen Demokratie in Russland, *Beilage, Archiv Für Sozialwissenschaft und Sozialpolitik*, XXII, (1921), *Gesammelte Politische Schriften*, Munich.

Subject Index

Academy of Sciences, 95, 117

agriculture, 17, 24, 26–7, 28, 32, 33, 35, 51–9, 100, 133–40, 162, 166, 178, 188, 201–4, 214, 238–41, 243, 254–6, 265–6

anarchism, 12, 51, 55, 74, 154, 170

'April Theses', 213, 233, 240

Army (Russian), 12, 14, 20, 31, 33, 47, 62, 63, 86, 91–2, 96, 102, 104, 105, 117, 165, 169, 172, 178–9, 180–2, 189–90, 192, 199, 215, 225, 232–4, 236, 242–6, 252, 263–5, 267, 273, 274, 275–9

Baku, 17, 35, 38, 80, 83, 94, 164, 166

Black Hundreds, 125, 127, 151

'Bloody Sunday', 85, 86–101, 113, 162

Bolsheviks, 11, 12, 13, 20, 72, 73, 74, 75, 95, 97, 109, 110, 111, 126, 127, 128, 130, 140, 141, 143, 144, 145, 146, 158, 163, 164, 177, 179, 183, 187, 188, 191, 195, 201, 205, 206, 208, 209, 212, 213, 214, 221, 223, 224, 225, 226, 227, 229, 230, 233, 234, 235, 236, 237, 239, 240, 242, 243, 244, 247, 248, 249, 250, 251, 252, 253, 257, 259, 260, 262, 263, 264, 265, 267, 268, 269, 270, 271, 272, 273, 274, 275, 276, 277, 278, 279, 280, 281

bourgeoisie, 23, 66, 67, 100, 107, 131, 141, 144, 145, 146, 147, 148, 149, 153, 185, 201, 209, 214, 221, 224, 225, 227, 233, 235, 248, 250, 251, 259, 268

bureaucracy, 12, 15, 29, 66, 82, 84, 141, 168

capital and capitalism, 16, 23, 27, 28, 29, 32, 33, 40, 44, 45, 64, 65, 67, 68, 72, 90, 118, 141, 144, 145, 149, 167, 213, 252, 281

Church (Russian Orthodox), 48, 64, 116, 172, 182, 258

communes, 30, 37, 40, 41, 52–4, 56, 58, 133, 134, 135, 136, 142, 147

Congress of Berlin, 25

constituent assembly, 19, 69, 95, 98, 99, 100, 106, 144, 194, 195, 201, 207, 215, 236, 237, 250, 255, 256, 272, 275, 278, 279

Crimea, 25, 26, 280, 281

Decembrist movement, 173

Disarmament Conference at the Hague (1899), 31

Donetz Coal Basin, 36, 177, 234

Duma, 64, 96, 100, 101, 104, 106, 109, 114, 115–32, 134, 140, 141, 144, 161, 163, 170, 171, 176, 181, 183, 184, 185, 186, 187, 188, 190, 192, 193, 194, 195, 199, 200, 201, 208, 239. See also municipal dumas

Ekaterinoslav, 17, 79, 125

Emperor, see Tsar

Empire (Russian), 11, 19, 25, 43, 60, 61, 93, 98, 119, 166, 177

entrepreneurs, 18, 23, 27, 35

factories, 35, 36, 37, 39–40, 41–5, 67, 72, 91, 103, 110, 132, 148, 165, 187, 188, 191, 199, 204–5, 209 235, 252, 253

famines, 17, 26, 32

February régime, 13

Finland, 81, 82, 93

Finns, 12, 19, 81, 184

Five Year Plan (First), 28, 281
foreign loans, 17, 24, 25, 28, 30, 32, 118
France, 17, 31, 118, 174, 179, 180, 280

Georgians, 19, 75
Germany, 17, 28, 31, 118, 174, 180, 242–3, 280
government (industrial) subsidies, 17, 24

Imperial Council, 117, 121, 130, 170–1, 183
industry and industrialization, 13, 15, 16, 17, 23–30, 31–3, 35–47, 52, 65, 67, 68, 160, 165–8, 178, 235, 253, 262, 281
intelligentsia, 18, 23, 41, 52, 74, 80, 96, 98, 100, 115, 141, 146, 151, 154, 155, 156, 158, 159
Italy, 17, 31
Ivanovo-Vosnesensk, 17, 75, 95, 108, 187

Japan, 61, 101, 103, 118
Jews, 19, 62, 64, 75, 79, 95, 98, 104, 106, 107, 124, 132, 152, 171, 184, 262
'July Days', 247 passim

Kadets, 121–2, 125, 127, 154, 184, 185, 193, 206, 218, 227, 239, 247, 250, 251, 256, 259, 261, 262, 269, 270, 278, 279
Kiev, 17, 79, 80, 84, 106, 129, 131

land, 16, 17, 37, 41, 51–9, 69, 79, 100, 104, 113, 122, 129, 133–9, 142, 202–4, 206, 214, 216, 239, 240, 249, 254–6, 265–6
landowners, 52, 55, 56, 57, 65, 79, 100, 115, 127, 151, 216, 254, 256, 265, 266
Lutherans, 19

marxism, 12, 37, 42, 126, 145, 149, 154
Mensheviks, 72, 73, 74, 75, 87, 96, 97, 105, 108, 109, 110, 126, 127, 128, 140, 141, 142, 143, 144, 145, 146, 163, 177, 186, 188, 191, 195, 199, 201, 205, 208, 212, 214, 215, 220, 221, 225, 226, 227, 228, 229, 230, 234, 235, 239, 244, 251, 256, 260, 261, 262, 268, 269, 270, 271, 274, 277, 278
Moscow, 35, 38, 39, 48, 49, 66, 84, 99, 102, 103, 111, 112, 116, 122, 131, 139, 148, 153, 157, 161, 163, 178, 185, 214, 234, 257, 259, 263, 269, 271, 273, 278
Moscow Soviet, 111, 112
Moslems, 19, 119, 120
municipal dumas, 25, 43, 180

national income, 17

October Manifesto, 64, 104, 105, 107, 111, 113, 115, 123, 128, 166, 172
Octobrist Party, 105, 154, 166, 172, 184, 190, 240
Odessa, 17, 26, 49, 84, 106, 131, 139

peasantry, 15, 17, 18, 20, 24, 25, 29, 30, 32, 33, 34, 36, 39, 40, 41, 42, 51–9, 62, 66, 69, 72, 79, 80, 84, 85, 93, 98, 99, 100, 111, 113, 114, 116, 118, 119, 129, 131, 133–40, 141, 143, 144, 146, 147, 148, 149, 151, 160, 184, 199, 201, 202, 203, 204, 206, 209, 215, 234, 238–41, 249, 254, 255, 256, 265, 266, 267, 268, 269, 271, 272
Peasant Bank, 56, 138, 139
Peasant Union, 100, 113
Petrograd (St Petersburg), 15, 35, 36, 37, 38, 42, 44, 47, 61, 66, 72, 79, 84, 86, 88, 89, 92, 94, 96, 101, 102–14, 115, 118, 122, 123, 125, 131, 148, 152, 161, 163, 164, 169, 172, 173, 175, 176, 177, 187, 190, 191, 192, 194, 199, 200, 201, 204, 205, 207, 209, 211, 213, 219, 220, 223, 227, 234, 235, 236, 237, 247, 249, 251, 253, 258, 259, 262, 265, 268, 269, 270, 271, 273, 274, 275, 276–7, 278, 279, 280
pogroms, 63, 79, 93, 106, 276
Poland, 26, 35, 44, 46, 81, 83, 93, 125
Poles, 19, 81, 119, 184
police, 12, 18, 44, 45, 46, 47–9, 87, 102, 104, 127, 163, 164, 165, 185, 189, 191, 215
population, 12, 15–17, 23, 32, 35, 55, 57, 66, 73

Populists, 24, 28, 33, 37, 69, 153
professional men, 15, 18, 71, 84, 95, 100, 102, 103, 127
proletariat, 13, 15, 16, 17, 18, 32, 35, 36, 72, 86, 93, 100, 109, 115, 133, 141, 144, 149, 160, 161, 188, 213, 251, 267, 268, 272, 275
Provisional Government, 172, 179, 193, 194, 195, 200, 205, 208, 209, 210, 212, 213, 214, 215, 217, 218, 219, 221, 222, 223, 224, 227, 228, 229, 233, 239, 242, 244, 248, 249, 260, 265, 270, 274, 275, 276, 277, 278

railways, 12, 16, 25–6, 29–30, 33, 58, 67, 94, 102, 103, 137, 165, 167, 177, 178, 181
Riga, 17, 131
Roman Catholics, 19, 120
Rostov-on-Don, 17, 271
Russo-Japanese War, 19, 81, 90, 93, 97–8, 101, 147, 151, 168, 173, 180, 281

St Petersburg, see Petrograd
serfdom, 38 passim
Siberia, 25, 57, 104, 139, 162, 278
Social-Democrats, 45, 48, 69, 72, 75, 88, 93, 95, 96, 100, 126, 127, 128, 131, 140, 141, 142, 144, 148, 154, 235, 279
Socialist-Revolutionaries, 69, 70, 72, 75, 82, 83, 86, 88, 100, 110, 114, 126, 129, 142, 154, 194, 195, 199, 201, 205, 208, 212, 214, 215, 225, 226, 229, 234–5, 239, 240, 241, 251, 255, 260, 261, 268, 269, 271, 275, 277, 278, 279
soviets, 45, 109, 111–12, 140, 143–4, 199, 200, 213, 214, 218, 220, 222, 223, 225, 229, 235, 236, 237, 240, 243, 244, 250, 251, 270, 272, 273–4, 275, 276
Soviet (St Petersburg), 106, 108, 110–11, 114, 115, 143, 172, 194, 195, 200, 204, 205, 207–8, 212, 221, 222, 223, 224, 228, 229, 233, 247, 248, 249, 251, 258, 259, 260, 270, 272, 274, 275–6
Soviet of Workers' and Soldiers' Deputies, 208, 224, 225, 240, 247, 258, 271

standard of living, 31–2, 55, 160, 188–9
strikes, 18, 20, 32, 42–5, 46–7, 79, 80, 88, 93–5, 96, 98, 100, 102–6, 110–11, 113, 148, 160, 163, 164, 172, 176, 187–8, 190, 191–2
students, 12, 15, 48, 66, 73, 79, 94–5, 103, 107, 132, 153, 155

tariffs, 17, 24, 27, 32
taxation, 17, 28, 31, 33, 37, 53, 54, 90, 133, 160
trade, 23–4, 32; balance of trade, 24, 55
trade unions, 18, 42, 44, 45, 47, 73, 87, 90, 103, 115, 144, 161, 163–4, 179, 184, 187, 189, 199, 235, 252, 270, 277
Treasury, 28, 29
Tsar (Nicholas II), 12, 15, 18, 19, 44, 51, 58, 60, 61, 63, 64, 65, 79, 83, 85, 89, 91, 92, 93, 96, 97, 99, 100, 103, 104, 106, 107, 111, 112, 113, 115, 116, 117, 120, 122, 123, 124, 125, 130, 170, 171, 173, 175, 181, 182, 183, 186, 190, 192, 193, 194, 204, 206
Tsarina, 60, 62, 171, 190–1
tsarism, 15, 18, 19, 23, 43, 48, 51, 60–68, 69, 75, 81, 95, 102, 103, 106, 109, 114, 130, 134, 141, 143, 144, 148, 150, 157, 168, 171, 174, 179, 184, 192, 196, 208, 209, 210, 216, 221, 228, 229, 281
Tsaritsyn (Volgograd), 17, 235

Ukraine, 26, 35, 75, 238, 254, 278, 280
Ukrainians, 19, 75
unemployment, 32, 253
Uniates, 19
Union of Liberation, 81, 83, 84
Union of Russian People, 63, 107, 125, 126
Union of Unions, 94, 98, 103
United Kingdom, 17, 28, 31, 118, 180, 259, 279–80
United States, 28, 31
universities, 15, 25, 79, 99, 103–4, 105, 117, 132, 153
Urals, 35

villages, 36–7, 51–9, 69, 135, 165, 202–4, 265–6

Vyborg Congress and Manifesto, 94, 122, 123; 126

wages, 37, 38, 40, 43, 44, 46, 162, 188, 189
Warsaw, 83, 94, 178, 180, 181
workers, 15, 24, 29, 31, 33, 34, 35, 36, 37, 38–9, 40, 42–3, 44–7, 48, 49, 50, 66, 72, 73, 79–80, 81, 85, 86, 90, 91, 95–6, 97, 102, 104, 110, 115, 116, 140, 143, 144, 149, 162, 163, 164, 165, 183, 189, 191, 199, 204, 205, 209, 214, 215, 224, 235, 236, 252, 253, 271, 276
Workmen's Association (of St. Petersburg), 88
World War I, 174–5, 176–85, 188, 189–90, 203, 216–24, 228–9, 232–4, 235, 236, 242–6, 258, 263–4, 270, 279–81

zemstvos, 25, 39, 43, 58, 64, 71, 81, 83, 84, 85, 98, 117, 141, 180, 184, 238

Name Index

ADORNO, Theodor, 151
ALEXANDER II, 51, 64, 133, 210
ALEXANDER III, 16, 30, 43, 64, 67
ALEXANDER MIHAILOVITCH, Grand Duke, 169, 190
ALEXEYEV, Admiral, 61
ALEXEYEV, General M. V., 207, 219, 220, 260, 279
ALEXIS, Tsarevitch, 116, 171, 191, 195, 206
ANASTASIA Princess (of Montenegro), 171
ANDREYEV, Leonid, 155
ANNENSKY, N. F., 91
ARSENEV, A. K., 91
AUDEN, W. H., 11
AVKSENTIEV, N., 257
AXELROD, Paul B., 73, 141, 215
AZEV, Evno, 70, 83

BAKUNIN, Michael A., 74, 157
BALFOUR, Lord, 211, 218
BAUDELAIRE, Pierre Charles, 155
BEILIS, Mendel, 171, 172
BELY, Andrey, 152
BERNSTEIN, Eduard, 147,
BISMARCK - SCHÖNHAUSEN, Eduard Leopold, Prince von, 48
BLOK, Alexander Alexandrovitch, 20, 152, 158, 159
BOBRINSKY, Count V. A., 25, 174
BOGDANOV, Boris, 260
BOGOLEPOV, N. P., 79
BOGROV, Dmitry, 124
BOMPARD, M., 15
BOSTREM, Vice-Admiral, 168
BRESHKO-BRESHKOVSKAYA, Catherine, 114, 177, 203
BRINK, Lieutenant-General, 168

BRUSILOV, General A. A., 179, 245, 258
BRYUSOV, Valery Y., 152
BUCHANAN, Sir George, 18, 190, 212, 220, 228, 244, 249, 259, 275
BUCHANAN, Meriel, 260
BÜLOW, Prince B., 11, 173
BULYGIN, A. G., 97, 106, 109
BUNGE, N. K., 24, 42

CACHIN, Marcel, 220
CATHERINE THE GREAT, 110, 121
CHEKHOV, Anton, P., 152, 153, 155
CHERNOV, Victor, 69, 83, 201, 208, 216, 226, 228, 255–6
CHKHEIDZE, N. S., 172, 212, 221, 226, 227, 270

DA VINCI, Leonardo, 155
DAN, Theodore, 216, 275
DEBAGORY-MOKRIEVITCH, Vladimir, 51
DENIKIN, General A. I., 243, 264, 279
DILLON, Dr E. J., 31, 82
DMITRY PAVLOVITCH, Grand Duke, 259
DMOWSKI, Roman, 98
DOLGORUKI, Prince, 99, 186
DOSTOYEVSKY, Fedor M., 23
DOUMERGUE, Gaston, 173
DUBASOV, Admiral F. V., 114
DURNOVO, Paul N., 80, 86, 106, 111, 112, 114, 174

ENGELS, Friedrich, 155, 268
ESSENIN, Sergei, 158

FIGNER, Vera, 210
FRANCIS I (Emperor of Austria), 29

GAPON, Father Georgei, 86–92
GERSCHENSON, Michael O., 155
GOGOL, N. V., 153
GONCHAROV, Ivan A., 17
GOREMYKIN, Ivan L., 134
GORKI, Maxim, 86, 91, 95, 273
GUCHKOV, Alexander, 172, 184,
 194, 207, 217, 221, 225, 226, 258,
 259
GURKO, V. I., 168
GVOZDEV, K., 226

HARPER, Samuel, 125
HENDERSON, Arthur, 220, 230
HERZEN, Alexander I., 66, 68, 74,
 146, 157, 176
HERZENSTEIN, Professor, 125, 128
HESSEN, V. M., 91

IVANOV-RAZUMNIK (R. V. Iva-
 nov), 158
IZMAILOVITCH, Catherine, 210
IZVOLSKY, A., 61

KALAYEV, 70
KALEDIN, General, 269, 279
KAMENEV, Leon, 214, 225, 237, 272,
 273
KANKRIN, Y. F., 29
KEDRIN, E. I., 91
KERENSKY, Alexander F., 172, 175,
 177, 194, 201, 205, 212, 222, 224,
 225, 226, 228, 242, 243, 244, 245,
 249, 258, 259, 260, 261, 262, 265,
 269, 275, 276
KHABALOV, General, 192
KHODSKY, Professor, 105
KHRUSTALEV-NOSAR, P. A., 111,
 112
KIRNOSOV, 129, 131
KNOX, Major-General Sir Alfred,
 218, 246
KOKOSHKIN, F. F., 206, 237
KOKOVTSOV, P. K., 96, 118, 119,
 120, 170
KONOVALOV, A. S., 172, 184
KORNILOV, General Lavr G., 258,
 259, 260, 261, 268, 269, 270, 279
KOTEN, Colonel von, 164
KRIVOSHEIN, General A. V., 173,
 180, 181
KROPOTKIN, Prince Peter, 55, 157,
 177

KRYMOV, General A. M., 190, 260
KRYZHANOVSKY, S. E., 126
KUROPATKIN, General Alexey N.,
 57, 81, 173

LAVROV, Peter L., 74
LENIN, V. I., (Ulianov), 12, 33, 42,
 45, 71, 72, 73, 74, 86, 87, 93, 107,
 109, 127, 140, 141, 142, 143, 145,
 146, 147, 148, 150, 172, 176, 196,
 206, 209, 210, 211, 212, 213, 214,
 215, 218, 219, 221, 224, 226, 230,
 233, 234, 235, 236, 237, 240, 241,
 243, 244, 247, 248, 249, 251, 253,
 258, 259, 260, 268, 269, 271, 272,
 273, 274, 275, 277, 278, 280–1
LEONTYEV, Konstantin, 23, 66
LIST Friedrich, 27
LLOYD GEORGE, David, 219, 230
LOBKO, General, 32
LUDENDORFF, Field Marshal E. von,
 242
LUKOMSKY, General A. S., 260, 279
LUXEMBURG, Rosa, 73, 74, 94, 98,
 148
LUZHENOVSKY, General 70
LVOV, Prince George, 123, 185, 193,
 194, 205, 206, 209, 211, 219, 221,
 222, 225, 226, 239, 242, 256

MAKLAKOV, N. A., 170, 172, 175,
 181, 183
MAKLAKOV, V., 186, 208, 237
MARKOV II, 174
MARTOV, J., 73, 108, 109, 221, 275,
 277
MARTYNOV, A., 108, 144
MARX, Karl, 11, 68, 147, 149, 155
MAXIMOVITCH, General, 114
MELLER-ZAKOMELSKY, General,
 112
MENDELSSOHN, Robert, 174
MICHAEL ALEXANDROVITCH,
 Grand Duke, 191, 193, 195, 206
MILITSA, Princess (of Montenegro),
 171
MILNER, Lord, 219
MILYUKOV, Paul, 71, 83, 121, 122,
 128, 155, 172, 174, 184, 185, 186,
 189, 190, 193, 194, 195, 201, 205,
 206, 209, 210, 211, 217, 218, 219,
 220, 222, 223, 224, 226, 228, 232,
 236, 249, 250, 259, 260, 279

MIN, Colonel, 112
MORGAN, J. P., 118
MOROZOV, SAVVA, 67

NABOKOV, Constantine, 230
NABOKOV, Vladimir, 80, 206, **207**, 217, 238, 261, 275
NEKRASOV, N. V., 19, 172, 194
NEVINSON, Henry, 110
NICHOLAS I, 29
NICHOLAS II, 18, 44, 60, 61, 63, 64, 66, 95, 116
NICOLSON, Sir Arthur, 15
NIKOLAI MICHAILOVITCH, Grand Duke, 175
NIKOLAI NIKOLAYEVITCH, Grand Duke, 175, 182
NIVELLE, General, 219
NOLDE, Baron B. E., 261

O'GRADY, James, 220
ONOU, Alexander, 219
ORLOV, Prince, 113

PALEOLOGUE, M., 173, 182, 184, 210, 212, 218, 232
PARES, Bernard, 124, 128
PARVUS, A., 147, 148, 149, 151, 176, 188, 210, 211, 249
PAUL ALEXANDROVITCH, Grand Duke, 191
PESHEKHONOV, A. V., 91, 226
PETER THE GREAT, 281
PETRUNKEVITCH, I. I., 99, 106
PILSUDSKI, Joseph, 98
PLEHVE, V. K. von, see von PLEHVE, V. K.
PLEKHANOV, George, V., 72, 73, 74, 144, 177, 211, 221
POBEDONOSTZEV, K. P., 63, 64, 66, 83, 104
POKROVSKY, M. N., Professor, 16, 67, 95, 168, 267
POLIVANOV, General A. A., 181, 183
POLKOVNIKOV, Colonel, 275, 276
POSTNIKOV, Professor, 240
POTEMKIN, Viceroy, 121
POURTALES, Graf, 173
PROTOPOPOV, A. D., 189, 191
PURISHKEVITCH, V. M., 126, 128, 174

RACHMANINOV, Sergei V., 20
RASPUTIN, Gregory Yefimovitch, 60, 171, 172, 182, 183, 191
RENNENKAMPF, General, 112
REUTERN, M. K., 24
RIMSKY-KORSAKOV, Nicholas A., 124
RODICHEV, F., 131
RODZYANKO, Michael V., 170, 180, 181, 182, 184, 192, 193, 194, 217, 259, 269
ROOT, Eliahu, 220, 244
ROZANOV, V. V., 156
RUTENBERG, Pinchas, 86, 92
RUZSKY, General N. V, 189

SAKHAROV, General, 114
SANDERS, William, 220
SAZONOV, Yegor, 82
SAZONOV, D. S., 175, 185
SELIVACHEV, General, 233
SERGEI, Grand Duchess, 177
SERGEI, Grand Duke, 70, 97
SHAKHMATOV, A. A., 91
SHCHEGLOVITOV, E. G., 183
SHESTOV, Leo, 156
SHIDLOVSKY, Senator, 96, 108, 110
SHINGAREV, A. I., 238
SHIPOV, D. N., 81, 106, 123
SHULGIN, V. V., 128, 172, 185, 187, 194
SIPYAGIN, D. S., 79, 152
SKOBELEV, M. J., 172, 226, 228, 235, 253
SOLLOGUB, General, 113, 156
SPIRIDONOVA, Maria, 70
STALIN, J. V. (Djugashvili), 28, 162, 248, 251, 252, 281
STANKEVITCH, V. B., 234
STEINBERG, Isaac, 267
STEPUN, Feodor, 152
STOLYPIN, Peter A., 62, 121, 122, 123, 124, 125, 126, 127, 128, 130, 131, 132, 134, 135, 137, 139, 142, 143, 160, 161, 173
STRAVINSKY, Igor F., 20
STRUKOV, General, 114
STRUVE, Peter, 71, 95, 279
SUKHANOV, N., 195, 200, 213, 217, 220, 247, 257, 267, 273, 277
SUKHOMLINOV, General, 169, 182, 183

SVERDLOV, L. M., 235
SVYATOPOLK-MIRSKY, Prince
Dmitry, 47, 82, 84, 91

TCHAADAYEV, P. Y., 74
TCHERNYSHEVSKY, Nikolai, G.,
74
TERESHCHENKO, Michael I., 172,
194, 226, 227, 228, 229, 242, 244,
249
THOMAS, Albert, 183
THORNE, Will, 220
TOLSTOY, Dmitry, 11
TOLSOY, Leo Nikolayevitch, 11,
23, 156–8, 177
TREPOV, General Fedor, 48, 105,
121, 210
TROTSKY, Leon D. (Bronstein),
68, 81, 106, 110, 112, 142, 146, 147,
148, 149, 150, 151, 175, 209, 210,
211, 213, 214, 215, 227, 234, 236
247, 249, 251, 259, 261, 262, 269,
270, 272, 273, 274, 275, 276, 277
TRUBETSKOY, Prince Eugene, 154
TRUBETSKOY, Prince Serge, 84
TSERETELLI, I. S., 127, 128, 225,
226, 228, 229, 236, 237, 242, 244,
248, 249, 258, 261
TURGENEV, Ivan Sergeyevitch, 51,
153

URUSSOV, Prince, 106

VANDERVELDE, E., 217
VASSILCHIKOV, Prince, 92
VERKHOVSKY, General, 264
VITTE, Sergei Ulievitch, 12, 16; 17,
18, 19, 25–34, 36, 40, 58, 63, 64, 65,
66, 67, 83, 91, 102, 103, 104, 105,
106, 111, 112, 113, 115, 118, 119,
130, 147, 174, 281
VOLKONSKY, Prince, 238
VOLODCHENKO, General, 264
von KOTEN, Colonel, 164
von PLEHVE, V. K., 43, 70, 79, 81,
82, 152, 173
VYSHNEGRADSKY, I. A., 24, 25, 33

WAGNER, Richard, 155
WEBER, Max, 16, 71, 74, 216
WILSON, Sir Henry, 190
WILSON, R. Woodrow, 219, 220,
280
WOYTINSKY, W., 265

ZASULICH, Vera, 210, 268
ZENZINOV, Vladimir, 107
ZHELYABOV, A. I., 51
ZINOVIEV, G. E., 235, 248, 272, 273
ZUBATOV, Colonel, S. V., 48–50,
66, 80, 87, 162

Psychology/Life Sciences in Paladin Books

A New Science of Life £2.50 ☐
Rupert Sheldrake
'An important scientific enquiry into the nature of biological and physical reality.' *New Scientist*.
'Immensely challenging and stimulating' – Arthur Koestler.
'The best candidate for burning there has been for many years.' *Nature*.

Genetic Prophecy: Beyond the Double Helix £1.95 ☐
Dr Zsolt Harsanyi and Richard Hutton
The past decade has seen many dramatic biological developments – genetic engineering, test-tube babies, cloning, all of them hotly debated, but none is likely to prove more controversial than *Genetic Prophecy*: the use of genetic markers to predict people's susceptibilities to various diseases.

The Diseases of Civilization £2.95 ☐
Brian Inglis
In the past decades there has been a growing disillusionment with orthodox medicine, while practitioners of alternative therapies began to boom. Why? In this powerfully documented critique Brian Inglis explains why we need a new approach to medical treatment.

Evolution from Space £1.95 ☐
Fred Hoyle and Chandra Wickramasinghe
In this startling book the authors argue that the evolutionary course of life on Earth has always been subject to cosmic influences. Its complexity attests to a guiding intelligence; in the final analysis God is a mathematical probability.

The Monkey Puzzle £2.95 ☐
John Gribbin and Jeremy Cherfas
Recent breakthroughs reveal that the genetic differences between chimpanzees, gorillas and humans is only one per cent; that we have evolved separately from the African apes for less than 5 million years; and that those apes may have evolved from human-like ancestors!

To order direct from the publisher just tick the titles you want and fill in the order form.

All these books are available at your local bookshop or newsagent, or can be ordered direct from the publisher.

To order direct from the publishers just tick the titles you want and fill in the form below.

Name _____

Address _____

_____

Send to:
Paladin Cash Sales
PO Box 11, Falmouth, Cornwall TR10 9EN.

Please enclose remittance to the value of the cover price plus:

UK 45p for the first book, 20p for the second book plus 14p per copy for each additional book ordered to a maximum charge of £1.63.

BFPO and Eire 45p for the first book, 20p for the second book plus 14p per copy for the next 7 books, thereafter 8p per book.

Overseas 75p for the first book and 21p for each additional book.

_____